RED
HORIZONS

RED HORIZONS

CHRONICLES OF A
COMMUNIST SPY CHIEF

by Lieutenant General
Ion Mihai Pacepa

REGNERY GATEWAY

WASHINGTON D. C.

LIBRARY OF CONGRESS CATALOGING-IN-PUBLICATION DATA

Pacepa, Ion Mihai, 1928-
  Red horizons.

  Includes index.
  1. Pacepa, Ion Mihai, 1928-   —Diaries.
  2. Intelligence officers—Romania—Diaries.
  3. Romania. Departamentul de Informatii Externe—
History. 4. Ceausescu, Nicolae—Journeys—United States.
  5. United States—Description and travel—1960-1980.
  I. Title.
  UB271.R62P337 1987   327.1′2′0924   87-26378
  ISBN 0-89526-570-2

Published in the United Staes by
Regnery Gateway
1130 17th Street, NW
Washington, DC 20036

Distributed to the trade by
Kampmann & Company, Inc.
9 E. 40th Street
New York, NY 10016

10 9 8 7 6 5 4 3 2

For Dana and Radu,
with love and hope.

Contents

viii CONTENTS

Gutta cavat lapidem,
non vi sed saepe cadendo.

A drop makes a hole in a stone
not by force but by constant dripping.

The conversations in this book have been written from memory by Lieutenant General Ion Mihai Pacepa. They are as accurate as any non-recorded, remembered conversations can be.

Introduction

WHILE I was still one of his top aides, Romanian President Nicolae Ceausescu often loved to watch a movie that showed a pro-Bucharest demonstration taking place in Washington, D.C. The beginning of the film showed a religious service being conducted by Romanian emigré clergymen from various denominations before a crowd of several hundred gathered around the Washington monument. In the audience were people wearing Romanian folk costumes, displaying armbands with the Romanian flag, and carrying placards hailing Bucharest's domestic and foreign policies, Romania's independence, and Ceausescu's wisdom. The movie then showed the demonstrators standing on the steps of the U.S. Capitol and later parading around the White House to the accompaniment of exhortations from portable loudspeakers calling for the renewal of most-favored-nation trade status for Romania.

The entire demonstration had been organized by the Romanian foreign intelligence service with the help of a few well-placed agents of influence. The emigré crowd, most of whom had never been to Washington before, had been specially transported in by their churches and social organizations, which were secretly financed and controlled by Bucharest. The placards had been made at the Romanian embassy, where the cassettes played over the loudspeakers had also originated. The movie itself had been filmed by two intelligence technicians especially sent to the United States for the occasion, and the narration had been done by the wife of the Romanian minister counselor in Washington, who was herself working for the intelligence service.

The demonstration was actually only a minor footnote to the

full range of influence operations conducted over the years by the Romanian foreign intelligence service to attract the Western political and economic support that Bucharest so badly needed to keep its ultra-orthodox Marxist system functioning. For Ceausescu, however, it symbolized another victory over Washington: a few weeks later the United States renewed the most-favored-nation status for Romania, despite its notorious abuses of human rights.

Since receiving political asylum in the United States, I have often related stories of this kind to call attention to the dangers of Communist influence operations. At the time I broke with Bucharest, influence operations had come to play the leading role in the Romanian foreign intelligence service's program, with the number of influence agents far outweighing the agents engaged in "classical" espionage to obtain classified information on the West. The political support, technological favors, and financial assistance that Bucharest's agents of influence managed to obtain from the West were the main thing breathing life into an otherwise stagnant economy and system of government.

With the passage of time, however, I have come to understand that the nature and purpose of devious Communist influence operations are often incomprehensible to the Western mentality. I have also come to understand that, fortunately or unfortunately, the Westerners whom the Soviet bloc generously rewards as its agents of influence are not subject to prosecution under Western espionage laws, even when they enable Communist countries to receive important political, commercial, technological, and financial benefits.

It took me many years before I could look back on my previous boss and his Communist system with the eyes of an American. It took me even longer to realize that individual Communist influence operations are not particularly worrisome to a Westerner unless he can visualize the whole, three-dimensional setting in which they occur. This book represents an attempt to provide that setting, in the form of a diary covering several weeks in 1978 when I was constantly at Ceausescu's side. It contains the story of my day-to-day life with a Communist leader who, during more than 20 years of absolute power, has built the most orthodox Marxist domestic policy in Eastern Europe and has clearly designated capitalism as his number one enemy. A leader who, cleverly using various influence operations, has simultaneously been able to gather enough Western political support and cold cash to keep his moribund, self-serving regime alive, and to build the first true Communist dynasty in history.

RED
HORIZONS

CHAPTER
I

IT was a cold, gray afternoon in March 1978, typical for that time of year in Bucharest. The lights were already on in my unlisted office at the Romanian foreign intelligence service, known as the DIE from its name in Romanian, *Departamentul de Informatii Externe.* Even though it had two French doors opening onto a balcony, the room was always relatively dark, as it was paneled from floor to ceiling in mahogany. I was placing a few new markers on an immense blue map of the world that took up the whole wall behind my oversize mahogany desk. Mounted on an invisible metal plate, the map displayed an army of magnetic markers in various colors and shapes spread all across the world, without any apparent logic. They stood for the top secret communications channels with Romanian embassies and other official representations abroad, with the DIE stations around the world, and with the centers for contact with DIE illegal officers in the West. They also represented various individual intelligence operations, such as the electronic surveillance of the United States Sixth Fleet in the Mediterranean.

There were seven telephones sitting on the table to the right of my desk, on top of another five scrambled radio telephone systems stashed away on two shelves underneath. Two of these were hot lines directly connected with the office of President Nicolae Ceausescu. Designed and installed by the Soviet KGB as a highly secure communications channel, the two-line telephone was part of an integrated system connecting the Warsaw Pact governments with each other. One line, called S for *short* because it had only three digits, was for Bucharest only. It was located in the offices and residences of Ceausescu, the prime minister, the rest of the Political Executive Committee[1] members living in Bucharest, the members of the cabinet, the chief and deputy of the DIE, the chief of the General Staff, and the Soviet ambassador to Romania. The other line, called *TO* because it went through a telephone operator, was for long distance. It connected the same people from Bucharest with Ceausescu's spring, summer, fall, and winter residences, as well as with members of the Political Executive Committee living in the 39 Romanian districts, the first secretaries of the district Communist Party committees, and with the local inspectorate chiefs of the internal security service, known as the Securitate. The Romanian *TO* telephone system was connected—via Moscow—with its counterparts in the other Warsaw Pact countries.

It was a few minutes after five in the afternoon when a telephone rang. I recognized the ring of the *S*, connected with Ceausescu's office.

"General Pacepa speaking," I answered.

"This is your servant, Boss. Constantin Manea. The Comrade wants you here right away. I'm sorry I've reached you. The weather is terrible here. I'll say a prayer for you."

"Okay, Professor."

I used to call Constantin Manea "Professor," because he had a doctorate in history. In the almost 15 years he had been Ceausescu's chief of staff, Manea had virtually never pronounced Ceausescu's name. "The Comrade" was how he always referred to him. I first became friends with Manea in the hectic days of the early 1970s, when I began planning Ceausescu's trips abroad. A good judge of human psychology, Manea was probably the only person who could really decipher Ceausescu's volatile nature and his unforeseen reactions. "The public Comrade is gentle, smiling, even warm and affectionate," Manea used to say of Ceausescu's truly Jekyll-and-Hyde personality. "The one I have to deal with every day, though, when he's not in a towering rage, is at best nervous, cloudy, impatient, and thoughtless of others."

During the last six years, when I was being called in by Ceausescu almost daily, not only on intelligence matters or as presi-

[1] In Soviet-style Communist parties, the supreme body is the politburo. After Nicolae Ceausescu came to power in 1965, he westernized its name in Romania to Political Executive Committee. In November 1974, he established the Permanent Bureau of the Political Executive Committee, composed of himself, his wife, the prime minister and another six members.

dential advisor, but also on the most unexpected family problems, such as gifts for his wife or difficulties in the private lives of his children, Manea spared me innumerable headaches. His bits of advice on when to try to solve a problem with Ceausescu and when not to, when to be aggressive and when to keep my mouth shut, were invaluable. He would often call me just to say, "The weather is terrible here. How is it there?" He meant that Ceausescu was in a furious rage, and that it might be prudent for me to get out of Bucharest for the rest of the day. Or he would say, "Why don't you dump some files into your briefcase and come on over?" by which he meant that Ceausescu was in a very good mood, and that he, Manea, was keeping a free moment in the schedule to slip me in.

Hastily opening my safe and taking out the notebook I used for meetings with Ceausescu, I left for his office at the Central Committee of the Romanian Communist Party, where he occupied the whole center front section of the second floor. As I came in, I saw Manea at the top of the stairs.

"'Romero' Must Be Recruited."

"The Comrade is with the minister of interior and Plesita," he said. The minister of interior was Teodor Coman. General Nicolae Plesita had for many years been the chief of Ceausescu's protective service and had recently been promoted to deputy minister of interior. "Even though the walls are a foot thick, I could hear the Comrade yelling at them," Manea added.

When I opened the door, Ceausescu was behind his desk, with Coman and Plesita standing at attention in the middle of the room. "Come in. These men can't remember anything. Who was that Western diplomat who got caught by the 'husband' at his 'mistress's' place in Bucharest that time?"

Ceausescu himself has the memory of an elephant, but over the past ten years he had also gained confidence in my unusually good memory. When I began elementary school, my father made me memorize one whole page of the telephone book every day. "Nothing will serve you better in the future than an excellent memory," he used to say, whenever I tried to object. The only way I found I could handle his demands was to memorize each page like a photograph, and I soon was able to recall the pages any time I needed to. I could usually say, for example, that such and such a telephone number was located at the bottom of page 183 on the lefthand side. This skill was enormously useful to me later on, when I began studying chemical engineering and had to memorize thousands of chemical formulas, or when I became in effect the head of the DIE, and had to memorize whole files. By now Ceausescu had learned that, in order to activate my memory, he had to describe a scene for me.

"Remember," prompted Ceausescu, "the 'husband' grabbed the fellow by the balls and threw him out into the main street, where there was some big party going on with a lot of drunks who almost killed him? You know, that Western diplomat who spoke Romanian and gave us so many headaches?"

"The Greek counselor, comrade," I immediately replied.

"That's it. And the 'husband' who caught him?"

"Colonel Marinescu, the deputy director of the Securitate's Surveillance Directorate," I shot back.

"That's it. The Greek counselor. That's it." Ceausescu left his desk and started pacing around the office. " 'Romero' must be recruited. I'm sure he'll succumb. After all, he's the one who took the first step. But if he should pull back, then you'll have to handle him as you did the Greek counselor. Instruct his Romanian girlfriend to invite him over to her room again. When they're right in the middle of a good fuck, the angry 'husband' should arrive on the scene. Marinescu should catch him naked in her bed, grab him by the balls and toss him out into the street, yelling that he raped his wife. Officers in disguise waiting outside should take care of punishing the rapist. You, Plesita, you do it, the way you did with Goma." Paul Goma is a Romanian dissident who has frequently evoked Ceausescu's wrath. "With Goma that time you used a fellow who was a boxer for Dinamo. Wasn't that it, Plesita?" Dinamo was the Ministry of Interior sports club.

"Captain Horst Stumpf. He's now assigned as a militiaman in Bucharest."

"Very good! Dress him up like a street sweeper or something, working there at night, and have him beat 'Romero' up, pour some brandy down his throat, and leave him on the street at dawn," said Ceausescu, scrutinizing each of our faces to see if we had understood. Looking into my eyes, he went on. "Your Disinformation Service, Pacepa, should then spread the word that 'Romero' was nothing but a common drunk, a womanizer, and so forth. They know how to do the job. Do you understand?"

"Yes, Comrade President."

"And you, Coman?"

"Yes, Comrade Ceausescu."

"That's all," he said, raising his arms as an unmistakable sign that the meeting was over.

"To the office," I ordered the driver a few minutes later.

Ceausescu's "Romero" was an intelligence officer assigned as a military attaché at the Italian embassy in Bucharest. He had recently fallen head over heels in love with a Romanian woman of easy virtue, who was a Securitate agent. A couple of months ago, "Romero's" wife had had to go back to Rome for family reasons, and he started spending most of his nights in his girlfriend's apartment. In recent weeks she had become more and more demanding, threatening to write the Italian ambassador about their relationship if "Romero" did not agree to share more of his life and his secrets with her. In an unexpected move a week earlier, "Romero" had asked for an urgent meeting with the Romanian minister of interior concerning "an exceptionally delicate and secret matter."

"Romero" told a long and tortuous story about a Western intelligence officer under cover as a diplomat in Bucharest who was having an affair with a young Romanian woman. She was starting to blackmail him, threatening to inform his ambassador if he did not buy her an apartment with foreign currency. His confused plea was that the minister of interior personally take the case in hand and stop the girl. "An uncompromised Western intelligence officer could be more useful to Romania than a compromised one," "Romero" slyly pointed out. It was, however, only after four more hours that he burst into tears, confessing that he was the subject of the case, and stressing that, if his ambassador were informed about the affair, he would be withdrawn from Romania and lose his career in the Italian military intelligence service.

Upon learning the outcome of the meeting with "Romero," Ceausescu ordered that he be recruited. Ceausescu's outburst of rage today was over "Romero's" having now changed his mind and decided he did not want to be an agent.

THE "HORIZON" OPERATION

Recruiting agents in the intelligence communities of NATO countries is one of Ceausescu's highest priorities, not just to honor his Warsaw Pact obligations but especially to protect his most highly classified secret, codenamed "Horizon." This was a vast influence operation he was personally running to gain Western political support, money, and technology.

It had all begun on the evening of February 22, 1972, when Ceausescu personally took over the management of the DIE. "Our experience shows that today the West is commendably eager to encourage the slightest sign of independence within the Soviet bloc. Let's take advantage of their eagerness," said Ceausescu cynically, in the memorable speech he made that evening in his office before the DIE's board of directors. "We must make cleverness our national trait. . . . Stop showing a sullen, frowning face and clenched fist to the West. Start making it feel compassion for us, and you'll see how fast Western boycotts change into magnanimity. Let's present Romania as a Latin island in the Slavic sea. . . . Our millenia-old traditions of independence are now up against Moscow's political centrism. . . . A pawn between two superpowers. . . ."

As was his wont, Ceausescu followed up his philosophy lesson with orders for its practical application: The DIE should start an organized influence offensive against the West. It should carefully plant little hints of independence—without affecting the fundamentals of Communism—and then hammer away at them, in order to stir up the West's sympathy for Romania and gain its political and economic assistance. The DIE's agents of influence should help Romania gain political and economic advantages in the West, turn Third World governments into political allies, transform hostile emigrés into supporters, sway the international news media. These agents should also use Romania's new prestige to unlock doors opening onto highly classified technology prohibited to Communist countries. Romania should make a substantial increase in its contribution to the defense not only of the Warsaw Pact but also of Peking and the whole Communist world.

The day after this historic speech, Ceausescu increased the DIE's table of organization from around 700 to over 2,800 intelligence officers, and he also upped its budget, paid in hard currency, more than eightfold. He relegated the DIE's traditional foreign intelligence activities to a back seat, establishing influence operations as the main task of the DIE.

"Horizon" was the code name Ceausescu himself gave to this operation, one of the many masterful deception and influence operations that he himself built up, brick by brick, starting in 1972. Its purpose was to give the West the illusion that his Romania was a new kind of Communist country, independent of everyone else, including Moscow, which deserved to be supported by the West, so as to create cracks in the walls around the Soviet bloc. Ceausescu's "Horizon" had everything: overt and covert propaganda in the West; hints dropped into concealed microphones discovered in Romanian embassies in the West and kept in place for sending misleading messages; documents "signed" by heads of foreign governments, counterfeited in Bucharest and "accidentally lost" in luxury hotels or leaked to the West in other ways; intelligence officers operating under the cover of the robes of ambassadors and archbishops; Swiss bank accounts rewarding high-ranking, corrupt Westerners who agreed to present Romania as a "maverick"; intelligence officers disguised as lovers, recruiting Western officials as agents of influence. "Horizon," contained in several bulky files arranged by geographic area, was the only place where one could find a distillation of Ceausescu's overall goals and concrete objectives for each non-Communist country of interest, starting with the United States and ending with the Central African Republic, as well as data on the most important influence agents created by the DIE over the years.

COMPROMISING THE AMBASSADOR'S WIFE

"Sixty-two, report to zero one. Repeat: sixty-two, report immediately to zero one," suddenly came out over my car's radio telephone. *Sixty-two* was the code for me, *zero one* for Ceausescu. Without a word, the driver made a U-turn, tires squealing as he pushed the accelerator to the floor.

"Sixty-two is on his way to zero one," the driver then answered the call.

Manea was waiting for me at the top of the stairs. "The good news, Boss, is that the storm is over and the Comrade is watching one of Moga's porno movies with Andrei." Lieutenant General Gheorghe Moga was the chief of the Securitate's Counterespionage Directorate, and Stefan Andrei the newly appointed minister of foreign affairs. "The bad news is that Comrade Elena is with them."

In Ceausescu's office the heavy velvet draperies had been drawn. Seated at the conference table between his wife, Elena, and Andrei, Ceausescu was watching a color movie that Moga was projecting on a portable screen. I was all too familiar with such compromising movies made by the Counterespionage Directorate from concealed cameras and microphones.

Seeing me come in, Ceausescu suddenly got up and started for the door. In his own way still the prudish peasant, Ceausescu detests sexual perversion. "Let's go," he whispered, as he passed behind me. I got up and followed him. He left the office without putting away any of the papers neatly laid out on his desk. That was Manea's job. The other people stayed behind to watch the end of the show. The presidential Mercedes 600, which, together with a whole fleet of security cars and motorcycles, was always waiting outside, sped at full throttle across the 50 feet from its parking space to the door. "Come over to the house with me."

The driver, a security colonel who had been with him for more than ten years, did not need to ask where we were going. He took off at a breakneck pace through the empty streets, the traffic always being brought to a complete standstill every time Ceausescu left his residence or office. Several hundred plainclothes security officers disguised as normal pedestrians, who regularly patrolled the route between Ceausescu's office and his residence, discreetly showed themselves along the way one by one, signaling that everything was under control.

Sitting in the front seat, Ceausescu was, as usual, glum and taciturn, absorbed in his own thoughts. He normally does not look out the car window, as the people on the street are of no concern to him. After ten minutes of racing through empty streets, Ceausescu's car reached its destination. The presidential residence, located on Primaverii Street, is entirely enclosed by a high wall of brick and concrete. The massive steel door opened automatically, and the car drove inside without reducing speed.

"Let's walk," said Ceausescu. That was always a sign that he had delicate business to bring up with me. He prefers to discuss very sensitive matters outdoors, not in his office or residence. As someone who has installed microphones in many homes and offices, he is very much aware of their uncanny ability to penetrate even into a person's innermost thoughts. His rose garden is the place where the most confidential decisions regarding Romanian intelligence and foreign policy are made.

He immediately set off, as fast as his short legs would carry him, through his immense garden, spread out over several acres and filled with rose bushes and artesian fountains and illuminated *al giorno.* "Turn off all the lights. Keep only my 'dwarfs,'" he commanded one of the bodyguards who were swarming all around. When he discusses secrets in his garden, he is always irritated by the indecent neon lights spreading a cadaverous white glow over everything. Suddenly hundreds of little lamps hidden among the bushes began softly outlining the paths.

"What's new?" Ceausescu asked. He always started his discussions with me this same way, even if he saw me ten times a day. He often said that his foreign intelligence service should always have something new to report.

"I've just received a message from Washington," I replied. "The station obtained a copy of a telegram hot off the wire from the American ambassador in Bucharest to the State Department."

"From 'W-12'?" That was the code name of an agent in the State Department.

"Yes, comrade. He turned over a decoded telegram that had just come in from their ambassador in Bucharest."

"What does the idiot say?" Ceausescu hated Rudolph Aggrey, believing that the State Department had snubbed him by sending a black as ambassador to Bucharest.

"Proposals for your visit to Washington."

"Any sign that they suspect 'Horizon'?"

"No indication."

"Send it to me tomorrow. What else is new?"

"Washington also reports that 'Richard' supplied a CIA report on Romania." "Richard" was a high-ranking official in the United States Department of Agriculture who had also been recruited by the DIE as an agent.

"Nothing about 'Horizon' in it?"

"No."

"Chalk up another point for us. Has Nicolae started recruiting agents of influence yet?"

"He's got a couple of cases in the State Department," I answered. Nicolae M. Nicolae was a brilliant engineer who had spent most of his life in the Ministry of Foreign Trade. In 1972 Ceausescu made him a deep cover colonel in the intelligence service, and in May 1976 he sent him to the United States as ambassador.

"Keep his feet to the fire. Did you recognize any of the faces in Moga's movie?"

"I don't think so, Comrade Ceausescu."

"The wife of the American ambassador."

"The current one?"

"His predecessor. The one I liked."

"Moga managed to have one of his officers who is an embassy driver shoved up under her skirt. Now he wants to send the driver to America, first for a visit, then for good. Get in touch with Moga. Maybe someday you'll have to have the DIE take over her handling."

"We've never acted against an American ambassador before, Comrade Ceausescu. I don't think anybody else has, either."

"We've never before had an American ambassador with a whore for a wife. What's his job now?"

"Head of personnel at Foggy Bottom."

"Couldn't be better."

MIDDLE EAST MEDIATOR?

"Tell me again what Sadat said."

Two days earlier I had gotten back from a trip to Cairo, where Ceausescu had sent me as his personal messenger to the Egyptian president, Anwar Sadat.

"That he had decided to accept Carter as the mediator between Egypt and Israel," I answered. President Jimmy Carter had been angling for this role.

"Just a few weeks ago Sadat agreed to meet with Begin here

in Romania." Ceausescu had been trying hard to mediate between Sadat and Israeli Prime Minister Menachem Begin.

"Now Sadat considers that Carter can exert a greater personal influence on Begin," I said. "And he says Carter will also bring the CIA into the game."

"I still don't believe it. Nor does Brezhnev. Yesterday I sent him your report, and today Drozdenko has already been here with a personal message from him asking me to foil Carter's plan." Soviet General Secretary Leonid Brezhnev's ambassador to Bucharest was V.I. Drozdenko. "If we can't keep Romania as the meeting place, he wants to transfer the Middle East peace process to the Geneva Conference and persuade Carter to recognize the PLO, or at least to agree to discussions with it."

I knew that it would not be easy to fit Yasser Arafat and his Palestine Liberation Organization into any peace process. "Arafat's not flexible enough to deal with Carter."

"I'll make him be! All you've got to do is bring him here as soon as you can." Ceausescu again lapsed into silence.

While passing by the residence, I could hear noisy rock music blaring forth, interrupted by small, repeated explosions. As we went by an open sliding door, I caught a glimpse of Ceausescu's son Nicu throwing unopened Scotch bottles against a wall. As they broke, they splashed liquor all over the furniture, and Nicu's laugh splashed all over the room. Nicu has been a hard drinker ever since his middle teens, when he would often disappear from home and be found days later, drunk as a lord, at a friend's house or in some seedy restaurant. At that time he would drink anything, from *tsuica,* a strong plum brandy similar to *slivovitz* (the Romanian national drink), to vodka, Cointreau, or champagne. Now he was 27 and drank only Johnny Walker Black Label.

Far behind us, I could see Elena at the front door. Spotting her husband, she sent a bodyguard over to call him to dinner. As he turned to go, Ceausescu asked me to have a *Kojak* movie shown afterwards. "I'll be in the movie theater at ten," I heard his voice trailing off out of the darkness.

Although Ceausescu has never been in a public cinema, he is a fanatical moviegoer. Each of his residences has a fully equipped projection room. His favorite movies are ones about Napoleon, who is his role model, and American police thrillers. "They shoot first and ask questions later," he would say about the American crimebusters. It was part of my job to get such movies for him from abroad. Like everything else at his residence, the movie theater is not small. The whole thing is done in light gray velvet. In the front row there are only two very large, deep easy chairs, which swallow you up when you sit in them, with low tables in front of each.

On the dot of ten Ceausescu came into the movie theater wearing a white turtleneck sweater, followed ten minutes later by Elena in a long, gray velvet dressing gown, half unbuttoned. Ceausescu is always punctual; Elena never is. A waiter served Ceausescu his special Moldavian yellow wine, which is produced only for him, and opened a chilled bottle of Cordon Rouge champagne, Elena's favorite drink.

During a movie at his private residence, Ceausescu is relaxed and entirely different from his public image. He loves to watch *Kojak* movies, not only because they are full of action, but especially because with his quick mind he has no trouble figuring out the denouement of a *Kojak* episode. At the end of this one the lights revealed Elena fast asleep, her mouth and her robe both having fallen indecorously open. Elena has never been able to stay awake till the end of a movie. On the other hand, I remember only one time that Ceausescu fell asleep during a show. It was at a stage gala given in his honor by Costa Rican President Jose Figueres in 1973, and Ceausescu was put to sleep not only by his jet lag but also by the dreamy ballet. *Kojak* is his style, not ballet.

After emptying another glass of wine, Ceausescu started off at his usual sprightly gait, making a sign for me to follow. His private study is filled with mahogany furniture inlaid with ivory. On the bookshelves are the complete works of Marx and Lenin, bound in blue leather, and of Ceausescu, bound in red.

"Arafat now holds the key," he began. "If I'm able to tell Carter, Sadat, and Begin that I can transform the PLO into a government-in-exile and persuade it to accept 242 and 338 in some way, I could be a mediator. We've got to force Arafat's hand." At issue were United Nations resolutions 242 and 338, which acknowledge the existence of the state of Israel.

"I want Arafat here," he went on. "Send my airplane to Beirut, and have Olcescu come with him." Colonel Constantin Olcescu was the Romanian chargé d'affaires and the DIE station chief in Lebanon.

"I want to get 'Annette' here, too," Ceausescu added. *'He* has more influence on Arafat than anybody else does." "Annette" was the DIE code name for a man very close to Arafat. When deep in thought, Ceausescu would often forget that he was supposed to say *she* for "Annette," even though he was his very favorite agent in the PLO.

While Ceausescu was talking, the heavy door to the office banged open. Elena appeared in the doorway, dressing gown entirely unbuttoned, hair in disarray, eyes red and swollen. "I've been looking everywhere for you, Nick. Where were you?"

"I've been talking with Pacepa. I want him to bring Arafat here."

Elena turned to me. "You'd better make him do what we want. We should see that the Comrade gets his Nobel Peace Prize. Like the one given to that idiot von Kissinger. Do you understand?" The honorary "von" that Elena gave the former American national security advisor, Henry Kissinger, was not meant as a compliment. She had hated Kissinger from the first moment she heard about his Nobel Peace Prize. Turning to address her husband, she said, "I want the ambassadress to be my own agent over there in America, with me pulling on her reins from here."

"The slut?"

"The bitch. Have you told Pacepa to get in touch with Moga?"

"Uh huh."

"That's why I love you so much." Slipping her hand under Ceausescu's sweater, she cooed, "I need you, Nick. Let's go to bed."

"Take care of what I told you, Pacepa," said Ceausescu over his shoulder, as he was dragged off by Elena.

It was after midnight when I left Ceausescu's residence to go home. The short walk to my house led under lime trees that had just started to bloom. Their aroma always reminded me of my childhood and the huge lime tree in front of my parents' house.

"ANNETTE": LIAISON WITH THE PLO

"Annette" was in fact Hani Hassan, Arafat's best friend. My acquaintance with Hassan dated from October 1972, when he first came to Romania, accompanying Arafat. I was in Ceausescu's office with Nicolae Doicaru, who was the chief of the DIE at that time, and with a DIE interpreter.

"This is my brother Hani el-Hassan," Arafat opened the discussion, placing his handgun on the table and pointing toward a middle-aged, well-built man with black hair and mustache, who was elegantly attired in European dress and who had an aura that inspired both calm and fear. He had the distinguished appearance of a doctor or lawyer, but his glassy eyes, his chunky hands and his gestures somehow made me think of a butcher.

"El-Hassan is my most devoted personal friend and my closest collaborator, although he is known only as one of my advisors," Arafat said. "Few people, however, know that he manages a whole foreign intelligence network. And even fewer know his real, deeply secret role in the Palestinian revolution. Fewer people than the fingers on this hand," Arafat emphasized, holding up his right hand with the fingers spread wide. "El-Hassan plays one of the most important roles in our struggle. More important than you or you," he went on, pointing to Doicaru and me, "because we are in a constant state of war. He is the one who, just a few months ago, prepared our answer to the Olympic Committee's decision not to allow a team of Palestinian athletes to participate in the Munich games. He is the brain who put our organization's name on the front page of every single newspaper." Arafat was referring to the September 5, 1972 massacre of 11 Israeli athletes by a team of PLO terrorists at the Munich Olympic Games.

Arafat detected a look of skepticism in his audience. "Don't be deceived by his elegant appearance," he cried. "Brother el-Hassan is not a gunman. He is a mind. He is a brain. He is our brain," Arafat concluded emphatically. I looked at Hassan, and I could no longer see the distinguished doctor or lawyer in him. His face was as impassive as stone. When I met his eyes, they were evil, piercing.

After that October 1972 meeting, an extensive liaison exchange started up between the PLO and the DIE. Hassan sent the DIE secret reports on Israel and Jordan that were by far the best information the Soviet bloc had ever obtained on those areas. Ceausescu approved—in excess amounts—every demand made by Hassan. Soon the DIE started providing him enormous quantities of technical intelligence paraphernalia, from electronic eavesdropping equipment for the secret monitoring of government institutions in Israel, Jordan, and elsewhere, to burst transmitters, secret writing materials, and other spy gear. "Moscow is helping the PLO build muscles. I'm feeding its brain," Ceausescu said.

In January 1975, Arafat and Hassan came to Bucharest in order to persuade Ceausescu to lend his personal support to a major PLO intelligence operation designed to overthrow and assassinate King Hussein of Jordan, making Jordan the home of a future Palestinian nation headed by the PLO. The most embittered against Hussein was Hassan. "More than half of Jordan's population is Palestinian," he said, "and according to the Palestinian National Covenant[2] the PLO is responsible for them. Palestine has become Jordan, however, and the king is swallowing up the Palestinians." Hassan's conclusion: "Hussein must die. He is no less dangerous than Israel to the Palestinian cause."

To which Ceausescu philosophically replied, "Monarchies and dynasties are antagonistic to revolutions."

SETTING UP KING HUSSEIN

After that meeting Ceausescu ordered me to prepare a trip to Jordan for him, and in April 1975 I accompanied him and Elena on their official visit to Amman. Going from the airport to the Royal Palace, we were surrounded by the most formidable escort I had ever seen. Mobile rocket launchers ahead of the motorcade, tanks around it, and antiaircraft artillery behind were only a part of the coverage we had.

"Has Your Majesty received any information connected with my visit?" Ceausescu asked. His first concern is always for his own skin.

"Oh, no, Mister President. This is routine. It's better to be safe than sorry."

The day after our arrival in Amman, Hussein himself piloted us in one of his airplanes to the Gulf of Aqaba. It was a weekend, and the king wanted not only to give the Ceausescus two relaxing

---

[2]The Palestinian National Covenant, or Charter, is a Communist-style declaration of principles about Palestinians, their homeland and rights. It was drafted in 1964 under the influence of Jamal Abdul Nasser and approved in its present form in Cairo in July 1968, together with the Constitution of the Palestine Liberation Organization.

days, but also to show them an ancient part of Jordan that he was personally trying to modernize. His passengers for the flight were Alya, his wife at the time; Ceausescu and Elena; Gheorghe Serbanescu, a DIE officer who was Hussein's former fellow student at the university and now Ceausescu's interpreter; and I. The beautifully clear day gave us an incredible panorama of this area of Jordan. The queen acted as our guide, pointing out Aqaba's landmarks and describing the international sports festival held there annually in mid-November, to coincide with the king's birthday.

At their tranquil villa in Aqaba, from which you could look out almost all the way across the Red Sea, everything was quite casual, without protocol. Hussein and Alya invited the Ceausescus to go out in their glass-bottomed boat to see one of the most beautiful coral reefs in the world, and finally they entertained the Ceausescus on one of their motor yachts. After the early dinner, which was individually ordered and eaten separately—"I love burgers, tacos, and Coke. You may have whatever you wish"— the king proposed a movie, his favorite evening pastime.

Ceausescu, however, had other ideas for the rest of the day. When he and Hussein met again after dinner, Ceausescu started putting Arafat's plan into action. He spoke out violently against the PLO's international terrorism, strongly condemning recent PLO attacks on Jordan's independence and Hussein's life. After less than two hours of talk, Ceausescu placed a file on the table containing biographic data on PLO terrorists, along with their photographs. Needless to say, he did not mention that it had come from Hani Hassan and had been especially compiled for Hussein. Ceausescu then proposed a "highly confidential" liaison between the Romanian and Jordanian intelligence services to protect their own personal lives and their two countries' independence. When Ceausescu had finished his performance, genuine to all appearances, the king remained silent for several minutes. His long history of problems with the PLO had made it a matter of life and death for him. Then Hussein shook Ceausescu's hand with his powerful, karate expert's grip and embraced him, still without saying a word.

The next day, Hussein informed Ceausescu of his agreement to a "fraternal liaison between our two intelligence services." A few hours later I had my first meeting with the chief of the Jordanian foreign intelligence service and his immediate staff. It quickly became evident to me that the PLO was almost as important a target for them as Israel was, and also that they had valuable sources at various levels and in different factions of the PLO.

By the time Ceausescu left Jordan, we had amassed several folders on the PLO, hastily pulled together by the Jordanian foreign intelligence service without taking time to protect its sources adequately. In his sincerity, Hussein ordered that a special file detailing the measures instituted by the Jordanian security and military forces to protect his life against foreign terrorism also be given to Ceausescu, as fraternal assistance to the Romanian security forces for protecting their president's life. At Hussein's personal command, a confidential liaison system was set up between the two intelligence services, including a special, bilateral, encoded radio communications system. A few days later, Hani Hassan received from Ceausescu's own hands a copy of every piece of paper obtained from the Jordanian king and his intelligence service. After that, Hassan periodically provided information to be given to the Jordanian service as ostensibly Romanian reports, and he continued to receive all the information secretly provided by Hussein's intelligence service transmitted during subsequent personal meetings in Amman and Bucharest, as well as via the encoded radio communications system.

In 1976, Ceausescu proposed to Arafat that they exchange intelligence advisors. The addition of a few PLO officers brought about a dramatic improvement in the terrorist component of the DIE, called "Service Z"—Z as the last letter of the alphabet representing the "final solution." To this service Arafat and Hassan assigned two teams of PLO professional terrorists, who had been especially trained for Romanian operations and were later used for kidnaping and assassination assignments in the West at Ceausescu's order. A DIE general, Constantin Munteanu, was transferred to Beirut as the head of a group of advisors who were to teach the PLO how to run deception and influence operations, in order to get recognized by the West.

"Annette" Is Recruited

By the end of 1976, Hani Hassan was formally recruited as a Romanian agent, based on the advisors' reports revealing his weakness for Western money. At Ceausescu's personal direction he got a feminine code name, "Annette." His DIE file should show that he has periodically been paid amounts of between $2,500 and $10,000 in cash, and that his information has been of considerable interest. The DIE analysts, for instance, found a wealth of data among the immense quantities of tapes resulting from the PLO's continuous interception of the telephone lines passing within East Beirut. According to "Annette," the PLO monitoring center—built for them by the Soviet KGB—was secretly wired into the Soviet embassy as well, giving the PLO a double-barreled operation. "Annette" also provided significant information about the secret training bases and camps organized for PLO terrorists in Bulgaria. His reports about the PLO training centers in the Yugoslav mountains were hugely enjoyed by Ceausescu and kept as evidence of Tito's duplicity. The most important contribution from "Annette," however, was the enormous quantity of Western arms samples, ranging from automatic weapons to tanks, he supplied the DIE. Most of them were captured in Lebanon, but some were acquired through capitalizing on the PLO's collaboration with the Japanese Red Army, the Italian Red Brigades, the West German Baader-Meinhof gang, and other similar groups.

From behind me I could barely hear the faint purr of my car's engine. Whenever I walked home at night, my driver would discreetly follow until he saw I was inside. My house was a two-apartment building, constructed just before World War II by the then famous architect Julius Prager for his two sisters. Ceausescu had me move there, to 28 Zoia Avenue, so that I would be close to his residence. I had the first floor, a luxurious apartment with a large garden and an outdoor swimming pool. The second floor, with its terrace gardens, was inhabited by the eldest son of the late Dr. Petru Groza, who in March 1945 had became the first pro-Communist prime minister and later president of Romania.

As I reached the house that evening, the militiaman guarding the Polish embassy across the street stepped out of his booth to give me a formal salute. When I unlocked the heavy metal gate, I saw a curtain cautiously moving on the second floor of my house. It was Groza's wife. She always stayed up to watch for me, no matter how late it was. Her husband had become a chronic alcoholic, and I had become her only diversion. A few months earlier she had blurted out that she had a crush on me and was fascinated with everything about me: my trips abroad, my appearances on television with Ceausescu, the parade of black limousines driving up to my home.

My apartment was completely dark. From the foyer I went directly to my study, where the desk lamp shone gently on the two large walls entirely covered with framed, enlarged color photographs. They showed me walking with Charles de Gaulle in Paris, dining with Willy Brandt in Bonn, fishing in the Caribbean with Raul Castro, accompanying Richard Nixon and Henry Kissinger as they were leaving the Romanian embassy in Washington, talking with Gerald Ford, shaking Hirohito's hand, debating with Ferdinand Marcos and dancing with his wife, Imelda, on their yacht, listening to Moammar Gadhafi in his patchwork tent, meeting Yasser Arafat at his Lebanon headquarters, talking with Anwar Sadat in his palace garden, visiting with Hafez Assad at his summer residence, and accompanying Ceausescu on more than thirty visits to North and South America, Western Europe, Asia, and Africa. At the left, a spacious, discreetly illuminated wall unit ostentatiously displayed the 39 Romanian and foreign medals I had accumulated over the years. The Latin American ones were the largest and the most spectacular, with their brilliant enamel faces and massive chains. The ones of heavy gold encrusted with large diamonds from the shah of Iran and from the Central African Republic's Jean Bedel Bokassa were the most valuable. Lying next to the medals was the Steiner violin I had gotten as a child as a birthday present from my godfather, the historian Nicolae Iorga, shortly before he was assassinated by the fascist Iron Guard organization in 1940.

I picked at some cold food set out for me on the dining room table by my daughter, Dana. The bedroom had heavy outside shutters hermetically sealing out the light. Sleeping no more than four or five hours a night for almost three decades, I had learned to drop off in less than one minute, but only if the room was pitch black.

CHAPTER

II

"BOTH of us want to influence America in our favor. Our methods are different, though. You, Brother Arafat, use arms. I use words."

"Struggle, Brother Ceausescu! Armed struggle and terror are the only things America respects."

"You, Brother Yasser, were here in 1972, and you are here now. You can see for yourself that nothing has changed in Romania in that time. We are still the same Communist country, where private property is not only prohibited—it is a disgrace. But the West now loves me. Two American presidents have come to Romania since I started my 'Horizon' operation, none before. Now, in the past six years alone, I have gotten twelve billion dollars in Western credits—two billion a year. Ten years ago, the most important technological intelligence Romania could pry out of America was about hybrid corn. Now Bucharest is one of the best in the Warsaw Pact at collecting high tech intelligence on America."

"Is that really true?"

"It's not only what *I* think, it's what Brezhnev just told me."

"Amazing."

"Before I started my 'Horizon' operation, I couldn't export anything to America. All I did was import their high tech. Now my exports almost equal my imports, and in ten years the balance will be ten to one in my favor. Five years ago I had barely a dozen intelligence officers over in America. Now I have five times that many, the ambassador included, and in a couple of years it'll be ten times as many. And what has America gotten out of it all? Shit, nothing but shit."

Using both hands, Ceausescu started to wolf down slices of tomato, onion, and feta cheese, his favorite dessert. When among close friends, he always prefers his fingers to a fork. So does Arafat, who took advantage of the pause to gobble down a dripping baklava that he had dunked into a jar of honey. Eating honey straight out of the jar is one of his favorite treats.

BROTHER CEAUSESCU, BROTHER ARAFAT

Yasser Arafat, accompanied by Hani Hassan, had arrived in Bucharest one hour earlier on Ceausescu's presidential airplane. Seated at the long table for 24 in the large meeting room were only five casually dressed people. On one side were Arafat and Hassan. Sitting between them was Gheorghe Serbanescu, the DIE interpreter. Ceausescu's only foreign language is Russian, which Arafat does not speak. Ceausescu sat on the other side of the table, and I was seated next to him, attending in my dual capacity as his personal advisor and acting chief of the Romanian foreign intelligence service.

The similarity between Ceausescu and Arafat was most striking. It was not only for political reasons or as a natural corollary to his anti-Semitism that Ceausescu was placing his bets on Arafat. Without Arafat's beard and slightly darker skin, it would be hard to tell them apart. They have the same shape face, the same expression around the mouth, the same smile, the same eyes that bore holes into you. They think and act the same. They are identically talkative, irascible, impulsive, violent, hysterical. This strong similarity struck both of them the first day they met and has played a significant role in their continued friendship.

Ceausescu had polished off everything on his plate and was now wiping it clean with a piece of bread. "In two weeks I'll be in Washington again, and I can swear to you that Carter will praise Romania as a great country and will call me a 'distinguished international leader.'"

"That's thanks to 'Horizon,' isn't it?" spoke up Hassan for the first time that evening.

"Can you think of anything better?" asked Ceausescu, looking at him with affection. Ceausescu considers Arafat to be his best friend and calls him "my clever fox," but he visibly admired Hassan, for his perfidiousness and coldbloodedness. Ceausescu took a whole tomato and bit into it like an apple, spattering juice and seeds. Then he stuffed his mouth full of onion and feta cheese, mechanically wiping his fingers off on the white damask tablecloth, all the while studying Arafat with his shifting, badger-like eyes.

"How are your influence operations doing?" he said, changing the subject.

"The advisors Hassan got from Brother Pacepa are true artists."

Ceausescu picked up on the idea. "Influence is indeed an art, a skill."

"At this very moment we've got something going in Vienna," Hassan intervened, "and the results might be a peace prize from Kreisky." Bruno Kreisky was the chancellor of Austria at that time.

Arafat burst into a peal of laughter. "A gift from a Jew to the PLO. Wouldn't that be marvelous?"

"We have another operation using Abu Nidal," Hassan added.

"Who would ever suspect that Nidal, my fiercest enemy, the very fellow who is killing off my men, could actually be doing things for me?" Arafat boasted.

"Congratulations," said Ceausescu. "How about pretending to break with terrorism? The West would love it."

"Just pretending, like with your independence?"

"Exactly. But pretending over and over. Political influence, like dialectical materialism, is built on the same basic tenet that quantitative accumulation generates qualitative transformation."

"I'm not the expert on Marxism that you are, Brother Ceausescu."

"Dialectical materialism works like cocaine, let's say. If you sniff it once or twice, it may not change your life. If you use it day after day, though, it will make you into an addict, a different man. That's the qualitative transformation."

"A snort of a pacifist Arafat day after day . . . ?"

"Exactly, Brother Yasser. The West may even become addicted to you and your PLO."

The friendly discussion kept on the same course for at least another hour. Over the last few months Ceausescu and Arafat had been most concerned with getting the PLO recognized in Western Europe by creating a moderate image for Arafat.

It was Ceausescu who first went to the heart of the matter. "I'll be in Washington in less than two weeks. That's why I've invited you here."

"Lay your cards on the table, Brother Ceausescu."

"Not long ago I told you about my scheme to bring Sadat and Begin to the same table, here in Romania. Sinaia is the place I chose for it, and I preached to them that nothing in the world could be more inspiring and secure than this secluded, picturesque mountain village. It's where the former king had his summer palace."

"I know. You told me."

"A few days ago I sent Pacepa to Cairo to discuss the details with Sadat, and when he came back I couldn't believe my ears. Sadat had changed everything! He said that Carter had come into the game and had offered not only Camp David as a meeting place and his personal influence with Begin, but also CIA support."

"Sadat hasn't breathed a word about it."

"He told Pacepa that nothing was more secret than that."

"Interesting." Arafat's fingers wriggled nervously.

"I immediately informed Brezhnev. You know, I don't like him as a person, but our common cause has always prevailed."

Both terribly vindictive by nature, Leonid Brezhnev and Nicolae Ceausescu had long ago begun hating each other. In 1953, Brezhnev became a two-star general and the deputy head of the Red Army's Political Department. Up until a year before that he had been the first secretary of the Central Committee of the Communist Party of Moldavia, a formerly Romanian region that the Soviets had occupied at the end of World War II. He was therefore considered an expert in Romanian matters and given the assignment of supervising the political indoctrination of the Romanian army. Brezhnev's sharp criticisms of the Romanian military deeply wounded Ceausescu, who was at that time also a two-star general and responsible for the political departments of the Romanian military and security forces. Ceausescu could not forgive him for this. When Ceausescu came to power, he ordered the DIE to make a detailed study of Brezhnev's activity as the Moldavian leader. A year later, in May 1966, when Brezhnev visited Bucharest, Ceausescu presented Brezhnev with documents showing that in the Russification of Moldavia in 1950–52, Brezhnev had deported more than one million Romanians to Siberia and replaced them with Russians and Ukrainians. The discussion was very hard-hitting and caused a break in their personal relationship. It was ten years before Brezhnev came back to Romania.

"What did Brezhnev say?" Arafat asked, his badger eyes moving rapidly from Ceausescu to me and back.

"In less than 24 hours Drozdenko was in my office with the Kremlin's message. They asked me to do whatever I could to diminish Carter's role and to help transfer the whole Middle East peace process to the Geneva Conference.

"That would not only automatically put Moscow in the middle of the scene, but it would also drag the whole story out forever. Geneva is famous for that." The Soviet Union and the United States are co-chairmen of the Geneva Conference.

"Now Carter has jumped in," said Ceausescu petulantly.

"He doesn't have any influence over me, and without Arafat there won't be any peace."

"That's what I want from you, Brother Yasser. Help me to show that I'm the only one who has any influence over you."

"It's in my own interest, too, for you to get the Nobel Prize, Brother Ceausescu."

"When I get to Washington, I want to put it to Carter that I, and only I, can change the PLO, and that I am willing to do so, if he agrees to transfer the negotiations from Camp David to Geneva."

"To change what?" Arafat interrupted suspiciously.

"Nothing serious, only a few cosmetic changes. Like transforming the PLO into a Palestinian government-in-exile. That would mean nothing to you, but it could erase with one stroke all the American pretexts for isolating you, and open Geneva's door to you, Brother."

Arafat stopped with his hand in mid-air, not seeing the honey that was starting to drip onto his suit from the spoon. Ceausescu went on: "It would be much easier to persuade the West to negotiate with a government-in-exile than with a terrorist organization."

Arafat glanced quickly at me, then started boring into Ceausescu with his restless, fretful eyes, while mechanically licking the empty spoon. "You're not serious, are you?"

"I'm not talking about any important change, only a fireworks display!"

"That's not easy."

"Do you think it's easy for me to have to sneak off secretly to Moscow, when I used to be received there with fanfares and the trooping of the guard?"

"I don't mind coming here secretly, Brother Ceausescu. That's for our cause. But we are a revolution, not a government. We were born as a revolution, and we should remain an unfettered revolution."

"And you will remain a revolution. The only thing I want to change is the nameplate on your door."

After pausing, Arafat launched into a long peroration. He said that the Palestinians lacked the tradition, unity, and discipline to become a formal state. That a Palestinian state would be a failure from the first day. That it was only something for a future generation. That all governments, even Communist ones, were limited by laws and international agreements. That he could not put any laws or other obstacles in the way of the Palestinian struggle against Israel.

"There is no doubt in my mind," Ceausescu said sympathetically, "that a war of terror is your only realistic weapon. In the shadow of your government-in-exile you can keep as many operational groups as you want, as long as they are not publicly connected with your name. They could mount endless operations all around the world, while your name and your 'government' would remain pristine and unspoiled, ready for negotiations and further recognition."

"What would be the political gain for me?" Arafat interrupted nervously, tearing a blank sheet of paper from his notepad into small shreds.

"You could capitalize on this credit, as I do," Ceausescu replied, snapping his fingers for a new bottle of wine for himself and another jar of honey for Arafat.

Under Ceausescu's pressure, Arafat finally agreed to go over these proposals with his closest collaborators and to send an answer through Constantin Olcescu, the Romanian chargé d'affaires in Beirut who doubled as the DIE station chief. "The sooner I get your answer, the greater the chance of my acting as your advocate in Washington," Ceausescu admonished.

"In less than 24 hours," answered the fidgety Arafat.

"If not in 24, then in 48. You may also think about giving some conciliatory hints to the West about 242 and 338." Those were the two United Nations resolutions that the PLO refused to accept.

"I will," said Arafat, winking at Ceausescu, before changing the subject. "I need some more blank passports from you, Brother Ceausescu. A hundred. Israeli, Jordanian, West European. A few American ones, if you can."

"What is mine is yours," said Ceausescu, going over to Arafat and affectionately kissing him on both cheeks. As they left arm in arm, the only sound to be heard was the rapid clicking made by Arafat's elevated heels and Ceausescu's thick leather soles in their short steps across the marble floor. Ceausescu is only five foot five, and Arafat just a few hairs taller.

When the automated sliding door had closed behind them, Hassan came up to me. "When can we talk?" he said in German. In the 1960s, Hassan studied engineering in West Germany and became president of the Union of Palestinian Students in Europe and of some affiliated workers' unions. In West Germany alone, there were over 3,000 Palestinian students and 65,000 workers. The vast underground intelligence network he formed in Western Europe was invaluable in Arafat's struggle to consolidate his position as head of the PLO. It was also a decisive step toward the very close relationship between the two of them and the absolute free hand Hassan got from Arafat.

"Olcescu will pick you up as soon as we can shake our bosses," I proposed. "Okay, 'Annette'?" Hassan registered an almost imperceptible shock at mention of his code name.

Once outside, we could see the two leaders walking in the garden, looking from behind exactly like Tweedledum and Tweedledee. They were wearing the same khaki sweaters and trousers, custom made in Romania for the PLO. The way they walked was identical, swinging their arms with the same movement. In their military-style outfits they looked out of place amid the marble statues, artesian fountains, and exotic shrubbery, all softly illuminated as if in fairyland. The garden belonged to a waterfront palace built 15 years earlier as a personal residence for the previous Romanian leader, Gheorghe Gheorghiu-Dej. The enormous presidential quarters and private offices were surrounded by numerous other amenities, such as a movie theater, plant conservatory, gymnasium, enclosed swimming pools, large boat dock, and luxurious apartments for Dej's long-time girlfriend, a well-known actress, and for each of his two daughters and their families. After Dej died, in 1965, Ceausescu attacked him for his personal excesses, termed his residence "unproletarian," and turned it into his guesthouse for top level visitors. The new residence Ceausescu himself built ten years later was, however, even more luxurious.

Hassan and I followed along behind Ceausescu and Arafat. After a few minutes, the two leaders shook hands, kissed effusively, pounded each other on the back, kissed again, and shook hands once more.

TAKING OVER ABU NIDAL'S "BLACK JUNE"

I left with Ceausescu on foot, his residence being only a few minutes away. Stefan Andrei was waiting at the gate. "No official meeting with Arafat, no press communique. He's leaving at daybreak so as to be in his office in the morning. As secretly as he came tonight," said Ceausescu *en passant*, without answering Andrei's greeting of "Long life to President Ceausescu," the most casual of the normal salutes given him and the one used by only his closest subordinates.

"You go on back, Pacepa," Ceausescu said to me. "Talk with Hassan. And don't forget, he loves Chivas Regal."

Andrei was still waiting at the gate. For this evening he had arranged an elaborate dinner to celebrate his appointment as minister of foreign affairs, and he wanted me to go with him. I explained that Ceausescu had given me one more order to carry out, but I assured him that I would be there later on.

It was a half hour later when I left Ceausescu's residence. "To

'Roma,'" I told my driver. "Roma" was the unofficial nickname for an old and elegant DIE safehouse I reserved for special cases. It was so called because of its location on Roma Street.

When I got there, Hassan, Munteanu, and Olcescu were already comfortably installed in blue velvet easy chairs. On the black cocktail table in the middle of the cosy room stood two glasses of Scotch on the rocks and one cup of "tea." Conspiracy was so deeply imbedded in Hassan's blood that even here his Chivas Regal had to be in disguise.

"Do you remember the 'Shuqairy' plan, Abu Munteanu," Hassan started out.

"Do I ever!" Turning toward me, Munteanu explained: "It's an influence operation we started together, General. Codenamed for Ahmad Shuqairy, the first PLO chairman, who drafted the National Covenant and the Constitution and who, during the Six Day War, escaped from Jerusalem disguised as a woman."

"The 'Shuqairy' operation is the Chairman's favorite," Hassan went on. "It's designed to make him look like a moderate. He personally recruited its first agent of influence, 'Solomon.' You do remember him, don't you, Abu Munteanu?"

"The doctor who organized the attack on the El Al bus at the Munich airport in 1970? The one who was secretly instructed by the Chairman to pretend reconciliation and approach the Israelis—but was then publicly denounced by him?"

"Yes. Do you also remember 'Helmuth'?"

"That Austrian agent of yours?"

"Well, then I have news for all of you. The Chairman dispatched 'Solomon' to Vienna, where, with 'Helmuth's' help, he made contact with some leftist Israeli politicians and started to float the 'reconciliation plan' past them." Looking at me, he explained: "The one we had set up together with Abu Munteanu. Then 'Helmuth' started blowing the story up and spreading it around. And now the big news: 'Solomon' and his Israeli partners will receive the Kreisky Prize, the one given for peace and human rights, or something like that. Isn't that interesting?"

"What's your political gain?" Olcescu asked, with a touch of suspicion in his voice.

"I instructed our people among the PLO hardliners to urge that 'Solomon' be reprimanded and told to renounce the prize or else resign from the Palestinian National Congress. Then Brother Kaddoumi and the Chairman will publicly defend him and praise Kreisky, even though he's a Jew. That ought to make it clear in Austria that the Chairman is a moderate, willing to negotiate."

"The student is about to outdistance his teacher," said Munteanu, looking at Hassan with professional pride.

"The 'Shuqairy' operation is the one mentioned by Chairman Arafat earlier this evening," Hassan explained to me.

"What's the next step?"

"The next step is your job. Your influence agents in the Austrian government should whisper into Kreisky's ear every day that he was the first Western leader to take a step toward the reconciliation between the Palestinians and Israel, and that he should also be the first to recognize the PLO officially. That such a gesture would make Arafat even more moderate. And that only someone who had good official relations with both parties could mediate in a conflict," said Hassan, unfolding his plans.

"The Comrade will like it," replied Munteanu. "It's exactly his style."

"I'm working on another operation, Abu Munteanu," Hassan continued. "It's a long-range one, but it looks very promising. Do you rememeber Sabry al-Bana?"

"The fellow who always had heart problems? The 'Father of the Struggle'?"

"Yes. His *nom de guerre* is Abu Nidal. He's the one who always wanted us to blast off at Israel every day of the week. There was no way we could do that, so in 1974 he decided to go it alone. He went to Bucharest with the Chairman once."

"I know him well," said Olcescu.

"After he left us, Abu Nidal approached Baghdad. He got more than ten million dollars from the Iraqis and used it to create the Fatah Revolutionary Committee, which some Baghdad circles immediately began calling the 'real Fatah.' A few months ago, Abu Nidal formed his own terrorist group, which he calls 'Black June,' after the June 1976 entry of Syrian troops into Lebanon. Last January they killed our representative at his Green Street office in London and announced that they were prepared to assassinate other PLO representatives."

"He was a friend of mine," said Olcescu.

"That wasn't Nidal's operation. It was ours."

"You killed your own representative in London?" Olcescu asked.

"In a revolution some people always die," said Hassan, a crafty glint coming into his eye. "Nidal himself is now spending more time in East German and Iraqi hospitals than he is standing on his own two feet. But we've taken over control of his 'Black June' through the agents I had there. All the top jobs under Nidal are held by my men. We're the ones who are really running 'Black June' now, not Nidal. We, not Nidal, now have the last word in setting its terrorist priorities."

"We, not Nidal, provide the intelligence support and the passports needed for its operations," Munteanu added.

"We, not Nidal, decide where to kill, where to act," Hassan continued, "and to top it all off, Iraq or Libya will foot the bill, as the Chairman says. They finance Nidal's Black June. The Chairman gave me the names of some of our people abroad that we could live without, and I've passed them to my men in the 'Black June.'"

"Why kill your own people?" Olcescu persisted stubbornly.

"We want to mount some spectacular operations against the PLO, making it look as if they had been organized by Palestinian extremist groups that accuse the Chairman of becoming too conciliatory and moderate."

"Isn't that a classic?" interrupted Munteanu.

"The Chairman asked the PLO Executive Committee to sentence Nidal to death as a traitor."

"I see," Olcescu remarked.

"I need your help, Brothers. I need some passports for 'Black June.' That's why the Chairman asked Brother Ceausescu for blank passports."

"'What's mine is yours,' is what the Comrade said," I pointed out.

"Thank you in advance, Brothers. The Chairman is now really hooked on influence. It won't be long before I'll be able to create a positive image for him in the West."

During 1985, Abu Nidal's name cropped up in the Western press linked to a new wave of Palestinian terror, after the November 1985 hijacking of the Egypt Airlines 737 jetliner to Malta ended with the death of sixty people. In early December, the

American media also reported that the PLO had publicly come out against Abu Nidal: "Earlier this month, Arafat's second in command, Khalil Wazir, adopted the . . . line that Abu Nidal is one who is a tool in the intelligence services of the Arabs. . . . Once he was in the hands of the Iraqis, now he is in the hands of the Syrians and Libyans."[1]

Only a few days after this PLO public declaration against Abu Nidal, on December 27, 1985, two simultaneous attacks took place against passengers in Rome and Vienna waiting to check in for El Al flights, leaving 18 dead and 121 wounded. Describing these terrorist operations, Time *magazine wrote: "In just ten terror-filled minutes last Friday, the civilized world was thus given yet another reminder of its vulnerability at the hands of suicidal terrorists, of the lethal instability that emanates from the Middle East and, finally, of life's terrifying fragility. Responsibility for the attacks was claimed by a dissident Palestine Liberation Organization splinter group. . . . Hours after the assaults, a man speaking in Arabic-accented Spanish called a radio station in Malaga, Spain, and claimed that both attacks had been carried out by the 'Abu Nidal organization.' . . . Abu Nidal is the code name used by Sabry Khalil Bana, 45, who quit Yasser Arafat's Palestine Liberation Organization in 1973, contending that Arafat had softened his opposition to Israel. Abu Nidal, in turn, was condemned to death by the PLO. Interviewed by Arab reporters recently in Libya, where he reportedly established a headquarters a few months ago for his Fatah Revolutionary Council, Abu Nidal has also been a frequent visitor to Iraq and Syria."[2]*

Just three days after these bloody operations, the Western press reported that Austrian Interior Minister Karl Blecha said "that he 'rules out' any involvement by Al Fatah, Yasir Arafat's branch of the Palestine Liberation Organization, in [the December 27, 1985] terrorist attack at the Vienna airport."[3]

Hassan's debriefing continued for another hour. When the meeting was over, Olcescu brought out a full bottle of Chivas Regal.

[1]Christopher Dickey, "Infamous Terrorist Suspected," *The Miami Herald*, December 29, 1985, p. 1A.

[2]"Ten Minutes of Horror," *Time*, January 6, 1986, pp. 74–6.

[3]Paul Lewis, "Chief Austrian Investigator Absolves Top P.L.O. Group," *The New York Times*, December 30, 1985, p. A6.

"Anything new on my friend 'Monique'?" Hassan asked.

"She's back on the job, lashing out at the Comrade as usual. I'm sure he'll soon be asking you to take care of her again," answered Olcescu, whose case it was.

"Monique" was a reference to Monica Lovinescu, a respected intellectual living in Paris who had been working as a United States government employee for Radio Free Europe. She had spoken out publicly and forcefully against Ceausescu's unprecedented personality cult and his efforts to build his own dynasty. On a brisk day in October 1977, Ceausescu called together his minister of interior, the chief of the DIE, and me for a walk in his rose garden.

"Monica Lovinescu must be silenced," he began. "Not killed. I don't need any uncomfortable French and American investigations. . . . I want her to become a living corpse. Use foreign hands, so that no evidence can turn up that could lead back to a Romanian connection." It was Ceausescu who decided that "Annette" should be used to carry out this operation. Hassan assigned three PLO officers to the job, one of whom, disguised as a French mailman, was to deliver a telegram to Monica's door. One chilly day in November, Bucharest received a wire from Beirut saying: "TELEGRAM HAS BEEN DELIVERED." According to a report later sent by "Annette," "Monique" had been severely beaten, but not badly enough to make her a "living corpse." His men had had to break off precipitously, when some of her neighbors happened onto the scene.

Leaving the safe house, Hassan put his hand on my shoulder and, speaking German, expressed his real pleasure at meeting me again, after so many years. Then he asked in a low voice, "I understand that Brother Doicaru is no longer with the DIE. Could that be dangerous for me?" Nicolae Doicaru, who had been Hassan's official DIE contact ever since that first meeting in Ceausescu's office in October 1972, had recently been removed as chief of the DIE.

I replied: "You know how much Brother Ceausescu respects you. You are in good hands."

"How many hands? Are there others who know about me?"

"Of course not," I lied, understanding Hassan's oblique reproach for today's unusual meeting, with three Romanian intelligence officers present. In fact, my little white lie was not very far from the truth, as no more than four other Romanians knew "Annette's" true identity.

When I came back from the door after seeing Hassan and Olcescu out, Munteanu was talking on the telephone. As he hung up, his face registered disgust.

"I just called the microphone monitoring center to ask about the 'Fedayee,'" he said. That had been Arafat's code name for a number of years. "After the meeting with the Comrade, he went directly to the guest house and had dinner. At this very moment, the 'Fedayee' is in his bedroom making love to his bodyguard. The one I knew was his latest lover. He's playing tiger again. The officer monitoring his microphones connected me live with the bedroom, and the squawling almost broke my eardrums. Arafat was roaring like a tiger, and his lover yelping like a hyena." Using his napkin, Munteanu wiped his hands, then his right ear. "I've never before seen so much cleverness, blood, and filth all together in one man."

That had become Munteanu's standard definition of Arafat. A few years earlier, Munteanu had spent months pulling together all the information the DIE had accumulated on him. He collected not only Romanian intelligence reports and the take from the concealed microphones targeted on Arafat during his visits to Bucharest but also the secret reports on him provided by the Egyptian, Jordanian, and Syrian intelligence services. "I used to think I knew just about everything there was to know about Rahman al-Qudwa," Arafat's true name, "about the construction engineer who made a fortune in Kuwait, about the passionate collector of racing cars, about Abu Amman," Arafat's *nom de guerre*, "and about my friend Yasser, with all his hysterics. But I've got to admit that I didn't really know anything about him," said Munteanu, when he brought me his finished study on Arafat. The report was indeed an incredible account of fanaticism, of devotion to his cause, of tangled oriental political maneuvers, of lies, of embezzled PLO funds deposited in Swiss banks, and of homosexual relationships, beginning with his teacher when he was a teenager and ending with his current bodyguards. After reading that report, I felt a compulsion to take a shower whenever I had been kissed by Arafat, or even just shaken his hand.

Nicu's Oysters

On leaving the safe house, I was dog tired and did not really
have much of a desire for one of Andrei's dinners. These bac-
chanalian orgies never lasted less than five or six hours, the time
Andrei needed to transform his usual athletic stride into a weav-
ing, wobbling slink. As Central Committee secretary for international relations since 1972, Andrei had the main say, after
Ceausescu and Elena, in making and renewing official assignments abroad, and he spared no effort to make this known among
the Romanian embassies. Andrei's office became a Mecca for the
members of the foreign service. All of them try desperately to get
assigned abroad and stay there for as many tours as possible, any
place being better than Romania, and Andrei started soliciting
favors in return for helping them. At first neckties, then fountain
pens, watches, and suits. All this booty lay piled up helter-skelter
at the back of his office. He put on a brand new suit or at least
a new tie every day, and he did not wear the same watch any
longer than a week, except for the gold ones. The ambassadors
and other diplomats also sent him delicacies in the diplomatic
pouch, in the form of ice chests full of lobsters, oysters, and other
seafood, along with cases of wine. It got to the point where he was
getting some of these delicacies every day from one or another
of the embassies. And so Andrei started giving exotic dinners for
a few friends almost every other evening, held in one of the
official guest houses.

This evening the dinner was different, because Andrei was
celebrating the accomplishment of his fondest dream, becoming
foreign minister. He had invited Ceausescu's son Nicu; his oldest
friend, Cornel Burtica, who had become minister of foreign trade
on the same day as he had been promoted to minister; Dumitru
Popescu, the Central Committee secretary for propaganda; and
his closest friend, Cornel Pacoste, the deputy foreign minister.

The affair was being held at the Party's guest house for foreign
Communist parties, an enormous brick building in the middle of
a manicured park on Kiseleff Chaussee. I got there shortly after
midnight. When Andrei came over to embrace me, he was pretty
unsteady on his feet, a good sign that the party would not go on
much longer. An instinct for self-preservation makes him always

leave his dinners under his own locomotion. Nicu was trying to pour Scotch from a bottle into one of Pacoste's ears. When drunk, Nicu is always either extravagant or aggressive.

"A spy among us!" yelled Nicu when he spotted me. He drank several slugs from his bottle, while trying to negotiate his way over to me. "Let me kiss our master spy. C'mon general." Nicu lunged toward me, trying unsuccessfully to push Andrei against the wall. Although they are the same height, Andrei has a much better build.

Popescu beckoned to me. Unusually intelligent, he was considered by Ceausescu to be a propaganda genius. Since his discovery, in 1968, Popescu had written most of Ceausescu's speeches, and that was why he had been kept in the same position ever since. Haughty and arrogant, he was famous for being comtemptuous and rude with his subordinates. "Don't ask why," he used to say when giving an order. "Just do what I tell you. I am your lord." That is why, among Party activists, his name became Popescu the Lord, and he was proud of it. The first time Andrei invited him to one of his dinners, Popescu accepted "only if you have Mateus rosé." Andrei got the wine, and since then they had been close.

"I've been talking with Burtica about the Comrade's visit to Washington. We want your advice," Popescu said to me.

"I'm closed, Lord. I'm hungry."

"Oysters for the general," screamed Nicu, noisily smashing a plate on the edge of the table to catch the waiter's attention. "Four dozen on ice. Where are you, you scum?" he addressed the waiter, throwing a glass that just missed him and crashed into the wall.

Another waiter came in with a drink for me. "I want to drink to our new foreign minister," I said, trying to get Andrei's attention.

"Hip hip hooray! Hip hip hooray! To our best foreign minister. And my best friend," yelled Nicu, now up on his feet and balancing uncertainly. He went behind Andrei's chair and started to sing. "Happy birthday to you. Happy birthday to you," while generously pouring out Scotch on Andrei's head. "When my old man gives up the ghost and my old lady craps, I'll make you my prime minister. And you, Pacepa, my foreign minister. You're all my friends."

Leaning on the table with one hand, the other wiping the Scotch off his face, Andrei stood up. "First of all, I want to thank Comrade Ceausescu for his confidence in me and to assure him through his son and you, comrades, that I will not betray his trust. Secondly, I want to thank our Communist Party for the help it has given me to arrive at this pinnacle." Bloated with alcohol, with Scotch dripping from his hair and face, Andrei was a wretched sight—vastly different from the person he is in his office.

A waiter came in with a silver platter full of oysters. "Put it here, in the middle," ordered Nicu, pointing toward the table. "Is there any seasoning on them?"

"They are just fresh and raw, Comrade Nicu," replied the waiter.

"They need seasoning, you idiot. This isn't a cat house, it's a VIP club." He precariously climbed up onto the table and started urinating on them, careful to "season" every oyster. "Come on, comrades. Let's have an oyster," he urged the guests, while unsuccessfully trying to pick up an oyster for himself. It took Andrei and Pacoste some time to get Nicu back into a chair. "Nobody's eating? Who doesn't like my seasoning? Nobody? Then I'll wash them off." And Nicu started squirting with a syphon bottle over the oysters and over the rest of us sitting around the table. Andrei and Pacoste, half intoxicated, thought it was funny. Burtica and the Lord, half sober, tried to protect themselves as much as possible.

Around three o'clock the party finally broke up. Two waiters and three drivers had a hard time helping Andrei and Pacoste into their cars. I left with Burtica and the Lord, both of whom were singing, but could also still walk. We left Nicu pushing a waitress toward the edge of the table while tearing off her blouse. "I want to fuck you, here. Right here on this table, you slut."

CHAPTER

III

IT was 8:30 AM when I entered Ceausescu's office to take him to visit IPRS/II, the Romanian version of the Soviet "city of microelectronics." Before I could even open my mouth, the heavy double door unexpectedly banged open, and Elena blew in like a hurricane, holding a slim file in her hand.

"I have this letter," she started out aggressively. "It just arrived."

"What letter?"

"Some woman in Germany wrote to me saying that I could understand it better than you could. That he's a spy and that she's going to go to the police and that he's going rot away the rest of his life in jail, unless I do something about making that whore let him out of her clutches."

"Slow down, Elena, slow down. Who is the spy?"

"Her husband. Who else?"

"And who is the whore?"

"Don't ask me. Ask Pacepa. You and he pull all the strings around here, behind your closed door."

"Give me the letter, Elena, would you?"

Ceausescu read the letter, then passed it to me. "Isn't this about 'the Scholar'?" he asked.

"It certainly is," I said, after glancing through it. "The Scholar" was Ceausescu's nickname for a DIE agent, a West German whose code name was "Malek." The letter was from his West German wife and his daughter, a lawyer, and was personally addressed to Elena. It was written in a careful but firm manner and stated that "Malek" had been trapped into a love affair in Romania and was being used by the Romanian intelligence service. It stressed that the two writers had hard evidence of his intelligence activities for Romania, but that they would not inform the West German security service, the *Bundesamt fuer Verfassungsschutz*, if Mrs. Ceausescu would order the Romanian intelligence service to break off all contact with "Malek" and to revoke his permanent entry visa into Romania.

"This is bad news. Have you ever met him yourself?"

"No, Comrade Ceausescu."

"Take a close look at the case and arrange to meet 'the Scholar.' " Ceausescu ordered me to show "the Scholar" the letter and ask what he thought would be the best solution. "He ought to have a better feel for it than we do. We need to save him—he's too important for us."

"Yes, comrade."

ROMANIA'S TECHNOLOGICAL CITY

"Let's go," ordered Ceausescu, abruptly leaving the room, followed by Elena with her duck-like waddle. By the time she reached the foot of the stairs, Ceausescu was already installed in the front seat of his Mercedes. Elena sat on the back seat by herself. I drove ahead in my own car.

Ceausescu had decided on this visit to IPRS/II a few weeks earlier, on his return from a secret trip to Moscow. There, Leonid Brezhnev had taken him on a visit to his "city of microelectronics," located not far from Moscow but so secret that their limousine had even had the curtains drawn across its side windows. "Now," he told me Brezhnev had said, "when our nuclear capability can destroy the Western hemisphere many times over, our first priority is to build rockets able to reach American rockets even before they are launched. . . . The most modern microelectronics is what we need for that."

Ceausescu told me that Brezhnev and his KGB chief, Yuri Andropov, had praised him for the Romanian penetration of Texas Instruments, saying that Moscow considered it one of the most valuable contributions to the Warsaw Pact's military strength. According to Ceausescu, the first technological intelligence on several Texas Instruments families of integrated circuits for military use, sent by Bucharest to Moscow, had been faithfully reproduced and given the name "Logika," and had caused a major improvement in the latest Warsaw Pact military equipment.

"I knew that electronics was the thing of the future, but I couldn't believe that those almost invisible chips could be so decisive for the very existence of Communism," Ceausescu ended his story. That very day he approved the inclusion of a visit to Texas Instruments in the official program of his trip to the United States.

The Soviet "city of microelectronics" is part of a very secret system of "technological cities" called GNTs, standing for *gorod nauki i tekhniki* (city of science and technology). Their purpose is to create new military technologies and weapons systems based on intelligence stolen from the West by the KGB and the GRU and their East European sister services. The GNTs are really small towns, but they are not recorded anywhere, not even on the Soviets' most highly classified military maps. They are built and run by the KGB, and their entire population, composed mainly of scientists and engineers, is on the KGB payroll, although some of them are on rotation from the Ministry of Defense and various scientific research organizations. By 1978, their combined population had reached more than 20,000.

Joseph Stalin himself ordered the construction of the first technological city, after the spies Julius and Ethel Rosenberg had supplied information on the atomic bomb. That "nuclear city," which put an end to the West's nuclear monopoly, was soon followed by others. The "cosmic city" became famous on April 12, 1961, with the launch of Vostok I, which made Yuri Gagarin the first man in space. Brezhnev created the "city of microelectronics" to turn the Soviet nuclear capability into a first-strike weapons system of American accuracy. The latest in the series was the GNT for *strategicheskaya oborona*, or strategic defense, charged with developing anti-ballistic missile systems, in line with the Kremlin's philosophy that he who controls space rules the earth.

Today's visit to the Romanian counterpart was intended to show Ceausescu the important new equipment for producing military chips recently smuggled out of the United States: diffusion furnaces, epitaxial reactors, mask aligners, pattern generators, photorepeaters. From all of this equipment the DIE had carefully removed the brand names and any other indication of its provenance. The members of the Romanian government present for the occasion were Prime Minister Manea Manescu, his first deputy, Gheorghe Oprea, and the ministers of national defense and of interior, Ion and Teodor Coman. Ion Avram, the minister of the machine building industry, which included the electronics industry, and General Teodor Sirbu, the director of the DIE section handling technological espionage, were the hosts. Everybody was lined up outside what was called "Pavillion TI," after one of Sirbu's in-house jokes. An electronics engineer himself, Sirbu had made the penetration of Texas Instruments a matter of personal pride.

When the presidential car pulled up, Ceausescu stepped out vigorously, shook a few hands, and immediately entered the building.

"Is it clean enough in there?" Elena asked me as she got out of the car. Her light green, flowered silk dress with matching high-heeled shoes was one of her favorite good luck charms.

When Elena caught up with Ceausescu, he was looking through a microscope mounted on a table in front of two brand new, large-scale integrated circuit testers. "Look, Elena. It's just fabulous!"

Elena went up to the microscope and peered down into it without adjusting the lens. "Fascinating!" she exclaimed, although she could certainly not have seen anything, as her eyesight is very different from Ceausescu's. "Texas Instruments?" she asked, pointing at the testers. She had picked up the name from the schedule of the upcoming visit to the United States and was anxious to show off her scientific knowledge.

"Fairchild Corporation," Sirbu automatically corrected, before perceiving his mistake.

Next to the testers was an exhibit of the various kinds of chips produced in that section. "We have all kinds of chips here," Avram's grating tenor rang out loudly and without warning, "from ones that will be used in our future rockets to ones that will modernize our wives' kitchens. The new washing machines and driers will put an end to the ugly rows of clothes draped over the balconies of our tall, new socialist apartment buildings."

Avram's demagogery was the secret of his longevity as a minister.

"Listen to him, darling," Elena jumped in. "Why washing machines, Avram? Just to protect your fat wife's manicure?"

"R-Romania i-is at w-war with capitalism," Ceausescu interrupted. He stutters when making an important point, as well as when he is nervous. "W-We c-cannot win with washing machines, comrades. D-Dollars are what we need, to protect the freedom of our people, and w-we c-can make a lot more d-dollars s-selling arms than w-washers and dr-driers."

"Pay attention to the Comrade, fatso," Elena stressed.

The visit went on for another hour or so. Ceausescu stroked every significant piece of equipment with his hands or caressed it with his eyes, talked with the engineers, and even cracked a few jokes. Elena's attention was directed more toward keeping her shoes clean.

After the Ceausescus had toured all the sections designated for the visit, they were invited to an exhibit room that was heavily guarded and protected by several alarm systems. Set up by the DIE, the exhibit contained the latest technological intelligence and hardware relating to a new generation of microelectronics for military use, the *very* large-scale integrated circuits. The intelligence and hardware had been obtained from the West.

When the entrance door had been relocked from inside, Sirbu burst out: "Comrade President of the Socialist Republic of Romania, Supreme Commander of the Romanian Armed Forces, and most esteemed Comrade Elena Ceausescu, this is the exhibit 'Romania 1984,' showing our beloved motherland at the end of the next five-year plan."

Ceausescu, now smiling broadly, walked over to a row of tables set up in the middle of the room.

"Here we have a three-dimensional display of the basic process for producing very large-scale integrated circuits, with samples for each intermediate stage," Sirbu began. Avram had played first violin during the visit inside the factory. Sirbu conducted the performance here, behind closed doors, as it was intelligence from the West, not Avram's research, that lay at the heart of the new development in microelectronics that was by 1984 to become a powerful military industry.

How to Steal American Technology

After Sirbu had finished presenting the display, he invited the Ceausescus to look at the opposite wall, where there were photographs of the most significant items of equipment Bucharest was in the process of obtaining to produce very large-scale integrated circuits.

"Without exception all this microelectronics manufacturing equipment is American," Sirbu began his new subject, "and all was obtained by the DIE and the DIA without the knowledge of the producers." The DIA was the military intelligence service. "Following the valuable guidelines given us by our Supreme Guide, Comrade Ceausescu, we are making wide-scale use of venal and corruptible East-West traders as well as of our own proprietary firms in the West for worming the equipment out of the United States."

Sirbu then presented several of the main scenarios for smuggling equipment out, using dummy firms or offices created in West Germany, Austria, or Japan by DIE illegal officers documented as Westerners. These companies allegedly imported the American equipment for some non-Communist country. Somewhere during the shipment, the markings and accompanying documents were exchanged for deceptive descriptions, representing the equipment as something innocuous like photographic or laboratory supplies, and the crates were then loaded onto Romanian commercial airplanes or ships. For security reasons, the dummy firms, which were also used for obtaining embargoed equipment requested by Moscow, were dissolved after several important operations and replaced by new ones. Sirbu emphasized that such firms were being widely used to obtain every kind of embargoed Western equipment, from robotics to military avionics.

Then Sirbu invited the Ceausescus over to a row of tables filled with samples of the most important integrated circuits produced in IPRS/II and of the military equipment in which they were, or would be, used. On the wall behind were statistics on the technical documents and hardware obtained by the DIE and the DIA for each type of chip, on the number of research man-years saved by their use, and on the gross savings in hard and national currency.

"Let's sit down for a moment," said Ceausescu, who, contrary to his custom, had not once interrupted Sirbu. He sucked the air in between his teeth several times and began to speak with visible emotion.

"Th-The tw-twentieth c-century is the c-century of pr-proletarian and Th-Third World revolutions," he said, beginning as usual with a Marxist sermon, then developing it until reaching his same old conclusion that selling weapons was the most desirable business in today's world. "We should not direct our industrial potential toward producing toilet paper and kitchen appliances as Avram just suggested. Let that be a task for future generations." He was now pounding the table. "Space radars and high-powered laser weapons are what we should put our efforts into. Today we have enough intelligence strength to obtain these American secrets. That would make us the most important and respected Soviet partner within the Warsaw Pact tomorrow," Ceausescu predicted.

A few years earlier, Brezhnev had sent his minister of interior, Nikolay Shchelokov, to Bucharest as his personal messenger. Besides asking for comradely help in supporting the "nuclear freezers" and the international peace movement as "ways to disarm the West," Brezhnev wanted technological intelligence on American anti-ballistic systems, space radars, and lasers. Later, Yuri Andropov, as KGB chief, had sent Bucharest numerous requests for intelligence in this field, and Ceausescu had become an eager pioneer here, too.

Ceausescu went on expounding his views on space lasers and other military equipment of the future, until his voice became hoarse. "W-we h-have here in th-this room a picture of Romania's bright and shining future. A Romania that, after 2050 years of struggle, will become, before our very eyes, one of the ten most important arms producers on earth. Invisible n-nuclear power and this l-little, insignificant-looking piece are the b-bricks that will be used to build our Communist order," he said, waving around a chip he had picked up from the table. "Weapons, comrades, are the most desirable items of trade in today's world!"

"How sensitive! What a shame we're not in a public meeting," Oprea whispered into my ear.

"That doesn't mean we shouldn't also smuggle plain chips out onto the Western market as American-made," Ceausescu added, winking toward us.

"We haven't spent any money on research," Manescu contributed. "We haven't paid for the license. We don't have to pay any royalties. And our labor costs are a fraction of those in the West. It wouldn't surprise any of us to see some Western firms in trouble soon. Especially Texas Instruments."

"Manescu took the words right out of my mouth," Ceausescu said, "but he didn't go far enough." Ceausescu always has to have the last word. "He should also have said that stealing from our deadly enemy is not only much cheaper, it is a proletarian duty, because we ought to defeat capitalism with its own weapons, comrades." Then he started handing out orders. He wanted a much closer connection between intelligence and production, for the rapid solution of any future technical difficulties. Concentrating exclusively on microelectronics for miltary use came next. The DIE was then firmly directed to shift the entire weight of its operations from Western Europe and Japan toward the United States, which was becoming more and more vulnerable to intelligence penetration. The IPRS/II experiment was ordered to be enormously expanded and directed toward the future of microelectronics, the very large-scale integrated circuits, which would soon change the face of the earth. "If I were to use an allegory, I would say that this very room was the place where Romania's future was today being spawned. We should continue to steal the best of everything capitalism has and put it to work for Communism. Don't misunderstand me, comrades. Stealing from capitalism is not like stealing out of our own pockets. Marx and Lenin have taught us that anything is ethical, so long as it is in the interest of the proletarian class and its world revolution," Ceausescu concluded.

As Ceausescu started mopping his forehead and the back of his neck, Manescu took the floor, eulogizing the "visionary Romanian leader," the "learned humanistic thinker," and the "supreme personality" and his views for the future. Flattering the top leader is a common factor in all the Soviet bloc countries, but Romanian fawning is overly effusive, in keeping with Romania's Latin temperament.

When he left, Ceausescu as usual got into the front passenger seat of his Mercedes, forcing Avram and me to crowd into the back seat with Elena. He was euphoric.

"What weighs more, Avram, a pound of gold or a pound of chips?" asked Ceausescu.

"A pound of your brains, Comrade Ceausescu," replied Avram promptly.

"You're not so dumb as you look, Avram," Elena chimed in. "Why aren't you taller and thinner?"

"If I could write laws," Avram came back at her, "I would make one that nobody should be taller than the Comrade. Period."

"Could you picture Napoleon being six-foot-two?" Ceausescu threw out from his front seat, turning toward us. "Or Stefan the Great being six-foot-three?" Both are Ceausescu's idols. The latter was a Romanian hero who was under five feet tall and who reigned in the fifteenth century, waging 47 wars and winning all but one of them.

When we got back to his office, Ceausescu signaled me to follow him in. "Over there," he said, meaning at IPRS/II, "I saw a lot of bright engineers from the Defense Ministry. We should quietly move them over to the DIE one by one. I'll give you five hundred more slots for technological intelligence. But only for military microelectronics." After a pause, he said, "Let's put some Texas Instruments chips in the heads of our DIE officers, Pacepa. That might make them smarter at swiping American technology!" followed by a peal of laughter.

The heavy double door of Ceausescu's office banged open, and the tall and slender Nicu, Ceausescu's younger son, came striding in, swinging his arms like a windmill, with Elena waddling behind him.

"Pana is an idiot!" Nicu exploded. "A total idiot. Unless he did it on purpose!" He threw himself into an easy chair, dangling one leg over the arm and clasping his other knee with both arms, while casually showing off his new gold Rolex on one wrist and a heavy gold bracelet on the other. After tossing his head to arrange his long hair gracefully on his shoulders, he negligently unbuttoned his jacket so that the gold French label of its lining could easily be seen. Everything Nicu wears is custom made in Paris or London.

"Why don't you lock Pana up in a madhouse, Papa? Or make

me his boss for a week," Nicu spat out in his very rapid, almost unintelligible manner of speaking. Gheorghe Pana was the minister of labor and the chairman of the General Union of Trade Unions.

"What did he do to my sweetheart?" exclaimed Elena, pursing her lips.

"I went to his meeting today—Papa said that I should. I told him I had a date with a skirt at ten, and what did the skunk do? Not a damn thing. His stupid meeting dragged on until just now."

"How many times have I asked you to be done with that numbskull, Nick? Remember how he told me to shut up that day at the airport?"

"That's all for today, Pacepa," said Ceausescu, interrupting Elena. "Take care of the things we discussed."

"I want to have a word with you, too," said Elena to me. "Meet me at the institute with Pana's file." The "institute" was the Central Institute for Chemical Research, which had been especially created for Elena. Actually it grew out of the old Institute for Chemical Research, known as ICECHIM, but it then got a new name, broader nationwide responsibilities, and a couple of additional new buildings.

ELENA'S AMBITIONS

When Ceausescu came to power in 1965, nobody had heard of his wife, but it did not take her long to develop a taste for fame. As the wife of the adulated Romanian leader, it was child's play for the ambitious Elena rapidly to accumulate scientific titles: chairman of the Section for Chemistry in Romania's Supreme Council for Economic and Soviet Development, headed by Ceausescu himself; vice president of the National Council for Science and Technology, which was especially created for her; full member of the Romanian Academy, the highest title for a scientist in any Soviet bloc country.

In 1973, I was with Elena in Buenos Aires when, fascinated by Isabel Peron's political ambitions, she decided to launch herself into active political life. In the unprecedented cult of personality created around Ceausescu, Elena rose rapidly on the political scene: member of the Grand National Assembly; member of the

Central Committee of the Communist Party; member of its Political Executive Committee (the Romanian politburo); and, only a year ago, member of its Permanent Bureau, Ceausescu's invention for concentrating power in the hands of himself and his wife. Today Elena is the number two in a hierarchy in which only the name Ceausescu has a firm place, the rest of the company being nothing but decorative flowers constantly shifted from one place to another, to prevent them from putting down roots.

Despite Elena's new political dimensions, she always kept her first title, director of ICECHIM. The main decorations in her office were Ceausescu's portrait hanging behind her desk and the volumes of his works, bound in red leather, lining the bookshelf on one side. The other two walls were covered with Elena's many Romanian and foreign scientific diplomas, together with numerous certificates belonging to medals for scientific, technical, or educational merit. Most of them were familiar to me, since in the last ten years the DIE had been deeply involved in obtaining them abroad for her. Elena greedily collects every scientific diploma she can, from honorary degrees to memberships in foreign scientific societies.

"Just look who's here waiting for me," Elena called out cheerfully to me in her nicest voice, as she plopped her new, pot-bellied alligator bag down on her desk. It matched her shoes, the stylishly pointed toes of which seemed to be pinching the large bones of her peasant feet. "Let's go over in the back," she said, taking my arm.

"In the back" actually meant the room to the right of Elena's office, behind a hidden door. Slightly smaller than her main office, the room was sparsely furnished and had only one telephone in it, the S line, connecting her with Ceausescu and a few other "privileged" persons, myself included. This was where Elena spent most of her time when she was at the institute, trying to keep out of the way of the professional scientists. "The Comrade is busy studying in the back," was her executive assistant's inevitable formula, whenever someone from the institute tried to reach her. There, "in the back," Elena would be either gazing boredly out the window or snoozing in her favorite easy chair, a copy of *Scinteia*, the official Communist Party newspaper, falling off her lap.

"Have you brought the Pana file?"

"Yes," I answered, putting the file of Minister Gheorghe Pana on the desk. The voluminous folder contained the current week of transcripts from the monitoring of his telephone and of the microphones installed in the Panas' home and offices. Pana was a man full of life and energy. His brilliant, laudatory speeches about Ceausescu had moved him from provincial Party activist to top member of the hierarchy. When he came to Bucharest, suddenly promoted one of the 11 secretaries of the Central Committee of the Communist Party, he had only one fault in Elena's eyes—he was married to a Jew. The Panas survived, however, and later Elena made peace and gave them a nicer house in the fanciest area of Bucharest. Every corner of the new house had microphones, but they never revealed anything but Pana's loyalty to Ceausescu and his wife's devotion to the Marxism she was teaching at the university. Elena eventually became bored with the Panas. "You'd better shove one of your sexy illegal officers up under her skirt," she told me. "I'm sick of her pretending to be the Virgin Mary." That did not work, however, and Elena's relations with the Panas soured again. Eventually Pana started drinking, and his wife started discreetly voicing her dissatisfaction with Elena's knowledge of Marxism.

Elena opened the file and started leafing through. "Has she bitten into the apple?" she asked me.

"Not yet." I tried to leave room for some hope.

"I'm tired of her. You have three more months to get her to hike her skirt up. Three months, in which I want her tape-recorded, photographed, and filmed. I want it all right here, in this file. Let me see her lying naked under your man. Wiggling her precious rear end till they reach an orgasm," said Elena nervously, slapping the file with her heavy, bony hand. "Three months," she went on. "Do you hear? In three months I want Pana out. If you can't get his *madame,* I'll get Pana himself." She was starting to yell. She can change her mood faster than anyone I have ever known, even Ceausescu or Arafat.

"I WANT AMERICAN MINKS"

The *S* telephone rang, and Elena's face lit up when she answered it. "Bring it in. Right now. And two plates." Turning to me she said, "I have a surprise for yo-o-ou. When I left home I

ordered a truffle pâté. I was sure the idiots had forgotten." I had
never had truffles before, and I was certain that Elena would
make me pay dearly for them now.

Sure enough, the bill was steep: "I've been told that America
has the best mink coats in the whole world. Isn't that true, darling?" I got the point. Every time I was preparing one of Ceausescu's visits abroad, Elena would ask me to arrange for her to
receive "nice gifts." For Japan the catchword had been pearls.
And she got them, many very expensive sets of pearls. Black was
at that time her favorite color. All those strings of black pearls
were paid for by Japanese firms interested in doing business with
Romania.

"I want some American mink coats," said Elena in an authori-
tarian voice. "Full length coats, and capes. You have a whole
army of people over there, darling, with nothing to do but to go
from one diplomatic reception to the next. Now let's put them
to work. I'm sure Madam Peanut hasn't the foggiest notion what
you do with a mink skin. I can't expect to get anything from her
but a basketfull of peanuts, can I, darling?" Elena asked, evidently hoping I would contradict her.

"As far as I know, Jimmy Carter wants to give you his book
Why Not the Best? and a volume of satellite photographs showing
Romania," was my modest reply.

"It's just as I told you, darling. The farmers try to pretend
they're intellectuals. What's the biggest private company we'll
be visiting there?"

"Texas Instruments. But I know that the Comrade has some
special thoughts about the visit there."

"There shouldn't be any connection between the Comrade's
getting what he doesn't have and my getting what I don't have,
if your 'instrument' is big enough." In private Elena's jokes could
be pretty crude.

For a few moments I was far away, trying to compose telegrams to the Washington and New York stations giving them the
good news that they had been blessed with the magic word
"mink coats" for the few days left before the visit. Finally I heard
Elena saying, "Are you upset, darling?"

"Just thinking, comrade."

"Don't you like mink coats?" Without waiting for an answer,
she continued. "Let's face it. Today Romania is better known in

the West than the Eiffel Tower, and more respected than the Queen of England. And it's all because of the Comrade and me. Everywhere we go, our hosts try to give us the red carpet treatment, but, unless we teach them, they don't know how. Remember the Germans? It was enough for you to drop the word 'car' as a hint, and everybody gave us cars. How many did we get?"

"The Mercedes 600 limousine for the Comrade, the 450 for you, a coupe for Zoia, two Audis for Nicu. And the 36-foot mobile home equipped as an office-on-wheels for the Comrade." None of these had ever been used, since the whole family had plenty of vehicles from the Romanian government.

"Or take that idiot, Hussein, darling. Don't you remember how it was with the yacht?"

Did I remember! It had happened in June 1975, when I was with Ceausescu and Elena at King Hussein's vacation residence at the Gulf of Aqaba, and he invited us onto his private yacht. It was the first time Elena had ever been on one. After dinner, Ceausescu and Elena asked me to join them in a walk on the beach.

"I want that yacht," was all Elena could blurt out through her tears, repeating it over and over. "I won't leave without it."

Ceausescu, visibly attracted to her idea, broke in. "Serbanescu is a good friend of Hussein's." Serbanescu was the DIE officer he always used as his interpreter at meetings with Arabs. "Just tell him how to put it to Hussein."

The next morning, when King Hussein asked for me, he was with Serbanescu. "You must understand that this particular yacht was my personal gift to Alya," he said apologetically. "But I'll immediately order a new one from the United States. I propose that she be named the *Friendship*."

One year later, I was informed by King Hussein that the yacht was ready for delivery. It was Ceausescu's wish that Hussein have it picked up from the United States and delivered to me in Istanbul. Three months more, and I was able to get the *Friendship* out of Istanbul and docked, under heavy guard, at a secret naval base in Mangalia on the Black Sea. The Ceausescus had never yet used it.

"Do you know what?" Elena interrupted my reveries again. "Don't forget my jewelry displays. I want one at Blair House, but one at the Waldorf Astoria, too. New York has always been better for jewelry."

"I won't."

During Elena's visits abroad, the DIE stations routinely had to persuade famous jewelery houses to display their finest collections to her. It was not a difficult task, though, because Elena always bought up unbelievable quantities, all paid for by the DIE.

"It looks like we're going to have a good visit in America, Pacepa."

"I'll do my best, Comrade Elena."

"Aren't you nice."

In a report for The New York Times News Service *on September 12, 1978, David Binder wrote: "Pacepa had been President Ceausescu's personal security advisor and helped prepare his state visit to the U.S. last [spring]. American officials recalled that his Rumanian advance party made numerous 'impossible requests.' One was a demand that when the President and his wife Elena visited the Texas Instruments headquarters in Dallas, the Rumanians 'expected' the company to present Mrs. Ceausescu with a fur coat."*

DEALING WITH AN UNWANTED BOYFRIEND

"What's new with Mihai," asked Elena, suddenly changing the subject.

"Business as usual," I replied.

Mihai was a young correspondent for *Lumea (The World)*, a Romanian magazine on foreign policy. A few months before, the microphone and surveillance coverage Elena had ordered me to keep on her daughter, Zoia, had revealed that Mihai had become her favorite boyfriend. Elena had rejected him long before Zoia started to talk about him. For one thing, his parents were too insignificant, uneducated, and unstylish. "Just look at the way they walk. Look at her bow legs and fat ass, and his pigeon-toed feet," Elena used to say, studying the clandestine photographs and movies made of Mihai's parents. It was, however, on the day she first saw a picture of Mihai wearing blue jeans that she really began to detest him. "Disgusting," was her verdict, and after that Mihai, too, was put under continuous coverage. Elena's hatred for him grew greater and greater, nourished by tidbits from the telephone intercepts, microphone transcripts, and movies secretly made of his sexual encounters with Zoia. Now just hearing Mihai's name made Elena nervous.

"I just don't want to have that bastard around here one single day more. I could kill him like a gnat. A car accident or something. But my harebrained daughter might blow it up into a big drama. I want him sent abroad and left there to rot," said Elena, whose voice had suddenly turned acidic. "I'm sick of having nightmares about him night after night."

Guinea was where Elena wanted to deport Mihai. "Remember when we were in Conakry?" she asked. "The ambassador told us about one of our tractor technicians whose head had just cracked open like a watermelon. It was found to be full of larvae and worms. Remember, the ambassador said that they had some kind of bug that laid its eggs through the skin of your head? I want a picture of Mihai's head cracked open like a melon."

Elena's ill-humored monologue about Mihai was finally interrupted by the ring of the S telephone. I could hear Ceausescu's voice asking if she wanted a movie for this evening.

"I don't want any movie. I want to talk to you tonight, *mon cher.* Right now. At home," answered an enraged Elena, before violently banging down the receiver. Snatching up her purse from the desk, she stalked off without another word and continued across the lacquered parquet and down the marble floor of the corridor, her heels clattering like a machine gun.

I had just gotten back to my office, when a jangling noise broke the silence. It was the special telephone connecting me with the Ministry of Foreign Affairs.

"Hi, Mike. How are you?" I heard Andrei's voice saying, as lively as ever. "I just got a telegram from Beirut. Something about a public statement on 242 that Arafat made today. A couple of Western ambassadors over there are already interpreting it as a sign of moderation in Arafat's policy. Aren't you clever! Did you call me earlier?"

"I tried to reach you first thing this morning," I said. "I just wanted to congratulate you on last night's party."

"Sorry you weren't able to come earlier. We had smoked salmon from London, lobster from Paris, rack of lamb from Athens, Kobe steak from Tokyo, cantaloupe from Istanbul, bananas and oranges from Tel Aviv, and Sachertorte from Vienna. How did Arafat make out with the Comrade?" Jumping from one subject to another, with no apparent relation, is quintessentially Andrei. It seems incoherent, but he does this intentionally to keep his interlocutor on his toes.

"As usual, Andrei. He'll never change."

"Nicu was in good form last night, wasn't he? The way he seasoned the oysters! And later when he squirted the starchy Lord! I almost shit in my pants."

"It wasn't exactly my dream."

"Come on, Mike, don't be such a square. Nicu is a real patrician. Can you imagine the fun we'll have when he's the boss? I just sent a courier over to you with all I have on the Comrade's visit to Washington. He said you'd be going over there soon to put on the finishing touches. When, Mike?"

"By the end of next week or so."

"We'll have a lot of fun there. I'll see you later."

I had not even hung up before Manea called me on the S. The Comrade wanted to see me right away.

When I entered Ceausescu's oversize office, he already had his overcoat on and was evidently about to leave for home. He was standing in front of his large desk inlaid with ivory and looking at the painting hanging behind it. Patriotically entitled *The Great Romania,* it depicted a beautiful young peasant girl walking through a rural landscape toward the viewer. Above it hung the Romanian seal. Underneath was Ceausescu's chair, raised a few inches higher than normal to make him look taller. Seeing me, he began pacing between his conference table for 12 and a wall unit containing the works of Marx, Lenin, and Ceausescu, passing under the Communist Party seal hanging over the entrance door, turning around, and suddenly sitting down at the low table flanked by two easy chairs that stood in front of his desk.

"Any news from Arafat?" he asked.

"I have an around-the-clock open line with Beirut," I began, "and I've had Olcescu go over to Arafat's headquarters every six hours, but the answer has always been 'not yet.' Punctuality has never been Arafat's main virtue."

"If you hear any news, call me at home. If after a few days we still haven't gotten an answer, send Munteanu to Beirut. My proposals have probably run into difficulties with Arafat's collaborators. He ought to use 'Annette' to solve them. Munteanu will just have to give her a rap on the knuckles, if she balks," Ceausescu ended, getting up and exiting through the room's side door.

MY ONLY FRIEND

When I arrived home, it was very late. The militiaman guarding the Polish embassy across the street did not come out of his booth for his usual formal salute. He was surely asleep. But the curtains on the second floor moved discreetly.

I went directly to the living room. Everything was still dark, except for a painting over the fireplace, which was illuminated by a small light attached to its frame. That light burned day and night, like an icon candle. From the frame an old man looked out at me with his large, warm, friendly black eyes. He was wearing a peasant's cap and his black Sunday suit. In his wrinkled face I could read sadness and suffering, but also wiliness. It was a painting dated 1937 by Camil Ressu, a Romanian classical painter, who had later become my daughter Dana's art teacher, and who was still alive.

The old man had had a place in my home for many years, among the many other paintings filling the walls. I had always loved art. When I was a little boy I used to do landscapes and portraits in watercolor and oil. My dream was to become a painter, but my father, who had not attended the university himself, since he had had to help raise seven younger brothers and sisters, had wanted me to become an engineer. In high school, my love for drawing found an outlet in a school newspaper I began editing. It was called *The Porcupine* and consisted of satirical cartoons. At the Polytechnical Institute, *The Porcupine* changed into a wall newspaper on a bulletin board. Its main character, a porcupine, became famous for its wry and disarming way of expressing human thoughts and feelings.

When I finally started working, I no longer had time for drawing, and my interest in art shifted to collecting. In time my walls became filled with paintings collected over almost 30 years, highlighted by those I had received from Dana, a recent graduate of the Art Institute who was now a professional painter. Until 1960 my old peasant friend was just one of my many paintings.

In the summer of 1960 Dana and I took a vacation on the Black Sea, where we learned about an artists' colony in a miserable little country village near the Bulgarian border. The village was May Ninth, named for World War II's V-E Day, but it certainly had nothing victorious about it. Writers, painters, sculptors, and poets rented rooms from the local peasants in the summer and lived the bohemian life, supposing themselves freer from government surveillance than in the city, even though they had to put up with the absence of such civilized amenities as running water and indoor bathrooms. At Dana's insistence we drove there and spent a day at the nearby beach.

In the afternoon, when we got hungry, we went into the village to the one grubby, state-owned restaurant and sat down in the garden. At a nearby table I noticed a very old man sitting by himself who looked familiar. I kept trying to place him, when suddenly his eyes struck a chord with me. I moved over to his table and asked if I could buy him a meal. He replied that he might be able to drink something, although he probably could not handle anything to eat, since he no longer had any teeth. Then I asked if the name Camil Ressu meant anything to him.

"Do I know Mr. Ressu, God keep him!" he burst out. "He painted me, and then he ran off with my wife!"

By now I was sure I had the old man of my painting. I was curious to learn more about him, but he was completely senile, and it was only with great patience that I was finally able to extract a few details. His name was Fedot Lily, and he had been a miller in that village in the 1930s. For several summers he had rented a room to the young painter Ressu, who had come there to paint the local landscape and its peasants. Ressu had spent many days painting Fedot and had ended up having an affair with Fedot's young wife and persuading her to run off with him.

Now that I knew who he was, the old man of my painting became my best friend. When I came home late in the evening, only Fedot would still be waiting up for me. I would tell him about my day—my thoughts, my anxieties, my hopes. He would listen silently, but his bright eyes would let me know that he understood and promised not to breathe a word of what I had said to anybody. I used to think that it would be good for every intelligence officer in the world to have his own Fedot Lily, with whom to share the daily ups and downs of a job that could not be discussed with anyone else. In fact, Fedot Lily became the only fellow in the whole world to know the real me.

Lying on the large cocktail table next to Fedot there was a printed invitation to the opening of Dana's art show. "My Beloved Dad" had been entered on the line for the name, penned in her feminine yet firm hand.

"Will I ever be able to take Dana with me on a trip abroad?" I silently asked my old friend. "Just once, Fedot." His large, warm, friendly black eyes turned unbearably sad.

CHAPTER
IV

"MIHAI should simply disappear without a trace," ordered Ceausescu as soon as he saw me.

It was shortly after six in the morning, and he was walking in the garden with Elena. Nervously he ordered me to have Zoia's friend Mihai immediately sent abroad for an indefinite period of time. Without letting Zoia know, without telling anyone else, without talking to his superiors at *Lumea*.

"Have Mihai recruited as a DIE agent and sent out on the first plane to Tunis."

"Let's have him sent to Guinea, Nick. Do that for me," begged Elena.

"To Tunis for now. Isn't your chief of station also chargé d'affaires there?"

"Yes, comrade."

"That's good. He should report only to you. And you to me and Elena. Nothing to the Ministry of Foreign Affairs."

"I'll die if I don't get to see Mister Blue Jeans in Conakry, Nick!"

"All in good time, Elena. I don't want those pigs from Free Europe or some stupid journalist poking his nose into my personal affairs." He especially hates Radio Free Europe.

"And if he keeps on trying to turn Zoia's head, even from there?"

"In Africa anything can happen. Some thug might leave him half dead on the street, or a car might. . . . We'll think about it."

"My patience has its limits, Nick." She was calm, but imperious.

DISAPPOINTING CHILDREN

Ceausescu's personal intervention in the lives of his children, two sons and a daughter, has been exceedingly rare. As a general rule he has delegated his responsibilities as a father. After 1965, he gave his oldest son, Valentin, then a teenager, into the custody of his ambassador to England, Vasile Pungan. Educated in London, Valentin learned nothing about Marxism, and when he got back home he was a great disappointment to his parents. His father urged him to study Marxism, but Valentin preferred science. It was the last straw when Valentin, against the will of his parents, married the daughter of a deceased rival of Ceausescu's, and he was immediately disowned. The visits of Valentin and his wife to the presidential residence now take place mostly when Ceausescu himself is not there.

When Zoia, the second born, turned 15, she was given into the care of Mircea Malita, who became deputy minister of education and later of foreign affairs, because Ceausescu planned for his daughter to start her life as an ambassador. Malita, an absent-minded professor who sometimes forgot to open his garage door and would drive his car straight through it, managed to get Zoia a master's degree in mathematics, give her a taste for logic and independent thinking, and allow her a few hours a week of freedom spent with other students. One of her fellow students, who became her boyfriend, pushed Zoia out of the shell Elena had carefully built to isolate her from common mortals. The long lines people stood in at the crack of dawn for their daily food and the indescribable difference between her meals at the presidential residence and the ones in the miserable student canteens astounded her. Such things shook her confidence in her father's public speeches, but she could not break through his busy daily routine to tell him what she had seen. She was able to talk only with her mother, who immediately labeled her boyfriend an anarchist and a reactionary. Zoia tried another boyfriend, but the lines were still there in front of the stores. When he had an appendectomy, Zoia for the first time put her foot into a hospital for ordinary people, where her boyfriend had to share a bed with another patient. The misery she saw there was even worse than that in the student dormitories, where each student at least had a bed to himself. Again she tried to reach her father. When she could not, the pedestal he had been on began to crumble, and her ideals about the society Ceausescu was building in Romania began to erode away.

In late 1975, Zoia was attracted to a group of dissident students. When the Securitate started arresting them, she herself became an outspoken critic of her father's personality cult and of her mother's machinations for power. In the end she refused to bear her father's name and would answer only to *Mademoiselle*. "The name Ceausescu has become a dirty word," Zoia repeatedly told all her friends. Her most grievous sin, however, was her obstinate refusal to be married off to any of the candidates carefully chosen by her mother. Zoia was determined to find her own husband, but every name she suggested was met only with fierce rejection as not being lofty enough for the future Ceausescu dynasty. That was the beginning of a bitter struggle with Elena, who eventually decided to monitor every minute of Zoia's personal life. Microphones were installed everywhere, from the bedrooms and baths of her apartments and her office to her white Mercedes coupe—a familiar sight at gatherings of Bucharest's chic young people—and the coverage was rounded out by around-the-clock physical surveillance. In 1977 she was turned over to my care.

Disillusioned with his first two children, Ceausescu pinned all his hopes for the future of his name on the youngest one. He gave Nicu into the custody of Stefan Andrei and Cornel Pacoste—"two brilliant examples of the new Communist intellectual," as he used to call them.

"I want Nicu to become foreign minister," ordered Ceausescu.

"Nicu should be a future Romanian president," was Elena's instruction to his mentors.

Nicu is entirely different from his older brother and sister. As a child, he disliked school. It was much more fun to spend his time with the bodyguards and security officers swarming around the presidential residences and to imitate their manners and vocabulary. As a young boy he became an object of derision for Valentin and Zoia, who had never seen him reading a book. His father and mother made it up to him, however. Merely by raising his voice, Nicu could have anything he wanted, and more. At 14, praised for attaining manhood by raping a classmate, and he was thereupon given his first car. At 15, he got his first boat. And at 16, he became a drunken rowdy, scandalizing all of Bucharest with his car accidents and rapes. Rumors about his "sickness" reached Ceausescu's ears. "We should work harder and better," is Ceausescu's usual prescription for curing the ills of Romanian society. "Stop drinking and start working," was the only help Ceausescu gave Nicu, when he found a few minutes for him.

THE AMBASSADRESS BECOMES "BERTHA"

When I arrived back at my office, General Gheorghe Moga was already there for our weekly discussion on cases of common interest.

Moga had been a DIE officer for 15 years. He was known for being tactless and for never saluting when he entered a room. Stolid, unfeeling, ruthless, and terribly stubborn was the description of him I had given Ceausescu five years earlier when he was looking for a DIE officer to make chief of counterespionage, in order to have that directorate work more closely with the DIE to recruit influence agents. "That's exactly what I want," Ceausescu decided. The next day, Moga was sworn in. After Moga had finished reporting on his cases, I asked about the ambassador's wife.

"When the ambassadress makes love with 'Teodorescu,' nobody would ever recognize her. She becomes a different woman," Moga began.

"Who's 'Teodorescu'?" I asked.

"My officer. The best ladies' man I've ever had. He works under cover as the American ambassador's driver."

"What about the ambassador?"

"Naive as they come. He knows as much about his wife as he does about Romanian politics. He's swallowed 'Horizon' hook, line, and sinker."

According to Moga, the Counterespionage Directorate had kept a much closer eye on the American ambassador than on any of his predecessors. He spoke Romanian, had many friends among Romanians, and was very sympathetic to Bucharest's trumpeted independence. His personal involvement in smuggling dissidents' manuscripts out of Romania in the diplomatic pouch, as well as his close relationship with the CIA officers working at the embassy, had raised suspicions that he might be a deep-cover CIA officer, just as Ambassador Nicolae Nicolae in Washington was a deep-cover intelligence officer. Moga had run several attractive and well-educated female agents against the American ambassador, without success. The astonishing result of the coverage was that his wife, not the ambassador, had the roving eye. That helped Moga to get the ambassadress and "Teodorescu" into bed together, and then to turn what had been a casual fling into a real love affair. Moga was now waiting for Ceausescu's approval to send "Teodorescu" to the United States to revitalize the affair and to to use the ambassadress' influence over her husband to facilitate the driver's emigration to the United States. "Teodorescu's" task in the long run was to continue developing the wife of the American ambassador toward recruitment as an influence agent. Her initial task would be to manipulate her husband in accordance with Bucharest's interests.

"Having an affair is a long way from being an agent. You know that, Moga," I said after he had finished.

"Not in the whore's case. The ambassadress is head over heels in love with 'Teodorescu,' who's already wormed a lot of things out of her that she's learned from her husband. I've got everything down on tape."

After Moga had left, I called in General Gheorghe Angelescu, the director of the DIE brigade responsible for the United States, and briefed him on the case of the U.S. ambassador's wife. Before leaving, Angelescu gave the ambassadress the code name "Bertha."

SCORNEA'S GIRLS

After reading through the incoming telegrams, I called to have Colonel Cristian Scornea bring me the file on "Malek," the man whose wife and daughter had written to Elena. As a teenager, Scornea had been adopted by a military unit and brought up by the soldiers. There he learned the worst side of army life: smoking, drinking, and wenching. Having had a German mother and a Romanian father, he grew up bilingual. During World War II he served as the interpreter for his military unit in dealings with the Germans. After the war, when the Communists took over the Romanian foreign intelligence service and purged it of its old officers, Scornea was among the first group of new recruits, selected from the army because of his clean record and his good German. Since then he had worked continuously for the German-Austrian Department of the DIE, spending more years of his mature life in Austria than in Romania.

Women were Scornea's favorite recruitment targets, and sex his basic recruitment method. He soon became famous for his female agents in the host country government, who would bring him documents out of their offices concealed in false compartments of their handbags. The DIE's section responsible for making the double-walled purses ended up being known as "Scornea's Section." Now he was assigned to the Ministry of Foreign Trade in Bucharest and had the task of recruiting visiting foreigners.

Like Moscow, Budapest, Prague, Warsaw, Sofia, or East Berlin, Bucharest has been transformed by the Communists into a marketplace for intelligence. In every hotel designated for tourists, telephones are tapped at the flick of a switch, microphones concealed in every room are activated as soon as a foreigner moves in, and closed circuit television provides continuous coverage of the dining areas, corridors, and even the public restrooms. Television cameras installed outside the most important hotels, such as the Intercontinental, the Athenee Palace, the Lido, and the Nord, together with infra-red equipment, are used to cover foreigners' movements outdoors. Surveillance officers posing as managers or waiters in the most important restaurants activate transmitters concealed in ceramic ashtrays on foreigners' tables. An army of prostitute agents is dispatched every day to the nightclubs, hotel lobbies, restaurants, theaters, opera and concert halls, circus arena, movie theaters, parks, and streets. Foreigners studying at Romanian universities who have been recruited as security agents—most of them black Africans—are directed to solicit illegal money exchanges or homosexual relations. Scornea had become an important part of this whole diabolical system.

RECRUITING "MALEK" WITH "ANDREA"

"Brief me on 'Malek,'" I said, when Scornea entered my office. He was panting a little under his load of files. Forty years of heavy smoking and almost thirty years spent developing agents in bars, restaurants, and bedrooms had taken their toll on him.

"The Scholar," as Ceausescu called him, was one of Scornea's most recent cases, and he could brief me on it without checking the files. "Malek" had been born in Germany, where he had become a chemical engineer. Investigation revealed that he had been a ranking Nazi officer in the chemical troops during World War II, and that after the war, allegedly to shield his activity as a Nazi, he moved to Portugal. There he started his own business as a "military consultant" and "arms engineer," dealing with various African and Asian countries. Later he built an arms factory in Cascais, Portugal, which produced air-to-surface incendiary bombs and artillery shells. These were exported, both legally and illegally, to certain Asian and African countries.

Years later, retaining his Portuguese passport and arms factory, he returned to West Germany, and not long after that he began handing out business cards showing himself as "NATO technical advisor." One such card was in the file. The investigation also revealed that "Malek" enjoyed a good financial position and was not vulnerable to monetary approaches, but that he appeared to be susceptible to an approach using a woman. In order to take a closer look at him, Scornea invited "Malek" to make several business visits to Bucharest. The take from concealed microphones and cameras led to the psychological analysis that he was at the "mid-life crisis" age and might be looking for a long-lasting romantic attachment.

With the help of the Securitate troops, Scornea selected "Andrea," a young girl living in the town of Brasov who was thought to be the ideal match for "Malek." She was then 21, a *cocotte* and local security agent, who was working as a waitress in a luxury restaurant, where the employees participated in the risqué shows. Previously she had been used successfully in other operations against West German visitors. She also had the operational advantage of having had a father who had been a political prisoner of the Communists' and had his property nationalized, thereby ensuring her a sympathetic ear from Westerners. Scornea armed "Andrea" with detailed data on "Malek," instructed her to become his girlfriend, and told her how to build a long-term relationship with him. A room equipped with concealed television cameras and microphones was ready and waiting at the luxury hotel Aro in Brasov, when Scornea brought "Malek" there for a week's vacation as guest of the Ministry of Foreign Trade.

"Andrea" became a passionate love story for "Malek," and Scornea his best friend and confidant. He got "Malek" a permanent entry visa for Romania and looked after "Andrea" when he had to be away on business. In return, Scornea asked "Malek" to give him samples of the military products made by his factory. Later he asked for their technology. By 1977 the recruitment was complete.

"Can you tell me about 'Malek's production as an agent?" I asked further.

Scornea, who was always in love with his agents, told me that "Malek" had made an important contribution to the modernization of the Romanian chemical troops. Based on his technological intelligence, which had been verified by Elena's Central Institute of Chemical Research, a super napalm factory was built in Bucharest. "Malek" had secretly transported numerous American air-to-surface bombs, artillery shells, and mines via Africa to Romania, where they were exhibited for several weeks in a room next to Ceausescu's office. These items were now being mass produced in Romania, with "Malek's" technical assistance. He had also helped to create napalm rain and other incendiary substances that were being tested by the commander of the chemical troops, General Mihai Chitac.

"A secret exhibit of military equipment produced in Romania based on 'Malek's' materials was presented to the Comrade just two weeks ago, when he was also given a demonstration of them. And this is only the beginning of our cooperation with 'Malek.' Military lasers and radar for low altitudes are only a few of the things he's working on now. We mustn't allow his stupid, estranged wife to destroy such a jewel of an agent," Scornea said with pathos, bringing his report to a close.

"Have you set up the meeting with him as I asked?"

"Yes, General. He's waiting in his hotel for my phone call."

"Ten o'clock in my other office. And leave 'Malek's' files here. I want to take a look at them."

My other office, corresponding to my other, unclassified hat as state secretary in the Ministry of Interior, was in the ministry's main building. It was located in a heavily guarded area on the second floor, with that of the minister and another three of his deputies. The fellow who now came in with Scornea looked exactly like the man he had described and the one in the numerous clandestinely taken photographs of "Malek"—dressed and undressed—I had seen in the files. Today he was elegant in his dark gray suit, white shirt, and silver tie. A diamond stickpin and gold-with-diamond cufflinks completed his *soigné* appearance.

I immediately made it clear that we were meeting at Ministry of Interior headquarters at the personal direction of President Ceausescu to discuss an important matter regarding "Malek's" secret cooperation with the Romanian intelligence service. After waiting for "Malek" to make a long peroration about how proud he was to serve Romania and its president and about how grateful he was for his new life in Romania with a wonderful young lady, I gave him the letter Elena had gotten from "Malek's" West German wife demanding that Romania stop using him as a spy.

As soon as "Malek" understood what the letter was about, he turned white as a sheet. He read on, his veins swollen and throbbing, his fists clenched, evidently under the pressure of a terrible rage. The strong, deep-seated conflict between husband and wife seemed to rob him of his voice.

When "Malek" was able to speak again, he was calm and rational. With German orderliness and pedantry, he presented a plan for dealing with the situation. Its bottom line was that his devotion to Ceausescu's government was boundless, and that no threat could put an end to his cooperation. More secrecy in his relations with Romania was called for, however, as a change of tactic. "Malek" offered to open an office in Vienna and to use it as a cover for his work on Romania's behalf. His idea was that the Vienna office should be an export-import firm, conducting legal activities that could provide cover for the smuggling of Western military and technological materials into Romania. "Malek" asked that "Andrea" be allowed to leave Romania for Vienna, where they could continue their life together. He accepted that, at this point, his permanent entry visa for Romania be canceled in his passport. In his view, that would calm his wife and daughter down and give him time to obtain a legal divorce.

"Mister State Secretary, my life is now for her and with her," he said of "Andrea." He took a picture of her out of his wallet. "And now she's pregnant!"

I deliberately asked to be received by Ceausescu a few minutes before noon. This was the best time for finishing something up quickly and, usually, without complications, since his lunch was religiously served at twelve-thirty.

"What's new?" I heard his usual question to me coming from behind the large desk inlaid with ivory.

In a few words I briefed Ceausescu on what I had found in "Malek's" files and on the proposals he had made during the meeting.

"We might be able to kill two birds with one stone," Ceausescu mused happily, as he gave me a conspiratorial wink. "We might solve the mess with his wife, as well as our need for well-covered export-import firms in third countries—like that one we created in Japan, so we could smuggle equipment for integrated circuits and chips out of the United States. Didn't I always say that 'the Scholar' had a German head? Hard, but well organized."

Ceausescu approved "Malek's" plan on the spot, including the exit visa for "Andrea" and $100,000 to open the Vienna office, which, he decreed, should use "Malek's" name but in fact be a DIE proprietary operation.

"Take care of 'Andrea,' too. She might be suspected abroad. What close relatives would she be leaving behind here?"

"Her mother and a brother, I think."

"After she leaves, have them arrested, harrassed, lose their jobs, or whatever. 'The Scholar' is too important a case, and we should help him move to America after a time," said Ceausescu. Then he went further into detail about helping "Andrea" to deceive possible Western investigators by arousing pity and tears instead of suspicion.

Emperor Bokassa I Takes a Romanian Agent as Wife

I was at the door, about to leave, when Ceausescu's voice caught me from behind. "First thing this afternoon I want to make a visit to the Star plant."

"Stars" was the euphemism Ceausescu and Elena used for diamonds. They were both so fascinated with diamonds that they personally set up and ran an operation against the Central African dictator Jean Bedel Bokassa for the purpose of getting mining concessions from him. In 1975, they invited Bokassa to make an official visit to Bucharest, where they saw to it that he would be shown a good time by a stunning Romanian girl, Gabriela, whom they had selected for the assignment. A few weeks later, at Bokassa's request, Gabriela was sent to Bangui on one of Ceausescu's own airplanes and accompanied by Ceausescu's chief advisor, Vasile Pungan. Gabriela Bokassa, Romanian wife of Emperor Bokassa I of the Central African Empire (now Republic), became one of Ceausescu's favorite examples of how an agent of influence could be infiltrated into a target country at the highest level. Because of her, Bokassa secretly accepted ten percent of the profits, paid into a Swiss bank account, from the diamond mines he arranged for Romania to operate on advantageous terrains. For a couple of years Gabriela was a successful agent, until she became so frightened of Bokassa that she managed to escape him and run off to Paris. The suitcases full of jewelry she took along helped her to begin a new, anonymous life in France. When certain rumors about Gabriela's disappearance from Bangui started circulating in France, Ceausescu ordered the DIE to spread the rumor that Gabriela had been sent back to Romania by the emperor. Ceausescu wanted to discourage French journalists from searching for her. This disinformation operation bore fruit. In November 1977, a French newspaper published the following: "The Romanian wife that Bokassa I at one time snatched away to his harem from the Bucharest Ballet deceived His Majesty, horrors! with a chauffeur-guardsman (bodyguard): the gardener [sic] was killed, and Lady Chatterly has been locked up on the other side of the iron curtain courtesy of Aeroflot."[1] This news item was later reprinted

[1] "Papa Bobos et la kermesse aux morts," *Le Canard Enchaine*, November 2, 1977, p. 5. (Translated from the original French).

in other French publications, including a biography on Bokassa, proving temporarily helpful in protecting Gabriela's anonymity in France and the secret about her activity as a DIE agent.[2]

"Stars" for the Comrades

In 1975, Ceausescu ordered me to obtain the technology and the equipment for producing synthetic diamonds. Large-scale intelligence operations mounted by the DIE produced results, and two years later I presented him with samples of diamonds experimentally obtained using that technology in a small pilot installation. Unexpectedly, Ceausescu ordered me to construct a "factory" and produce synthetic diamonds secretly in Romania. "It is not your job," he said, "but I am afraid no one else could do it and at the same time keep it a secret."

I built the plant as a capitalist would, making do with an old, unused automobile service building instead of constructing a huge, eye-catching new one, as is the fashion in the Soviet bloc, and I fitted it out with a lot of computers instead of workers. By the fall of 1977, the plant was at the technological testing stage, and at the beginning of January 1978 it started industrial production on a large scale.

When Elena saw the first samples of very clear diamonds, she made a long face and immediately asked that a jar "so big" be filled with synthetic diamonds in preparation for Ceausescu's sixtieth birthday celebration, on January 26, 1978. At Elena's initiative, every Romanian institution, from the prime minister's office down to the smallest kolkhoz, was asked and importuned to prepare valuable gifts for the Supreme Guide, sparing no expense. She instructed the DIE to use its powers of persuasion to get Western companies to send expensive gifts. To encourage the flow, a national museum of gifts received by the Ceausescus was hastily opened—although it contained only copies or photographs of the most valuable items.

The birthday results were amazing, the value and quantity of

[2]Pierre Pean, *Bokassa 1er*, Paris: Editions Alain Morean, 1977, pp. 25–6.

gifts received by Ceausescu incredible. The Ministry of Mines produced one enormous, 24-carat gold ingot, with the words "CEAUSESCU AND THE PEOPLE" formed in bas relief on top. The Ministry of Agriculture offered solid-gold ears of hybrid corn. The Ministry of Interior gave him a television and hi-fi stereo unit with a platinum remote control device. The DIE offered a custom-made rifle from the famous British hunting arms producer Holland & Holland, in addition to the jar, weighing over 20 pounds, of synthetic diamonds. The jar remained on display in Ceausescu's office for only a few days. Ever since that birthday, Ceausescu had been very anxious to visit the "Star" plant.

It was a little past two when Ceausescu, refreshed from his daily after-lunch nap, left with me in my car, followed by only one security vehicle. The "Star" plant was at that time one of the most secret industrial units in Romania. Ceausescu spent the whole afternoon walking around the gigantic presses producing the temperature and the enormously high pressure needed to transform the specially imported graphite and chemically pure cobalt into diamond crystals. He was impressed by everything, but I cannot forget the look of absolute astonishment on his face when I opened the vault and showed him the first hundred pounds of diamonds produced there.

Ceausescu did not say anything at the plant. "I like your creation," he said when we got back to his office. "Now let's go into the diamond business in a big way. Your DIE has to sell the 'Stars' secretly on the Western market— the same way it does with the cocaine in transit from Asia to Europe that we confiscate at the border." Romania and Bulgaria had long been smuggling drugs to the West. The smugglers now began selling the diamonds to Western Europe.

"OIL, JEWS, AND GERMANS, OUR BEST EXPORT COMMODITIES"

Suddenly Ceausescu threw out a question. "How much cash do we have in the TA-78 account?"

Reading from my pocket notebook, I told him the exact amount. It was around $400 million.

"Deposit the money we make on the 'Stars' into the same TA account. Understood?"

"Yes, comrade."

"We've also got to up the price Tel Aviv and Bonn are paying for Jews and Germans." That meant the price of exit visas. "Oil, Jews, and Germans are our most important export commodities," Ceausescu added, voicing his favorite slogan. For another hour or so, until Elena came to take him home, Ceausescu kept on instructing me in how to milk more money out of Israel and West Germany.

Jewish emigration has long been a burden for Bucharest, and the huge numbers asking to leave Communist Romania have been a black mark against it. In the late 1950s, a British businessman, Henry Jacober, who had had commercial dealings with Romania for many years and had been recruited by the DIE, asked for an emergency meeting. He told his case officer, Gheorghe Marcu, that he had informed the Israeli foreign intelligence service about his contact with Romanian intelligence, and that they wanted to use him for a special, very secret operation. His message was that the Israeli service was ready to pay the Romanian government a certain confidential amount of money for each Jew allowed to emigrate, based on an unwritten gentlemen's agreement between Jacober and Marcu.

Bucharest turned down this proposal, considering it a provocation, but Jacober was persistent. A few months later he proposed building an automated chicken farm in Romania, free of charge, if 500 Jewish families would be allowed to leave. The Romanian leader at the time, Gheorghe Gheorghiu-Dej, eventually approved the proposal as a one-time experiment. Before the end of the year, a modern chicken farm was discreetly installed in Peris, a small village north of Bucharest, on property owned by the Ministry of Interior. When Gheorghiu-Dej made a visit there a few days later, he liked it, approved 500 exit visas for Jews, and ordered five more chicken farms.

By the end of 1964, the Ministry of Interior had become the largest meat producer in Romania. It owned chicken farms, turkey farms, and pig farms producing tens of thousands of animals a year, several cattle farms, and other farms with some 100,000 head of sheep—all with automated slaughterhouses, refrigerated storehouses, and packing plants. To transport the packaged meat it also had a TIR fleet of refrigerated Mercedes trucks. In early 1965, a Kellog's Cornflakes factory was added to the ministry's food line.

All of these farms and food processing plants were paid for by Henry Jacober, in exchange for exit visas for Romanian Jews. They were built in the same area of Peris and staffed by political prisoners, a pool in which the ministry could usually find the required veterinarians and engineers. "If you cannot find the people you need in the jails, just arrest the ones you need and then use them," was Gheorghiu-Dej's usual answer, when the minister of interior, Alexandru Draghici, would complain that the farms needed more manpower than he could provide. A deputy minister of interior, Alexandru Danescu, was placed exclusively in charge of the farms, the production from which was earmarked for export to the West only. Henry Jacober helped this export both directly and indirectly. After the early 1960s, the annual number of emigration visas for Romanian Jews was entirely dependent upon the eggs, chicken, turkey, pork, beef, and cornflakes exported to the West.

Year after year, the DIE became more deeply involved in Jewish emigration. It had not only to manage the "Jacober-Marcu gentlemen's agreement" but also to obtain the best breeds of animals and to transport them to Romania on chartered airplanes, also paid for by Jacober. The diplomatic pouch was carrying more bull sperm, obtained with Jacober's help and money, than it was secret information.

By far the most spectacular DIE livestock operation, however, was the one run between 1958 and 1965 smuggling live, uncastrated Danish Landrace pigs out of Denmark, with Jacober's help. The white, lop-eared Landrace pig found in Central and Eastern Europe had been transformed in Denmark into a superior hog by selective breeding. The Landrace pigs were the key to Denmark's export trade in Wiltshire bacon to England. Denmark maintained its monopoly and extremely high prices by strictly prohibiting the export of Landrace pigs for breeding. Over a period of seven years, however, the DIE smuggled thousands of piglets out of Denmark. They were anesthetized and transported, first in diplomatic automobiles, then in special diplomatic pouches, and finally in large TIR trucks protected by diplomatic seals. By the beginning of 1965, Romania was producing

50,000 Landrace pigs a year, all exported to the West as bacon and ham with Jacober's help.

The "Jacober-Marcu gentlemen's agreement" was kept in the deepest secrecy. The prime minister, Ion Gheorghe Maurer, who was also Gheorghiu-Dej's personal best friend, did not know a thing about it. Ceausescu himself learned of this operation only in 1965, when he came to power after Gheorghiu-Dej's death. He denounced it as "outrageous," abolished it, transferred the animal farms to the Ministry of Agriculture, fired Marcu from the DIE, and drastically reduced Jewish emigration.

Two years later, Ceausescu had second thoughts—as he usually does—and asked if Jacober was still alive. Soon after, Marcu was reinstated in the DIE, promoted in rank and position, and ordered secretly to resume the contacts with Jacober. This time, however, the exchange was not for animal farms but for hard cash, in dollars. The operation now became more secret than ever. Because of my position I was one of the very few who were aware of it.

After Jacober had died of cancer, the deputy director of Israeli intelligence for immigration, a native Romanian with an Israeli diplomatic passport bearing the name Yitzhak Yesahanu, became the new partner in the "gentlemen's agreement." Ceausescu was happy finally to have a direct connection with the Israeli government, but he ordered that it be maintained simply as a personal relationship between two people and be made even more secret than before. In 1972, after Ceausescu took over the intelligence service and became its immediate supervisor, he decided to remove the DIE's name from the new Yesahanu-Marcu gentlemen's agreement. A disinformation story was spread that Marcu had been removed from the DIE, and soon he was officially appointed deputy director general of the "Institute of World Economics," a cover institution staffed by DIE officers.

The new, still unwritten Yesahanu-Marcu gentlemen's agreement provided that Bucharest would be paid, in cash, a certain amount per head, depending on age, education, profession, employment, and family status, for each Jew allowed to emigrate. In July 1978 this payment amounted to between $2,000 and $50,000 per person. In some individual cases, Yesahanu was asked to pay up to $250,000. The meetings between Marcu and Yesahanu took place monthly at the Romanian embassies in West

Germany, Austria, or Switzerland, where Marcu brought lists containing the names of the Jews approved for emigration, and Yesahanu turned over suitcases full of U.S. dollars. In 1974, one of these suitcases got lost at the Zurich airport, where it was finally found only after a couple of days. It was still intact, containing over $1 million. Over the years, the Yesahanu-Marcu agreement netted Bucharest hundreds of millions of dollars, together with several additional large credits issued by various Western banks, with part of the interest payments defrayed by Yesahanu.

Encouraged by the results, Ceausescu ordered the DIE to initiate a similar operation for selling ethnic Germans. This he considered potentially even more advantageous, Romania having almost a million ethnic Germans within its borders. The sale of Romanian ethnic Germans was arranged along the same lines, based on a personal agreement between the same Marcu and "Eduard," who represented himself as an undercover intelligence officer and personal representative of Hans Dietrich Genscher, the West German minister of interior, who was directly involved with facilitating the emigration of Germans from Eastern Europe. "Eduard" continued in this secret role even after 1977, when he said he had been elected to the Bundestag. Suitcases full of U.S. dollars were transported monthly to Bucharest via the Romanian airline TAROM, and special credits, with part of the interest paid by "Eduard," were periodically issued to maintain or stimulate Ceausescu's enthusiasm for the emigration of *Volksdeutsche* to the fatherland.

In February 1972, Ceausescu decided that additional benefits could be extorted from this hideous sale of human beings, unique in modern history. "No Romanian citizen of Jewish or German descent," he ordered, "should be given an emigration visa unless he has signed a secret agreement with the security forces and has agreed to act as an intelligence agent abroad." Two new components were then added to the DIE, one for the recruitment of Jews asking to emigrate, the other of Germans, but up until 1978 only a few thousand had in fact been recruited. Most of the Jews and many of the Germans who emigrated never did use their secret communications systems and simply disappeared as agents. Some of them, however, were heard from. In reflection of this new operation ordered by Ceausescu, the annual reports on espionage published by the West German Ministry of Interior showed that after 1972 the greatest number of agents uncovered in West Germany had been sent by Romania.

At the end of 1977, Ceausescu decided to wrest one more advantage from his trade in human beings: He ordered Marcu to ask Yitzhak Yesahanu to supply Western arms samples in exchange for an increase in Jewish emigration. An American or British tank was his top priority.

CEAUSESCU'S SECRET FUND

Ceausescu has never received a penny of wages during his entire adult life. Before World War II he was an apprentice to a shoemaker, who paid him with room and board and Marxist indoctrination. During the war Ceausescu was in and out of jail as a Communist and became a Party activist immediately after its end. Since he has been Romania's supreme leader, it has been a matter of pride for him to emphasize that he has never been paid for what he has done. "My whole life has been devoted to the World Revolution of the Proletariat," is Ceausescu's favorite definition of himself.

Ceausescu is also proud of the fact that he has never purchased anything for himself from a store. In fact, it was not until October 1970 that Ceausescu, mainly under pressure from Elena, set foot in a department store for the first time. This happened on an official visit to New York, when he accepted an invitation from the management of Macy's to visit their main store at Herald Square. Ceausescu was astonished.

"How long did it take them to set up that show?" he asked, when he got back to the Romanian Mission to the United Nations.

"Macy's is the largest department store in the world," hedged a puzzled ambassador.

"I mean, to fill up the store with all that stuff we saw there?"

It finally dawned on the ambassador that Ceausescu believed the whole store had been stocked just as a show for him, and the ambassador started to explain what he knew about Macy's.

"Do you subscribe to *Scinteia, monsieur?*" Elena interrupted suspiciously.

"Of course, comrade. Everybody does."

"Then you ought to read it. Read it, *monsieur*, and learn something about America. It's written there in black and white that American stores are nothing but window dressing, that Americans can't buy anything unless they borrow money. And that after they buy something they get laid off and everything is taken away from them again. Show, *monsieur*. Everything is show, to cover up the poverty, to hide how people are sleeping in the streets. Read *Scinteia*, you peasant, you *mascalzone!*"

"Everything I know is from *Scinteia*," the ambassador said, trying to expiate himself.

"When you're talking with me, keep your mouth shut!"

"Let him speak, Elena. He lives here."

"Don't listen to his garbage, Nick. He ought to be sent back to Bucharest and enrolled in a political course."

The next morning Ceausescu told me to check Macy's out and report back to him with the truth. A year later he opened the first—and only—department store in Bucharest. On the day of its inauguration by Ceausescu himself, the store was chock full of merchandise gathered from all around the country. A few days later, its shelves were virtually empty. Periodically the store was "prepared" for visits by high-level foreigners or by Ceausescu himself. It would be closed off to the public and stuffed with merchandise. For his part, Ceausescu has never really believed that Macy's was not especially stocked for his visits.

In 1971, Ceausescu began taking a careful look at money for himself, as insurance "for a rainy day." In that year his old friend Juan Peron, then living in exile in Spain, came to Bucharest begging for financial assistance. Peron badly needed funds to mobilize his labor union bastions in Argentina in preparation for a return to power, and also to maintain his elegant residence in one of Madrid's most fashionable suburbs and to support his wife's pretentions. A special diplomatic pouch that I set up began carrying monthly bags of cash to Madrid for Ceausescu's exiled friend. As a sign of gratitude, two weeks after Peron's reinauguration as president of Argentina he invited Ceausescu and Elena to come to Buenos Aires on an official visit. I was there in the presidential palace when Peron told Ceausescu: "The first time I was president, I thought it would last forever. Now I've learned that everything is ephemeral but money."

By the end of 1973 Ceausescu had opened his own highly

secret account, prosaically codenamed "TA." It contained every penny of cash obtained by the DIE from its special "OV" operations. ("OV" stood for the Romanian *Operatiuni Valutare,* meaning foreign currency operations.) The "TA" account for 1973 was called "TA-73." Thus, for the current year it was called "TA-78." The money the DIE obtained from the West in the form of cheques or bank transfers, which could be legally controlled, was immediately deposited at the Romanian Bank of Foreign Trade, known as BRCE, and credited to the national budget. But the money obtained by the DIE in hard cash—most of it from the export of Jews and Germans—was recorded only in Ceausescu's TA accounts. Cash received in other currency was exchanged into dollars, usually in Zurich. The dollar bills received from Bonn and Tel Aviv were first "laundered" into new ones, in case the numbers had been recorded, and then were kept in a DIE underground vault. It constituted Ceausescu's secret slush fund, and he occasionally withdrew money from it, buying Western cars for his children or ordering a custom-built, armored Mercedes for himself—outlays that were kept secret in Romania. He also used the money for Elena's diamond collection and for the jewelry she bought during her official visits abroad. So far he had spent no more than $4 million from this fund, a negligible sum compared to the total amount accumulated, which was in the neighborhood of $400 million.

"This is for a rainy day," he used to whisper. In 1977 he ordered the DIE to open several secret bank accounts and safe deposit boxes in Switzerland. Only Ceausescu could use these accounts, but as far as I knew there had been no withdrawals from them. They were just kept for "a rainy day."

The facts seeping out after the overthrow of former Philippine President Ferdinand Marcos brought back memories of my days with Ceausescu and the rapaciousness for Western lucre that was growing in him in the mid-1970s. After Marcos and his retinue precipitately left Manila in February 1986, their first stop, on Guam, was as common mortals. But when they left the Andersen Air Force Base commissary with over $12,000 worth of goods without paying for them, they were not acting like common mortals. It is difficult, if not impossible, for someone who has been an absolute dictator for twenty years to become a normal *human being again. Ceausescu and his family have also never paid for anything in the past twenty years.*

The total value of the fortune Marcos managed to divert out of the Philippines may never be learned, but it is probably not far from what Ceausescu has by now stashed away. The only apparent difference is that Marcos had a salary as Philippine president, even if only $5,700 a year. Ceausescu has none.

Late in the evening I called Ceausescu at home to report that there was still no word in from Arafat, and that Munteanu was ready to leave for Beirut, as he had ordered.

"Come here," he commanded, and hung up.

When I got there, Ceausescu was walking in his rose garden, and I fell into step with him.

"Take one of my airplanes and go to Beirut with Munteanu. Give Arafat a copy of the latest messages between me, Carter, and Begin." Ceausescu always put himself first in any company. "And the blank passports he asked for. Give him an even hundred, including American ones. Both facsimiles made by the DIE and genuine passports we've gotten from Gadhafi."

Suddenly stopping and grabbing a button of my jacket, but looking straight through me, Ceausescu added: *"I* ought to be the mediator in the Middle East. I *ought* to be. Can you understand that?"

I was not happy about this trip. The Middle East was not my favorite place to visit, although traveling with Munteanu would make it both pleasant and productive. He had for many years been the chief of the DIE's Middle East Brigade and a close personal friend of Arafat's. In 1977 Ceausescu had approved his retirement but had kept him on as a "special DIE Middle East advisor" for very important contacts with Arafat.

It was soon after midnight when I arrived home. Everything was as usual there. The militiaman from the Polish embassy came out from his booth for his formal salute, the house was dark, and Mrs. Groza was peeking out from behind her window curtain. In my apartment, only Fedot Lily's light was burning.

CHAPTER

V

IT was before seven o'clock in the morning when the *S* telephone rang. Elena had just learned from Ceausescu about my trip to Beirut. She wanted Olcescu to buy her 12 complete sets of damask table linens from Syria, each for a setting of 24, and "some big stars" from Beirut. After I had hung up, my executive officer, Vasile Pop, reported that General Munteanu was there. "Have him come in, and bring him a cup of tea," I ordered.

PORTRAIT OF A MIDDLE EAST EXPERT

Munteanu bounced in, exhuberent and full of energy as usual. "Long life to the General! Your fat, old, semi-retired spy is ready and waiting for another dirty job."

Tall and corpulent, Munteanu was elegantly dressed in a dark, pin-striped suit with a gold watch hanging on a chain draped across his vest, making him look like an old-fashioned American businessman. His large eyes, continuously moving behind the six-dioptic lenses set in heavy black frames, betrayed his inner vitality and the dynamic mind that was under constant pressure and in constant agitation.

"Last night," he said, "Radio Yerevan finally gave the answers to two old questions from listeners: What should we do in case of a nuclear attack, and can you drive a Volga car around a 90-degree curve at 80 miles an hour? You probably didn't catch them. You're a busy general."

The perennial jokes about Radio Yerevan, supposedly broadcast from the capital of Soviet Armenia, are all the rage in Eastern Europe. "Tell me," I encouraged.

"In case of an American nuclear attack, every single Yerevan inhabitant is to place a large white bedsheet over his head and quietly proceed to the nearest cemetery, being careful not to provoke any panic."

"And the Volga?" I prompted. One of my service cars was a Soviet-made Volga.

"The answer is that you can certainly drive a Volga around a 90-degree curve at 80 miles an hour, but only once!" laughed Munteanu.

Pop came in and said he had put the hundred passports for Arafat in two Samsonite briefcases sealed as a diplomatic pouch, which he would load onto the airplane. Placing my travel briefcase on the couch, he added: "It has the same numerical key as always. You have everything there: passport, money, the papers for the pouch. I've put your Walther in too. You're going to Beirut." He was referring to my personal handgun, one a high Nazi official had used to commit suicide with in Bucharest in 1944. I glanced toward Munteanu.

"To have a gun in my hand is more disgusting for me than to hold a stinking, dead rat," Munteanu once told me, and at the time I thought those words well described his benign nature. A few years later, though, I happened to go to the DIE firing range very late one night and found him there alone, practicing with a Colt 45. When I looked at his target, I saw all the bullet holes were in the bull's-eye. "When in Rome . . . ," he whispered to me, visibly embarrassed. His best weapon, however, was undoubtedly his ability to judge people. He always devoted an inordinate amount of time to studying his human targets, watching their gestures, searching their souls.

A pharmacist by training, Munteanu was only 22 when he became an intelligence officer. He spent his first nine years in New York and Washington. The death in the early 1960s of one of the DIE's Middle East experts unexpectedly caused Munteanu to become the station chief in Cairo. The recruitments made by his station at the highest levels of Egyptian society and his personal relationships with the Egyptian rulers, especially Gamal Abdul Nasser and Anwar Sadat, had long since made him the most competent Romanian expert on Egypt. During the confusing, nebulous hours following Nasser's unexpected death, Munteanu literally moved into the presidential palace, mourning Nasser's death, bewailing Egypt's fate, and trying to do something useful to help anybody he could, even to carrying around tables and chairs for the foreign delegations arriving in Cairo for the funeral. "It was a once-in-a-lifetime opportunity to catch the eye of the up-and-coming leaders," he told me when he got back.

Just one day after the official Romanian delegation returned from Nasser's funeral, the Soviet ambassador in Bucharest gave Ceausescu a personal request from Soviet leader Leonid Brezhnev for a "comradely, fraternal evaluation of the new Egyptian leader." "Embassy Counselor Munteanu" was mentioned only orally by the Soviet ambassador, who commented that perceptive observers in Cairo had been amazed at the familiarities noted between him and President Sadat.

"What the devil is your Munteanu up to in Cairo?" Ceausescu asked me one hour later, visibly disturbed that somebody else's name had been interposed between himself and Brezhnev. "If he is so omnipotent, ask him to bring Arafat here to see me. That fellow who claims to represent the Palestinians."

In late 1970, Munteanu did bring Yasser Arafat, the new chairman of the PLO, to Bucharest. At that time the PLO had not been officially recognized by any Communist country. The fact that he was able to talk directly with Ceausescu, the first Communist leader he had ever personally met, made Munteanu grow in Arafat's eyes.

FLIGHT TO BEIRUT

I turned to my executive officer. "Get the 'Flotilla 50' duty officer on the phone for me," I ordered.

One minute later the commander of "Flotilla 50," General Calomfirescu, was himself on the line. "With your agreement, General," he reported in his high and affected but still warm and polite voice, "I'll be your flight captain today."

"Flotilla 50" was the code name for Ceausescu's special airplane fleet, which, based on the Soviet model, came under the Ministry of Interior. As in the other East European countries, the presidential fleet was composed of Soviet-built airplanes, among which were two brand new Ilyushin-62s—at that time the largest Soviet-built passenger airplane—and two older Ilyushin-18s, fitted out with sleeping compartments and salons for long flights, as well as two Antonov-24s and two helicopters for short trips inside Romania. Recently "Flotilla 50" had also received a custom-built Boeing 707. I was in charge of furnishing it and loading it up with American communications and flight equipment, obtained legally or illegally, in order to make it a faithful copy of the United States president's Air Force One.

We set off for the airport around 7:30 AM. After the car had left headquarters, Munteanu remarked prophetically: "It won't do any good."

"Okay, Abu," I said, using the name Arafat had given him. "Give me your lecture."

"What the Palestinians don't need is an Arafat with spectacles perched learnedly on the end of his nose presiding over government meetings. Terrorism is the Palestinians' way of life. They want a vengeful, bloodthirsty, unscrupulous leader who can craftily kill off their enemies. When Arafat stops living up to this image, he'll be killed. But Brother Yasser is slyer than a fox. He knows all this far too well to start changing his tune now, just because the Comrade asks him to. That's my sermon for today."

The headquarters of "Flotilla 50" is on the south side of Bucharest's Otopeni International Airport, unnoticed by its normal passengers. The hangars housing its airplanes and helicopters seem to be just part of the commercial airport. Only one white IL-18 with the Romanian seal on its tail was standing outside under guard. "The crew of the presidential IL-18 are ready for their mission. I am the commander of 'Flotilla 50,'" announced General Calomfirescu, saluting at the foot of the airplane's ladder.

With Calomfirescu in the pilot's seat, the clumsy four-engine airplane took off smoothly and was now at its cruising altitude. Two stewards, dressed in gray uniforms—Elena's favorite decorator color at the moment—and wearing white gloves, served breakfast.

"What do we have for Yasser?" Munteanu asked.

"Words from the Comrade and the passports he asked for—an even hundred."

"Those'll not only be useful for his 'Shuqairy' operation, they're also as good as gold for their relations with the Baader-Meinhof and the Red Brigades. Any American ones?"

"One."

"Finally. It's been one of Arafat's fiercest ambitions to pull off an anti-Israeli operation involving Americans. This might give us a leg up with him, if anything really could. But I still don't see any hope for the Comrade's idea of transforming the PLO into a government-in-exile, any more than you can make a mummy dance." General Munteanu paused while a stewardess refilled his teacup. "As the leader of a government, even one in exile, Arafat would have to adhere to international agreements and proclaim a minimum of laws, and that would be suicidal for him."

Calomfirescu joined us for lunch. "Are we going to pick up the Chairman?" he asked Munteanu, referring conspiratorially to Yasser Arafat.

"No drama today. Just the two of us. Do you remember our first flight with the Bearded One, back in '70?"

Calomfirescu smiled timidly. "You and the crew were the only civilized human beings on board that time. When I came back to visit the passengers, as now, I was literally surrounded by his bodyguards, a couple of dozen ferocious-looking creatures, armed to the teeth, with their guns pointed straight at me."

"I was in the same boat," interrupted Munteanu. "Brother Yasser was sitting somewhere in the middle of the cabin, surrounded by those two dozen fedayeen, who kept their guns on their knees throughout the whole flight. I couldn't get any closer to him than ten feet away."

"It was a night flight," Calomfirescu went on reminiscing. "After takeoff, we served dinner, but nobody even touched it. They had brought their own food and drinks. And afterwards, we needed a whole day to clean up the plane and get rid of the stench."

Munteanu, who was evidently looking forward to meeting Arafat and Hassan again and to seeing his other old PLO friends, was in an excellent mood and told a lot a jokes. Toward the end of the lunch, when we had just started attacking the platter of French cheeses, Calomfirescu excused himself. "I want to bring the plane down myself. I probably know Beirut better than anybody else." The airplane landed softly and rolled toward the main building. Through the window I spotted Olcescu, surrounded by a group of people to whom he was busily giving orders.

THE SMUGGLING NETWORK

At five-foot-five, well built but not fat, with dark hair and very tanned skin, suited out as usual in first quality cloth but affecting casual negligence, Colonel Constantin Olcescu was beginning to look more and more like a Palestinian. For several years he had been the Romanian chargé d'affaires in Lebanon, as well as the DIE chief of station and Ceausescu's liaison officer with Druze leader Kamal Jumblatt and with Yasser Arafat's headquarters. An energetic and enterprising man, he soon became so accustomed to the front atmosphere of Beirut that, when a rocket fell on the embassy one day, he first shaved himself, then asked Jumblatt to have his Druze militiamen collect the scattered documents and stand guard over the building, and only after all that did he get around to reporting the incident to Bucharest.

Stepping inside the airplane, Olcescu said, "Welcome to destroyed Paris," an allusion to the epithet "Little Paris" generously accorded to both Beirut and Bucharest in the past. "Everything is all set. The border formalities taken care of, customs likewise. Arafat has an escort for you, General. And Jumblatt has one for the plane. We're sinking enough money into them. Shall we go?"

I was relatively familiar with Beirut, although it was still always a surprise for me to see how, after each devastation, with the buildings still steaming smoke, business and social life was able to start up again in almost its normal course and vitality. This time, however, was different. Everywhere there were barricades, roadblocks, and checkpoints, manned by unshaven fedayeen wearing some semblance of a uniform and the traditional towel on their heads. On the streets, scruffy-looking Palestinians and children negligently holding Kalashnikov submachine guns harassed the pedestrians. Cars without license plates careened around chaotically or were parked anywhere, without order.

"It looks different, doesn't it?" Olcescu asked, seeing my surprise. "That's because of our PLO friends. They are a revolution, not a government. They can destroy, but they can't rebuild. We don't have any regular mail service any more, the electricity and water come on at random, and traffic rules and policemen have been done away with. The stores are more closed than open, since our friends started just helping themselves to what they wanted."

"What about these new Mercedes cars you see everywhere?"

"Smuggled out of Germany. There aren't any customs for the PLO to go through in Lebanon."

On our way to the embassy, Olcescu told us that the meeting with "Annette" was set for four that afternoon at the Romanian embassy, which he regularly visited under his cover as Arafat's political advisor and Farouk Kaddoumi's deputy. Arafat had secretly left by car the day before to meet with President Haffez Assad in Damascus, but there he had been informed that I was coming and had agreed to be back by evening, if we would send the plane there to get him. Munteanu immediately offered to fly to Damascus to get Arafat. "If I don't go along to snag him, the plane could sit there for days waiting for him to show up." I approved.

The meeting with Hani Hassan took place at the embassy as planned. His report was short and unequivocal. Arafat was firmly against Ceausescu's proposal, considering it unrealistic and absurd, for reasons of both principle and pragmatism, but especially because it was dangerous for himself. The transformation of the PLO into a government-in-exile should be approved by the National Congress, together with a new constitution. With all the different factions inside the PLO, Arafat considered that too risky and had decided not to rock the boat. He had so far discussed Ceausescu's proposals with only Farouk Kaddoumi, his chief political advisor, and had decided not to spread it among any other collaborators. It was also not a topic for today's discussion with Assad. According to Hassan, Arafat would do anything to be recognized by the West but was not willing to risk his actual position.

Before leaving, Hassan reported that he had just received the latest shipment of arms from West Germany, and that he now had enough samples of arms and military equipment to fill another ten-ton truck.

Right after the meeting I got off a telegram ordering the DIE to send a TIR truck to Beirut within 48 hours. That way the arms samples collected by "Annette" could be secretly transported to Romania under the protection of the international TIR agreements and diplomatic seal.

TIR is the name given to a Romanian foreign trade organization handling the overland trucking of export merchandise to foreign countries. It takes its name from an international organization—the Transport International Routier—that regulates its activities. The DIE took over direct control of the whole Romanian TIR land transportation system, based on the model set up by Bulgaria, which has one of the largest TIR fleets in Europe. The Bulgarian TIR fleet, officially responsible for the rapid transportation of exported fruits and vegetables, is deeply involved in the trafficking of drugs and arms from Bulgaria to the West.

By 1974, most of the drivers of the Romanian TIR trucks were also DIE officers under cover. Like their Bulgarian counterparts, they had been trained for the clandestine transport of people, arms, and drugs and for emptying dead-drops loaded with espionage materials by DIE foreign agents and illegal officers along Western highways. By 1978, the DIE was making full use of the TIR trucks for secretly bringing high-technology materials and military equipment into Romania, as well as for smuggling unmarked arms and drugs to the West. Most of these movements are carried out under the protection of international TIR agreements and foreign customs seals. Over the years every kind of seal and form sheet used by Western customs authorities has been duplicated by the DIE and kept on hand to use to replace any original customs seals destroyed along the way for operational reasons.

"May Munteanu stay on here for a few more days and go back to Bucharest with the TIR truck?" Olcescu asked, after reading the telegram I had written. "I can give him an embassy car and driver to go ahead of the truck. The addition of Munteanu's brashness, along with his diplomatic passport and his rank of political counselor, could provide extra protection at the Turkish border."

That was true. "Annette" would surely see to the truck's smooth departure from Lebanon, and the Bulgarian border would present no difficulty, as the Romanians had secret passwords they could use there. The current wave of anti-terrorist measures presented a risk that the truck might be opened at the Turkish border, however, and that might provoke an outburst in the Western press. I approved the proposal and ordered the additional protection of using the embassy's pouch seal and diplomatic courier documents personally signed by Olcescu in his capacity as chargé d'affaires.

Having taken care of the truck, I sent a brief telegram to Ceausescu: "MEETING WITH ANNETTE NEGATIVE."

In no time I had an answer back: "COMRADE PODEANU: 1. YOUR REPORT WAS PRESENTED TO THE SUPREME GUIDE. HIS ORDER IS TO PERSEVERE WITH THE FE-DAYEE, ACCORDING TO THE INSTRUCTIONS HE PER-SONALLY GAVE YOU. 2. AFTER YOUR MEETING WITH THE FEDAYEE YOU SHOULD GO ON TO TULCEA TO DE-LIVER A WRITTEN MESSAGE FROM THE SUPREME GUIDE TO THE BEDOUIN. YOU SHOULD GO ALONE RE-PEAT ALONE, WITHOUT THE DEAN, TO SEE THE BED-OUIN. 3. SEND THE AIRPLANE TO THE BASE. IT WILL IMMEDIATELY RETURN TO BACAU, WITH THE WRITTEN MESSAGE FOR THE BEDOUIN. CAROL."

Under the periodically changing substitution code used in telegrams for additional encipherment, at that time the *Supreme Guide* was Ceausescu, *Carol* was Minister of Interior Coman, *Podeanu* was my code name, and *dean* meant ambassador. The *Fedayee* and the *Bedouin* had been used for Arafat and Gadhafi for quite some time. Foreign city names were usually encoded using Romanian city names that began with the same letter of the alphabet, as *Tulcea* for Tripoli and *Bacau* for Beirut.

Meeting the "Fedayee"

When Munteanu got back, he went with Arafat directly to PLO headquarters. Olcescu and I left from the embassy in one of Arafat's Mercedes cars, which took off like a bat out of hell, escorted by four more cars bristling with fedayeen heads and Kalashnikovs sticking out through the windows. The cars raced through the roadblocks and checkpoints without even slowing their speed, providing proof of the PLO radio system's efficiency and an unexpected sign of discipline in an otherwise totally chaotic West Beirut. We came to a halt in front of a building that had its windows and doors protected by concrete blocks and sandbags. The sidewalks and streets were full of unshaven, carelessly dressed young Palestinians with their fingers resting on the triggers of cocked submachine guns. From the doorway, however, we were accompanied by two well-mannered officers.

Arafat, who was drinking tea with Munteanu, got up and came toward us, donning his fixed smile.

"I am very happy to receive my brother Ceausescu's messengers," he began, speaking rapidly in his lilting English and occasionally spattering saliva around, after embracing me and leaving two gooey spots of mucus on Olcescu's cheeks. "We are at war. When we finally drive Zionism out of Palestine we'll have a real home. Until then, I have to receive you here and there," he whined in mock apology, offering us a chair.

"I understand from Abu Munteanu that Brother Ceausescu has sent the passports I asked for," Arafat began, without any other introduction.

"Yes, Chairman, he has, along with his best wishes for success in your struggle. They are in there," I responded, pointing to the two Samsonite briefcases Olcescu had placed on his desk and opened up.

Arafat turned his shifting, badger-like eyes to take a look inside, then began rifling quickly through the passports. "How many?"

"One hundred, Chairman."

"That's generous. These briefcases will help write a new page in the glorious history of Palestine," he proclaimed emphatically, while continuing to flip through the passports. "There it is! Abu Munteanu told me that I was getting one American passport, too. I've never had a blank American passport before."

"You've got one there, Chairman. But you can't use it by yourselves. *We* would have to write in the names and everything else with a special typewriter the Americans are using, and we have only one such machine. If you don't mind our knowing the identities of your holders, you can have as many U.S. passports as you want. If you do mind, just forget it."

"Brother Ceausescu is my closest friend," Arafat said, admiring the U.S. passport. "I don't have any secrets from him."

"I have something else for you, Chairman," I said, changing the subject and putting an envelope on his desk. "Here you have the English text of the most recent messages between Comrade Ceausescu and Carter and Begin."

"That is very helpful," Arafat replied, pasting on his studied smile. "We will study them very carefully." He leafed through the documents, obviously without reading them, then closed the two briefcases with the passports and suddenly exploded theatrically.

"I know. I know," he blurted out in short bursts, gesticulating with both arms. "I know that I am late with my answer, but I had to discuss it with all my collaborators. And with Assad. That's why I went to Damascus—to discuss Brother Ceausescu's proposal."

"Arafat tells a lie in every sentence," is how Munteanu used to describe his regular discussions with the PLO chairman.

"Ever since I left Bucharest," Arafat went on, "I've been advocating Brother Ceausescu's proposals of transforming the PLO into a government-in-exile. All of my closest collaborators agree that we have to have our own country, and certainly our own government, too, but they cannot say how soon that will be. I know that my brother Ceausescu is always in a big hurry. But we are at war here, and we can't act so fast, you know. All I can say is that I fully agree with my brother's idea to have a government. That is what you should tell him."

"What about a government-in-exile?" I ventured.

"Until such time as we can rout Zionism out of Palestine, we will always be in exile. That is what you should tell my brother."

It was clear that Arafat was playing dumb and trying to keep Ceausescu well disposed toward him, with Ceausescu's visit to Washington just a few days away.

"Just let me see if I've understood you, Chairman. Should I tell Comrade Ceausescu that the time is not ripe for transforming the PLO into a government-in-exile?"

"That's your way of saying it," he replied, going over to use a telephone sitting on his desk.

"I've just called Abu Lutf," he said when he came back. "He's the main one against Brother Ceausescu's and my proposal. Hear him out."

Abu Lutf was the *nom de guerre* of Farouk Kaddoumi, one of the "group of eight" who in the early 1960s formed the Movement for the Liberation of Palestine, which Yasser Arafat headed. When he arrived, in traditional Palestinian dress, I could hardly recognize the PLO "foreign minister," who usually wore only perfectly tailored Western suits.

In his demagogical style, Kaddoumi led off with praise for Ceausescu. "I don't want to speak today about his boundless political support to the Palestinian cause. I want to speak now about his humanitarian help, about the Romanian airplanes filled with medical supplies secretly sent to Beirut every month, about Brother Ceausescu's professional and material assistance, about the Romanian advisors and technicians sent here to improve our over forty Samid factories and workshops, about our first group of fifty Palestinians just sent to Bucharest to be trained in managing the Samid business." Then, without any apparent connection, one of his favorite stylistic tricks, Kaddoumi gave a long dissertation on the fact that between the Palestinians and the existence of Israel there was an irreconcilable antagonism, which could be overcome only by the destruction of Israel as a state.

"The Palestinians have three watchwords: national unity, national mobilization, and liberation. No one can change them— neither Chairman Arafat, nor the Executive Committee, nor even the National Congress. And none of us can add a fourth watchword: compromise," Kaddoumi wound up emotionally.

"I'll never compromise," Arafat jumped in. "I cannot, and I will not. I am a revolutionary. I have dedicated my whole life to the Palestinian cause and the destruction of Israel. I will not change or compromise. I will not agree with anything that recognizes Israel as a state. Never." Arafat was beginning to raise his voice. Like Ceausescu, he can get furious over nothing. "Nobody, neither friend nor foe, can force me to compromise."

Arafat had become truly violent, and Kaddoumi tried to calm him down. "We know that Brother Ceausescu doesn't want a compromise. We know his real feelings toward Israel. We know he is moving all Jews out of sensitive government jobs. We know that he only wants us to give him something for public consumption, something that will get Carter to lean in our direction. But we simply cannot transform our revolution into a bureaucracy."

"That's the delicate position I'm in," said Arafat, suddenly rational again. "But I am always willing to make the West think that

I want what Brother Ceausescu wants me to do. Will you take this back to Bucharest as my answer?"

"That's why I'm here, Chairman."

"If that's settled, let's go have something to eat," said Arafat, jumping to his feet and inviting us to dinner. He took us to a nearby room furnished like a military barracks. There waiting for us was Hani Hassan, together with a man whose face was very familiar to me, but I could not put a name to it.

"You ought to know him," said Arafat, putting his hand on my shoulder. "He is our national hero, Abu Daoud. He told me that on his last visit to Bucharest he was given a magnificent dinner. That's why I asked him to prepare this one for us now. You've got the cream of the PLO here: its spokesman, Abu Lutf, its brain, Abu Hassan, its mailed fist, Abu Daoud. And its chairman."

"Do you know the story about the four parrots that were for sale?" Munteanu jumped in.

"No," answered Arafat.

"An old fedayee went to the bazaar to sell his four parrots, which were all nice-looking birds, with beautiful, colored feathers. 'How much do you want for this one?' asked a buyer, pointing at the red parrot. 'Two thousand pounds,' answered the fedayee. 'What? Is it made out of gold?' 'No, Brother, but it can speak Arabic and English.' 'And how much for the blue one?' 'Four thousand pounds, Brother. It also speaks German. The yellow one is six thousand, because it speaks four languages.' 'I see,' said the buyer. 'And what about that one over there that has feathers of all different colors?' 'That one costs twelve thousand pounds, Brother.' 'What? How many languages does he have?' 'None. He's the chairman of the team.' "

"Give me a gun," called out Arafat in mock rage, as he choked on a bite of food.

It was after midnight when we left PLO headquarters. Back in the salon of the embassy, I wrote a short telegram for Bucharest reporting that the discussion with the "Fedayee" had taken place in a "friendly atmosphere," and that "Podeanu" would be leaving for Tripoli in the morning. "Friendly atmosphere" was the code for unsuccessful.

"What do you think about having Kaddoumi but not 'Annette' present at our discussions with Arafat?" Olcescu broke the silence.

"I'm not surprised," Munteanu cut in. "One of Arafat's main concerns is to keep it a secret from his own men what 'Annette's' real job is. He appeared only for the protocol part, the dinner—and then as Kaddoumi's deputy.

Yasser Arafat has always been eager to protect Hani Hassan's cover as one of his political advisors and to keep his name out of any of the Palestinian terrorist operations secretly prepared by Hassan. It was only during the October 1985 hijacking of the Italian liner Achille Lauro, *with its 123 passengers and 315 crew aboard, that Hani Hassan's name was first publicly linked with a PLO terrorist operation. His presence in Cairo, as reported in the press, fully demonstrates that influence operations are still his secret job. According to* Time *magazine, Egyptian President Hosni Mubarak was "eager, perhaps overeager, to demonstrate that Arafat was a moderate opposed to terrorism by involving him in the hostage mediation. Arafat was just as eager to comply. On Monday evening, one of his closest advisors, Hani el-Hassan, already was in Egypt."*[1]

PLO ATTEMPT ON GOLDA MEIR

"I'm dying for a glass of Scotch," Olcescu lamented. "Can you believe that I'd never met Abu Daoud before? After all these years I've spent in Beirut." He took a bottle of Scotch out from a sideboard. "Do you remember the telegram about him that Munteanu and I sent during Golda Meir's visit to Bucharest?" he went on. It had been a tough day for all of us, and we needed a little Scotch and chitchat.

The events had taken place in May 1972. Munteanu was in Beirut to deliver a very confidential message from Ceausescu to Arafat. It contained details of Ceausescu's April discussion with Egyptian President Anwar Sadat in Cairo, including the latter's suggestion that he, Sadat, meet personally with the Israelis as a first step toward peace. At the end of his message, Ceausescu informed Arafat that he had been asked to act secretly as media-

[1]*Time*, October 21, 1985, p. 25.

tor between Egypt and Israel, and that in a few days he would be having secret talks in Bucharest with Israeli Prime Minister Golda Meir. This news made Arafat's headquarters seethe with rage.

On Friday, May 5, 1972, I was the acting chief of the DIE. Around four-thirty in the afternoon I received a flash telegram from Beirut saying that four Arabs had left Cairo for Bucharest to assassinate Golda Meir when she went, on foot, to the Chorale Synagogue, where she was scheduled to attend a religious service that evening. Just a few minutes before that, Ceausescu had called to tell me he had finished a second meeting with Meir—bringing the total time of their closed-door discussions to 14 hours—and that she was about to set out on her walk to the synagogue. Ceausescu was enthusiastic, probably already picturing himself as the mediator in the Middle East, and eventual recipient of the Nobel Peace Prize.

If the information from Beirut was correct, it was almost too late to do anything. I immediately checked with the electronic monitoring center for any new information obtained through the microphones copiously planted by the Securitate everywhere around Meir, as well as in the home of the chief rabbi, Dr. Moses Rosen, in the synagogue itself and in its courtyard, but nothing suspicious turned up. There was not enough time to alert the Securitate and the army, which were formally in charge of Meir's security. The bureaucratic chain of command and the sluggishness of the Romanian military system were not compatible with swift reaction. I decided to use the entire manpower of the DIE's anti-terrorist unit, which was kept on constant alert to prevent attacks on DIE headquarters, Romanian embassies abroad, or commercial airliners. At approximately five-thirty, four Arabs, surprised and overwhelmed, were arrested on a street close to the synagogue, without having been able to use their submachine guns and hand grenades. All of them were carrying Egyptian passports.

A few minutes later I was in Ceausescu's office. He turned white as a sheet, afraid that his dream would suddenly fall apart, and ordered: "Kill them! Say that they offered armed resistance." But before I left his office Ceausescu had changed his mind. He did not want any publicity that might compromise Bucharest as a future meeting place between Golda Meir and Anwar Sadat. At about eight that evening the Arabs were secretly photographed as they enjoyed a lavish dinner, complete with black caviar and champagne, in a government guest house. The next morning they left Bucharest on a Romanian commercial airplane. It was months before the DIE was able to identify the leader of the terrorist team in the Meir operation from secret photographs as Abu Daoud, the field commander of the 1972 terrorist attack on the Israeli Olympic team in Munich. Only then did the DIE fully understand that the attempted assassination of Golda Meir had been plotted by the PLO.

On that day in May 1972, however, the passports found on the arrested terrorists convinced Ceausescu that Cairo had been the instigator of the attempt against Meir, but he decided to keep it a secret from her. He sent me to accompany Meir on her walk from the Israeli embassy to the synagogue. After the religious service, she saw the thousands of people gathered outside the synagogue behind the security fences. They were all silent, afraid they would be brutally driven away if they opened their mouths. As Meir came closer, they began to take out hidden yarmulkes and, cautiously looking around, to put them on their heads. Although yarmulkes are not legally banned in Romania, wearing them is frowned upon. Meir ventured a "Shalom." "Shalom!" came back enthusiastically from several thousand throats. Hebrew songs poured forth in a spontaneous demonstration of affection. As Meir got into her car, she had tears in her eyes.

Before Meir left Bucharest, Prime Minister Ion Gheorghe Maurer, a passionate hunter, gave her a huge black bearskin at a farewell ceremony. Winking at her, Ceausescu cautiously suggested that this trophy might also symbolize the skin the "Bear" stood to lose in the Middle East conflict. On that day Ceausescu launched what would become one of his favorite strategies for winning over Western leaders: the use of the innocuous anti-Soviet joke.

"In 1972," Olcescu declared, "the Bearded One just struck out blindly, when he first learned that Sadat might meet Golda Meir."

"His hatred of Israel is literally in his blood," Munteanu added. "After I gave Arafat the Comrade's message about a possible Sadat-Meir meeting, he first exploded with rage. But then he turned physically sick."

"What do you think about Arafat's message to the Comrade?" Olcescu asked curiously, looking at Munteanu.

"I expect that we'll see the PLO's policy toward the West becoming a game of 'Now you see it, now you don't' for the time being," Munteanu concluded prophetically.

Arafat is still playing the game of denying today what he gave someone to understand just yesterday. Describing the January 1986 discussions for peace in the Middle East between Jordan's King Hussein and Yasser Arafat, who was accompanied to Amman by his "aide" Hani Hassan, the American press wrote that "Arafat emerged from a morning meeting hinting that he was ready to accept two U.N. resolutions considered key to Mideast peace efforts if Israel first agrees to a multinational conference to oversee the talks. Arafat has repeatedly gone to the brink of, and then pulled back from, accepting the two U.N. resolutions."[2]

[2]Juan O Tamayo, "Progress seen in Mideast peace talks," *The Miami Herald*, January 28, 1986, p. 1A.

VI

"THIS is your captain speaking," General Calomfirescu said using the airplane's loudspeakers. "On our left we now have the Suez Canal. In a few minutes we'll be coming up on the Nile delta and the city of Alexandria."

It was not yet eight o'clock in the morning, and I was still eating breakfast. Before we had left Beirut, Calomfirescu had promised to fly low and follow the coastline, to give me a bird's-eye view of Egypt and also of Libya, which were not on my regular travel route.

COURTING GADHAFI

Ceausescu has been fascinated by Gadhafi ever since the latter seized power in Libya in 1969 at the age of 27. Ceausescu's interest stemmed in part from the fact that he himself had been considered youthful when he came to power in 1965, at the age of 47—a very young age compared to Kremlin leaders. Furthermore, he had also begun his political career in the army, and he shares Gadhafi's volatile nature. Their most important similarity, however, is in their dreams. Gadhafi has gigantic plans to build up Libya as an international power and himself as the undisputed world leader of Islam. Ceausescu wants to place his country at the center of world politics, to make himself an international figure, and to become the leader of the Third World. Libya's vast supply of oil money has also been high on Ceausescu's list of Gadhafi's admirable qualities. In the early 1970s, Ceausescu finally decided he ought to meet Gadhafi in person, but long before his first visit to Tripoli I had to triple the size of the DIE station there, in order to provide the weekly reports on Gadhafi he demanded.

Ceausescu has always been concerned with studying the character of foreign leaders. He made a long and careful study of Richard Nixon before deciding to receive him in Romania with full state honors in 1967, after Nixon's first retirement from politics, when he was nothing but a private citizen. Merely a practicing attorney in New York City, Nixon had been snubbed on a visit to Moscow and not received at any official level. In August 1969, only a few months after his inauguration as president, Richard Nixon paid Ceausescu back by becoming the first United States president ever to visit Romania. The visit was an important coup for Bucharest.

In his memoirs, Henry Kissinger, Nixon's national security advisor after he became president, recalls that, "The President had 'very pleasant recollections' of his meetings with the Romanian leaders when they received him warmly as a private citizen. . . . Nixon never forgot courtesies of this kind." According to Kissinger, in 1969 Nixon himself "suggested including Romania on his around-the-world trip. . . . For the first time an American President would visit a Communist nation in Eastern Europe."[1]

Nixon's visit to Romania was followed by an avalanche of Ceausescu visits to Washington—in 1970, 1973, 1975, and 1978—and by President Gerald Ford's coming to Bucharest only three weeks after having received Ceausescu at the White House.

Similarly, Ceausescu had the DIE make a minute study of French President Charles de Gaulle before inviting him to Bucharest. On arrival, de Gaulle found the same black Citröen limousine he was accustomed to in France, a bed identical to the custom-made one he had at the Elysee Palace in Paris, and the same foods he was used to eating at his early morning breakfast and late evening dinner. De Gaulle was deeply touched. By the end of his visit, he had quietly agreed to unlock some of the doors to the West's microelectronics and computer industry for Romania. On another occasion, a thorough psychological dissection

[1]Henry Kissinger, *White House Years*, Boston: Little, Brown and Company, 1979, pp. 156–7.

of Pakistan's Zulficar Ali Bhutto enabled Ceausescu to obtain Bhutto's confidential agreement on secret cooperation between the two countries' foreign intelligence services to obtain Western intelligence on nuclear weapons.

When Ceausescu finally concluded that he had a good picture of Gadhafi, he ordered his minister of foreign affairs to arrange a visit to Libya. The first official discussion with Gadhafi was scheduled to take place immediately upon Ceausescu's arrival in Tripoli, but Colonel Gadhafi had simply disappeared from sight and could not be found. When he finally did come back, the unfriendly and suspicious Gadhafi abruptly got up and, without saying a word, walked to the other end of the large conference room, where he fell on his knees and began to pray. The Romanian ministers and the ambassador froze in their tracks, expecting Ceausescu to explode. He, however, smiled broadly and indicated serenely that he would wait as long as need be.

When Gadhafi finally returned to the conference table, Ceausescu said: "I have great admiration for people who believe. You believe in the Koran, I believe in Marxism. But both of us believe in the independence of our own countries. You threw out the American bases, I the Soviet. You are building an independent Moslem country, I an independent Marxist one. We should help each other."

Gadhafi spent long minutes looking into Ceausescu's eyes. The rest of the meeting then continued without incident, Gadhafi spending that whole day with his Romanian guest. Utterly contrary to his normal pattern, Ceausescu did not talk at all that day. He merely listened attentively and admiringly to Gadhafi. When the two leaders had finished their scheduled time together, Ceausescu informed Gadhafi that his personal aide-de-camp and his presidential airplane had to fly back to Romania and return during the night to bring him an important document.

The next morning Gadhafi arrived punctually, an unusual occurence in those days. When the two leaders came together, Ceausescu had a large, antique, chased silver box in his hands. Opening it, he took out a very old, handwritten book. "This is the original manuscript of the first translation of the Koran into the Romanian language, made hundreds of years ago. We have only this one copy, but I have only one real brother. It is for you to keep, my brother."

Colonel Gadhafi dipped greedily into the beautiful old book. Visibly moved, he literally could not speak. Eventually he managed to stammer, "My brother! You are my brother for the rest of my life!" at the same time vigorously embracing Ceausescu.

The Koran manuscript was the gift Ceausescu had planned all along for Gadhafi. "Going by the feel I've gotten for Gadhafi, there's nothing that would hook him better than our antique manuscript of the Koran," he explained to Nicolae Doicaru and me. Doicaru was the chief of the DIE at that time, and he was personally running this operation. "And nothing," Ceausescu continued, "would impress him more than for me to present it to him spontaneously, as if in reaction to the force of his personality." The scenario for transporting the Koran to Tripoli during the night had been worked out long before Ceausescu left Romania.

After that day, Ceausescu held nothing back in his efforts to overwhelm Gadhafi. He threw open Romania's doors for Libyans to enter its universities and sent thousands of teachers to Libya to help Gadhafi fulfill his ambitions of wiping out illiteracy and of creating a new intelligentsia devoted to himself. A large modern hospital was built and equipped and staffed with Romanian medical personnel. Ceausescu's maxim—"The money spent on Gadhafi will soon be paying fat dividends"—proved to be correct. Gadhafi became one of Ceausescu's closest friends and allies. Before long he was asking Ceausescu to join him in his "Green Revolution," aimed at transforming the Libyan deserts into agricultural lands, as they had been during the days of ancient Carthage, when Libya was an important granary for the Roman Empire. The Green Revolution envisioned not only a nationwide campaign to fertilize the land but also the transformation of the nomadic Bedouins into farmers. With Gadhafi's dollars, Romania constructed farms all over Libya and made a fortune.

American Passports for Libya

The year 1974 marked the beginning of intensive cooperation between the two security forces, and the exchange of foreign passports became its most important aspect. In order to stage terrorist acts abroad without involving Tripoli, the Libyan security forces had amassed a vast collection of passports that had been confiscated or stolen from foreigners working in or traveling through Libya, as well as ones taken from indigent Arab workers who had died in Libya. The DIE received many such passports, which were used in terrorist operations run by the PLO or by itself. In turn, the DIE gave Tripoli American and other Western passports that the DIE had counterfeited.

The Libyans are to this day organizing terrorist missions with the help of this passport collection. The terrorists who made an attack at the El Al checkout counter in the Vienna airport on December 27, 1985, were traveling with stolen Tunisian passports. According to the press, "the Tunisian Interior Ministry said in Tunis that two of the passports used by the terrorists to enter Austria were confiscated last summer by Libyan authorities from Tunisian workers in Libya who were being expelled. The third passport was reported lost by a Tunisian worker in Libya in 1977. The Ministry said that 'several hundred' Tunisian passports were confiscated recently by the Libyans from Tunisian workers being sent home."[2]

"This is your captain speaking." Calomfirescu's voice rang out over the loudspeakers again. "On your left are the Gulf of Sidra and the port of Bengazi. I have informed the control tower of the exact time of our arrival in Tripoli and asked them to pass it on to our embassy."

When I arrived, the short, pudgy, mustachioed "Riyad"—that was the DIE's code name for the Libyan first deputy minister of interior—was at the airport to greet me, as usual. Next to him stood Romanian Ambassador Nicolae Veres, DIE Chief of Station Anton Anton, and "Jarnea," the embassy's Arabic speaker. The ambassador did not know that "Jarnea" was a deep cover lieutenant colonel in the DIE. Together with them was General Romeo Popescu, an old DIE hand who had been chief of station in Belgium, then director of the Illegal Brigade at headquarters. He was still a DIE officer, now under cover as the Romanian Ministry of Interior's general director for visas and passports. Popescu had arrived in Tripoli an hour ahead of me, on a routine visit to help the Libyans counterfeit passports for their terrorist operations in the West, and to obtain new samples of foreign passports from them. "Riyad" drove Popescu and me to his office.

As always, "Riyad's" desk was covered with folders and loose papers. "I may have to disturb your order here," Popescu began, giving "Riyad" a wink as he searched for a place to open up his enormous, accordion-type briefcase. "This is for you," he said, emptying a large envelope full of blank Western passports fabricated by the DIE and selected for the Libyans in response to their particular requests.

"Riyad's" face suddenly lit up. "This will make the Colonel more than happy. You know, a blank passport is like a blank cheque—its value is without limit."

"Here are some more gifts. Also something like blank cheques," Popescu went on, pedantically setting out a whole row of rubber stamps on "Riyad's" desk. "You cannot use a blank cheque unless you fill it out, and here you have the writing tools for your passports, *mon cher ministre.*" There were large stamps for diplomatic or tourist entry visas for various foreign countries, and small ones used by foreign border points to mark the date of entry or exit. "In this box you have several dozen samples of the ink used by each country for every kind of stamp and signature, and in this envelope the instructions for their use. Some countries use red ink on Mondays, others may use a blue fluorescent one on Fridays," he added, with a touch of superiority in his voice, before concluding with emphasis: "The Colonel's intelligence officers won't have to visit the United States or Western Europe as Libyans any more."

GADHAFI'S JOINT VENTURES AGAINST "AMERICAN IMPERIALISM"

During lunch "Riyad" received word that the Colonel would see his "guest" at three o'clock. When we had hastily finished our meal, a helicopter took "Jarnea" and me to the heliport of a military unit, somewhere near Tripoli. A black Mercedes heavily escorted by "Riyad's" cars was there waiting for us. After a short drive, we slowed down and entered a military compound. Two jeeps immediately took us in tow, guiding us through a military unit on the alert. Everybody was wearing a helmet and carrying a Kalashnikov, the road was guarded by jeeps with machine guns, and tanks under camouflage nets were ready to move at the least sign. Next we were stopped at a high green iron gate, the only opening in a concrete wall reinforced with sandbags for as far as we could see. Only the black Mercedes was allowed to pass through the green gate, and it was now escorted by half a dozen foot soldiers armed with submachine guns. We came into a large walled courtyard, in the center of which, far away, we could make out a square building surrounded by military tents. The road to it was blocked at intervals by tanks with their engines running. The tanks straddled the road crosswise every 500 yards or so. Our car was stopped in front of each tank and checked over by an officer, until we got to the door of the building.

Inside, everything was green, even the dress of most of the men. "It symbolizes Gadhafi's Green Revolution," "Jarnea" enlightened me, as we finally were invited into a green waiting room, decorated only with a color portrait of Gadhafi wearing a green military uniform. We had waited less than an hour when a man in a green uniform came in and escorted us to the Colonel, who was alone in an immense room. He was standing looking out a window in an evidently calculated pose, placing his profile in bold relief. I could hear the door being quietly closed behind us, but I could detect no sign that Gadhafi was aware of our presence. Like his tents, the room had walls covered with colored leather pieces sewed together like a patchwork quilt and was furnished with bright green sofas and easy chairs. I waited a long time before deciding to try a cough. As if surprised, Gadhafi turned his head slowly in our direction, seeming to study us for some time, and then began speaking in Arabic.

"I am always thirsty for his excellency my brother's wisdom. How is he doing?" "Jarnea" whispered the translation into my ear. Gadhafi was wearing an extravagant, custom-made, dark green uniform with many loops of gold braid across his chest, and high heeled shoes. His dark sunglasses, partly covered by the large visor full of "scrambled eggs" from an oversized, Italian-style military hat, did not conceal but rather highlighted the pancake makeup on his face.

After making a few conventional introductory noises, I tried to give him Ceausescu's written message, but I was stopped by a firm gesture Gadhafi made with his hands, displaying gold rings with large emeralds on most of his fingers. "Tell me what it says," he ordered imperiously. Like Ceausescu, he does not like to read anything himself.

"President Ceausescu gave me the honor of reporting to you, Excellency, his full acceptance of one of your earlier proposals," I began, trying to stick to the formal tone he had set. Gadhafi threw me an inquiring look. I politely reminded him that, a few weeks earlier, he had offered Ceausescu $400 million for importing a modern oil refinery that would be located on the Black Sea.

"Of course I know," Gadhafi interrupted, his eyes glistening triumphantly. "I offered to pay for a modern refinery imported from the West for processing only Libyan crude—with the products to be exported as Romanian—as a safety valve for me, in case of a Western boycott of Libyan oil. I also told Brother Ceausescu that I was willing to finance a second and then a third refinery immediately."

I nodded and continued with Ceausescu's message. "Expressing his deep solidarity with Libya's revolution and cause, the Romanian president not only agrees with Colonel Gadhafi's proposal but has also found a way of substantially reducing the time needed to bring it to life. President Ceausescu is prepared to put an existing refinery at Libya's immediate disposal, one that was recently imported from the West, if Colonel Gadhafi can deliver the $400 million promptly."

"Is that true?" asked Gadhafi. "Of course I will pay for it, if my men find the refinery satisfactory. You know that I have money, don't you?"

Ignoring his interruption, I continued with Ceausescu's message, explaining that he also asked Gadhafi to obligate himself to send Romania the necessary flow of crude to keep the refinery running at full capacity. At the same time, Ceausescu informed his brother that the refinery's profits in foreign currency had to be shared, in order to pay for the Romanian work force.

"There is no question that I agree to everything Brother Ceausescu asks of me," said Gadhafi, unexpectedly becoming less suspicious upon learning that he would have to pay hard cash in return for Ceausescu's favor. Evidently happy with the news and suddenly remembering that he was still standing, Gadhafi pulled over an easy chair for himself and gestured for "Jarnea" and me to do the same. A green uniform came in bringing buttermilk for all of us.

"What else is in my brother's message?" asked Gadhafi, after the green uniform had left.

I reported that Ceausescu also wanted to know if Gadhafi had been able to come to a decision on Ceausescu's proposal regarding financing a tank industry in Romania.

"It's the German one, isn't it?" he asked. "The one my brother said you have enough technical intelligence on to copy and produce in Romania. What's the difference between it and the new Soviet tank?"

"President Ceausescu considers the West German Leopard II better than the Soviet ones—stronger, lighter, faster, and substantially more reliable in submerged fording. But his real reason for building a tank of our own is that it could be exported without any restriction."

"He's right on that. I paid good money for my Soviet tanks, but the Kremlin always tries to stop me from doing what I want with them. What was my brother's proposal?"

"A joint venture to produce the Leopard II. Romania would cooperate with all the technological intelligence it has as well as with confidential West German assistance given to support Bucharest's independent foreign policy. Romania would also provide the Romanian-Libyan joint venture with all the buildings, work force, and every other logistical need. President Ceausescu is asking you, Excellency, to finance the import from the West of all the necessary equipment and tools for the new factory as well as the cost of the license and of the special steel and other imported materials."

"What license? I understood the tank was NATO property and no license could be bought. Am I wrong?"

"No, Excellency, you are right. For many years President Ceausescu had a priority intelligence operation aimed at reproducing the Leopard II, because it could not be imported. During those years, he accumulated tons of blueprints and technical specifications. The Romanian technicians now have almost everything their West German counterparts had when they started to build the Leopard II, and a lot more. Even an original model."

"So why do you need a license?"

"The key problem for the Leopard II is its engine, Excellency. We recently smuggled out an extra engine sample, which we dismantled and studied. The conclusion was that the compact, light aluminum engine was such a precision instrument that it was much too complicated for Romania's current technological level. That is why President Ceausescu has decided to find a way to cooperate with the West German manufacturer."

"And the NATO approval?"

"President Ceausescu has found a way to do without it. He gave me a personal message for the manufacturer, a prestigious West German corporation, asking in ambiguous terms for help in bolstering Romania's independence and promising, in exchange, additional business in the future. With this message in hand I contacted one of the manufacturer's leaders, the head of the engine factory. This man, who has been given the code name 'Leopold,' had been assessed in our intelligence reports as being sympathetic to Romania's foreign policy."

"'Leopold' from 'Leopard'?"

"Yes, Excellency. 'Leopold,' after having been fully briefed by me, agreed to cooperate in resolving what he called 'this delicate matter.' Several days later—that means early last January—we left together in his company's jet plane for Bucharest, where he was scheduled to join Chancellor Schmidt as a member of his official delegation. President Ceausescu sent you a personal message about the discussions he had with Schmidt at the time."

"A month or so ago."

"Yes, Excellency. During the flight to Bucharest there were only the two of us there on the plane, and 'Leopold' explained that the Leopard II had been developed for NATO with German federal funds, and that therefore it was not possible for it to be a direct object of trade without federal government approval, which would never be given to a Communist country. Recently, however, his company had designed a new diesel engine that was entirely based on the Leopard II engine. The one basic difference was its lubrication system, because it was designed for use only in a horizontal position, essentially for mobile drilling units. But the new engine did not belong to the West German government any more. 'Leopold' could sell its license and a production line to Romania."

"If this engine is good for mobile drilling units, I may be able to use a whole army of them."

"Certainly. That would, however, have to be a separate arrangement."

"But let me ask you: How could such an engine be used in a tank climbing at an angle of twenty-five degrees or more?"

"In addition to the official contract, 'Leopold' would sign a confidential agreement, under which a Swiss firm especially set up by himself for this one-time contract would design and deliver the special lubrication system necessary to transform this engine into one for a tank. It would secretly be a branch of his company. Every employee of this branch would be one of his retirees, with experience on the Leopard II engine and its lubrication system, handpicked by himself. They would receive the entire original technical documentation from him. According to 'Leopold,' the only thing different would be the stamp on the blueprints."

"Any guarantees for fulfilling the secret agreement?"

"Ten days ago I was in West Germany to firm up the secret contract. 'Leopold' drove me in his car back to the Romanian embassy in Cologne, and when we got there he asked me to help him unload the trunk. It was full of heavy boxes, which he opened inside the embassy. They contained the original lubrication system of a Leopard II engine and a prototype of a similar lubrication system for the new engine."

"He's got it!"

"Yes, Excellency. According to 'Leopold,' the so-called civilian version of the Leopard II engine was conceived from its very beginning not only for mobile drilling units but also for armored vehicles. He does not yet have the right to sell it openly for military use, so the Swiss firm will be nothing but a cover for the NATO authorities."

"Is $300 million enough, General?"

"Actually, $350 million is what President Ceausescu needs for starting the process. Cash."

"All right. I want, however, to share the production on a fifty-fifty basis from the very first day."

"I shall report exactly that, Excellency."

"There was something about a similar joint venture for the military aircraft industry in one of my brother's earlier messages. What kind of airplanes?"

"There are two. One is a Fokker commercial plane, the FK-614, designed for medium range, able to land anywhere, even on the sand. Fokker has several military versions of it in blueprint: reconnaissance, bombardment, and parachute launching."

"It sounds perfect to me. The second one?"

"Fokker has developed a VTOL—vertical take-off and landing. President Ceausescu thinks that a joint venture with Fokker for producing the commercial 614 would open the doors for Romania to steal the VTOL blueprints."

"Is another $350 million enough?"

"President Ceausescu does not have a firm estimate. But may I report that Your Excellency wants to finance the project with at least $350 million?"

"Yes. My minister of defense could discuss this matter on his next visit to Bucharest."

"I don't believe that President Ceausescu will be prepared for that until after his visit to the United States in the middle of April. I have a message from him connected with his visit."

"I'm listening."

No Peace for the Middle East

"President Ceausescu's visit there has three major objectives. The first is to consolidate the most favored nation status Romania has just received. The second is aimed at opening new doors to American technology prohibited to Communist countries and also to you, Excellency."

"That's good. What is his priority there?"

"Microelectronics and computers."

"That's over my head, but it's all the rage now."

"The President will brief you after his visit, as usual. His third and most important goal is peace in the Middle East."

"Why peace? There will never be peace as long as Israel continues to exist and I am still alive."

"President Ceausescu considers that peace is now more fashionable than war, and he wants to be in on it—as a mediator. He is going to propose a step-by-step plan to President Carter. First, Israel's complete withdrawal from the territories it occupied after the 1967 war and also from southern Lebanon. Second, the

Palestinian people's right to self-determination and to an independent state of their own. President Ceausescu will emphasize at the White House that without a lasting solution to this question there will be no viable peace agreement in the Middle East, nor any guarantee of independence and security for any state in the region, Israel included," I continued emphatically.

"There will never be territorial independence and security for Israel. That should be clear to my Brother Ceausescu."

"As a fourth step, President Ceausescu wants to use Carter to urge that the Israeli government show more receptiveness to President Sadat's initiative."

"Sadat is a fool! He should either step down or be bumped off."

"The last step he envisions is the resumption of the Geneva peace conference, where the Soviets are the permanent co-chairman. He will insist that the conference include Syria and Jordan, and the Palestine Liberation Organization as the authentic representative of the Palestinians. I may also inform you that, in Washington, President Ceausescu wants to torpedo Carter's maneuvers to mediate between Begin and Sadat."

"Begin should be assassinated. And that fool Sadat should either step down or be bumped off."

"Brother Ceausescu wants to remain the mediator between them," I continued, ignoring Gadhafi's interruption. "His trump card is that, as you know, he is the only leader in the world who has diplomatic and personal relations with both Israel and Egypt, and personal friendship with Chairman Arafat."

"Arafat is a stupid fool!"

"Brother Ceausescu wants to persuade Chairman Arafat to show concilation toward 242 and 338 and to change the nameplate on the PLO's door to read government-in-exile, but he has run into difficulties. Could you help him, Excellency?"

"I do not support peace in the Middle East. And I do not support Arafat. He is a stupid, incompetent fool!"

"You once supported him, didn't you, Excellency?"

"The stupid fool is a zealot, a warrior, and a clever one. But he doesn't accomplish anything."

"What should I report to my president?"

"Tell Brother Ceausescu that our views differ on the Middle East and on Arafat. And that I want him to give me an absolutely clean South American passport. It should be so clean that my brother himself would have the confidence to use it. You know who it's for—'Carlos.' And I want my brother to tell me of a Western airport Carlos could safely use to get to the West."

"What else should I tell President Ceausescu?"

"That, despite our entirely different ways of fighting American imperialism, he has my full support. As long as his silly 'Horizon' works, he'll have my money to support it. The day it doesn't do the trick any more, he can count on my arms."

Gadhafi suddenly rose from his chair and took a handkerchief out of his pocket, with which he wiped his forehead and the back of his neck. "What is the status of our 'Brutus,' General?" the Colonel asked a few minutes later.

"Brutus" was the code name for bacteriological weapons. The day after launching an international appeal for the abolishment of all chemical weapons, Ceausescu called in General Mihai Chitac, the commander of the chemical troops, and me, and ordered that an ultra-classified component for bacteriological weapons be immediately created within the chemical troops and developed with the DIE's help. Later this component was given the code name "Brutus" from *brucellosis,* the first bacteriological weapon it produced, which became Ceausescu's favorite. Promising eventually to share the product with Libya, he persuaded Gadhafi to invest large sums of money to develop "Brutus," although in reality no foreign currency was needed for this project.

"I don't have anything about 'Brutus' in President Ceausescu's message," I ventured to answer.

Gadhafi spun toward me quick as a flash. His transfigured face turned hard as granite, and his eyes shot daggers at me. "Don't play games, General. There's Libyan money in there, and I want to know what it's doing." As "Jarnea" translated into my ear, he whispered that Gadhafi's voice betrayed a nervous tremor. Although Gadhafi was speaking Arabic, I could easily sense the menace emanating from him.

"Tell that to Brother Ceausescu," Gadhafi added in the same voice. Then he went slowly over to the window and, carefully turning his profile toward us, remained there without saying anything more, just staring out into the night. I understood that the meeting was over.

From Gadhafi's office I went to the embassy, where the chief of station, Anton Anton, was waiting for me in the main salon.

"Bucharest keeps asking if you've come back," he said. "The Comrade is waiting for your report." A few minutes after I had written out a telegram saying just "BEDOUIN FAVORABLY DISPOSED," Anton reported that "Riyad" was downstairs waiting to take me to an official dinner being given for General Popescu and me.

HELPING "CARLOS"

"Riyad's" dinner took place at the Ministry of Interior's club, which was as cold as a casemate. It was attended by his deputies and several other high-level officers. On the long bare wooden table were four roast lambs, surrounded by silver bowls full of green rice pilaf and numerous bottles of green lemonade. The dinner started out in a silent, morose atmosphere. The few jokes Popescu tried out were followed only by his own laughter. After a couple of hours the mood warmed up a little, but by then "Riyad" had led me out to his car. "Let them enjoy themselves without their bosses," he said.

We pulled up to the entrance of a luxury hotel, where the uniformed doorman who came to open the door was thunderstruck when he spotted "Riyad." "This is another result of our liaison," "Riyad" said to me. "Our ministry has taken over this hotel and others that are used mostly by well-heeled foreigners. Every telephone is monitored, we've put microphones in every room and at most of the dining room tables, and the personnel are our officers under cover. Just like what I saw at your Athene Palace and Intercontinental hotels."

We spent the rest of the evening talking at a solitary, remote table, where, without being asked, the waiter filled our teacups with Scotch, served from a copper teapot. In proportion to the number of cups, the real "Riyad" began to emerge from the shell of the taciturn, monosyllabic one who spoke only rarely and never said what he was thinking. The fanatical anti-Zionist and frenzied anti-American that I had seen once before, in a Bucharest nightclub in the summer of 1977, began to come to life again.

The secrecy that governs any intelligence service, either in the free world or in a totalitarian country, prohibits its officers from discussing their work with laymen. But there is also an unwritten law that, when two intelligence officers get together, the only thing they can talk about is their clandestine business. Terrorism had been "Riyad's" main job for the past five years. That's what he had talked about in Bucharest a few months earlier, and terrorist operations were what he started to reminisce about now. Today he talked about the infamous terrorist "Carlos," also known as "the Jackal." Ilich Ramirez Sanchez, his real name, was the son of a wealthy Venezuelan. He became a revolutionary, then an active supporter of the Popular Front for the Liberation of Palestine, a Marxist terrorist group, and finally a personal friend of Gadhafi's.

"As long as 'Carlos' continues to live here," said "Riyad," "I have unlimited funds to cover all his expenses for the rest of his life." Only after draining his teacup did he continue: "'Carlos' is nervous, restless, can't sit still. Now he wants to organize a new operation in the West. Did the Colonel ask you for a passport?"

"He did."

"We've asked our Bulgarian friends for a South American passport for 'Carlos,' but the Colonel also wants Romanian help. You know, we have excellent relations with Sofia, but Ceausescu is the Colonel's brother."

It was after midnight when we left for the airport. As soon as the airplane had reached its cruising altitude, Calomfirescu came back to the salon. "Try to sleep for a couple of hours, General. The presidential bed is waiting for you," he said, after we had finished a late candlelight dinner prepared by himself.

As always, once in bed I said my prayers. I have been a devout Christian all my life, and I have never gone to sleep before giving thanks to God. Ever since religion had become prohibited, however, I had said my prayers only in my mind. Over the years I had learned to concentrate until I could clearly see the image of Christ crucified on the cross. That was my church, my altar, my icon for almost 30 years. It was to this Christ, Whom I saw so clearly in my mind's eye, down to the least detail of His face and body, that I always said my prayers.

It was almost six o'clock in the morning when I finally got to Bucharest. Coming back from my trips to the West, Otopeni International Airport always used to strike me as a strange, threatening place, belonging to a different, primitive world. From the air you can see the anti-aircraft cannons and heavy machine guns installed by Ceausescu to prevent any hijacked airplane from leaving the country. The airport building, drowned in darkness to save electricity, swarms with security officers and militiamen carrying submachine guns. The officials, from the border guards and customs officers down to the doormen, are all equally unfriendly and suspicious. The passengers, timorous and frightened, try to wait or walk around without drawing any attention to themselves. On this particular cold and rainy morning, however, the airport actually looked inviting to me, compared to the world I had just come from.

Pop, my executive officer, was there to give me a quick briefing on what had happened during my absence. After finishing his report, he told me that the "Professor" had called several times the day before—Ceausescu had wanted news from me. Now he had left word for me to be at his office "the first thing in the morning." That meant eight-thirty, the time Ceausescu always got there, with the punctuality of a Swiss watch. I gave Pop my briefcase and left to go home. On the way my driver, Paraschiv, talked mostly about my daughter, Dana, and her fiancé, Radu. Yesterday had been the opening day of her exhibit in Bucharest. A lot of people had been there. She had been so excited. . . . In the afternoon Paraschiv had taken her to Radu's sculpture exhibit. A lot of visitors there, too. . . . They were so cute together.

CHAPTER

VII

"WELCOME home, Boss!"

"Am I glad finally to see a human being, Professor!" I replied in answer to Constantin Manea's effusive hug.

Ceausescu's suite of offices and meeting rooms was empty at that early morning hour. The only other people there were the team of technicians responsible for doing the daily security sweep of Ceausescu's office. A rule introduced long ago by the Soviet KGB requires that the Communist Party leader's office and residence be regularly and systematically checked for Western monitoring devices or other operational coverage. Every morning all telephones are replaced by identical-looking ones that have been checked out and sealed. The telephone lines are checked daily to detect any foreign connection or potential interception. The radiation detection system concealed in the door frame is tested every morning, as are the Geiger-Mueller counters and other radiation meters hidden inside the office. Once a week the walls, ceiling, and floor are x-rayed in a supplementary search for hostile microphones.

"Let's go inside, Boss. There isn't another place on earth safer for a chat than the Comrade's office," Manea said, winking in the direction of the officers doing the sweep. He pushed me into the presidential office, where he began setting out on Ceausescu's desk the things with which he usually starts his day, in a specific, invariable order: the DIE's daily national intelligence reports on top, the folder containing the embassy telegrams selected by the minister of foreign affairs underneath, the report on the Radio Free Europe broadcasts in Romanian next under them, and on the very bottom the Agerpres news bulletins especially prepared

115

for him, containing information from the Western press that has not been published in Romania.

"We haven't had much business the last few days, Boss," said Manea. "The Comrade had a meeting with the minister of defense and his staff to congratulate them on their recent maneuvres. Do you know who our best man was? General Militaru won all the medals! Remember what a spectacular performance he made when he opened the last National Day military parade? There he was, like Prince Charming, riding in his open car and saluting unit after unit and then reporting to the Comrade. All the girls went wild over him, didn't they?" Nicolae Militaru, one of Ceausescu's favorite generals, was the commander of the most important Romanian military district, which included Bucharest.

"What about the trip to the United States?"

"It begins on April 12th, as you know, and nothing's been changed in the schedule you proposed to the Comrade."

"The Comrade has just left his residence," a security officer reported from the doorway. "And he is in a good mood, according to what the chief officer at the residence said." Ceausescu's unpredictable moods and rages were proverbial.

"Austria's the Soft Spot"

Manea was standing in the open doorway, facing the stairs, when ten minutes later Ceausescu strode past, handing him the black hat he always wears for the office from the beginning of spring until the onset of winter.

"You are finally home, Pacepa. Come inside," exclaimed Ceausescu with obvious good humor. "What's new?" he began as always, after installing himself on the raised chair behind his desk and picking up his favorite black felt pen.

I reported on my mission in Beirut, trying to be brief and to the point. Despite Ceausescu's lengthy speeches and propensity toward garrulousness, he has no patience with wordiness in others.

Ceausescu remained silent for a long time after I had finished. When he raised his quick-moving eyes toward me again, the legal-size pad in front of him was full of unintelligible geometrical figures drawn in thick, black ink. "For five years I've been trying to break Arafat of lying, but my old fox just can't live without it. If he can't tell at least one lie, he doesn't enjoy the day," Ceausescu said, visibly embarrassed. Losing is what he hates most. "The truth is that Arafat is courageous toward Israel and the Americans but a chicken with the Arab world. He's got a long way to go within his own PLO before he can even begin to think about changing it." Ceausescu rose from his chair. It is not his way to complain. He took a notebook bound in black leather from his personal safe, one of the few documents he used to keep there.

"If we can't have a government-in-exile, we should try to get Arafat's PLO recognized in the West the way it is. As 'Annette' said, for the moment Austria looks like the best soft spot. Let's see what the 'Bible' says." The "Bible" was the name he gave to a handwritten book made by the DIE in only one copy, just for him, which contained cryptic descriptions of its most important agents in the West. "Let's see. Austria. Here it is. The Federal Chancellery. Isn't that Kreisky's office?"

"Yes."

"Under the Federal Chancellery it gives three agents: *'Bodor'—Ministerialrat—money;* *'Berthold'—Ministerialrat— money;* and *'Stumpf'—Hofrat—money.* Tell me about them."

"Those are three of Kreisky's personal advisors. Same thing I am."

"I hope better," Ceausescu winked.

"Me, too, comrade. *Rat* is the German word for advisor. *Ministerialrat* and *Hofrat* are two Austrian bureaucratic ranks."

"Can't they work on Kreisky?"

"'Stumpf' has only supplied classified documents from the Federal Chancellery. As good as you can expect, for Austria. 'Bodor' and 'Berthold' have done both information and influence, for dollars in Switzerland. They don't want Austrian schillings in Vienna."

"Write them down. There's another name here, *'Orlando'— Referent Kreisky's personal office—money.*"

"A bureaucrat. Perfect for information. He's made photocopies of every scrap of paper that's come into his office from or for Kreisky and given us everything. Fifty dollars apiece, by the bale. The Yugoslavs are crazy about them."

"The first name under the Vice Chancellery is *'Daniel'—execu-*

tive officer—gold watches, gold desk sets. Who is the vice chancellor?"

"Androsch is vice chancellor and minister of finance. 'Daniel' is in the final stages of the recruitment process, rewarded with gifts but not yet with money."

"Where else should I look?"

"The Ministry of Foreign Affairs?"

"Here it is. There are more names here than you need to make up a soccer team. Pick out two or three who could put a bug in their minister's ear. They should be able to get to him at least three times a day, and once more in the evening." Ceausescu started nervously flipping through the pages, evidently bored with the "Bible."

"Well," he exclaimed, after a pause. That was an unmistakable sign that he was ready to dictate orders, which he would do to the accompaniment of his right fist pounding the desk at intervals. And so it was. "All in good time," he began. "We should now mount an influence operation designed to convince Kreisky that recognizing the PLO would be the best protection for his nonaligned, unarmed Austria against terrorist attacks. You have a whole army of agents around him and enough experience to do that. Ask Belgrade for help, too. From what Tito has told me, he can do whatever he wants with Kreisky. Vienna should not only recognize Arafat but also establish diplomatic relations with the PLO, as we have done."

Then Ceausescu ordered that rumors be cleverly spread in the West suggesting that Arafat was becoming more moderate and even implying that he was considering a "more realistic approach" to Israel and to the United Nations resolutions on the Middle East. "I don't want the rumors based on tittle-tattle. I want serious documents, made for or by heads of state. Tell Ilie what to do. He's the expert." General Mihai Ilie was the chief of the DIE's Disinformation Service. "He'll also find the best way to leak them. Remember the Western diplomat visiting Bucharest for two days who found a briefcase in his hotel room?"

"That was last year."

"He locked the briefcase in his luggage, went down to the desk and learned that there had been a Syrian general staying in his room who had just left that morning." Ceausescu laughed. "Tell Ilie to mount another clever operation. Disguise one of your illegal officers as an Egyptian dignitary traveling through Austria and have him 'forget' his document in a Vienna hotel. Money is no object."

ROMANIAN ARMS FOR THE THIRD WORLD

Ceausescu changed the subject. "What about Libya?"

After I had finished filling him in on the discussion I had had with Gadhafi, he continued silently drawing black, geometrical lines on his pad, as if there were no one in his office. When he finally looked up at me, his eyes were shining, his face beaming.

"The news is go-o-od. And $750 million coming in here on one day alone!" He closed his right hand tightly, as if literally holding onto the millions he was talking about. "The refinery is not your problem. I'll take care of that later," he concluded, ordering Manea to have the minister of petroleum and the minister of the chemical industry come to his office at two o'clock. "But the military industry is all yours. It's your responsibility until the first tank rolls out of the factory. And until the first Fokker built in Romania takes off," he decreed. "How many of Gadhafi's dollars do we really have to spend on the tank?"

"Almost nothing. If we buy the German license for the mobile drilling units, 'Leonard' will charge us almost nothing for the adaptation of their engine."

"I always like killing two birds with one stone," Ceausescu said with a smile. "It's expensive to keep Communism alive today. I've already got a huge foreign debt staring me in the face, and I can't reduce it by exporting tomatoes or toilet paper. We should be making dollars any way we can. And we should be exporting arms any way and every way, openly and secretly, legally or by smuggling—I don't care how." Ceausescu was putting his broken record on again. "Do you remember the last exhibit the Secret Service set up for me at Blair House? They didn't have a single American submachine gun on display. Their agents all carry Uzi submachine guns, because they are better for their needs. Uzi is now a symbol of anti-terrorism, and the Israelis have made both a name and a fortune with it. We should be building our own 'Uzis.'" He got up and started to walk from one side of his office to the other, with me shuttling along at his side.

"The Third World is basically divided between two large arms producers, but it is reluctant to rely on either American or Soviet arms. We should mount influence operations to increase the spread of anti-Soviet as well as anti-American sentiments. And then, bang! we should pull out our 'Uzis.' A modern Leopard tank made in an independent Romania. A multi-purpose Fokker military plane made in an independent Romania. A fighter plane created by independent Romania and Yugoslavia. And behind the scenes, in secret, a bacteriological missile built by an independent Romania. The Israeli Uzi has become a symbol of anti-terrorism. Our 'Uzis' should become a symbol of independence."

Ceausescu stopped in the middle of the room, turned toward me and caught at my jacket button. "How about 'Cega' as a name for our new tank?"

"From *Ce*ausescu—*Ga*dhafi?"

"Think it over."

Ceausescu went back to drawing geometrical symbols on his pad, forgetting my presence. That was his way of concentrating. "We do have some South American passports, don't we?" he finally spoke up. "I mean of our own, not ones we've gotten from Moscow or somewhere else."

"Yes, we do."

"As secure as what Gadhafi wants?"

"We haven't had any problems with them so far."

"We've also got some original Spanish passports, haven't we? The ones Santiago Carrillo gave us?"

"Yes, comrade. We have 500 blank passports. Originals, obtained by his Communists working in the Spanish police. He said they were very secure."

"Give Gadhafi a couple of those too. Do we have the safe airport in Western Europe Gadhafi wants? It's to get 'Carlos' into Europe, isn't it?"

"Yes, comrade. We have several. One is at Frankfurt in West Germany. There we have 'Rudy,' a *Bundeskriminalamt* officer who's a recruited agent. Currently he's the chief of one of the border guard shifts, the people who check passports. His last dead drop held a dozen films containing the West German and Interpol "Wanted List" issued to the border points."

"Any other way to get 'Carlos' into Europe?"

"'Rolf.'"

"The one who's helping us with the Fokker negotiations?"

"Yes. He has several airplanes, and he could bring somebody into West Germany using a private airport or the section of a large airport reserved for private airplanes. The border and customs controls are very casual there."

The heavy double door of Ceausescu's office unexpectedly slammed open and shut, and Elena blew in like a cyclone. "Where've you been, Nick? I've been looking all over for you," she asked, just to say something. As soon as she spotted me, she began screaming. "I'll crush you like a louse. You'll curse your mother for ever having brought you into this world."

"What has happened, Elena?" Ceausescu broke in.

"I have something to settle with this louse," she yelled in my direction. "I had a million things for him to do. And he, the miserable worm? He goes off to swim in the Mediterranean."

"Leave him alone, Elena. He just got in, and he's dog tired."

"In that case, make him bark. I had a lot of things for you this week, Pacepa," she went on. "The meeting with the Venezuelan ambassador, for instance. You set everything up, but then you left just before he got the medal for me. Nobody knew anything. It was a disaster."

"Come on, Elena. It was perfect. What more could you ask?"

She suddenly changed the subject. "Have you at least brought me something nice from your trip?"

I reported that Olcescu had simply not had the time to go to Damascus and buy the tablecloth sets, but that he would be sending everything along in a day or two.

"Olcescu never has time for me," Elena mewed affectionately. "And what about the 'Stars'?"

"Olcescu talked to his men—those fellows he uses to flog cocaine. They promised several exceptionally large diamonds by tomorrow. I'll get them in the diplomatic pouch."

"That's probably all for today, Pacepa," Ceausescu said, interrupting Elena's grilling.

Service D, as in Disinformation

It was not until late in the afternoon that I was able to visit the Disinformation Service, as Ceausescu had ordered. Disinformation is one of the most secret activities of any East European country, where the very word is tabu. Thus Service D was known within the Securitate as a small "Documentary Archives" unit, and its headquarters was hidden away on the fourth floor of an out-of-the-way Ministry of Interior building. The normal Securitate officers thought Service D was just an office with three teller-like windows for receiving documentary requests from different intelligence units and replying with information found in its secret archives—as it did in fact actually do, for cover reasons. When I got there, a duty officer took me inside through an inconspicuous door, punching out a combination on its electronic lock to open it. After crossing a buffer zone that looked like an archives room, we entered the actual Disinformation Service.

"Comrade General, the service is carrying out its routine program. I am Colonel Valentin Leonte, deputy director of Service D," came the maladroit report, evidently given by somebody who was unfamiliar with military conventions. "You know, General, I have two left feet when it comes to anything military. Ilie just called to say he would be a couple of minutes late. He hasn't been feeling well again."

Valentin Leonte was the code name for Colonel Valentin Lipatti, an old-time DIE officer who had spent most of his career working under cover as ambassador-at-large in the Ministry of Foreign Affairs. Although a bourgeois and the brother of Dinu Lipatti, a well known pianist who spent all his life in Switzerland, Leonte had been recruited and kept in the DIE as a unique exception because of his devotion to Communism, talent for diplomacy, perfect French, and special understanding of the West.

"Until Ilie gets here, let me show you my new computerized system for our collection of letterhead stationery," Leonte suggested. Without waiting for an answer, he opened a nearby door and invited me to enter.

The main purposes of disinformation services in the Soviet bloc are to conceal the countries' real military strength, to distort the true dimensions of their arms buildup, to mislead Western governments and media about Communist intentions with fabricated stories, and to launch rumors for specific tactical purposes. Ceausescu had gradually transformed Romanian disinformation into his personal Marshal Potemkin. Just as Catherine the Great's marshal had to create sham villages for her, to make her Russia look the way she wanted it to, so Service D had to create phoney Western classified documents for Ceausescu, presenting Romania as an independent maverick within the Soviet bloc.

Over the years, Service D has collected several hundred thousand examples of letterhead stationery and appropriate signatures from all around the West. Based on direct DIE procurement augmented through exchange with other Warsaw Pact services and with the Yugoslavs and Libyans, the collection now contains stationery and signatures of almost all non-Communist chiefs of state, heads of government, ministers, and leading figures in the intelligence services, political parties, newspapers and magazines, private corporations, and even charitable institutions. The Vatican was represented as well. There is also a huge font containing copies of the keys used in the typewriters of these Western institutions at certain specific time periods. As in an art museum, every new item is carefully checked, assessed, and preserved. The collection is considered a very important intelligence asset, and no expense is spared to update and complete it with the rarest items available.

These materials are used to create "original" Western documents containing false texts, which are skillfully manipulated for the best effect. In the previous eight years, for instance, Romania's Disinformation Service had successfully created documents signed by various Western leaders. Each of these documents, touching on various innocuous matters, also contained carefully worded references "confirming" Romania's independent stance toward Moscow, the genuineness of its approach to the West, its economic and political difficulties stemming from its independence within the Soviet bloc, and the importance of Western help for Romania to encourage other cracks within the Soviet bloc. Carrying various degrees of classification, such "original documents" were skillfully surfaced in countries other than the ones in which they supposedly originated. They were "forgotten" in a briefcase left in a luxury hotel, presumably by a high-level Western government official; or seen on the desk of a Western official who was actually a Romanian influence agent; or discreetly leaked to a journalist by some Western civil servant who doubled as a DIE agent.

Among the latest was an operation that had used West German Chancellor Helmut Schmidt's official visit to Bucharest the previous January, on his return to Bonn from Cairo. Service D carefully created a file about Ceausescu, which appeared as though it had been put together by the BND—the *Bundesnachrichtendienst,* the West German foreign intelligence service—as briefing material for Schmidt. Besides personal data on Ceausescu and his family, the file contained critical comments on his personality cult, his orthodox Marxist domestic policy, his attitude toward German emigration from Romania, and his foreign trade policy. But it also outlined Ceausescu's genuine independence from Moscow and Romania's economic difficulties generated by the Soviet reaction to it. Written on BND letterhead, classified *streng geheim,* with each page numbered and stamped as registered, the file could easily have been taken as legitimate by somebody outside of the BND. On January 8, 1978, only hours after Schmidt had left Bucharest, a Westerner making a transit stop in Bucharest found a "forgotten" copy of this official-looking West German file in his room at the Athenee Palace Hotel. Another copy of the same file, embellished with Schmidt's own marginal notations, was "left behind" at the Cairo hotel where members of Schmidt's delegation had stayed.

Leonte's collection also helped Romania reduce its hard currency imports from the West. The first successful operation of this kind was predicated upon a long and acerbic rivalry between the French Schneider-Creusot corporation and a West German industrial group composed of AEG, Siemens, and Schloemann A.G. over exporting metallurgical equipment to Romania. Every document brought to Bucharest by the French and West German representatives during the many months of negotiation was secretly photographed, and their telex and telephone communications were constantly monitored. Toward the end of the technical discussions and the beginning of the financial negotiations, an offer purportedly made by the West German group was cleverly leaked to Schneider-Creusot, which thus learned that its prices were more than 20 percent higher. The French corporation drastically lowered its prices, and its new offer, giving prices much lower than the actual ones, was leaked to the Germans. This gambit went on for seven more months and netted Bucharest a price reduction of several million dollars. Subsequently, this operation was copied in dozens of cases, allowing Bucharest to reap significant financial benefits.

"This is my baby," said Leonte, sitting down at a computer terminal connected to a microfilm reader. "Suppose we want Jacques Chirac's signature, his letterhead, and the typewriter used for him in 1974. We take the codes for him from this catalogue," he continued, typing them out on the computer keyboard, "and everything starts to come up on the screen, including a reference to the shelf where we can find the original." Delighted with his show, Leonte beamed at me, then tried the name of Cyrus Vance, the U.S. secretary of state. "Look, General. Here we have a letter signed by Vance on State Department stationery." Leonte typed out another code, and the image on the screen changed. "And here, General, is another one, signed by him on his own, personal stationery. They're both from this year. Whenever we need something by him, all I have to do is provide the text, in flawless American English with a touch of State Department jargon. Our print shop will produce the stationery and type the letter, and our graphological lab will take care of the signature."

The duty officer reported that General Ilie's car had just driven up. Mihai Ilie had had a long and diversified career in Romanian security. After the war, he, together with Soviet KGB advisors, organized the infamous espionage show trial in which the Vatican was presented as a spy network and forced to close its representation in Bucharest. A few years later Ilie became the deputy chief of the Securitate's Counterespionage Directorate, responsible for the English-speaking countries. There he was the brains behind every important operation against the United States and British embassies. His career in foreign intelligence started as an officer in the London station and ended as deputy director of the DIE. An advanced case of diabetes prompted doctors to give him no more than two years, when, in the mid-1960s, he was sent out as chief of the Paris station, mostly so he could seek French medical treatment. His record there, together with that of his deputy, Mihai Caraman, surpassed all expectations. Two spectacular recruitments at NATO headquarters provided tens of thousands of the most sensitive Western military documents, which were transported directly from Bucharest to Moscow on special military flights and were paid for with gold coins from the Kremlin. A recruited code clerk furnished the French code system, also immediately sent to Moscow.

Ilie's career abroad was brought to an abrupt end by the defection of his favorite officer, Ion Iacobescu, who was under UNESCO cover in Paris and defected to the United States in 1969. A year later, Ceausescu appointed Ilie chief of the Disinformation Service and ordered the DIE to pay for his medicines and foreign doctors. He was now working no more than four hours a day, but his presence at the head of the Disinformation Service dramatically increased its efficiency.

"Sorry I'm late, Boss," Ilie said, walking slowly into the room. As usual he was wearing a black overcoat draped across his shoulders and a black hat negligently pushed toward the back of his head. "I was supposed to be dead long ago, not to keep torturing my friends and myself," he continued, to the accompaniment of a strange wheezing noise caused by a severe angina he had developed.

Alone with Ilie in his office behind its heavily padded door, I briefly informed him about my discussions with Arafat and about Ceausescu's order for an "ingenious" disinformation operation "à la Ilie" for inducing Chancellor Kreisky to give Arafat's PLO official recognition.

"I get it, Mike," he said after I had finished. He remained silent for a long time, and I could almost hear the wheels of his alert mind clicking away. "I'll find something. Maybe a Jordanian intelligence service report to Hussein. The bitter rivalry between Arafat and Hussein will lend special weight to every positive word written in there about the PLO leader." He took another long pause before continuing. "I think I'll also have Sadat's written comments in the margin of a confidential report on the PLO from his foreign minister. And Andreotti's on his minister of interior's report about the kidnapping of Aldo Moro. I can easily sprinkle the Comrade's ideas about Arafat through them and leak them to Kreisky in various corners of the world." Ilie's efficiency was proverbial among the handful of people who knew his real job.

"In a few days," Ilie changed the subject, "I'll have something else to give you, Mike. A new report from 'Ovidiu.' More than 150 savory pages of information on actions and operations being planned against Comrade Ceausescu's June visit to Great Britain. And a lot of biographic data on people he has spotted for either recruitment or 'neutralization.' I got it through 'Ana,' as usual."

According to Ilie, "Ovidiu," a writer and prominent anti-Communist Romanian emigré, had been recruited by himself in Paris. For his own security, "Ovidiu" refused to meet with DIE officers in the West, and his only contact with the DIE in France was through his sister, "Ana," living in Romania, who visited him in Paris one or two times a year. "'Ovidiu' has published a book in the West that has made a name as a devastating description of Romanian 'gulags.' I helped him write it," Ilie went on. "Now 'Ovidiu' has become a kind of Romanian Solzhenitsyn. He looks like a genuine, rabid anti-Communist. Conservatives and skeptics trust his words more than anyone else's," Ilie droned on in his monotonous voice. "I'll now have his pen scratching out only one of the Comrade's ideas—that Romania is a maverick inside the Soviet bloc. Very carefully. As with 'Titus' in London. Who would ever suspect these tough anti-Communists of being our men?"

CHAPTER

VIII

CEAUSESCU had long ago set this date for his visit to the exhibit arranged for him and Elena by the Securitate's DGTO (*Directia Generala de Technica Operativa* or General Directorate of Technical Operations). It was set up in a couple of large rooms next to Ceausescu's office at the Communist Party's Central Committee headquarters in Bucharest.

The DGTO is a huge outfit. It conducts microphone and telephone intercepts and mail censorship throughout the country and makes surreptitious entries into private homes and public institutions. It also covers all Western embassies and other Western representations in Romania, including their radio and telex communications, and it monitors the NATO communications in the area.

Created in the early 1950s by the KGB, the DGTO has grown enormously in the last ten years. Ceausescu considers it his most important weapon for controlling the domestic population, much more effective than the hordes of Securitate agents created within every Romanian organization and the "block" and "street" committees of informants covering all social, economic, and residential areas. He has always been deeply interested in all of the DGTO's activities, but he has a special thing about microphones.

POWER THROUGH MICROPHONES

Ceausescu's fascination with microphones was born in the early 1950s, when he was the military forces' political commissar, responsible for replacing the Romanian capitalist army with a

128

new, Communist one modeled after the Soviet Red Army. The Directorate for Military Counterintelligence, known as Directorate IV, was among the first intelligence units the KGB set up in Romania. Microphones were in those days the most efficient weapon Directorate IV had, and it is still true today, when over 90 percent of the Romanian officers have their offices and homes electronically monitored at least periodically. When in 1954 the Moscow-educated General Ceausescu became secretary of the Communist Party in charge of military and security forces, he was intensively instructed several times by Nikita Khrushchev himself in the use of microphones.

From my position in the Ministry of Interior, I myself saw how the instructions Khrushchev had given to Ceausescu were gradually put into action. In 1965, when Ceausescu became the supreme leader, population monitoring grew into a mass operation of unprecedented scope. Hundreds of thousands of new microphones were silently put to work from their hiding places in offices and bedrooms, starting with those of the Politburo. As in the Soviet Union or any other Communist country, corruption and prostitution reigned at the highest levels in Romania, and the microphones relentlessly recorded everything. Like Khrushchev, Ceausescu also ordered a monitoring room built behind his office, so he could personally check on the take from the microphones. They were the key to his power.

The number two man in the Romanian hierarchy, Gheorghe Apostol, who had once been a general secretary of the Party himself, was Ceausescu's main rival. The microphones on him showed Apostol to be a devoted Marxist-Leninist with nothing to reproach him for except not having enough regard for Ceausescu. Coincidentally, however, they also revealed that Apostol's wife was throwing frequent parties with her colleagues, very rarely attended by Apostol himself. His new minister of interior presented Ceausescu with clandestine photographs of these parties. Ceausescu then personally dictated an "anonymous" letter, written as if from a friend of Apostol's, in which Apostol was described as a bourgeois whose conduct was incompatible with his position as number two in the Party. Ceausescu ordered that the letter be handwritten, put in an envelope together with several of the clandestine photographs, which he personally selected, and "mailed" to the first secretary of the Romanian Communist Party—Ceausescu himself. On December 10, 1967, during a break at the National Conference of the Romanian Communist Party, Ceausescu confronted Apostol with the "anonymous" letter and asked him to resign from the Politburo. Fearing an obstinate refusal, Ceausescu immediately convened an emergency meeting of the Politburo. After a 20-minute discussion, the Politburo, caught off guard by Ceausescu's aggressiveness and the unusual "evidence," agreed to remove Apostol temporarily from his position and to appoint him as chairman of the national trade union organization. Once he was no longer number two, Apostol was finished. In May 1977 he was demoted for his "bourgeois lifestyle" and appointed ambassador to Argentina. When Ceausescu gave me the order to have microphones installed in all his rooms there, he remarked in an aside, "Apostol might save us a lot of trouble if he would just become a victim of the terrorist wave" that was overwhelming Buenos Aires at that time.

Once Apostol was replaced in the Politburo with a Ceausescu supporter, the rest was not difficult for the ambitious new leader. He convinced the number three man in the Party hierarchy, Chivu Stoica, a former president and prime minister, that he had a drinking problem that might make him an embarrassment to the Party. Stoica resigned on Ceausescu's promise that he would be held up as an honorary figure for the rest of his life. On February 18, 1975, however, Stoica was called in by the Central Committee and accused of having sexual relations with a 22-year-old niece. He quickly realized that he had microphones in his own home. That same night Stoica committed suicide by firing his hunting rifle into his mouth. A suicide letter addressed to Ceausescu was found on his desk and given to the addressee. Its contents were never disclosed; however, after he read it, Ceausescu was said to have ordered first alcohol for his hands, and then champagne.

A few other leaders from the "old guard" were blackmailed, recruited, and finally installed as the "new guard." Compromising materials and microphones were kept hanging over their heads like swords of Damocles to ensure their loyalty. The most important of them was a four-star general, Emil Bodnaras, who was a member of the Politburo, former minister of national defense, and Ceausescu's mentor. Blackmailed for his personal admiration of Stalin and for his secret membership in Lavrenti Beria's state security organization, Bodnaras agreed to transfer his loyalty to his former subordinate. The microphones installed all around him proved that he really did remain loyal the rest of his life.

In 1967, Ceausescu replaced the former 17 Romanian administrative regions with 39 smaller districts, thus killing three birds with one stone: new leaders came in on the regional level, each of them had far less personal power, and Romania as a country looked larger than ever. The whole group of army senior commanders were also replaced. It was the most dramatic turnover of power since the Communists had taken over the government. The real and only reason for these changes was Ceausescu's policy of putting his own men in everywhere, a strategy designed to last until the end of his life, and until that of the dynasty he envisions passing the scepter to.

In March 1974, Ceausescu finally removed the last pawn from the old guard. He blackmailed his prime minister, Ion Gheorghe Maurer, with "anonymous" letters condemning his liberal views and his wife's behavior and persuaded him to resign for reasons of health.

Soon after he came to power, Ceausescu decided that every member of the old guard, whether removed or kept in office, should be electronically monitored for the rest of his life. He also secretly ordered that new Politburo members and government ministers be covered by microphones in their offices and homes from their first day until their removal, when they would be treated like the old guard. "We should not trust anyone, family members included, before checking on their thoughts," Ceausescu said to me in 1972, when he appointed me to supervise the unit monitoring the Politburo and the "old guard."

Based on the knowledge I have gained from experience, I can find no substantive differences in the way Ceausescu became leader for life and the way it was accomplished by Leonid Brezhnev, Todor Zhivkov, Janos Kadar, and other Soviet bloc leaders. But the way Mikhail Gorbachev has gone about seizing absolute power in the Soviet Union today truly makes him look like Ceausescu's alter ego. Like Ceausescu, when Gorbachev became supreme leader he was the youngest member of the Politburo, with

only domestic experience. Ceausescu's only expertise was in mili-
tary and security matters, as an instant general; Gorbachev's was
in agriculture, as an engineer without on-the-job experience.
Their views on foreign policy were unknown. Soon after Gorba-
chev's nomination, rumors were heard in Moscow that Grigory
Romanov, his main rival for supreme power and the number two
in the hierarchy, had a penchant for the easy life, and that
Catherine the Great's dinner service, borrowed from the Hermit-
age Museum, had been smashed at his daughter's wedding party.
Then Romanov was tacitly demoted from the Politburo and has
since disappeared from public life.

Premier Nikolay Tikhonov "resigned" for reasons of health,
and Andrei Gromyko, whose name was far better known abroad
than the new leader's, was "promoted" to an honorary job, with-
out executive power. Almost half of the members of the cabinet
were replaced in Gorbachev's first year. A new generation of
military and naval commanders took over, constituting the most
rapid turnover at the top of the Soviet military since 1945. Over
40 percent of the regional Party first secretaries on the oblast or
kray level were replaced between March and December 1985. The
explanations for the changes were exactly the same as Ceau-
sescu's: old age, poor health, a need to end corruption, a desire
to make the economy more efficient. There is also a startling
similarity in the way the two dictators have portrayed themselves
to the West. Both Romanian "Horizon" and Soviet glasnost de-
pict a supposedly liberal and reasonable Communist dictator
with whom the West should think it can do business.

Monitoring the thoughts of the entire Romanian population
has been Ceausescu's major domestic policy goal, for which he
has spared no expense or manpower. When he came to power in
1965, the Romanian security forces had one central and 11 regional KGB-designed electronic monitoring centers and five central mail censorship units around the country. The new exhibit
showed that the DGTO had, as of March 1978, ten central and
248 peripheral automated electronic monitoring centers, plus
over 1,000 "portable" units covering small towns, vacation re-
sorts, and the picturesque, historical monasteries favored by
Western tourists, as well as 48 mail censorship units.

*   *   *

When I arrived at the exhibit, only Generals Ovidiu Diaconescu and Istichie Geartu were there. Both electronics engineers, the former was the commander of the DGTO, and the
latter the chief of its huge research institute. Geartu was a
scholar, living with and for his inventions. Diaconescu, in contrast, was a sly old fox who had spent all his life in the electronic
monitoring business. I had gotten to know Diaconescu better in
February 1972, when we both went to Moscow for discussions
with the KGB. Our schedules in the Soviet Union contained a
visit to Leningrad together, including a day at the Hermitage
Museum and an evening at the Kirov Ballet to see Ulanova herself in Swan Lake. On our arrival in Moscow, however, we got the
unpleasant news that the Leningrad trip had been canceled and
replaced by a visit to some kolkhozes. At the end of the first day
in Moscow, when we got back to the KGB's luxury guest house,
we asked for Armenian cognac. For over two hours, we both
pretended to get increasingly inebriated, as we loudly speculated
about why our trip to Leningrad might have been canceled,
winding up with the drunkenly brilliant conclusion that it was
Brezhnev's hatred of everything cultural that had stood in our
way. The next morning we were unexpectedly taken for a short
meeting with KGB Chairman Yuri Andropov, who told us that
the Leningrad visit was on again, apologizing for the actions of
some stupid bureaucrats. Diaconescu was in seventh heaven.
"Microphones are the most efficient intelligence weapon there
is," he said, repeating his favorite maxim.

How to Monitor an Entire Nation

Ceausescu came in at ten o'clock, on the dot as usual, together
with Elena. Ungainly in the military uniform he seldom wore
because of the secrecy of his job, Diaconescu stepped up and said,
all in one breath, "Comrade Supreme Commander of the
Romanian Armed Forces, the exhibit 'DGTO in 1984,' set up
according to your personal order, is ready to be presented. I am
the commander of the DGTO, Lieutenant General Ovidiu
Diaconescu."

Although Ceausescu loves to hear these formal reports and his
title of supreme commander, omission of which can ruin his

whole day, he made a modest sign with his hand, as if to say that all this was not necessary. "Time is precious. Stop talking and let's get to work," he said.

Diaconescu, who was as good a judge of human nature as he was an engineer, continued unperturbed. "Comrade Supreme Commander and Highly Esteemed Comrade Elena, the theme of our exhibit is the future development of the DGTO, so as to carry out your orders to monitor the entire population of our beloved country, the Romanian Socialist Republic."

"I like your accent. Where are you from?" asked Elena, smiling broadly with all her yellow teeth.

"Oltenia. Not far from where the Comrade and you were born," answered Diaconescu, discreetly wiping the perspiration from the back of his neck, after all the effort he had put into loading his first few words with every hint of Oltenian accent he could muster up.

"Your general's sweet," Elena whispered to me.

"This is a telephone device that has been perfected by the DGTO after ten years of work," Geartu started out slowly and methodically, in sharp contrast to Diaconescu's rapid manner of speaking. He held an innocuous looking, beige colored telephone. "This is not just a normal telephone. It also serves as a very sensitive microphone, capable of recording all conversations in the room where it is installed. If this telephone is approved as the only kind legally allowed in Romania, it will open a new era of broad-scale electronic surveillance, without the tedious need for surreptitious entries into private homes to install microphones."

"Could it have different models?"

"We have three models and five colors, and we can have as many as you wish to order."

"That's what I've been waiting for. How good is it?"

"Excellent," broke in the fast talking Diaconescu. "Much better than anything we've seen to date. We have samples of similar instruments discovered in our embassies abroad—American, British, and West German-made. Ours is clearer. Please listen to these comparative tapes."

"Can we use it on a wide scale?" asked Ceausescu, ignoring the request that he listen to the tapes.

"We are only waiting for your command, Comrade Supreme Commander."

"Approved. Starting today, March 28, 1978, this is the one and only telephone approved for use in Romania. Period. How many old telephones do we have in use today?"

"More than three million," Diaconescu promptly replied.

"Replace them with the new ones," Ceausescu ordered.

"I don't understand, Nick. What's the difference between this one and the black one I have in my office?" Elena asked, a little embarrassed. She knows nothing about how the tapes are made that she so avidly listens to in the back room of her office.

"The d-difference is t-that *you* will never have the new one, neither in your office nor at home," Ceausescu answered, winking toward us. He also stutters when pleasurably excited.

"May we do a demonstration, Comrade Supreme Commander?" asked Diaconescu.

"Go ahead," approved Ceausescu, with a large smile on his face and a glow in his eyes. Being addressed as "Supreme Commander" is even more exciting for him than having sex, or so Diaconescu had told me a few days earlier.

"To this portable monitoring center we have hooked up four phones that are installed in four different, randomly selected apartments. Two are the kind we use now, and two are the new model. The monitoring center is voice-activated, so it will automatically start recording when any one of the phones is in use. It's recording one conversation right now," said Diaconescu, pointing to a moving recorder. The conversation could clearly be heard in the exhibit room when he pushed a button. "The recorder stops when the conversation is over, as it just did. That's all we can record with the old phones. But now let's listen to the new one."

Diaconescu dialed a number and asked if it was the National Theater. "Wrong number" came from the other end of the line, but the tape recorder did not stop after the telephone had been hung up. A woman's voice could be heard asking who had called. "Some idiot who put his finger in the wrong hole. Let me finish what I was listening to on Radio Free Europe about the trip the Dictator and his old bag are making to the United States," the man's voice replied, before being cut off sharply. Diaconescu's hand, darting out faster than a snake, had flicked off a switch. He always did have good reflexes.

The deadly silence was interrupted when Diaconescu flicked another switch. A fuzzy noise together with heavy breathing and short yelps came suddenly out of the speaker, but Diaconescu's quick hand immediately shut it off.

"Turn it back on," Elena ordered with biting voice. Her experienced ear was almost as good as Diaconescu's. "They should be arrested," she ordered, after listening a few more minutes. "At eleven in the morning, working people should be out working, not making love."

Ceausescu moved along a few steps. Geartu was holding up a normal-looking telephone outlet, explaining that inside its plastic body there was a concealed mini-microphone, which could not be found without the outlet's complete destruction. It was to be used in other rooms that did not have the telephone device in them, so that a whole apartment could be covered. The same display contained several other new pieces of equipment designed by the DGTO for use in villages where people often had no telephone. Ceausescu's eye was caught by a television set with a built-in transmitter that could be activated by a remote control matching its code.

"We propose introducing this microtransmitter in all television sets that are to be sold in rural areas. One advantage with having it there is that it would have a constant source of power, eliminating the need for batteries. And for another thing, a television set is silent eighty percent of the time." Romanian television programs are on the air only a few hours a day.

"If we're going to use this hocus-pocus, we could even shorten the daily program. Some news and a film about the Party is all the people need, isn't that so, Nick?" asked Elena.

"Approved," Ceausescu said, moving on to a display showing monitoring equipment for restaurants. The ceramic ashtrays and flower vases caught his attention. Geartu reported that, by the end of the next five-year plan, every restaurant would be equipped with only ceramic ashtrays and vases containing thin, battery-activated micro-transmitters. They could be turned on by any surveillance officer or waitress-agent, who needed only to pull out a needle-like pin.

First invented by the Soviet KGB, ceramic ashtrays and flower vases containing microtransmitters are now secretly used by all East European security services for monitoring discussions in restaurants and hotel lobbies. The American journalist Hedrick Smith humorously describes what he witnessed in a Soviet hotel by the Caspian Sea, when word came down that a delegation of foreign ambassadors was about to make a visit there. "Like the provincial bureaucrats of Gogol's rich satire *The Inspector General*, the staff scurried about in a frenzy to make the hotel more presentable. . . . The regular glass ashtrays disappeared from the dining room tables and new, more decorative ashtrays appeared. Large, white carnations were placed on each table."[1] It evidently did not occur to Smith that the new ashtrays and flower vases were not only for show. Their use as portable monitoring devices is still one of the best kept secrets within the Soviet bloc.

Ceausescu and Elena went slowly from one display to the other, listening with growing interest about new ways of performing electronic monitoring, daytime and nighttime clandestine photography, indoor and outdoor video-taping, and faster and more complete mail censorship. Then the Ceausescus came to a display of equipment designed for use abroad. Geartu and Diaconescu began presenting the prototype of a new electronic monitoring center for use in Romanian embassies, along with passive systems, lasers, and encoded ultra-high-frequency transmitters for installation in such targets in the West as government institutions, military units, and private homes.

"Show them to Arafat and 'Annette.' To Gadhafi, too," he whispered into my ear. "And give them as many as they want."

A BEAUTIFUL NEW LIFE

It was noon when the Ceausescus arrived at the end of the exhibit. Taking a noisy deep breath, Ceausescu looked around and asked: "How many people will we be able to monitor simultaneously by the end of our next five-year plan?"

"I can only report, Comrade Supreme Commander and Esteemed Comrade Elena," replied Diaconescu, "that, if our proposals are approved today, then as of January 1, 1984, we will

[1] Hedrick Smith, *The Russians*, New York: Quadrangle/The New York Times Book Co., 1976, p. 17.

be able to monitor ten million microphones simultaneously. Assuming that our population will keep the same rate of increase in the next five years as in the last five, our estimate is that every single family could be periodically monitored during each calendar year, with the suspect ones continuously covered."

"How many children do you have, comrade?" Elena interrupted Diaconescu.

"One, Comrade Elena. One soldier for the Party."

"That's why our population isn't growing. You should have at least four soldiers for the Party, dear comrade. Add a ten to fifteen percent population increase to your estimates, General. By 1984, Romania should have at least thirty million inhabitants. I'll take care of that, and you take care of your microphones."

Ceausescu sucked in air between his teeth several times, then began. "We are now building a beautiful life for the Romanian people, comrades. A new and independent life, which our people deserve, after two thousand and fifty years of struggle and humiliation." Elena led the applause. "For the past decade, each year has marked something new in our Communist history. Let us make 1984 another cornerstone. Let us again be unique in the Warsaw Pact. Let us be the first in the entire world, comrades. In a very short time we will be the only country on earth able to know what every single one of its citizens is thinking. Five years is all that separates us today from a new, much more scientific form of government." He looked meaningfully at his audience before continuing.

"Why is American imperialism so unpopular? Because it does not know what its people think, because it is not scientific. What you are doing here, comrades, is the real science of government. It is a true public opinion survey. The Communist system we are creating together is the most scientific ever, I repeat, comrades, *ever* to be put at the service of mankind."

Diaconescu opened the applause. Ceausescu raised his arms, asking for silence. "It is too bad that we cannot tell our working people how the Communist Party is looking out for them, comrades. Wouldn't the miners go out and dig more coal, if they could just be sure that the Party knew what their wives were doing every single instant? They would, comrades, but we cannot talk about our system today. The Western press might accuse us of being a police state. That's imperialist propaganda, comrades.

We do not have a police state, and we will never have a police state. We are a proletarian dictatorship preserving our ideological purity. Communism is the only real democracy, and history will attest to that for generations to come." Applause.

"But someday we *will* be able to talk about what we are doing here. Someday, when our proletarian world revolution defeats the capitalist hydra, and our red flag is flying everywhere on earth!" Ceausescu finished dramatically.

MUZZLES FOR SECRETS

Before leaving, Ceausescu beckoned me over. "I want the 'muzzle' for our visit to Washington." The "muzzle" was an odd piece of equipment designed for Ceausescu to use in holding secret conversations abroad, in places where "bubbles," or acoustically protected rooms, were not available. As one who knows the capabilities of hidden microphones only too well, Ceausescu is terribly afraid of being monitored himself.

When I left Central Committee headquarters, it was already late afternoon. "To the LM," I ordered, closing the door of my car.

"The general wishes to be driven to the First of May Boulevard headquarters," my driver echoed, guiding the car out of the heavily guarded area.

"LM" was the designation for the DIE's Technical Directorate, a special unit that worked around the clock, seven days a week, to develop and apply all kinds of espionage paraphernalia, ranging from a photocamera concealed in a coat button to a miniaturized burst transmitter capable of sending pages of encoded information over thousands of miles in only fractions of a second. "Who is the director on duty?" I asked the security officer who unlocked the door of the main building for me.

"Colonel Aurel Sandu," he answered, while electronically relocking the door.

An electronics engineer, Sandu had made a name by uncovering microphones planted in Romanian embassies, as well as by installing them in DIE targets in the West. When Ceausescu ordered that influence and disinformation become a more important part of the DIE's activity, Sandu mounted several spectacular operations. Using high-tech equipment, he was able to locate hostile listening devices in Romanian embassies and residences abroad without touching the walls, so the listeners did not know their microphones had been discovered. Cologne, Brussels, Ankara, Athens, Cairo, and Budapest were only a few of the places where he had been successful. That allowed the DIE to stage special conversations so as to feed the listeners carefully prepared disinformation material.

Sandu's room, crammed with electronic equipment, looked more like a scientific laboratory than the office of a director. When I entered, he was sitting at a work table, deeply engrossed in an oscilloscope. In his light gray overalls, with his glasses perched on the end of his nose as he fiddled with his equipment, Sandu looked more like a scholar who cared about nothing but his research. Only when he starts to speak does the enterprising intelligence officer in him come out.

"Sorry, General," said Sandu, jumping to his feet as if set off by a spring, when he finally realized that I had been standing in his office for some time. "I was trying to filter out the street noise from the tapes we made at Turkish military intelligence headquarters in Ankara. Do you remember the operation?"

"Yes, Sandu, but I'm here now to see about your 'muzzle.' The Comrade wants to use it on his trip to Washington."

"I've got it!" Sandu said, his dark face lighting up. "The AZ-11 is being put through an endurance test twenty-four hours a day. Come with me, General." He led me to a nearby conference room, where ten officers sat with things resembling oversize oxygen masks over their mouths and unusual earphones entirely covering their ears. They were arguing with each other in utter silence.

"Give it a try, General." Sandu pulled out a chair for me, while handing me a mask and earphones. He took another set for himself. I was able to communicate perfectly with everyone else around the table. Wearing the mask and earphones was a little uncomfortable, though.

"Do you see these microphones?" Sandu said, pointing to six different ones on the table. "None of them can pick up any intelligible sound from our conversation. Even with very powerful amplifiers. That's all spelled out here," he explained, patting a fat file he had brought in with him.

As I took off my mask and earphones, Sandu picked up a Samsonite suitcase. "I've got two AZ-11's in suitcases, ready to go," he
said. "They're all set to work in Washington or wherever." Catching my reproachful examination of the shabby suitcase, he explained. "It's new, General. We made it look old and grubby on
purpose. As if it had been carting somebody's old underwear
around for five years, not some brand new electronic equipment."

"I'll take one for the Comrade," I said, intending it as a compliment.

"There's one already in the trunk of your car," the energetic
Sandu cut in, always trying to be one jump ahead of the game.
"I'm happy to see the general smiling," he continued, and I
thought I caught a hint of irony in his voice. He was probably
thinking about the same thing I was—the picture of Ceausescu
sitting in Blair House in Washington with the "dog muzzle" on
his face.

CHAPTER
IX

'W-WHEN d-did you become CIA agents?" exploded Ceausescu, his stutter a telltale sign of his terrible rage. "Take this sheet of paper and write everything down, right this minute. All of you!" he yelled, hurling a stack of blank paper to the floor.

The minister of interior, Teodor Coman, his first deputy, Nicolae Plesita, and I stood dumbfounded in the middle of Ceausescu's office. Moving from one side of the room to the other like a caged tiger, Ceausescu started pacing furiously. "I gave you an order to have microphones installed in every one of Kiraly's rooms, and up his ass, too, and to have him surveilled day and night. How much did the CIA pay you for letting Kiraly send this new letter abroad?" he bellowed at Coman, who stood stock still, flabbergasted. "How did he manage to get this appeal out to the West?" he screamed, for once forgetting all about his delicate throat and fragile vocal chords. "How much did the CIA pay you for not catching his letter abroad? For letting it fall into the hands of a journalist?" he raged on, now at me.

Ceausescu began to calm down after a while, but not before having decided that the ministers of foreign affairs and justice, who were later called on the carpet, were also CIA agents. He stepped over to face Coman. "Kiraly is an idiot," he decreed solemnly. Gone was the stuttering and yelling. "An idiot who hasn't learned a thing. I've tried to be generous, keeping him on as a member of the Grand National Assembly, letting him run free, but that beast just couldn't understand that my patience does have its limits." Ceausescu ordered that Kiraly immediately be moved to the other end of the country, at the border with Yugoslavia, far away from all his Hungarians. He was to be surveilled 24 hours a day, "openly and brutally." He was to be scared out of his wits and kept under constant pressure, so that he would understand not to play games with the dictatorship of the proletariat. "And beaten to death, if he tries to slip away or to send another letter abroad." Finally, Ceausescu ordered that the Securitate find a non-political pretext to arrest Kiraly. "Give him 'Radu' the first day he's in jail," Ceausescu instructed his minister of interior. "Radu" was the code name for a lethal means of silencing critics when they were in jail.

When we left Ceausescu's office an hour later, neither Coman nor Plesita said a word.

"Where does the general wish to be driven?" asked my driver, Paraschiv.

"Wherever you like. I just need some air!"

HATRED FOR HUNGARIANS

Ceausescu has always been a fanatical nationalist, but nowhere is this more evident than in his personnel policies. Only ethnic Romanians going back two generations and born within the Romanian borders are allowed to hold Party and government positions affecting national security. For the job I had in the DIE, the requirement was pure Romanian blood going back three generations. Romanians of other ethnic backgrounds, even though their families may have lived in Romania for generations, are strictly prohibited from holding positions in the sections for national defense of the Communist Party's Central Committee, in the DIE, at Securitate headquarters, or in the General Staff of the Armed Forces. Even Romanians married to people of other ethnic groups were silently removed after Ceausescu came to power. Only a few token Jews, Hungarians, and Germans have been kept for propaganda purposes in high positions, but despite their high-sounding titles they have no access to Ceausescu's real secrets. His increasing efforts to purify the blood of the Romanian government ominously recall Hitler's attempts to create a purely Aryan nation.

The Hungarians living in Romania are the ethnic group most hated by Ceausescu, because of their number and cohesion. After the collapse of the Austro-Hungarian monarchy, many Hungari-

ans ended up under foreign rule. According to Hungarian reports, there were at that time 15 million Hungarians living between the Alps and the Carpathian Mountains, only 10 million of
whom were in Hungary proper. This estimate may well have
been exaggerated, but the fact remains that some two million
Hungarians were living in Romania's Transylvania. In the late
1960s, Ceausescu began taking the Hungarians concentrated in
Transylvania and quietly dispersing them throughout Romania.
"Why shouldn't we do exactly what Brezhnev did?" he asked,
referring to the period when Leonid Brezhnev had dispersed
over one million of the Romanians living in the Moldavian Soviet
Socialist Republic to Siberia. At the same time, concerned with
creating the illusion of a balance of Hungarian representatives in
Romanian political organizations, Ceausescu has been preoc-
cupied, ever since he came to power, with finding Romanians of
Hungarian origin who would be loyal to him.

Carol Kiraly was one of Ceausescu's own discoveries. An avid
hunter, Kiraly garnered political credentials by organizing exclu-
sive hunting parties, where Ceausescu bagged impressive trophies. When Romania's 17 regions were replaced by 47 districts,
Ceausescu appointed Kiraly first Party secretary for Covasna, a
district with an almost exclusively Hungarian population. Soon
afterwards, in Covasna, Ceausescu brought down the largest
bears he had ever shot, and it was not long before Kiraly became
an alternate member of the Political Executive Committee. I just
happened to be in Ceausescu's office with the minister of interior
on the day in 1972 when the latter gave him a letter in which
Kiraly objected to discrimination against the Hungarian minority
and resigned from all his Party and government positions, an
event without precedent in the history of Communist Romania.

I shall never forget Ceausescu's stupefaction, the long minutes
of leaden silence during which he stared at us with popping eyes
and then his great explosion of rage. When he calmed down, he
ordered that the letter be kept in strictest confidence, that microphones immediately be installed in every inch of Kiraly's house,
including the bathroom, and that incriminating materials be
carefully collected on him. Ceausescu also ordered Kiraly's public compromise in the near future, his arrest for non-political
reasons, and eventually his quiet liquidation in jail.

In the Soviet Union, arresting political opponents for non-political reasons became a fact of life after Stalin's death, when Moscow refused to admit the existence of any political opposition. The rest of the Soviet bloc soon followed Moscow's example. "All our prisoners are simply criminals," is what Ceausescu proclaimed in the fall of 1967, when he decided to spread the word in the West that Romania no longer had any political prisoners. A few days later, in a very confidential walk in his garden with Ion Stanescu, who had just been appointed chairman of the newly created State Security Council, Ceausescu made it clear that nothing had changed. "Every suspected political opponent," I was told by an enthusiastic Stanescu after his meeting with Ceausescu, "must be just as forcefully neutralized as before. 'With inventiveness and creativity,' the Comrade said, 'we can find countless ways to get rid of political criminals, without giving the Western media any reason to squawk about us. We can arrest them as embezzlers or speculators, accuse them of dereliction of their professional duties, or whatever else best fits each case. Once a fellow's in prison, he's yours.' The Comrade spoke like a real professional," Stanescu marveled. Then he went on in a low, conspiratorial voice. " 'Listen, Stanescu,' the Comrade said to me last night. 'It's not only on the street that accidents can happen. It's not just free men who get sick and die.' Imagination and creativity, that's what the Comrade expects of me," Stanescu summed it all up. Thenceforth, "imagination and creativity" became magic words in the Securitate.

LETHAL RADIATION IN JAIL CELLS

To liquidate some of his critics during their jail detentions on non-political charges Ceausescu uses the Securitate's Service K, a relatively small component responsible for counterintelligence work within the national penitentiary system. In Romania, the latter is subordinate to the Ministry of Interior, not to the Ministry of Justice. Created by the Soviets in 1950, based on the KGB model, the Romanian Service K does the dirtiest work against jailed prisoners, monitoring microphones and running stool pigeons in the jail cells to elicit damaging information and to frame prisoners into making incriminating statements. In some cases, it secretly liquidates them, staging alleged suicides or using poison that causes what looks like a natural death. In the spring of 1970, Service K added radioactive substances supplied by the KGB to its deadly arsenal. Ceausescu himself gave the procedure the code name "Radu," and he would issue the order, "Give 'Radu' to Popescu." The radiation dosage was said to generate lethal forms of cancer.

"'Radu' should be given to Kiraly the first day you have him in jail," Ceausescu said on that day in 1972, winding up his orders and giving the minister of interior a conspiratorial wink.

For a long period of time the microphones on Kiraly revealed nothing significant. No political discussions, no compromising activities, nothing. Until the end of September 1977, when the intensive coverage supplied some information on Kiraly's deep concern over not yet having been able to get in to see Ceausescu and discuss how Hungarians were being discriminated against in Romania. Because of this, Kiraly had started drafting a memorandum documenting the government's earlier abuses and oppressive measures against ethnic Hungarians, Germans, and Jews. Minister of Interior Coman and I were again witness to Ceausescu's rage, when he was informed of this. He immediately called the first vice prime minister, Ilie Verdet, and ordered him to see Kiraly and calm him down. "Try to drag his future plans out of him, and promise him whatever it takes to calm him down for now. Later, who knows? Even useful people may die in a hunting accident. Or," he added, "they may come down with cancer."

On October 4, 1977, Kiraly was received by Verdet, as well as by Political Executive Committee member Petre Lupu, Minister Teodor Coman, and Ion Vinte, an old Party member of Hungarian descent who was vice-chairman of the Council of Working People of Hungarian Nationality. During that meeting, which was taped, Kiraly was persuaded to give Verdet the draft of his memorandum about the situation of Hungarians in Romania. "The Party will take steps to remedy the mistakes that have been committed," promised Verdet, to keep Kiraly quiet, but no attempt was made to live up to this.

In January 1978, the microphones on Kiraly suddenly went dead. When on January 24th Securitate agents found him hiding out in an obscure hotel in Bucharest, it was too late. That same

day the London *Times* and the Manchester *Guardian* simultaneously published a report from Belgrade saying that, in a letter
smuggled out of Romania, Carol Kiraly claimed that the
Romanian Communist Party and government were practicing a
discriminatory policy against Hungarians and other minorities
living in Romania. The next day the whole Western press published articles about this, and Radio Free Europe read excerpts
from Kiraly's letter over and over. Minister of Interior Teodor
Coman and his seven deputies, including myself, were called in
by Ceausescu the minute he heard about it. And now today,
Ceausescu had learned that Kiraly's letter in its entirety had
reached the United States Congress, which had voted to give
Romania the "most favored nation" status, and that the members
had reacted with stupefaction or revulsion, depending on which
way they had cast their vote.

Suddenly the radio telephone interrupted my reverie. "Sixty-
two, report immediately to zero one. Repeat: sixty-two, report to
zero one." Dumitru Popescu, Party secretary for press and propaganda of the Party's Central Committee, was waiting for me at
Ceausescu's door. When we entered his office, Ceausescu was
gazing out at the deserted street, the broad avenue across from
his office being closed to traffic. Turning toward us, he ordered
that the Romanian press immediately be flooded with articles on
the equal rights of minorities in Romania, on their proportional
representation in all political and governmental organizations
from the Central Committee and the Grand National Assembly
down to individual kolkhozes. "Use the data I gave Wallach yesterday," said Ceausescu, taking from his desk a file with the text
of an interview he had just given the American journalist John
Wallach of the Hearst Newspapers and starting to dictate from
it: "The composition of the Grand National Assembly is conclu-
sive in this respect: of its 349 members, 29, i.e. 8.2 percent, are
Hungarians, 8, i.e. 2.21 percent, are Germans, and 3, i.e. 0.9
percent, belong to other nationalities."[1] Ceausescu emphasized
that these figures very accurately reflected the population per-
centages of these groups. He went on to dictate other figures,
grossly exaggerated, which he had sprinkled throughout his in-

[1]*President Nicolae Ceausescu's State Visit to the U.S.A.: April 12–17, 1978*, (English
version), Bucharest: Meridiane Publishing House, 1978, p. 37.

terview. "Make sure the American press prints all of Wallach's interview," Ceausescu said to me at the end.

After Popescu left, Ceausescu grabbed me by the arm and began to pace around his office. "It's not Kiraly who bothers me. I can crush him like a louse any day. It's Kadar. I know that Jewish pig is behind the whole thing. I can feel him breathing down my neck. He wants Transylvania ceded back to Hungary. That'll never happen without a war. In the First and Second World Wars the Romanians occupied Budapest, and we'll do it again and again."

When Ceausescu is mad he uses the pejorative words for Hungarian and Jew. Instead of calling Kiraly an *ungur* he said *boanghen*, and Kadar was not an *evreu* but a *jidan*. This is roughly equivalent to using *Hunkie* and *Kike* in English, or worse.

When he had vented his rage, Ceausescu stopped and caught at one of my coat buttons: "Before my visit to Washington we ought to set up an exhibit of Romanian books that have been translated into Hungarian, German, and other minority languages, to show the equal rights of minorities here. Get to work on that." Further, he wanted the DIE to obtain approval for a photographic exhibit on 'Romania Today' at the State Department, graphically presenting his "tireless domestic and international activities." Still hanging onto my button, Ceausescu continued: "In the meantime we should be keeping a watchful eye on all the *boanghen* pigs we have at home."

The facts that later came out underscore the seriousness of the Kiraly case. On Thursday, June 5, 1980, Congressman Richard T. Schulze of Pennsylvania raised the Carol Kiraly case in the House of Representatives. "Last January I visited Romania and intended to meet Mr. Kiraly to get his opinion firsthand. However, the Romanian authorities denied me the opportunity to meet him on the most flimsy pretexts. His voice of protest, however, could not be silenced. Last February, he sent another extraordinary protest letter to Romania's prime minister, Ilie Verdet. The letter reveals the promises he received from the Romanian leadership in an obvious attempt to silence him after his first letter of 1977. All of those promises have been broken, and the campaign of cultural genocide continues unabated."

In October 1984, a Western human rights activist finally saw Kiraly in person. In the interview, Kiraly stated: "The atmosphere of terror is beyond description. It permeates every aspect of everyday life. . . . Distrust is so prevalent that no one dares to communicate to anyone."[2]

CONTEMPT FOR JIMMY CARTER

It was after six in the evening when the ominous ring of the S telephone interrupted a meeting I was conducting in my office.

"General Pacepa speaking."

"This is your servant, Boss," I heard Manea's unflappable voice saying. "How do you feel?"

"Alive!"

"Me, too. But I'm off now. The great meeting with the People's Council chairmen has broken up, until tomorrow morning. The Comrade just left here, and guess what he ordered?"

"Oh, no!"

"Oh, yes! But the weather is much better now."

When I arrived at Ceausescu's residence, he was walking outside. The garden was dark, only the paths being illuminated by the dwarf lights in the labyrinth of bushes.

"What's new?" asked Ceausescu, when I stepped into stride with him.

"Mihai has arrived in Algiers."

"Who?"

"Zoia's friend, Mihai."

"Oh. Keep him away from here, dead or alive. And give Zoia somebody else. She's just a dumb little girl playing her stupid game of independence. What else?"

"Munteanu has left Beirut with a TIR truck full of Western arms.

"The ones from 'Annette'?"

"Yes, comrade."

"Keep me informed. Do we have an answer to our request to visit Texas Instruments?"

"Yes, comrade. An affirmative one."

---

[2]Cited in the testimony of the International League for Human Rights before the Subcommittee on Human Rights and International Organizations, May 14, 1985, p. 12.

"Excellent. I'll be the first Communist president ever to set foot in that microelectronics empire." As the walkway led past an empty bench standing in front of a 2 story building, Ceausescu automatically said, "Good evening." For years an octagenarian woman used to sit there every evening in the spring, summer and fall, all alone, wearing a block shawl around her shoulders and a black kerchief around her head. It had been Ceausescu's mother, who had moved there after her husband's death. A new house had been built for her, elegantly furnished and full of servants, but she had always seemed to be a stranger there. She would spend hours waiting on that bench to catch a glimpse of her son walking with someone in his garden, although before she died Ceausescu, absorbed in his own thoughts, never greeted her. It was only after her death a few months earlier that he had begun noticing his mother's absence.

"I read through that file you gave me on Carter and his family. Twice. I can see that, despite his innocent smile, soft voice, and shy manner, Carter is not easy or predictable. But he's not so contradictory as you describe him, either." Ceausescu emphasized that, although Carter had graduated from the Naval Academy in only 60th place, he evidently had a brilliant mind, a fantastic memory, and an unusual capacity to absorb masses of information, as well as being a good listener and a very hard worker. Ceausescu, who himself had never graduated from the university before becoming a political leader, saw no contradiction there. Furthermore, Carter's rivals accused him of hiding a high degree of stubbornness and vindictiveness behind his smile, and Ceausescu found that perfectly natural also.

"In my opinion," Ceausescu said, getting to the heart of his analysis, "Carter's weak points are other things. One is his ridiculous religiosity, which makes him act morally superior and keeps him from making friends, especially in Congress. Isn't it significant that Tip O'Neill, that old fox from his own party, doesn't conceal his contempt for Carter? Another weakness is his intense inner life, which detracts from the dynamism a president needs. Then there is his lack of pragmatism, which may make it difficult for him to move away from abstract goals toward the constructive, day-to-day management of priorities. And finally, his modesty and lack of confidence in himself—a president shouldn't be modest."

Then Ceausescu made his main point. "Carter's biggest disadvantage is that he is totally inexperienced. What can you expect from somebody who spent his life growing peanuts?" To Ceausescu, that was one of the worst things about the American system of government. Anybody with money and a nice smile could become president, but then, just when he was starting to learn the job, he would have to leave office. "The Americans just can't understand that being head of state is a profession. Anyway, that's their problem, isn't it? All in all, I would say that Carter looks like a friendly, low-key fellow whom I'll be able to work on, just the way I did with Nixon and Ford. Only we have to move fast. In his inexperience and naiveté Carter could quickly get himself into political hot water."

Ceausescu continued his walk for a long time before he suddenly asked: "When was the last time you prayed to the Lord?" Caught off balance, I did not know what to answer. There was no way he could have learned about my secret morning and evening ritual, when I would concentrate until I could clearly see the face of the crucified Christ and say my unspoken prayers to Him.

"Come on. Don't you know when you last went to church?" I heard Ceausescu saying.

"Oh, yes, comrade. When I was in elementary school," I answered.

"Good, good. So did I," replied Ceausescu. "Now we may be going to church again, if need be. Not here—in America." Ceausescu laughed. "I've been reading in your file on Carter about how close he is to his Baptist minister. I don't care how you do it, but you have to find a way to use that minister." Ceausescu emphasized that the minister should be brought to the point of remarking on Romania to Carter every day—that Romania did not have rich and poor, nor kings and beggars, but only free people whose education, jobs, medical assistance, and retirement pensions were guaranteed by the government.

"Yes, comrade. The Washington station is working on it, through a confidential agent who is said to be an honorary chairman of the Baptist Church organization for the United States and Canada."

"Twist his arm!" Ceausescu ordered, and then went on instructing me about how the agent should be used to influence Carter's minister and what else he should be whispering into

Carter's ear, "day after day, and day after day, and day after day again. Do you remember the motto for our 'Horizon'?"

"*Gutta cavat lapidem, non vi sed saepe cadendo?*"

"Exactly. A drop makes a hole in a stone not by force but by constant dripping. Let's make Carter's minister be the drop to make a hole in his head. Understood?"

"Yes, comrade."

Abruptly he changed the subject. "When Carter was elected, I told you to open a commercial office in Atlanta."

"We did."

"No problem getting American approval?"

"None."

"We'll be buying peanut shipments from Carter, and we're going to need some people there. A small but clever outpost of your men, to deal with Carter's farm."

Ceausescu made a long pause before he started talking again, with no apparent connection to what he had been saying before. "Have you seen Coman today?"

"Yes, comrade."

"He's still the same tractor driver he's always been. A total nonentity. If I replaced my minister of interior, the West might read domestic problems into it, though. So I'll keep him on, but I'll take the power out of his hands." Ceausescu said that he had decided to gather all internal security into one single department, put a new man on top of it, and subordinate the whole thing to Elena.

"Do you know Postelnicu?" he asked abruptly.

"Tudor Postelnicu, the first secretary in Buzau?"

"Don't wrinkle up your nose. Postelnicu is very close to Comrade Elena, and he's particularly close to Nicu. The three of them ought to be able to take care of our domestic security. Postelnicu will get in touch with you tomorrow. Give him a hand with writing up a decree for the new department, like the one you made for the DIE."

"May I use Luchian? He worked on the DIE decree." General Eugen Luchian had the rank of deputy minister of interior and was also the prime minister's legal advisor.

"Good idea."

"I've been looking all over for you, Nick. Where were you?"

asked Elena, rushing out to join us as we passed the main entrance.

"Pacepa's just been telling me some interesting things about the American president," Ceausescu said, winking at me. "Carter looks unexpectedly nice, even distinguished, with great esteem for his wife and devotion to his family."

"Go soak your head, Nick! Have you ever seen a *distinguished* American?" Elena squawked, trying to put all her knowledge of English into the last two words. Name me just one movie where you've seen such an American and I'll eat it, Nick. And you," she went on, jumping on me, "don't you go filling the Comrade's head with your intrigues and fantasies!" Then, turning back to Ceausescu: "Come on to bed, Nick. Don't waste the night away on fairy tales."

"All right, Pacepa. You should leave for Washington as soon as you can. Take care of the finishing touches on my program, and wait for me there. Let's go after Carter!"

Upon leaving Ceausescu I called my office. "Have Badescu get me an American visa," I told Pop. Colonel Gheorghe Badescu was under cover as chief of the Consular Directorate in the Ministry of Foreign Affairs. "And ask Luchian to be at my office by nine tomorrow morning."

When I left the residence, I asked my driver to head for Tunari, the club for the Ministry of Interior's top executives, known as the "generals' club." That evening there was to be an intimate dinner given there by Minister of Interior Teodor Coman to celebrate Minister of Defense Ion Coman's 52nd birthday. Tucked away in the middle of the Baneasa forest, the Tunari Club was about a 15-minute drive from Ceausescu's residence. As the car raced along, so did my thoughts.

In Ceausescu's view, an American president was someone on whom no investment effort should be spared. "All I need is a personal meeting with Carter," Ceausescu decided, after the 1976 elections in the United States. He ordered his minister of foreign affairs and the DIE to work out a complex series of moves culminating in an official visit to the United States as soon as possible.

Nine days after Carter's inauguration, however, these operations were suddenly disturbed by an open appeal to the signers of the Helsinki accords made by Paul Goma and eight other Romanian dissidents. Ceausescu ordered that Goma immediately be arrested and savagely beaten in his jail cell. That same day I attended an extraordinary meeting of the Political Executive Committee, at which, in less than half an hour, Ceausescu's proposals were approved for nationwide censorship of mail and telephone connections with the West and for the frustration of all contact between dissidents and diplomats in Romania. In short order, President Carter conveyed to Ceausescu his concern about the human rights situation in Romania. That was the first contact between the two men, and Ceausescu simply could not believe that the new American president, who was in his view nothing but a farmer, could take such a firm position.

At Elena's suggestion, Ceausescu decided to take Vasile Pungan out of mothballs. Pungan had previously been a diplomat in the United States and ambassador in London. In England, he arranged for special, extended studies for the Ceausescus' oldest son, Valentin, and then an invitation for the other son, Nicu, and the daughter, Zoia. According to the DIE's chief of station in London, the story was that, during Elena's numerous trips to London to visit her children, Pungan, a widower, had become her lover.

Ceausescu temporarily released Paul Goma, and on February 24, 1977, President Jimmy Carter received Special Envoy Vasile Pungan, who explained that the Romanian leaders understood his concern about human rights, and that Romanian President Nicolae Ceausescu in particular shared his views. Pungan also stated that the rumors alleging the arrest of dissidents in Romania were concocted lies, and that the writer Paul Goma was in no way under arrest. When I showed Ceausescu the decoded text of Pungan's telegram from Washington, which confidently stated that Carter had believed Ceausescu's message, he immediately called Plesita in. "I want Goma beaten up today. Have him beaten until he's scared out of his wits." The next morning, Plesita gave me a blow-by-blow description of how militia officer Horst Stumpf, the ex-boxer, had creamed Goma at his home. Ceausescu was now extremely anxious to worm himself into the good graces of the new American president.

In April 1982, Matei Haiducu, a naturalized French citizen, admitted to the French authorities to being a Romanian illegal officer. He confessed that Bucharest had given him the assignment to "eliminate by any means" Paul Goma and Virgil Tanase, two dissident emigré writers living in France who were ridiculing the cult around Ceausescu and his family. Haiducu's only important instruction from Bucharest was that the Romanian government not be compromised by their assassinations. He turned over to the French a fountain pen loaded with a toxic chemical that he had been given in Bucharest by General Nicolae Plesita, in the name of the Romanian president. It was an extremely strong poison developed in Moscow that causes death through cardiac arrest, leaving no trace. Haiducu's operational scenario, worthy of a spy thriller novel, is minutely detailed in his book entitled I Refused to Kill, *published in 1984.*[3] *The irrefutable evidence presented by Haiducu caused French President Francois Mitterrand to accuse Bucharest and to postpone a scheduled official visit to Romania.*

THE COMRADES AT PLAY

My car did not slow down until we began to approach the zoo gardens, a crowded popular attraction for the inhabitants of Bucharest, who are not spoiled with many public diversions. Now it was a peak time, and the arriving and departing buses looked like bunches of grapes, with people dangling from every side. Hordes of sweaty people were swarming around the food vendors selling grilled *mititei*—the skinless sausages that are Romania's national dish—along with beer to wash them down.

A few minutes after passing the zoo, we were in the open country. Vast agricultural fields stretched away to the right, where patriotic workers were toiling by lamplight. On the left were peasant houses, which became increasingly humble the farther they were from Bucharest. As everywhere in the Romanian countryside, the road lay in total darkness, in order to save electricity.

[3]Matei Pavel Haiducu, *J'ai refuse de tuer: Un agent secret roumain revele les dessous de "l'affaire,"* Paris: Librairie Plon, 1984.

After several more miles, my car stopped in front of a heavy wooden gate, which was always locked and guarded by uniformed armed sentries. Spread over some ten acres and tucked away between a kolkhoz and a forest, the Ministry of Interior's executive club was completely enclosed by a high, innocuous-looking wooden fence. No common mortal could catch the slightest glimpse of what was inside. At first sight the club looked like an immaculately maintained copy of the Versailles gardens, with a labyrinth of paths adorned with statues and cast iron benches set against manicured bushes and carefully tended flower beds. Artificial lakes, artesian fountains, and graceful gazebos stretched out on every side. Discreetly hidden behind the hedges and ornamental trees, however, were a number of buildings and other facilities. For specially imported films there was an intimate movie hall, where almost invisible black-suited waiters hovered around with cakes, ice cream, and beverages. In another corner there was a bowling alley that had its own picturesque little café housed in a glass conservatory filled with palm trees and tropical plants. Behind another hedge was an elegant indoor firing range with a bar that had its padded velvet walls done in blue—the Ministry of Interior's color—where the men could relax between rounds in comfortable, deep easy chairs, also of blue velvet. For special occasions there was a banquet hall and a ballroom. Tennis courts and volleyball courts and riding stables completed the picture.

Sprinkled throughout the gardens were a dozen attractive villas, where top executives could bring their families for a night, a week, or a month of relaxation. The club's most popular attraction, however, was its restaurant with its small, candlelit dining rooms manned by white-clad waiters wearing white silk gloves and red carnations in their lapels. Two musical ensembles, one for chamber and one for folk music, provided atmosphere while the diner selected from a menu that featured a richness found nowhere else in the country, with malosol caviar, gooseliver paté, and wild truffles being only its palest offerings.

Access was strictly limited to club members and their immediate families. On Saturday evenings and Sundays it was most heavily used, but it was only on special occasions, such as May Day, National Day, and especially New Year's Eve, that it would be packed full. Nicu Ceausescu was one of the club's most frequent visitors, not for its luxurious appointments or elegant table, but for its firing range and large supply of his favorite Johnny Walker Black Label. "Shooting bullets and Scotch at the same time is even more fun than screwing," he used to say, firing off a submachine gun with one hand while guzzling Scotch from a bottle held in the other. Nicu's visits invariably ended with his getting roaring drunk.

The party was being held in a separate building that contained a large banquet hall and a few smaller rooms at either end, divided off by wooden accordion doors. To the left, immediately inside the entrance, it had a large foyer, followed by a room containing a stage for a band and a circular marble dance floor. To the right of the banquet hall there was another room, this one with low cocktail tables and blue velvet easy chairs, where one could retreat for coffee, cognac, and gossip. The dinner had been set for seven o'clock, and now it was almost eleven, but, as my car drew up to the entrance and I counted the black Mercedes cars parked outside, each with its driver fast asleep at the wheel, I saw at a glance that all the main guests were still in attendance.

The foyer was full of waiters and waitresses passing food and drink. In the next room, a few guests stood around gossiping, glass in hand. General Constantin Olteanu, the chief of the Central Committee's Section for Armed Forces and Security, was playing the piano with one hand while his other busily explored under the skirt of a waitress sitting on his lap. Olteanu comes from Elena's hometown, and she has made him what he is today. Nicknamed "General Cognac," he wound up every party getting very drunk. On the dance floor, General Vasile Milea was barely able to maintain his equilibrium as he cavorted with one of the entertainers from the Ministry of Interior's musical ensemble, his right hand inside her blouse. He was well oiled, as usual. Milea, the military commander of the Patriotic Guards paramilitary organization, was more often to be found tipsy than sober. When I had last visited him at his office a couple of weeks earlier, he had half-filled his cup of coffee with cognac at only nine in the morning. He was, however, Elena's best source of information inside the Ministry of Defense and her principal favorite there.

The banquet room was swathed in cigarette smoke. The Ministries of Interior and National Defense were the only Romanian government institutions allowed to spend Western currency in cash, and then only for espionage purposes. Personal gifts for the Ceausescus and American cigarettes and Scotch whiskey for the two ministers were among the very few other tacitly allowable items that dollars could be used for. During a special party like this, American cigarettes were usually placed all around the table, and everyone present, whether smoker or not, would puff on them non-stop. In Romania, American cigarettes are as much a curiosity as opium joints are in the West.

Through the fog I could see the wife of the minister of defense waving for me to come over. "Come here, Uncle Spy. I've saved you a place." With her quiet sense of humor, Coman's wife had years earlier begun calling me "Uncle Spy," after her husband had reprimanded her for addressing me as "General," that being my classified DIE title.

A terrible commotion was coming from a few chairs to my left. General Plesita was playing his favorite parlor game with a group of deputy ministers of defense and interior. Introduced by Plesita himself after a visit to the Hungarian Ministry of Interior, this inane game was supposed to amuse by getting people drunk. Each participant had to drink a full glass of wine while standing up and reciting: "I am the wine captain, and I will empty this glass in three draughts." Before the second swallow, he had to say: "I am the wine-wine captain, and I will empty this glass-glass in three-three draughts." If he omitted a word, or forgot to double the words *wine, glass,* and *three,* he had to empty his glass at once and start over from the beginning with a new one. Before the third swallow, the words had to be tripled. At the end, if he could get that far, he had to recite the last sentence backwards: "Draughts three-three-three in glass-glass-glass this empty will I and captain wine-wine-wine the am I." This game had become a regular diversion at the club's parties, but recently it had been slightly modified. The wine was replaced by Scotch, and the game always ended with heavy intoxication. At the moment Plesita's victim was Tudor Postelnicu, who was visiting the club for the first time.

My neighbor at the table was Vice Prime Minister Gheorghe Oprea, one of the Ceausescus' closest confidants. "What a sensitive party, Mike!" he exclaimed to me. Pulling his chair up close, Oprea began whispering in his most conspiratorial tone. In the afternoon he had had a very confidential discussion with Ceausescu and Elena about personnel changes, and everything was still very secret. The minister of defense, Ion Coman, was to be promoted to secretary of the Central Committee for the armed forces, security, and justice. Constantin Olteanu would replace him as minister of defense. Vasile Milea would become the chief of the General Staff. And I was to be appointed chief of the presidential palace, a new position somewhat similar to that of the chief of staff at the American White House, but with more substance. The whole DIE and the Securitate's Directorate V, responsible for the protective security of the president, would be removed from the Ministry of Interior and given to the presidential palace. Everything would be directly subordinate to Ceausescu, with me as the acting administrator. "The Comrade believes in you as much as he does in himself, Mike," Oprea finished, effusively kissing me on both cheeks.

A few minutes later, Emil Bobu, Romania's vice president, rapped on his glass with a knife, signaling for silence. "Comrades, as someone who has coordinated the Department for Cults, I have been told that priests and rabbis have to pray to their God, whoever he may be, in the morning, in the evening, and at least once during the day. We, however, are atheists, comrades. We believe only in the most beloved, esteemed, and illustrious son and daughter of the Romanian people, Comrade Ceausescu and Comrade Elena." Bobu portrayed Ceausescu as a knight who, instead of the Bible and the cross, was carrying Marx's *Das Kapital* and Stefan the Great's sword. Elena was Minerva, the goddess of wisdom, the personified power of the mind. In only a few days they would have to do battle in the very lair of savage imperialism, in Washington, where the Comrade would have to confront the proletariat's number one enemy. When Bobu ended his speech ten minutes later, the room erupted into applause, followed by chants of "Ceausescu and the People!" to the accompaniment of rhythmic clapping. General Olteanu was quietly crying onto the piano, while General Milea stood teetering unsteadily on a chair, trying to kiss the portrait of Elena hanging on the wall. Bobu always was a master at fawning over Ceausescu. Minister of Interior Teodor Coman, by now unsteady on his feet, threw off his jacket and necktie and tried to get a *hora* going, which soon caught up most of those present in its circle. Folk dancing is the only kind Ceausescu knows and likes, and in recent years it had become patriotic and almost required to dance the *hora* on such occasions.

The "wine captain" game was attracting general attention, as usual. Postelnicu, completely besotted, was lying on the table, roaring and crying at the same time. Generals Vasile Ionel and Vasile Moise, also drunk, were arguing loudly over the two ministries' soccer teams. General Marin Nicolescu, the commander of the rocket forces and artillery, whose turn it was now, had to keep starting over from the beginning and was cursing like a horse trader.

When the dinner broke up around two o'clock in the morning, the drivers had a hard time helping their bosses leave the room and get into their cars. They managed it, however, as they were all well trained at that. Only Olteanu's driver needed assistance, as his boss was now violently beating up on a waiter.

"I have a s-spy on a c-cassette f-for you. G-Get a c-cassette player in here r-right away," said General Gheorghe Moga, stepping unannounced into my office. He stutters most when he has either very good or very bad news, so I did not know how to take this unexpected visit.

Five minutes later we were sitting in my back room, listening to Moga's cassette. The date-time indicator announced that the recording had been made the night before, around midnight. The loud background noise indisputably proved that it had been recorded at a restaurant. A warm female voice was speaking Russian with a man whom I judged, even with my very limited knowledge of Russian, to be a Romanian speaking quite good Russian. According to the written translation Moga brought with him, the discussion consisted in recalling their passionate relationship when he had been in Moscow as a student at the Soviet Military Academy. It ended with a new date set for two days later at Bucharest's Lido restaurant.

"Point one," prompted Moga, as the recording ended, "that's the beginning of the recruitment of a Romanian officer by the Soviet KGB or GRU. Two, yesterday there was no Russian woman or Romanian military officer staying at the Athenee Palace Hotel, where the restaurant is. Three, there was a dinner there given by the Ministry of National Defense for the Warsaw Pact military attachés. Four, the only Romanians there were very high-ranking generals, one of whom is now a spy, or will be by tomorrow. Five, catching him is your job, not mine, because I'm not in charge of the top hierarchy. Six, I've prepared a report for the minister of interior, who will have it on his desk by tomorrow morning. So don't bury the case."

Moga left as unexpectedly as he had come. I turned the cassette player on again and had the strange feeling that I knew the man's voice, although I could not put a name to it. From my back room I placed a call to Colonel Iosif, saying that I would meet him at his office in the afternoon. "I have something important for you, too," he said.

SILENCING A BROADCASTER

When I got back to my office, Eugen Luchian was there, studying a file while sipping his favorite drink, espresso coffee "cooled" with two teaspoonfuls of Chivas Regal, which Pop had just fixed him. Major General Luchian was the only other non-DIE officer allowed access into its main headquarters. His official position was that of permanent secretary of the National Commission for Visas and Passports, with the title of deputy minister of interior, and of chief legal advisor to the prime minister. Besides Ceausescu and Minister Coman, Luchian was the only person who knew the DIE's whole structure. It was he who drew up the presidential decrees reorganizing the service, which Ceausescu signed in 1972 when he took it under his personal supervision.

"We just had another telephone discussion with Emil Georgescu in Munich," Luchian started off, as he shook my hand with his enormous bear paw. "Soon I'm going to bring Georgescu to his knees." He slapped a fat gray file with his huge palm.

Emil Georgescu had been working for the United States government as a supervisory program editor in the Romanian Department of Radio Free Europe since January 1974, shortly after his defection from Romania to West Germany. His public denouncements of the personality cult in Romania and of abuses committed by the Romanian security forces had spelled his doom. On the evening of August 22, 1976, the eve of Romania's national day, the minister of interior, the then chief of the DIE and I had been summoned for a walk in Ceausescu's rose garden.

"Emil Georgescu must be silenced forever," Ceausescu ordered. "He should have his jaw, teeth, and arms broken, so that he will never be able to speak or write again." He added that the job should be done by foreign criminal mercenaries, without any possible connection with Romanian authorities, and that no written record be kept of this conversation and the operation against Emil Georgescu.

Ceausescu can be terribly violent when he holds a grudge. Soon after he came to power, he had his first taste of biting public criticism, given by a Romanian emigré leader, and his immediate reaction was, "Kill him without attribution." The man who had criticized him, Gheorghe Zapartan, was an emigré priest living in West Germany, who had denounced Ceausescu's personality cult in both public speeches and church sermons. Shortly after the priest had died in an automobile "accident," the Romanian prime minister at the time, Ion Gheorghe Maurer, who was experienced in international law, went to Ceausescu. "Nick," said he, "as Romania's supreme leader you can do anything. Good or evil. But one thing don't do. Don't give the order to kill. That's first degree murder. It doesn't matter if the one giving the order is a beggar or a king." Ceausescu got the message. Since that day he has preferred to have his political opponents beaten to the point of becoming living corpses, although occasionally he forgets Maurer's advice and gives the order to kill.

On October 19, 1976, Emil Georgescu was seriously injured in an automobile accident staged by a team of French drug smugglers working for the DIE. They were not able to deliver the beating, because two West German cars unexpectedly pulled over and stopped at the accident site. That was why six months later Georgescu was able to be back full time at Radio Free Europe, again lashing out at the Bucharest government. Ceausescu immediately ordered a disinformation operation to compromise Georgescu's professional integrity. Through DIE sources in France, West Germany, and the United States, as well as through signed and anonymous letters sent to Radio Free Europe, the DIE insinuated that Georgescu had received illegal monies from Romanian emigrés and had been involved in dishonest fur and jewelry deals. Several scare letters were sent to Georgescu himself, threatening that he would be killed and his home burned down if he resumed his activity for his "Jewish masters" at the radio. These letters were written as if from a terrorist wing of the illegal Romanian fascist organization in exile, the Iron Guard, and were signed "Group V." Group V was created out of whole cloth by the DIE. To make the group more credible, menacing letters carrying the same signature were sent to other anti-Communists living in the West, such as the late Noel Bernard, former director of the Romanian Department of Radio Free Europe, who had become extremely popular in Romania because of his caustic criticism of Ceausescu's personality cult; Paul Goma and Virgil Tanase, two active dissidents living in France; the former king of Romania, Mihai von Hohenzollern, who lives in Switzerland; and the prominent playwright Eugene Ionesco, a member of the French Academy. A blackmail operation was also directed against Georgescu, trying to force him to resign "voluntarily" from his job in return for an exit visa for his old mother living in Bucharest. Eugen Luchian, as permanent secretary of the National Commission for Visas and Passports, was put in charge of this blackmail operation.

Bucharest was evidently not able to compromise Emil Georgescu, who continued his vehement criticism of Ceausescu over Radio Free Europe. On the morning of July 28, 1981, Georgescu was stabbed 22 times by two French smugglers while leaving his Munich home. The annual official report published in 1983 by the West German Minister of Interior on the most significant activities of the Bundesamt fuer Verfassungsschutz *comments: "Only through prompt assistance could the severely wounded victim be saved. The perpetrators were arrested and sentenced to several years in prison. They stubbornly refused to give any information on who had hired them. After the failure of this assassination attempt, other persons from the Romanian intelligence service are said to have been given the assignment of liquidating the Romanian emigré once and for all."*[1]

Rising precariously from his chair, Luchian came up to my desk. "Before I forget, I'd like to invite you to my house Saturday evening. Oprea and Voicu are coming, with their wives."

"Isn't Oprea in Belgrade now?"

"Yes, Mike, but he'll be back by Saturday evening." Gheorghe Oprea, the first deputy prime minister, was Luchian's boss, and

[1]*Betrifft: Verfassungsschutz '82*, Bonn: Der Bundesminister des innern, April 1983, p. 210. (Translated from the original German.)

violinist Ion Voicu, the director of the Bucharest Philharmonic, was a friend of mine.

"I have a job for you from the Comrade," I changed the subject. Then I told Luchian about the new decree he had to draft up, and about Tudor Postelnicu.

"That freak? That dwarf? That lush?"

"Careful, Luchian. He's your new boss."

"No problem. I've got his number. Whenever I used to go through the town of Buzau I would stop at his office to leave a carton of Kents or a bottle of Scotch on his desk. He would become all milk and honey, and I never left without having the trunk of my car full of wine. Wine is all they've got in Buzau, and that's the only thing he knows."

We spent a couple of hours defining the structure of the new Department of State Security and noting down everything that needed to be specified in the presidential decree. It was Luchian's job to draw up the final wording, and he was an expert at it.

A Tank in the Diplomatic Pouch

When Luchian left, Pop told me that General Constantin Munteanu and Colonel Constantin Olcescu had crossed the border from Bulgaria not long before and should be at my office in less than an hour. Just as I started skimming through the incoming telegrams, the *S* telephone rang.

"Lieutenant General Pacepa speaking," I answered it.

"This is your servant, Boss." I recognized Manea's voice. "I'm sorry to disturb you, but the Comrade wants you to give him a call."

I got Ceausescu on the telephone. "Has Munteanu arrived at the border yet, Pacepa?"

"Yes, comrade. He crossed it some half hour ago."

"Without any incident *en route?*"

"Not that I know of. He'll be at my office in less than an hour. May I report to you afterwards?"

"Yes." I heard the click of the telephone as he hung up.

Shortly thereafter, Pop came in to tell me, "General Munteanu and Colonel Olcescu are here." I stepped into the outer office, shook hands, and ushered them into my office.

"Welcome home," I started out, after they had settled into easy chairs.

"We just got in from Beirut," Munteanu opened. "The trucks are parked outside of Bucharest, guarded by two officers in civvies."

"You mean the TIR *truck*," I specified.

"I mean the *two* trucks we came with," answered Munteanu.

"I sent you only one truck," I persisted.

"That's why I came along, too," Olcescu interjected with his deep bass voice.

"I'll explain everything," said Munteanu. "As you know, in Beirut we were given several dozen wooden boxes full of military equipment supplied by 'Annette.' We just loaded them onto the truck, filling it up to the top. Now you can tell him the rest." Munteanu stopped, clutching at his chest, and motioned to Olcescu.

"Just as we were about to leave," Olcescu launched into his story, "'Annette' asked for a new meeting. She said they had just captured a new French tank, and that she had maneuvred to have it crash through the wall of a house and into a hole, where it sat covered over with tree branches. She said it was ours if we would take it out during the night. My Commercial Office said we had a TIR truck there in transit. As chargé d'affaires, I ordered that the shoes it was carrying be unloaded, I put my driver in it, and shortly after midnight we found the house where the tank lay hidden. We had a few problems getting the tank onto the truck, but in the end everything worked out okay." He asked permission to light up a cigarette, and we took a break as Pop came in with coffee.

"In Beirut," Munteanu took up the story, "Jumblatt gave us an armed escort. We drove ahead, in our car, and the diplomatic pouch documents, together with Olcescu's chargé d'affaires title, opened every border for us."

"'Annette' asked me to give you his best regards," Olcescu said, starting to sip his coffee. "He gave me an oral message from Arafat for Comrade Ceausescu, following up on the one sent through you. The bottom line is a suggestion that Willy Brandt be used to induce the West to recognize the PLO." At that time, former Chancellor Brandt was the head of West Germany's Social Democratic Party. "Arafat wants Brandt to use his position as chairman of the Socialist International to get it to recognize the PLO. He also wants him to work on Kreisky to support the 'Shuqairy' operation. 'Annette' insisted on your personal help. She knows you get along well with Brandt."

I saw that Munteanu was dead-tired after two nights and one day of continuous car travel. "Thank you for a job well done," I closed the meeting. "Now, Munteanu, you go home and take a long rest. Olcescu, if you can stay on your feet for a few more hours, I'd like you to take the trucks over to the DIE school in Branesti and unload the goodies there. I'll come over there in the evening."

"I'm dying to take a look at the tank by daylight."

After they left, I picked up the *S* telephone and dialed 105. "Long life, Comrade Ceausescu. This is Pacepa."

"Go ahead."

"Munteanu and Olcescu just left my office. Everything was okay on the trip back. There's just one thing. . . . "

"Oh, no!"

"I sent them one truck, and they came back with two. There's supposed to be a tank in the second one."

"What the hell are you talking about?"

"I haven't seen it yet. I've sent both trucks to the DIE school in Branesti. I'll be there this evening."

"I think I'd like a *Kojak* tonight. At home. Be there by nine-thirty. With the news." The click of the telephone told me that the conversation was over.

It was shortly after 3:00 PM when I left my office for Iosif's. He had the most secret unit in Romania, known to only a handful of people. It conducted the around-the-clock monitoring of Romania's top *nomenclatura*, starting with Ceausescu's own family and the members of his Political Executive Committee. Iosif's unit was even so secret that no DIE driver was allowed to know of its existence.

"Home," I ordered Marcel. When we got there, I told him he could take off. "Be back here at six." I crossed through the house, exiting out the door of Dana's little apartment. My house was located between two streets, the main entrance being at 28 Alexandru Avenue, and the entrance to Dana's apartment on Zoia

Avenue. With my briefcase under my arm, I strolled down the street, determined to enjoy the perfume of the lime trees as long as I could. Located next to the West German embassy, Iosif's unit was barely a 15-minute walk from my house.

A LADY CALLED OLGA

The Romanian Ministry of Interior, like the other intelligence and security services in the Soviet bloc, is wrapped in a cloud of secrecy, although in recent years the public has been given a few glimpses of its workings. There have always been three versions of its intelligence and security structure, all three personally approved by Ceausescu. The first, for public consumption, is carefully drawn up by the Disinformation Service to conceal every function given to the services that contravenes the Romanian Constitution, such as mail censorship and telephone monitoring, although the components responsible for that were among the largest in the Securitate. The privacy of correspondence and telephone conversations is stipulated in the Constitution.[2] Furthermore, Article 17 of the Constitution reads, "The citizens of the Socialist Republic of Romania, irrespective of their ethnic origin, race, sex or religion, shall have equal rights. . . ."[3] Accordingly, the Securitate counterintelligence units concerned with the Jewish, German, and Hungarian minorities and with religious worship must also be concealed. The second version is classified Top Secret and lists all internal Securitate units that are subordinate to the collective leadership body of the Ministry of Interior, composed of the minister and his deputies. The third version, the real one, is classified Top Secret Of High Interest and is always handwritten. It is known only to Ceausescu, to the minister of interior, and to the chief and deputy chief of the foreign intelligence service. In addition to the DIE and Iosif's unit, it contains two other very clandestine departments: one for counterintelligence within the Central Committee of the Romanian Communist Party and the Council of Ministers, and the other for counterintelligence within the Securitate itself.

[2]*Constitution of the Socialist Republic of Romania,* (English translation), Bucharest: Meridiane Publishing House, 1975, p. 12.
    [3]*Ibid.,* p. 8.

Iosif's unit had something over 1,000 officers and was used by Ceausescu and Elena for testing the loyalty of their closest relatives and collaborators. The unit's real power lay in the fact that it had its own, ultra-secret electronic monitoring center, its own mail censorship service, and its own surveillance section, so that it could keep the identity of its targets absolutely to itself. No other Securitate or Militia unit has such a capability, as everyone else uses the services of the Ministry of Interior's General Directorate of Technical Operations. The technical capacity of Iosif's unit was 600 targets for telephone interception, 400 targets for microphone monitoring, and practically unlimited mail censorship targets.

Iosif himself was waiting for me in the lobby of his building. He was five-foot-nine, with a strong build, wore size 11 shoes, and had a head as round as a billiard ball, with fringes of hair only on the sides around his protruding ears. He lumbered toward me, encumbered by the rheumatism that sent him off to take mud baths every summer in his native Tekirghiol, a little fishing village on the Black Sea. Behind the heavy frames of his glasses, two piercing black eyes moved constantly, trying to decipher my mood.

"A long and healthy life to you, Comrade General, and to your family," Iosif greeted me. He had a certain amount of difficulty expressing himself. Twenty-five years in the Securitate and the DIE could not entirely compensate for his lack of education and his early years spent as a tractor operator in a kolkhoz. "I think I have a new case," he continued cautiously, closing the padded door behind us as we went into a small room heavily shielded from electronic monitoring.

"I also have a case," I said, giving him the cassette I had received from Moga.

The equipment in the room made it look like a broadcasting studio. "I want you to listen to this tape," he said. "It was made last night. A Soviet tourist bus arrived in Bucharest the night before last, and, as usual, we surveilled it to see if anyone would try to contact one of our targets. An elegantly dressed lady we'll call Olga discreetly left the group early yesterday morning. Before seven o'clock she made a call from a public phone booth, but we missed it. Then she spent the rest of the day window shopping. Around nine-thirty in the evening she walked into the

Athenee Palace Hotel and had dinner, paying in Romanian lei, even though she hadn't exchanged any money here. The surveillance team had an ashtray transmitter put on her table 'just in case.' After Olga had gone back to her hotel, the surveillants returned to their headquarters and routinely screened the tape. They discovered there was a man on it. The team is sick over having missed him."

Iosif's tape had the same thing on it as the one Moga had given me in the morning. Iosif went on to say that Olga had spent today with her group. He proposed covering her meeting with the man tomorrow night at the Lido restaurant, using both microphones and cameras.

Iosif then briefed me on several of his priority cases. Ceausescu's daughter, Zoia, was still not using the apartment prepared for her by Elena, being afraid that it was bugged. When she had learned about Mihai's sudden disappearance, she had gotten high on vodka and had sex with one of her other boyfriends in her white Mercedes coupe. Nicu had gotten drunk again last night and smashed up a bar. The prime minister had given a party at home that had lasted until three in the morning. Two of his guests, one a relative, had told jokes about Elena. Cornel Burtica, the minister of foreign trade, had made love to one of his secretaries again.

Shortly before six, I stopped Iosif's recital. I loaded up my briefcase with the files for my meeting with Elena the next day, and then I called my office.

MONITORING THE ROMANIAN NOMENCLATURA

"Nothing important here, comrade," Pop reported.

I took my leave, accompanied by Iosif as far as to the main door. "To Branesti school," I ordered the driver waiting in front of my house. From my briefcase I took out the file containing handwritten excerpts from the microphone and telephone coverage of Ion Gheorghe Maurer, his wife, and their friends. For more than 20 years Maurer had been Romania's prime minister. He was in Ceausescu's way, however, and was retired in 1974 for health reasons. Only because of his international prestige and popularity was Maurer allowed—contrary to the general rule—to keep his huge residence with indoor swimming pool, his two cars with drivers, and his protective security coverage; however, microphones were kept installed in each of his rooms and in his vast garden. Although retired, Maurer continued to be considered the number two in the Romanian *nomenclatura*.

To the ordinary Romanian people, the word *nomenclatura* means the elite, a social superstructure recognizable by its privileges. *Nomenclatura* people do not travel by bus or streetcar. They use government cars. The color and make of the car indicate its owner's status in the hierarchy: the darker the color, the higher the position. White Dacias[4] are for directors, pastel colors for deputy ministers, black for ministers; black Audis for Nicu; black Mercedes for the prime minister and his deputies; and black Mercedes 600, Cadillac, and Rolls-Royce limousines for Ceausescu. *Nomenclatura* people do not live in apartment buildings constructed under the Communist regime. As I did, they get nationalized villas or luxury apartments that previously belonged to the capitalists. *Nomenclatura* people are not seen standing in line to buy food or other necessities. They have their own stores, and black car people can even order by telephone for home delivery. *Nomenclatura* people are not seen in normal restaurants fighting for a table or listening to a disagreeable waiter saying, "If you don't like it, stay home." They have their own special restaurants, and they can even go to the ones for Western tourists. During the summer, *nomenclatura* people are not seen on Bucharest's crowded, sweaty public beaches. They either go to special bathing areas or have weekend villas in Snagov, a resort located 25 miles outside Bucharest. *Nomenclatura* people do not spend their vacations packed like sardines into Soviet-style colonies. They have their own vacation homes.

The darker the car, the closer the house is to Ceausescu's vacation residence, and black car people also get cooks and servants. They do not stand in line outside Soviet-style polyclinics, where treatment is free but you are yelled at by everyone from the doorman on up and may not spend more than 15 minutes with the doctor, who has to see at least 30 patients in his eight-hour shift. They do not go to the regular hospitals, where people may

[4]The Dacia was the only car being produced in Romania as of 1978. It was a copy of the Renault 12, which had been discontinued by the French Renault company.

have to double up two to a bed. They have the luxurious, Western-style Hellias hospital, built as a private foundation in the days before Communism.

The microphone coverage on top members of the *nomenclatura* is without doubt the best kept secret in the Soviet bloc. "For us, only Comrade Brezhnev is tabu," KGB Chairman Yuri Andropov told me when I was visiting Moscow in 1972. "Keeping a close watch on our *nomenclatura* is the KGB's most delicate task. Take Shchelokov, for example." General Nikolay Shchelokov was the Soviet minister of interior. "We all respect him, but through the microphones we learned that he was drinking too much. I reported it, and Comrade Brezhnev is now trying to help him. The same thing happened with Ustinov." Marshal Dmitry Ustinov was the Soviet minister of defense.

The KGB's *nomenclatura* coverage is imitated throughout the whole Soviet bloc. Every East European country has its own top secret "Iosif's unit," where a faceless army of little security people record everything for the supreme leader, even the way a *nomenclatura* man moans when he is making love.

I was sure Maurer's file would delight Elena. For the past four years she had been in charge of electronically monitoring the *nomenclatura's* top level, and she had become a real professional at working the listening equipment set up in the back room of her main office at the Central Committee.

The file covering Maurer's past two weeks did not show anything involving national security. Maurer was still a loyal Communist. It did, however, contain new data on the *History of Contemporary Romania* that Maurer was then writing, in which he gave his version of what he called Ceausescu's alterations of history. The file held whole passages from the book, as Maurer read them aloud to his wife. One in particular caught my eye.

"On Monday, March 19, 1965, I paid my daily visit to Gheorghiu-Dej. He could no longer speak, because of his throat cancer, but he jotted down several words on a notepad with his favorite violet pencil and gave the note to me. I read: 'It is my final wish that Comrade Maurer be my successor.' After reading it, I tried to tell him how I felt. His eyes were closed. Dej was going." There was a break on the tape, in which you could hear pages being turned, according to Iosif's transcript. Then Maurer's voice continued. "The Politburo meeting the next morning was brief. I presented Gheorghiu-Dej's note, but I turned down the position of leader. In an effort to avert a violent succession crisis, I proposed that 'the youngest man' be appointed temporarily, until the next Party Congress, which had to elect the Party leader. My proposal was seconded by Emil Bodnaras and was accepted. At the funeral Nicolae Ceausescu, 'the youngest man,' publicly took an oath proclaiming loyalty to the deceased's policies."

Mrs. Maurer's voice broke in, continued the transcript. "Why are you reading me that now?"

"Because today is March 20th," he explained. "Today it's been thirteen years since Nick was appointed."

"You would have been better off stinking for two days after eating a bucketfull of shit thirteen years ago, instead of proposing the Dictator. Now you'll stink for the rest of your life!"

I went on thumbing through the file. A couple of Maurer's usual jokes about Ceausescu's personality cult. Some of his wife's backbiting gossip. Something about Elena's snobbishness and political incompetence. An unsuccessful attempt to make love. I could picture Elena's smirk on reading the file. She was always dying to hear titillating stories.

THE SPY SCHOOL IN BRANESTI

The car sped away from Bucharest. Gone were the drab, uniform apartment buildings lining the streets, the long lines in front of the stores, and the people carrying their shopping bags, where they had tucked away whatever they had been able to buy that day. Now we were in the country, with poor little houses standing along the side of the road and weary people trudging along on muddy sidewalks. From time to time there was a tavern, with drunks leaning around it.

"Sixty-two B, your position, please, for the base," came Pop's voice over the DIE's radiotelephone. The code for me was *62*, and *62B* was for my driver.

"Sixty-two B is five minutes from eight zero five."

"Sixty-two B, please ask sixty-two to call one zero two from eight zero five," Pop finished, telling me to call Elena after I got to the school.

The car soon turned onto a road with a round, fluorescent "Do Not Enter" sign. At the end of this road was a group of buildings surrounded by a forest of gigantic omni-directional and logarithmically periodic shortwave antennas, each with a red light on top of it. The DIE school was under the cover of a civilian radio communications center. The surrounding antennas were, however, not just cover but belonged to the DIE's new National Center for Enciphered Communications, which also served the Ministries of Foreign Affairs, Foreign Trade, and National Defense, as well as the Central Committee of the Communist Party, reaching out to the farthest embassy abroad.

The school was another project I had spent years on. Until the mid-1960s the DIE, like any other Soviet bloc foreign intelligence service, had sent its officers to a special two-year school in Moscow. In separate courses for each country, the officers learned two foreign languages, the basics of Soviet-style espionage work, and the use of Soviet-made espionage equipment. In 1964, the Romanian leader at the time, Gheorghe Gheorghiu-Dej, asked me to create a similar Romanian school. At first it was located in Snagov. A few years later, when Bucharest decided to put the jamming of Western radio broadcasts in Romanian on ice, the DIE school was moved into the huge, vacated premises of the national jamming center in Branesti. Over the years the new school came to be looked upon more as a resort than as a university campus. There the students live exactly like Americans, Frenchmen, Germans, or whatever. They have Western-style golf, tennis, and swimming clubs, movie houses showing foreign-language films, and Western-style cafeterias. The students have to immerse themselves in the foreign atmosphere and live there as if in a foreign country, dressing and speaking like natives.

As my car approached, the massive metal gate opened automatically. Evidently the school had been watching our car through the hidden video cameras installed everywhere. I was met by the school's deputy director, a colonel, at the entrance to the main building. "Comrade General, the professors and students of the DIE school are working according to schedule," he reported formally.

From the director's office I telephoned Elena.

"Hi, darling," I heard her say sweetly. "Tomorrow would you

like to bring me the file you have on the fat old fuddyduddy, the one you helped to keep alive on her last visit here?"

"Yes, Comrade Elena. I will."

She knew I understood she meant Golda Meir.

"And don't forget the old bag." That meant Mrs. Maurer.

"She's in my briefcase," I replied.

"Good. I'll see you tomorrow. Bye."

Before I left with Olcescu to look at his goodies, I called Pop and told him to get Golda Meir's file ready for the next morning. She was not Elena's type. Meir's modesty and ascetic way of life were not for her. But Golda Meir's ascent to the supreme power position in Israel still fascinated her. Ever since Elena had met Isabel Peron on a visit to Argentina in 1973, she had been fascinated by female political leaders. When Isabel became president of Argentina, I heard Elena say, as if talking to herself, "If a whore from a Caracas nightclub could do it, why not a woman of science?"

TESTING THE STOLEN TANK

"I've gotten almost everything out of the boxes and put it on tables in the military museum," Olcescu informed me when I finally was able to see him. The "military museum" contained everything connected with NATO's military strength, ranging from scale models of Western military airplanes and aircraft carriers sold in the West as children's toys, to the latest piece of military hardware the DIE had been able to smuggle out.

The museum's main room was now full of tables Olcescu had arranged in an orderly array. They held several dozen handguns, rifles, machine guns, and submachine guns, from West Germany, Belgium, France, Italy, England, Japan, and the United States, which he had unpacked from "Annette's" boxes. A good portion of the items were from Israel, however. Other tables were full of infrared and light amplifying equipment for use during the night by infantry, artillery, and armored cars. There was also a precision rifle fitted out with night vision equipment. Ceausescu had wanted one like that for when he went hunting in the early morning, when the bears are out but hidden by darkness. In one corner there was an American mobile radar installation. In another, an American laser aiming device for tanks. Spread out in a separate room was a complete computerized command center for the artillery.

"The tank is sitting beside the firing range," Olcescu filled me in. "Its outside was covered with blood—they don't give up easily! But now it's all washed and clean. It may be just what the Comrade is looking for to export to the Third World—it's medium-sized, fast, and built for warm climates."

The tank was indeed still "warm," as "Annette" had said. A pair of eyeglasses were lying on the floor, evidently lost when the operator was killed. One glove was resting on a shelf; the other was probably on his hand. The machine gun was loaded with a round of ammunition. On a conveyor were shells waiting to be fired. I started up the engine and began driving the tank around. It went much faster than I had expected. I tried to manipulate the gun but could not get the hang of it. "Call the tech," I ordered, turning off the engine.

Sandwiches and beer were waiting in the director's office. As I was about to leave, the tech came running up. He looked unusually pale. "The gun was still loaded with a live shell," he reported.

Before nine-thirty I was at Ceausescu's residence. He was outside, walking at a fast clip along the paths marked only by his dwarf lights. I fell into step with him and reported everything I had learned.

"That's good. 'Annette' is a hard worker. He's paying me back for everything I've done for him." Ceausescu has conspiracy in his blood, but he does not devote much attention to detail—like the gender of "Annette."

"I want you to get together a military exhibit for when we get back from America," he went on. "On one side put every piece of arms equipment that we've produced based on technological intelligence. On the other side put all the military samples we've gotten from 'Annette' and any other ones that have not yet been used for producing new weapons so that we can decide what we should concentrate on. We ought to plant the idea in everyone's mind that arms should become our number one product, and that intelligence should be its main source of inspiration. Do you understand me?"

"Yes, comrade."

"When are you leaving for Washington?"

"The first of next week."

"On your way there, make a stop in Bonn and see if you can't brainwash Brandt to give Arafat a hand. I'll give you a message from me to take along, inviting Brandt to Bucharest as my private guest. That might help."

Suddenly and without apparent connection, Ceausescu lashed out: "Jewish money is taking over America. If it's not stopped, the Zionist conspiracy will soon take over the whole capitalist world." He paused for a moment, then continued: "I'm sick and tired of all these pressure tactics for letting Jews emigrate from Romania. They—are—my—own—citizens. They—are—not—Americans!" he proclaimed deliberately, punctuating each word with a slash of his right hand. I knew that, in a break during the People's Council congress that afternoon, Ceausescu had had a confidential meeting with the chairman of the World Jewish Congress, Nahum Goldmann. "It's a conspiracy against Romanian independence and my personal prestige. I can't fight the Zionists openly—Arafat and 'Annette' have to take on that job. But we should be helping them a lot more than we are." Turning on his heel, he left abruptly for the movie theater.

Ceausescu's new anti-Semitic outburst did not surprise me. As I had learned from Teodor Coman, just a day before my return from Tripoli Ceausescu had firmly instructed both the minister of defense and the minister of interior: "Every single Jew must be discreetly and secretly removed from all command positions in the military and security forces by the end of the year. If you have questions, you should not be in your jobs." All Jews had been gone from the DIE since 1972.

When *Kojak* was over and the lights had come back on, Elena sat up with a start. With drowsy eyes and face puffy with sleep, she looked dazedly around and then suddenly grabbed Ceausescu by the arm and started pulling him. "Let's go to bed, Nick."

It was late when Paraschiv pulled up in front of my house and the militiaman guarding the Polish embassy gave me his formal salute. While I was unlocking the iron gate, I could feel a pair of eyes following my motions. I glanced up toward the second floor. Sure enough, there she was.

XI

"LOOK who's waiting for me," I could hear Elena saying, her voice dripping with syrup. "With a bag full of goodi-i-ies." As she appeared in the doorway she drawled "Goo-ood mo-orning," showing off all her stubby teeth and holding out her right hand for me to kiss. She was wearing a lilac two-piece outfit of floral-patterned silk, and her bony feet were fairly bursting out of the brand new lilac silk shoes. Her clothes had just come from Paris.

A SESSION WITH COMRADE ELENA

Friday morning was always reserved by Elena for me to give her news from the microphones installed in the offices and homes of the top *nomenclatura.* Her office, only slightly smaller than Ceausescu's, had the seal of the Communist Party behind her desk instead of that of Romania. The wall facing the desk had a life-size portrait of Ceausescu. Against one side wall was a large set of bookshelves filled with Ceausescu's works bound in red leather and several copies of "her" book on chemistry. On her desk was only his photograph, in a gold frame. No files or other papers. Elena does not like to read. The only exception I ever saw was Iosif's files. She loved them, even if to read them she secretly had to get out her glasses, which she never let be seen in public.

"Show me," Elena said, trying to find a comfortable position in her oversize chair. "What's new with Violeta?"

Violeta was the wife of Stefan Andrei, the minister of foreign affairs. She was a little painted doll, an affected young actress who always paraded around as if she were on stage. As soon as Elena had ordered microphone coverage put on Violeta, several years earlier, the first recording of one of her casual love affairs was made. It was with a student. There had been many others since then, always handsome young men with an athletic build. "Just look at the minx!" Elena burst out that time. "The Party gave her one of its top people as a husband, but she runs around hiking up her skirts at every tarzan who throws her a smile." It was in the mid-1970s when Elena mused, "What do you think Violeta sounds like when she's making love?" The following week I put a cassette recorder on Elena's desk, and she played it over and over. "Just listen to the minx, darling," she said, breathing heavily. "When she comes in here, she always minces around and lisps off the tip of her tongue, but on the tape it's enough to break your eardrums the way she cries and screams." Since that winter day I always had to have several Violeta cassettes in my briefcase. By April, Elena was asking that professional listening equipment be installed in her back room, and after that she started keeping the Violeta cassettes. And others.

"Don't you have anything on Violeta today?" Elena cried out, staring at me. "Is she dead?"

"Violeta went to East Berlin, where she was to perform in a co-production with East German actors."

I could almost hear the air going out of Elena. She turned red in the face, her hazel eyes narrowed to callous slits, and her mouth formed itself into one sharp, lipless gash. "So what? Whether it's Berlin or London, she's still the wife of our foreign minister, and we ought to know what she's doing." Elena thereupon gave me strict orders to have Violeta monitored around the clock, in Romania or abroad, no matter where she was.

Elena flicked through the rest of the files without her usual interest. Only Maurer's caught her attention. After she had finished leafing through it, she picked up the S telephone.

"I miss you, darling. How are you?" Elena cooed sweetly, when Mrs. Maurer answered the telephone. "Oh, I see. Call me back after your guests leave. I want to have a nice chat with you. The last time I saw you I couldn't really talk, because there were other people present. My dear, you looked so pretty that day. Just like a virgin, my dear. Yes. All full of pimples. You don't still have sex, do you? At seventy-five it's not much fun any more, is it? Fifty-five? Oh, I didn't know." I heard a click. Evidently Mrs. Maurer had hung up on her.

"I've got Golda's file here," I offered, holding up a file on Golda Meir in an attempt to avert an outbreak of hysterics. "You asked me for it last night."

"Give it to me." She grabbed the file. "Has she gotten rich?"

"I don't think she cares about money."

"What about Indira?" she asked, meaning Prime Minister Gandhi.

"That's another story."

"I want to see Indira's file," Elena went on. "Before you leave for Washington."

"You'll have it. Here's a file I have for you on the visit to the United States. It contains everything about your schedule there."

"Big deal! A week wasted on Mister and Madam Peanut." Then she sweetened her voice. "Are you going to have any diplomas there for me, darling?"

"Yes, comrade. A certificate of honorary membership in the Illinois Academy of Science," I offered, hoping to improve her mood.

"Illi-what?" she screamed, jumping to her feet. "Who do they think I am? Mother Teresa? I want an academy in Washington. Or New York. Let Mister Peanut put that in his pipe and smoke it!"

I tried my best to explain that the American president did not have the same power that the Romanian did. The only result, however, was Elena's wrath. "Come off it! You can't sell me on the idea that Mister Peanut can give me an Illi-whatsis diploma but not any from Washington. I w-i-l-l n-o-t g-o t-o I-l-l-i-what-ever it is. I will not!"

"The diploma will be awarded to you at Blair House, in Washington, by Professor Merdinger, representing the board of the Illinois Academy of Science," I tried to calm her down.

"Who?"

"Professor Emanuel Merdinger, a native Romanian."

"Why not the whole board, darling? They never have had and never again will have an international scientist and political leader in one and the same woman. Come on, darling. I want the whole board."

Silence is golden, I thought to myself, remembering the earlier telegrams from both the Washington and the New York stations saying that it was simply unrealistic to try for an academic degree for her.

"Is your professor a Jew?" asked Elena, a note of suspicion creeping into her voice as it suddenly became sweet again. "Isn't Merdinger a Jewish name, darling?"

"Professor Merdinger is a friend of Romania, Comrade Elena."

"We don't have Jewish friends. I don't want my diploma smudged up by Jewish fingers."

"Comrade Ceausescu received him in 1972 and had good words to say about him," I tried, playing what I thought was my best card.

"That was politics. We are now talking science."

I had had similar discussions every time the DIE was able—and not exactly easily—to arrange for a new diploma for Elena. And as soon as she had one in her hands, she immediately forgot how hard she had had to push me to get it. One time on the airplane leaving the Philippines, she confided with an air of absolute ingenuousness: "I don't think you know, darling, but their university insisted on giving me an honorary doctorate. I kept refusing, but do you know what they did? They may be little yellow people, but they can use their heads. They got Imelda to take me there. What could I do then, darling? What a sweet soul she is." Only the DIE chief of station in Manila and I knew that it had been impossible to sway the university's board, until we got help from President Ferdinand Marcos's closest confident, General Fabian Ver. Only Ver's promise that Imelda would accompany Elena to the ceremony and make a substantial donation to the university changed the board's mind. Another time, when we returned from a trip to Asia and South America, where she had garnered quite a number of honorary titles, brought off by the DIE with considerable effort and money, Elena gushed to the Romanian prime minister's wife: "Do you know what, darling? There were exhibitions of my scientific works on display everywhere. Everybody wanted to give me a diploma. I finally just had to put my foot down, darling. After all, I had certain political obligations to fulfill, too."

"I've got some news for you," said Elena, clumsily getting up out of her chair and clumping over to the bookshelf. "I was sitting over at the institute writing my new book, when a very distinguished-looking man, a foreigner, insisted on seeing me. It was the president of Leipzig University, in person!"

"Leipzig or Darmstadt?" I asked, knowing that she had met the *Rektor* of the Darmstadt Technical Institute. Elena always has trouble distinguishing between East and West Germany.

"Whatever. He had come all that way—can you guess why? To bring me the German translation of my book."

"My book" had been written by a team of researchers and engineers, some completely unknown to Elena, and was based on the latest technological intelligence obtained by the DIE on the synthesis mechanism of various macromolecular components.

Elena rattled on and on about her meeting in a suspiciously excited way, until she baldly came out with it:

"Darling, so many people all over the world are so grateful for my scientific effort. I feel that the scientific mind I was blessed with shouldn't be used just for the well-being of my own country but for all mankind. I should invent something that will last forever, like fire or nuclear energy."

Elena urged me to put the DIE's whole technological espionage network in the West, numbering hundreds of foreign scientists and engineers who had been recruited as agents, to work on the problem. She wanted information on the most important research in the West that was in the process of being patented. She would select a few of these projects as hers and have them patented in Romania, backdated to before their first registration in the West. Afterwards, Elena would use these Romanian patents to obtain international ones. "Your DIE will have to do that until I take charge of the Romanian patent, classification, and standardization system."

According to the Romanian press, in December 1984 Elena became the chairman of the apparently insignificant new "Classification, Standardization, Norm-setting, and Quality Control Council." She has always been dogged in the pursuit of her personal ambitions.

CONTRADICTING THE CONSTITUTION

It was noon when I left Elena and went up to General Luchian's office, one floor higher. For over a year he had been there every Friday waiting to see me after my weekly bout with Elena.

"I'm trying to get better figures on emigration," Luchian began, "for your discussions in Washington. It's not so bad with the Germans—the Comrade's limit for this year is a headcount of 10,000. But you're going to be in hot water with the Jews. The Comrade approved only 1,200 for the whole of 1978, and you won't have any more than three hundred for the first quarter." As permanent secretary of the National Commission for Visas and Passports, Luchian was the expert on emigration. Incredibly pedantic, he was respected for the accuracy of his figures, despite constant pressure from everyone, Ceausescu included, to have them show only the sunny side of the picture.

"I have a marvelous story for you," Luchian began again. "Yesterday I called Postelnicu and invited him to come over so we could work on the decree together. 'Since when should the mountain come to Muhammad?' he asked, and hung up on me. I couldn't believe my ears. Mike, in Buzau he always saw me to my car and danced around me and could never do enough for me. I immediately hopped over to his office to see what the matter was, and what do you think he said? 'From now on, you should come here only when I call you. Be here at seven tomorrow morning with the decree finished. And keep it short, because at eight I've got a breakfast with the prime minister.' Can you believe it?"

"Careful, Luchian. You're going to have him as your boss."

"I'd rather be a waiter in some third-rate restaurant than his underling." He banged a heavy paw down on the table. "I worked through the whole night, and this morning, on the dot of seven, I put the file down on his desk. He didn't even open it. At ten o'clock he called me back and said it was a mess. Briefly, what he wanted was for me to include mention of the DGTO and other security units whose names have never been written down on paper before."

"In a public decree?"

"I told him that a public decree could not have anything in it that contradicted the Constitution, and that the wording he wanted would only make the Comrade explode. Do you know what he said? He said the Comrade was too busy to read it and would just sign off on it. Poor idiot. He certainly doesn't know the Comrade." After pausing for a moment, Luchian continued. "I tried, Mike. I tried to help Postelnicu as a friend. The best I could. And guess what he said? 'Go back again, comrade. Write out the decree the way I told you to, put it in a sealed envelope, and make sure that it is on my desk before eight this evening.' Can you even in your wildest dreams conceive of putting the DGTO's functions down on paper?"

Always cool and collected, Luchian had now become nervous and red in the face. "I had my suspicions," he said, "but now I've just gotten confirmation that that tricky old fox General Diaconescu was behind the whole thing." He meant the chief of the DGTO, General Ovidiu Diaconescu. "He's always been trying to catch the Comrade's signature on any scrap of paper approving mail censorship and telephone interception. He and his thousands of officers are doing a job that is contrary to the Constitution, without having *any shred* of paper to cover their rear ends, I know that. If someday Free Europe or somebody else bursts the bubble, Diaconescu will be in extremely hot water."

As I was leaving, Luchian saw me to the main door. "Don't forget," he reminded me. "Tomorrow evening. At my house. With Oprea and Voicu."

FRIENDLY LETTERS FROM GENERAL VER

"To the office," I ordered my driver.

A few minutes later, Paraschiv reduced speed as he went by the United States embassy, allowing the wrought iron gate at the nearby DIE headquarters to open automatically and let us drive through. We stopped in front of an imposing gray office building. A few steps led up to an old-fashioned, etched glass door. On the other side of this door everything was locked and covered by closed circuit television. My plastic magnetic card, similar to an ordinary Western credit card, with an intricate drawing on one side and my signature in my operational alias, Mihai Podeanu, on the other, set a huge, circular iron door in motion, the only way to enter the building. (Mine was also the official signature on that of every one of the other 3,000 DIE officers.) The elevator for DIE officers was to the left of the circular door.

To the right, a wide staircase with a red runner led up to the third floor, reserved for the DIE's chief and deputy chief. The chief duty officer took several formal steps toward me, stopped when he was two yards away, and gave the ritual report: "Comrade General, during my tour of duty nothing unusual has occurred. I am the chief duty officer for the Department of Foreign Intelligence, Colonel Victor Dobrin." His real name was Victor Daisa, but everyone working for the Romanian espionage service had a secret operational alias that he used inside headquarters and in connection with his job, so that no one working with him could learn his true identity. Abroad, however, officers usually used their true names.

When I opened the door facing the stairs, Colonel Vasile Pop, my chief executive officer, and his deputy, Captain Popescu, jumped up like jack-in-the-boxes. They shared a room filled with special telephones, radio stations, telex machines, radiophoto transmitters, and safes.

"Here are the general's telegrams," said Pop. "And here is today's diplomatic pouch mail for you. It includes a very confidential report from Tel Aviv, General. And an envelope and this cardboard box from Manila, both with the Philippines presidential seal on them and addressed to you personally."

The Tel Aviv report was from the chief of the cryptographic team sent there a few months earlier, who reported that the Israeli code used for surveilling the Romanian embassy and its personnel had been broken and that the station was now running disinformation operations. The envelope from Manila contained a friendly letter from General Fabian Ver. As usual, he started by reminiscing about our days together. This time he recalled the flight he and I had made to the American war monument in Bataan. The point of his letter, though, was to invite me to spend a vacation as his guest at Malacanang Palace. He enclosed a large photograph autographed by Imelda showing me walking arm in arm with her and Elena Ceausescu at Malacanang Palace. A light blue, silk pilot's uniform was in the cardboard box; it was identical to ones Ver and I had worn on that flight to Bataan.

I first met General Ver in the winter of 1975, when I went to

Manila to prepare Ceausescu's state visit. On my arrival, the DIE chief of station, who was also chargé d'affaires, reported that the DIE technical team from Bucharest had discovered microphones in every room of the Romanian embassy. Instructions had just come in from Bucharest asking that I raise the matter personally with President Ferdinand Marcos as soon as possible.

At my meeting the next day with Marcos, also attended by Ver, I placed a few of the microphones on his desk and read him a note of protest. After whispering with Ver for a few moments, Marcos replied that they had been installed by the American CIA.

"They are the ones doing such things here. We don't have anybody who speaks Romanian in all the Philippines," said Marcos, asking me to send his personal apology to his friend Ceausescu. "General Ver will tell you a lot more about all this."

Ver did tell me a lot more. That evening he had me to dinner at the palace. He did most of the talking, mainly about the secret agreements the Philippines had had to sign with the United States government in order to receive financial assistance, and in particular about the CIA's operations in the Philippines. That evening I heard more about the CIA than I had ever heard in my life, and the comments were not of the friendliest nature.

It was after midnight when I finally returned to my room in the palace. Two cute young girls, almost naked, were snuggling up on the bed waiting for me. I called the chargé d'affaires, and he took me to a hotel. When I came down to the lobby early the next morning, there was Ver. Since that day he had been extremely friendly with me. He was constantly with me the rest of the time I was in the Philippines, and the program he worked up for Ceausescu's state visit was carried out without a hitch and went beyond all expectations. Most important for the Ceausescus' mood during the visit were the top medals and fabulously expensive gifts he arranged for them to be given by the Marcoses, as well as honorary diplomas for Elena's collection.

When I went back to the Philippines in April with the Ceausescus, Ver again tried to perform the impossible, so as to make the visit a success. Toward the end, however, his excess of zeal almost ruined everything. He arranged a breakfast for the Ceausescus on board Marcos's yacht that went on to become an all-day and all-night party, with theatrical performances, music, dance, parlor games, a semi-striptease by Imelda, fireworks, and mountains of food and drink. Ceausescu was indeed overwhelmed. Elena, however, went into hysterics every time Imelda appeared on the bridge wearing a new outfit, while Elena had to sit there with no chance to change into anything else.

Since that visit, I had seen Ver only once, but he sent me friendly letters every other month. And I would reply.

"WE SHOULD RECRUIT BILLY CARTER"

When Pop came back into my office it was past six. "The Comrade has just left his office and sent a radio message from his car for you to meet him at home."

At Ceausescu's residence, the duty officer reported, "The Comrade is waiting for you in the rose garden."

"What's new?" Ceausescu asked without looking at me, as I fell into step with him. Not waiting for my answer, he continued. "In your file on Carter's family I see that his brother Billy is some kind of lush, a corruptible fellow trying to turn a fast buck." Ceausescu had become obsessed with the idea of recruiting Billy Carter as an influence agent. "I see also that the DIE has a man in a position to build up some business relations with Billy. Isn't that the Liberian who has an export-import company in London, managed by his brother?"

"Yes, comrade."

Ceausescu stopped, caught at a button of my jacket and, looking me straight in the eye, went on in a conspiratorial tone. "We should recruit Billy, using a 'foreign flag.'" Ceausescu directed that the Liberian agent make Billy his official representative for export-import business in North and South America and pay him generously. "We'll supply the cash. Let Billy make some money off of us, develop a taste for it, and then, wham!—we recruit him, telling him the money wasn't British or Liberian, but ours. We need to hurry though to get to him before others do."

Ceausescu let go of my button and started walking again, rigidly swinging his arms. "Remember the shah's brother?" he continued. "I spotted him on a visit to Iran that time, and we made him into our representative for importing oil from Iran. Then you gave him a percentage for exporting Romanian products to Iran. And then, wham!—you had him recruited and eating out of your hand. Are you interested in knowing something about the Iranians' relations with the Americans, the Soviets, or the Israelis? Who could know that better than the shah and his brother? Do you want to know something about their army or Savak? The brother is their supreme commander. Do we need to win the bidding to sell something to Iran? The brother gives you the sealed bids from all the interested parties, you secretly open them, make copies, and then, wham!—I submit a bid that's five dollars cheaper. So I get to build a tractor assembly plant there. What if I do have to pay the brother ten percent? What's two million dollars to me? A tenth of the value of the tractors we assemble and sell annually in Iran. Of course, you also pay him another two million for the locomotives he helps you sell there, and more for the railroad cars and for geological research equipment, or whatever else, but we still make a lot of money. Ten or fifteen million dollars a year paid to him in Switzerland is enough to make him develop a taste for more. Isn't that it?"

"Yes, comrade. Exactly."

"Or take Rifaat Assad. Hafez is one of my best friends. I wouldn't even think of trying to recruit him. But his brother is an entirely different matter. I spotted him during a visit to Syria. We followed the same scenario as with the shah's brother, and now Rifaat is also eating out of our hand. Do I need lucrative exports to Syria? Rifaat will take care of it, because he knows the taste of my dollars, and he wants you to deposit more and more to his personal Swiss account. Now he is our man. Do I need a back channel for secret political communications? A way to inform Hafez secretly about my future discussions with Carter? Do I need to have somebody disappear in the West? Rifaat will take care of it. Now he can't do without my money."

Ceausescu stopped short and, punctuating the air with both his arms, then said, "In our relations with the non-Communist world, politics without influence is like Marxism without Lenin. Nobody will give you anything unless you know how to grease his palm."

ORDERS TO KILL

Ceausescu walked along in silence for a time. Then he said, "What's new?" This time he meant it.

"There's a problem with Stan."

"What kind of problem?" he asked, looking up quickly at me. General Nicolae Stan was the chief of the Securitate's Directorate V, responsible for the protective security of Ceausescu.

"Stan's sister is married to a Party activist whom the DIE has been training for assignment to Israel as an illegal officer."

"I didn't know Stan had any Jewish relatives."

"His brother-in-law changed his name from Schwartz to Negru."

"Send him out as an "X" officer to work with the Israeli Communist Party underground there."

"The problem is that, when Stan heard about it, he formally asked the minister of interior to have the operation canceled. Coman did so, but now Negru and Stan's sister want to go to Israel on their own."

"Wha-a-at?"

"They found a way to tell the Israeli embassy about how Stan had had their exit visa canceled. Negru also has written a letter for broadcast by Radio Free Europe in which he asks you to approve their emigration to Israel as their human right."

"'R-R-Radu'! T-Tell C-Coman t-to g-give them 'R-Radu.' H-Have t-them arrested for a few h-hours and g-given 'R-Radu,'" he howled desperately with drooling mouth, as he stopped in the middle of the path. "T-That's d-defection, and d-defectors s-should b-be k-killed—all of t-them; b-beaten to a p-pulp and k-killed l-like animals b-before t-they s-start p-publishing anything." Although the evening was chilly, his forehead suddenly began to drip perspiration.

Nothing scares Ceausescu more than defections. It is not the compromise of information that he considers the most damaging. For him, as for the other Soviet bloc leaders, the far greater consequence lies in the long range effects of the very fact that one of their most trusted officials could defect to the West and publicly tell the world what Communism is really like. I remember that the information provided the CIA by the Romanian intelligence officer Ion Iacobescu, who defected in France in 1969, caused the arrest of important Romanian agents inside NATO and the French government, but the real value to the West of his defection went far beyond that. A book published in France about his case, combined with ingenious measures by the French security service, undermined Bucharest's credibility so badly that nine years later Romania had still not been able to recruit any other agents in NATO or the French government. The 1972 defection to the United States of Constantin Dumitra-chescu, the station chief in Tel Aviv, magnificently exploited by the Israelis, caused so much damage to the DIE's prestige in Israel that for the next six years it was unable to recruit any new agents there.

For a while I trotted along in silence beside Ceausescu. When he resumed speaking, he was calm.

"We've got to have all our defectors killed without a trace. Has the Mafioso left for Washington?"

"'Felix'?"

"Yes."

"He has. A week ago." The Mafioso was an American citizen active in the Mafia who had been recruited by the DIE and codenamed "Felix."

"Ask him to kill Rauta. He's making a lot of noise in Washington right now and should be the first to be killed. Then Goma. And have him blow Free Europe sky high—with bombs." Constantin Rauta was a DIE engineer when he defected to the United States, and he had begun visibly lobbying the United States Congress for support in his efforts to get his wife and daughter out of Romania.

After issuing these orders, Ceausescu began refining them with minutely detailed instructions, as is his usual practice. He was finally interrupted by a bodyguard sent by Elena to summon him for dinner.

"When do you leave for Washington, Pacepa?"

"I don't have a visa yet."

"Push them. I need you over there."

Outside it was calm but cold.

"Where does the general wish to be driven?" asked Paraschiv.

"To Pescarus." That was a picturesque lakefront restaurant very close to Ceausescu's residence, run exclusively by the DIE and the Securitate because of its attraction for Western tourists.

Over dinner, I could not help thinking about Ceausescu. After 13 years in power, he looked upon Romania as something that he and his family literally owned. His wife, Elena, was on the rise, and nobody in the whole country was now being appointed to a high or middle-level position without her blessing. Ceausescu's brothers, Ilie, Nicolae, and Ion, controlled the armed forces, the DIE, and agriculture. Elena's brother ran the General Union of Trade Unions, which had control over all the working population of Romania. Their son Nicu was the head of the Union of Communist Youth. And this was just the beginning. There is no system of government more susceptible to nepotism than the Communist one.

I had just gotten to dessert when my driver came in alarmed. "A radio message just came in saying you should immediately report to zero one." So much for my dessert.

Ceausescu was pacing around his office like a caged tiger.

"I don't want to have Rauta killed before my visit to Washington. Nor Goma. They should be rubbed out afterwards, along with Free Europe. Understood?"

"Yes, comrade."

"That's all for now."

The duty officer at the entrance to Ceausescu's residence silently opened the door for me, giving a military salute.

"To the office," I told Paraschiv.

CHAPTER

XII

IT was not yet seven in the morning when Iosif arrived. His suit was all rumpled, his face was gray, and his eyes were swollen from lack of sleep.

OLGA IN THE FLESH

"I have a film for the General," Iosif said wearily as he removed a large roll of 16mm film from his briefcase. When the projector started up in my back room, there was Olga in the flesh. She was just leaving her hotel early that morning. Although no longer young, she was a petite, attractive woman with a bouncing blonde pony tail and a sexy swing to her hips.

The concealed camera had tenaciously followed Olga all day long, and the film showed excerpts. She walked, took streetcars, hailed a taxi, visited museums and stores, all the while trying to act very casual. I could spot the Soviet intelligence touch, however, in her attempts to shake off suspected surveillance.

When Olga entered the Lido restaurant, the time noted on the film showed a few minutes before eight. She picked out a dim corner, from which she could easily watch the entrance. Suddenly it turned into a sound film, spliced together with the tape from the transmitter in the ceramic flower vase on her table. Shortly after eight-thirty a man came up to her, affectionately kissed her hand and sat down. As the concealed camera faced Olga, it picked up only the man's back. He was about my build, and something about his gestures and demeanor seemed familiar. Olga became more and more affectionate as she recalled the fabulous days and passionate nights of their past. First one of her feet, then finally both of her legs began maneuvering under the table.

Olga tells about how she has given up her teaching job at the Military Academy for one in the Foreign Ministry. She has just been assigned to the Soviet embassy in Sofia, where she will begin working in a couple of weeks. They could meet again on weekends. "It's only a few hours' drive." She doesn't want to telephone him; that wouldn't be wise. But an old friend at their embassy in Bucharest, "also in the military," could act as intermediary. "You'll recognize him. He was a friend of yours, too. I asked him to come here before ten, so you and he could set up some kind of arrangement." Olga says she will have to leave in the morning with the group of Soviet tourists.

When Olga's Soviet friend arrived, the time noted on the film was exactly ten o'clock. The Romanian man stood up to shake his hand. "Thunderation!" I heard myself saying softly. The camera had moved in for a close-up, and, as I saw the broad smile of a familiar face, I automatically reached over to freeze the projector. In my mind's eye that face was superimposed on another one wearing a military hat loaded with "scrambled eggs." I could see it riding along in a Soviet-made Gaz convertible, going from one military unit to another on Stalin Square for the formal greeting, and then stopping in front of the official tribunal during the August 23rd National Day parade: "Comrade General Secretary of the Romanian Communist Party, President of the Romanian Socialist Republic, I am the commander of the National Day parade, Lieutenant General Nicolae Militaru."

I restarted the projector. The close-up faded slowly back to normal, showing Militaru pleasantly surprised and giving the newcomer a friendly handshake. They immediately began talking about the days when they had both been students at the Soviet Military Academy. The Soviet, "Vanya," had just been appointed to Bucharest. "Yes," he said, "I'm a military attaché here now. We have perfectly good reason to get together now and then."

Militaru gave the man his private telephone number at the office, "so you won't have to go through my chief of staff. If I'm not there, no one will touch it."

They ordered another round of cognac. "When Olga makes

another trip to Bucharest," Vanya said, "I'll give you a call. As soon as you answer, I'll hang up. Then I'll call back and let the phone ring once. When she is going to the Black Sea, I'll let it ring twice." Militaru and Olga were to set up meeting arrangements in advance. They were already standing, ready to leave, when Vanya seemed to have an afterthought. "Could you do me a favor? Just between old friends? It would be a tremendous help if you could lend me the General Staff telephone book. I'm so new here, I don't know anybody."

Militaru seemed to be intensively studying his shoes. "I suppose you know I'm not allowed to make a xerox copy of it." The General Staff telephone book included the Directorate for Military Intelligence (DIA) and was classified Top Secret.

"I just need it for two or three hours, so I can become familiar with the departments and people I'll be dealing with. I may take a few notes, but no xerox copy. Word of honor." They finally agreed that on Monday Vanya would officially ask to be received by Militaru, who would arrange to be alone in his office for a few minutes and would slip the telephone book into Vanya's briefcase. "I can drop it back into your mailbox that same evening," Vanya suggested.

"Okay. Here's my card with my address on it," Militaru said, as the three of them started for the door.

At this point Iosif stopped the projector. "I have a lot more film," he said, "but it's not worth it. General Militaru left with Olga in his car. They spent the night at a small motel on the highway to Brasov. And I got lucky. When they ordered mineral water, I had it sent in to them in an ice bucket—you know, one of the ceramic ones with a built-in transmitter. Iosif placed three cassettes on the table. "They made love the whole damned night. Comrade Elena may be interested. The chief of the monitoring center says he's never had such sexy cassettes before. And you know he's heard plenty!"

Iosif went on to say that, after leaving Militaru and Olga, Vanya went to the station and caught a train for Brasov. Shortly after arriving there, he hopped onto another train going back to Bucharest and got off in Ploiesti. A car and driver from the Soviet embassy were waiting for him. "My boys took pictures of him the whole time," said Iosif, placing a file on the table. "We don't know all that much about Vanya. He just got here. But that trick with the train, to shake surveillance, is typical GRU." It was clear that it was a Soviet military intelligence operation.

Nicolae Militaru had been a member of the Central Committee of the Romanian Communist Party since 1969, and commander of the Bucharest Military Region since 1970. His brother, Aldea, was also a member of the Central Committee, as well as a member of parliament. Nicolae Militaru was Ceausescu's personal choice for commander of the Bucharest Military Region after the Soviet invasion of Czechoslovakia. Ceausescu was so satisfied with Militaru's performance that just a week before this he had decided to promote him to deputy minister of national defense. The appointment was scheduled to take place before Ceausescu's departure for Washington.

THE SERB CASE

"It's nothing but a repeat of the Serb case. Almost down to the last detail," said Iosif.

"What are the differences?" I knew of the case of General Ion Serb, but I did not know all the specifics, as the Serb investigation had been started by the Securitate's Directorate IV, responsible for counterintelligence in the military.

"Let's see. Like Militaru, Serb also went to military school in the Soviet Union. In Romania he had also risen to become chief of the Bucharest Military Garrison, when he was contacted by his former Moscow girlfriend."

"Did she also come as a tourist?"

"Sort of. She came as a tourist guide. We called her 'Nastasia.' "

"Where was their 'accidental' meeting?"

"Also in a first-class restaurant. That was their bad luck, too. Just as now, everything there was being live monitored. Nastasia said she would be coming back to Romania on a regular basis, as an Intourist guide."

"Did she introduce Musatov?" The Soviet case officer had been Colonel F. A. Musatov.

"Yes. Exactly as Olga did with Vanya, at the end of dinner. She would let Serb know through him every time she was coming back. He also happened to be a Soviet military attaché."

"When did Musatov start pushing for something?"

"Just like Vanya. The GRU likes to strike while the iron is hot. At his first meeting with Serb, while Nastasia was pressing Serb's legs between her knees under the table, Musatov asked Serb for some innocuous-sounding classified documents. Just wanted to take a look at them. No copy."

"What did Serb give the Soviets?"

"Musatov moved in very fast. He cranked out that old ploy about doing a doctoral thesis. In it he was writing something about defending an East European capital against a NATO attack using conventional weapons. He was using Bucharest as his example, and the Bucharest defense plans would be a big help for him."

"Serb's reaction?" I wanted to know.

"Just for a few hours. No copies."

"Then what?"

"When Musatov asked for the plans, Directorate IV secretly took them out of Serb's personal safe that night and replaced them with the disinformation version they always have on hand."

Directorate IV prepares all military disinformation items, ranging from phony traffic signs around important military installations, to incorrect markings on the military equipment used in military parades for the bafflement of foreign military attachés, to the more sophisticated items. Every time the minister of defense presents an important military plan to Ceausescu, Directorate IV is also supposed to present its disinformation version to him. It has to look identical to the original plan, so that it could not be distinguished from it. Only the most important strategic and tactical data are changed, for the purpose of misleading an enemy who might surreptitiously obtain it. This Kremlin-generated paranoia for secrecy had been succinctly formulated by KGB Chairman Yuri Andropov, at my last meeting with him: "The most sacred Soviet-bloc secrets are military, and disinformation is the best way to keep them."

"So was it only the disinformation version that Serb gave Musatov?" I asked.

"Yes, General. Moscow got caught at its own game. This time the GRU is smarter, though. I'm sure nobody from Directorate IV has prepared a disinformation version of the telephone book."

"What was the Comrade's reaction to the Serb case?"

"Black!"

"Meaning?"

"He wanted Serb scattered to the four winds. But it had already been publicly announced that Romania didn't have any more political prisoners, so the Comrade decided to have him neutralized for violations of the secrecy law. Classified documents prepared by Directorate IV were hidden in his house during a surreptitious entry, and he was immediately arrested when they were found."

From that point on I knew Serb's case in detail. He was court-martialed behind closed doors for violations of the secrecy law, stripped of his rank, and sentenced to seven years in prison. A few days after the trial, Ceausescu ordered me to launch a disinformation operation in the West, spreading the rumor that Serb was the first Soviet-bloc general to have been executed as a Soviet spy. "You could hardly find anything more convincing than that to support 'Horizon' in the West," Ceausescu said at the time. As a first result of the disinformation operation, in February 1972 the West picked up the news that Serb might no longer be a general. In a few days Serb became an international case, with the Western media publishing reports that Romanian General Ion Serb had been arrested and executed for having passed military information to the Soviet Union. As part of the disinformation, an undercover DIE officer posing as a spokesman for the Romanian embassy in Vienna stated publicly that he had learned only that Serb was no longer a general; he refused further comment on reports that Serb had been shot as a spy for the Soviet Union.

Ceausescu ordered that Serb's real fate, known to only a handful of people, be one of Romania's best kept secrets. In August 1976, upon his return from the Crimea after a conciliatory meeting with Leonid Brezhnev, Ceausescu ordered that Serb be forced to sign a secrecy agreement, then released from prison and sent to work in a kolkhoz far away from Bucharest. As I reviewed Serb's case in my mind, I was trying to think of recommendations to make to Ceausescu when I gave him Militaru's case, although I knew Ceausescu had never asked for anyone else's suggestions on anything. I picked up the *S* telephone and dialed Manea's number. "Hi, Professor. I have a sudden urge to come over and see you. How's the weather?"

"Eat your own shit, Boss, if that's all you can find to do. There's an earthquake going on here. Nine on the Richter scale, with everything rattling around. Postelnicu and Luchian are inside. I can hear it from here."

"I have to see the Comrade."

"Comrade Elena's in there, too," continued Manea in his expressionless voice, ignoring my insistence.

"I'll take your advice, Professor."

"If I survive, I'll call you back later, Boss."

HANDWRITING SAMPLES OF THE WHOLE POPULATION

It was around eleven when Manea got back to me. "Sorry for you, Boss. There's another hurricane raging here, and the Comrade wants to see you right away. He even ordered me to send a helicopter after you, if you weren't close by."

"I'll be right there, Professor. With the news I've got, I can only make the weather worse."

Before opening the door of Ceausescu's office for me, Manea managed to whisper that Coman and Plesita had been inside for some time and that Elena had just joined them. She always had a nose for trouble.

"Didn't I tell you they were all idiots?" I heard Elena saying, as I opened the door. "How many times have I asked you to fire them and call in the army?"

"H-How c-can your army learn who the author of an anonymous letter is, w-woman?" Ceausescu screamed from behind his desk, purple with rage.

"If they can't figure it out, then they'll just shoot every other suspect. Believe me, nobody will ever write another anonymous letter after that."

"T-Take t-this g-garbage away," he said to me, sprinkling spittle over everything on his desk. He threw a file onto the floor. The stuttering was always an ill omen. The sprinkling forecast a thunderstorm.

When I picked the file up, I could see that it was bulging at the gills with anonymous letters addressed to Radio Free Europe in Munich. They were full of criticism of Ceausescu's and Elena's personality cult. I got the picture. Evidently the letters had been picked up in the mail censorship and presented to Ceausescu by Coman and Plesita as evidence of their vigilance. Now Ceausescu wanted the writers' scalps.

"I want to get their names. I'm as sure of it as I live and breathe—Free Europe knows their names. Everybody knows them, except for me and the Securitate."

"Bunch of idiots," muttered Elena.

"You are to pull their names out of the Free Europe files," Ceausescu told me. "Immediately."

Glaring furiously at us, Ceausescu jabbed violently at a button on his telephone table. "Call Luchian in here. Now!" he yelled, when Manea appeared in the doorway.

"I'll give you three months to get handwriting samples for the whole Romanian population, starting with children in the first grade. No exceptions. Get the autobiography from every employee's personnel file." Handwritten autobiographies are the rule for employees in Romania, as they are everywhere in the Soviet bloc. "Invent some new kind of form that retirees and housewives and other non-workers will have to fill out. Use your head—do I have to teach you how to do it?"

"No, comrade. We have such a collection," Plesita tried to say.

"If you can't identify the authors of these anonymous letters, you don't have the handwriting samples you need. In three months you ought to be able to catch every anonymous letter-writer and find some reason to put him in jail." Ceausescu's thumb was again pressing the buzzer. When Manea came in, Ceausescu said, "Write down: 'Coman and Plesita. Handwriting samples.' Report the results to me three months from now," he finished.

When Luchian came in, Ceausescu had calmed down somewhat. "I want every typewriter belonging to the state to be registered, starting with the ones in my office, and I want samples of their type to be kept by the Securitate. I also want them to be locked or sealed when they're not being used." After a short pause, he continued, looking at Luchian. "You are to write an order to every state and cooperative organziation, and have the prime minister sign it. Clear?"

"Yes, comrade," said Luchian in his bass voice.

"I also want you to draft a Decree of the State Council saying the following: The renting or lending of a typewriter is forbidden to all Romanian citizens. No one may own a typewriter without authorization from the militia. Those who already have typewriters should immediately ask for such authorization; if it is refused, the owner must sell the typewriter to someone who has an authorization or surrender it to the militia. When an authorization is approved, the owner must present his typewriter to the militia for samples of its type to be made. The typewriter should be presented to the militia annually and after every repair, for new type samples." Ceausescu waited for Luchian to catch up with him in his notes, which he printed in a large hand. "Is that clear?"

"Yes, comrade, but it might not be legal."

"Wha-a-at?"

"We can issue such an order for all state agencies and organizations, because their typewriters are our property. But not for private individuals."

"Why not?"

"It might be against the Constitution."

"D-Did the C-Constitution m-make us, or d-did w-we m-make it?," asked Ceausescu rhetorically, his badger-like eyes darting from Luchian to the rest of us and back again. "W-We m-made the C-Constitution. W-We'll c-change it, if we h-have to." That was one of his favorite axioms.

Ceausescu's attitude toward the law was typical of Communist leaders. Konstantin Simis, a practicing lawyer and law professor in Moscow before being forced to emigrate in 1977, described a similar situation in his book. In the 1960s, when Khrushchev ordered Soviet black market speculators to be sentenced to death, the public prosecutor general of the Soviet Union, Roman Rudenko, explained to him that the law did not permit the courts to do that. "Khrushchev then spoke the wonderful sentence that sums up the attitude of Soviet power to legality: 'Who's the boss: we or the law? We are masters over the law, not the law over us—so we have to change the law; we have to see to it that it is possible to execute these speculators!'" On July 1, 1961, the Presidium of the Supreme Soviet of the

USSR issued a decree introducing the death penalty for the crime of speculating. [1]

"You w-write the d-decree I ordered, and I'll t-take c-care of the C-Constitution," Ceausescu ordered nervously. When he pointed his finger at the door, looking at us, Coman and Plesita melted away as if they had never been there, followed by Luchian, his heavy step rattling the glass holding pencils on Ceausescu's desk. A few minutes later Elena left also. I held my ground.

Ceausescu started pacing around his office, and then, as if trying to postpone another piece of unpleasant news, he asked: "Is Luchian an idiot, or does he just play dumb?" Without waiting for my answer, he continued. "If your news is as bad as Coman's, you'd better leave, too."

"I'm sorry to say it is," I replied, without moving.

"Well, go ahead," he said, sitting down on his special chair that made him look taller. He started doodling with his favorite black pen.

I presented the Militaru case, making it as short as I could. When I got to the meeting at the restaurant, Ceausescu froze, his right hand suspended in the air. As I pronounced Militaru's name, the pen fell from his hand, making a deadened thump as it hit the desk. The silence in the room was so thick you could cut it with a knife.

When I finished, Ceausescu was literally speechless. His face became a contorted mask, with twisted mouth and eyes narrowing into slits. His hands were paralyzed into claws. His slumping torso shrank down into the chair at an almost imperceptible pace. After many long minutes, he precipitately left the office for his back rooms, leaving the door open. I could hear him vomiting.

When Ceausescu came back, he was an old man, wearing a suit that was too large for him. He looked at me. "I just met with Brezhnev. He kissed me when I left."

After another long silence, Ceausescu pressed a buzzer, and Manea immediately came to the door. "A glass of water. And the decree I signed for Militaru."

[1]Konstantin M. Simis, *The Corrupt Society: The Secret World of Soviet Capitalism*, New York: Simon and Schuster, 1982, pp. 29–31.

Ceausescu emptied the glass at one gulp. Then he violently tore to shreds the presidential decree appointing Nicolae Militaru deputy minister of national defense.

"Whore! Son of a bitch!"

He exited the room through the side door, not saying another word. I was still sitting on my chair when a puzzled Manea opened the door. "What's going on here, Boss?" he asked in his flat voice. "The main gate just called me, saying the Comrade has left and all's well."

"Let's pick up these scraps of paper. And burn them."

"Too bad for him," Manea said without emotion. "He was great as head of the National Day parade."

Gossip at the Dinner Party

It was late in the afternoon when I called home. Dana answered the telephone. "I'm working with Radu, Dad. A new painting."

"May I ask a favor, Dana? Could you come with me tonight? Dinner at Luchian's. Eight o'clock."

"That's okay, Dad. I'll be ready and waiting for you by seven-thirty."

The ring of the S telephone broke the Saturday afternoon silence of my office.

"General Pacepa speaking."

"Hi, Mike." It was Oprea's tenor voice. "I don't know if I can make it to Luchian's on time. Would you like to pick up Mary?"

"Yes, Prime Minister. You know I've always had a crush on Mary." Oprea loved to be called *Prime Minister*. In fact, he was indeed the one who ran the government, Prime Minister Manea Manescu being more of a figurehead.

"Thank you so much. I'll be there as soon as I can."

I had known Gheorghe Oprea since 1949, when he, a mechanic at the time, was in the first group of workers sent by the Party to become engineers in a two-year concentrated course at the Polytechnical Institute, where I was studying. When Ceausescu came to power, he picked out Oprea as a worker turned engineer and appointed him deputy minister in the Ministry of Heavy Industry. Nobody could recognize the apprentice of 1949 in today's tall, distinguished man in dark gray pinstripes, with his gold-rimmed glasses and scholarly look. A calm, low-key man, Oprea has always been grateful to his benefactors. In his new position he became a workaholic, and his gelatinous personality soon transformed him into Ceausescu's boundless admirer. Later he turned into a very convenient yes-man, and that caused Ceausescu to keep promoting him. By the time of Luchian's dinner party Oprea had recently been raised to first deputy prime minister, and Ceausescu had just told me in confidence: "Your old friend will soon be our new prime minister."

I was thinking that it would be a curious gathering at Luchian's that evening. Oprea, a little man who spent every hour serving Ceausescu and craving titles. Titles at any cost. And Ion Voicu, a phenomenally talented violinist, who obstinately refused all titles.

My close relationship with Voicu was a natural result of my own love for the violin, which I began studying when I was seven. The first time I came across Voicu's name was when I heard a young, unknown gypsy-like fellow play Lalo's *Symphonie Espagnole.* His eyes were closed from the moment his bow touched the first string until the very last note. To a faultless technique he added an incredible warmth, which I could feel going all through my body and through the concert hall. After a time, Voicu's unusual talent was discovered by the Communist government, and he was sent to Moscow to study with David Oistrakh. When he was back, I never missed any of his concerts. Once, after he had finished a superb rendition of Paganini's "La Campanella" and the public was applauding frenetically, I saw a fat old lady wearing a flowery dress and hat jump to her feet in the first row and start yelling with all her lungpower: "Quiet! Quiet! Don't scare him." After a pause, bursting into tears, she added, "He's my only son." Her son also impressed the former Romanian leader, Gheorghiu-Dej, who in 1959 ordered the DIE to provide $40,000 to buy him a Stradivarius. In the course of carrying out this order, I came to know Voicu well, and we became fast friends.

After Romania's last real orchestra conductor defected, and an upcoming talent, Sergiu Commissiona, finally got permission to emigrate—later making a successful career with the Baltimore and Houston symphonies—Ceausescu decided that Voicu should become both the conductor and the director of the Romanian National Philharmonic. Voicu tried to refuse, saying he wanted to remain just a fiddler, but he lost the argument. His first appearance on the podium was not encouraging. When Voicu cried on my shoulder, I got Ceausescu's permission to invite Sergiu Celibidache to visit Romania. A native Romanian living in Sweden, he was a mathematician who had become a conductor of international stature. Voicu's talent and charm persuaded Celibidache to tackle the job, and in less than a year he created a marvelous orchestra and trained Voicu to wield the baton.

When Dana, Mary, and I arrived at Luchian's, Voicu and his wife, Madelaine, were already there. Dana, as usual, first went over to pay her respects to a painting called *The Future*. Although it depicted a banal subject—the portrait of a young man and behind him in the gray mist a very old face, representing himself at the end of his life—it was done with enough sensitivity to impress the artist in her. Oprea arrived just in time for the dinner, which was sure to be delicious. Both Luchian and his wife, Silvia, loved to cook. During Luchian's dinners, his guests had to tell stories.

"I want to tell a story about Madame Aslan," Luchian's bass voice boomed across the room. "Is anybody interested?"

Everybody in Romania is interested in stories about Dr. Ana Aslan. Years ago she invented the controversial vitamin H3. It was first put on the market as "Gerovital" pills, which, she claimed, were a strong preventative against aging. When she later put a lotion containing H3 on the market and claimed it would prevent baldness, she became an international name. West Germans, in particular, fell hard for it. In the early 1970s she came out with Gerovital injections for sexual rejuvenation and became famous. The fact that Gerovital was not medically approved in most of the Western world only made it more desirable and expensive. By the mid-1970s, it had become a national treasure, although Western scientists maintained that Gerovital was nothing but a hoax. In 1975, I accompanied Ceausescu on a long official trip to South America. Toward the end, during our flight from Brazil to Mexico he remarked to me that, if the Mexican leaders would also insist on talking only about Dr. Aslan, he would call off the whole visit. As it turned out, they did indeed talk more about Aslan than about Ceausescu, exactly like all the other South American leaders we had met on that trip.

"Well," Luchian launched into his story, "I just got a phone call from Madame Aslan. She asked me for help, because she had been arrested at the Bucharest airport for hiding $800 under the large bun she wore her hair in."

"Is that true?" squeaked Oprea, looking over at me.

It was indeed. Despite her fame, she was not allowed to keep any of the money she made in foreign currency. That is the general rule in all the Soviet bloc, and Ceausescu is particularly anxious to enforce it. "It's a true story," I answered. "She asked me for help, too."

"What she did is a disgrace, a national disgrace," said Oprea in revulsion.

I told a story about Nadia Comaneci. "It was in Japan, shortly after the Montreal Olympics, that I first met Nadia in person. She was there as the star of a fund-raising gymnastics show. It was her fourteenth birthday that day, and I presented her with a huge cake."

"How nice of you," Silvia Luchian broke in. "What did she do with all the cakes she must have gotten there?"

"Mine was the only one. Unfortunately, I didn't know that she had an eating compulsion that was bad for her, and that her devoted coaches, Marta and Bela Karoly, were making a desperate effort to protect Nadia from herself. The Karolys let her blow out the candles but wouldn't even let her taste the cake."

"Is it true that her mother is nothing but a cleaning woman in some school, and her father a drunk?" asked Silvia.

"That's correct."

"Oh, no, Mike," Oprea broke in. "How could you do that? Don't you know the Comrade wants to keep that a secret? He's such a sensitive man."

By the end of 1977 Ceausescu had decided to change Nadia's coaches. "I don't want to share Nadia's fame with a couple of dirty *boanghen*," he said. Marta and Bela Karoly are of Hungarian descent. "We have to find Romanian coaches for her. People of Romanian blood." Soon thereafter, Nadia was moved from her native Onesti, a town in Moldavia, to Bucharest, where she was turned over to a collective team of coaches especially created and approved by Ceausescu. A Party activist was its head, and a Securitate officer his deputy.

I went on with my story. "Some weeks ago the minister of sport and tourism reported to the Comrade that Nadia had been missing for several weeks and nobody had been able to find her. 'You can't tell me that such a person can simply disappear in our country,' the Comrade told the minister of interior, ordering him to search to the ends of the earth until he found her."

"Is she dead?" Silvia screamed, almost hysterically.

"She was found last week. She'd gotten herself a boyfriend and was hiding out in his apartment."

"Such a sweet child," Mary interjected.

Now for my punch line. "I saw her that same day. She was obese, more than thirty pounds overweight. Her eating compulsion had gotten to her."

"Does the Comrade know?" asked Oprea.

"I was there when he was informed."

"Oh, dear. And he's so sensitive."

Marta and Bela Karoly, the coaching couple who discovered and created Nadia Comaneci, became virtually jobless in Romania, and in early 1980 they defected to the United States, where they are making a fabulous career for themselves. One of their first results is Mary Lou Retton. The other day I was looking at Mary Lou, so full of life, bouncing through a television commercial, and I could not help comparing Nadia to her. Mary Lou's bright and self-sufficient future shines out through every pore of her body. In contrast, Nadia was finished before she could even become an adult. There in Romania she will not be given a second chance. Only her name will be around for years, while Nadia herself will be housed and fed like a creature in the zoo.

"I'm sorry, but I don't have any stories about famous people," Voicu started out. "The National Philharmonic is scheduled to begin a tour abroad next week, and some butterfingers dropped our only French horn, which now has a crack," he complained. "Since we don't make French horns in Romania, I wrote a memorandum to the chairman of the Council for Socialist Culture and Education, asking for approval to import one. 'We don't have any foreign currency available,' came back the answer. So I sent a

Rosalyn Carter and Elena Ceausescu laughing together, with Pacepa looking on.
Mrs. Ceausescu later privately called Mrs. Carter "the peanut head."

Nicolae Ceausescu speaking at a National Press Club luncheon on April 13, 1978.
He was called upon by reporters to release from Romania the family of defector
Constantin Rauta.

President Jimmy Carter
toasts Romanian President
Ceausescu at a White
House dinner. Elena
Ceausescu is on the right.

Lt. General Ion Pacepa, left, with Henry Kissinger at President Ceausescu's arrival in the White House garden on April 12, 1978.

Hungarian-Americans outside the White House on April 13, 1978 protest the treatment of Hungarians living in Romania. One demonstrator waves a Hungarian flag with the center cut out.

AP/WIDE WORLD PHOTOS

WANTED

FOR THE MURDER OF HUNGARIAN TEACHERS IN RUMANIA

nti-Ceausescu demonstrators fill a New York City street. During his April 16-17 sit there, protest leaders were ordered to be killed by President Ceausescu.

OTO COURTESY OF HUNGARIAN HUMAN RIGHTS FOUNDATION

Elena and Nicolae Ceausescu, left, meeting with a group of Romanian Americans
Ceausescu's New York hotel room. Ion Pacepa is in the original photograph (top),
standing in front of the double doors. But when the photo was published in a
Romanian book after Pacepa's defection (bottom), his image was removed.

memorandum to the Comrade. It came back yesterday with the order to 'have it mended immediately.' And that's where I stand now."

"I can help you," Oprea broke in kindly. "Just tell me where it can be mended, and I'll give the order."

I gave Dana a stern look, and she swallowed the laugh on her lips.

Voicu brought his story to an end. "When Celibidache heard that I might have to go to the Berlin Concert Hall with a French horn that had been glued back together, he almost had a heart attack."

As we rose to leave the table, Oprea looked happy that dinner was over before it was his turn to tell a story. Cognac glass in hand, he dragged me conspiratorially over to a corner.

"I have an extraordinary piece of news. This evening the Comrade gave me the order to cut our arms budget by fifty percent. He said that military expenses should appear to be less than five percent of our national budget. You know the Comrade. He is such a lover of peace." Oprea started whispering in my ear about the discussion he had had with Ceausescu. "Do you know what he said about the Leopard II tank we're going to start building? He said, 'Put its cost in the civilian budget, as expenses for tractors.' Isn't that marvelously simple?" Oprea emptied his cognac glass, wiping his mouth with the back of his hand. "Mike, you can't imagine what the Comrade said about the new incendiary industry we're now developing with 'Malek.' He said, 'Show the money for it as being for new detergent factories.' Why can't I come up with just half the ideas the Comrade has in his head?"

Within the Warsaw Pact, the published defense figures are coordinated by the Kremlin and formally approved by the politburo of each member country. These figures, which are far from the real ones, have only propaganda and disinformation value. They are basically intended to provide political meat for nonruling Communist parties in the West and for international peace movements, as well as to shield the true defense effort from Western analysis. The real, unpublished defense budget has the highest possible security classification, and only a handful of people have the right to know it in its entirety. In Romania, Oprea and I were among them. And now Ceausescu was trying to fool even these few. It probably would not make much difference though, as in Communist countries the monetary amounts given in the national currency have little real value anyway.

When the dinner was over, Luchian came downstairs with us. In the lobby of his apartment building—another elegant old vestige of capitalism, now used to house high-ranking government officials—he caught my arm. "About the decree I wrote for the new Department of State Security the Comrade wants to create. Last night, exactly at eight, as he had asked, Postelnicu had the decrees on his desk."

"Decrees?"

"Yes. I sent him two, the one I wrote and another the way he wanted—you know, with the DGTO and all the other secret units in it. On top I put a note giving him my personal views on his version."

"It's good you stated your position in writing."

"The devil it is. It wasn't yet nine o'clock this morning when the Comrade called me in, with the Constitution. There was the Comrade standing behind his desk, with *Madame* next to him and Postelnicu in the middle of the room. 'Read me Article 33,' the Comrade shouted, before I had even closed the door. I didn't need to read it. I know the Constitution by heart. After all, I wrote it. Article 33 says flatly that, 'The secrecy of correspondence and of telephone conversations shall be guaranteed.'[2] That was enough to make the Comrade explode. 'How could you send me a decree referring to telephone intercepts and mail censorship? Just to have my signature on it and send it to Free Europe?' I respectfully replied that it was not my decree but one ordered by Postelnicu, and that I had given Postelnicu another version of the same decree omitting all reference to the DGTO. 'That's a lie,' I heard Postelnicu saying. 'He didn't give me anything else, Comrade Ceausescu.' Then he turned to me: 'Why are you trying to compromise me in front of the Supreme Commander and Comrade Elena, Luchian?' The Comrade stared at both of us, as if trying to figure out which one of us was lying, and then he ordered me to submit a new decree Monday morning that was in conformity with the Constitution, and to show it to you first, Mike."

"Thanks. That's all I needed!"

[2]*Romanian Constitution*, p. 12.

"Before I could get away, *Madame* jumped on me," Luchian went on. "She said that it was all my fault and that I should be trying to protect the Comrade, and herself, and Postelnicu, that that was my role, and so on and so forth. But I'm not made of stone, either. I said once more, loud and clear, that I had told Postelnicu everything, but that Postelnicu was stubborn as a mule."

"Did you really say 'mule'?"

"Of course I did. *Madame* became furious and started yelling at me, but I just walked out," Luchian added, with a nervous tremor in his voice. I could just picture this big, calm bear with Elena jumping down his throat, and I could hear him arguing with her in his deep, bass. But I was afraid for him. Elena never forgets.

CHAPTER

XIII

"COME see me." The click of the telephone being hung up was just as unexpected as its ring had been. When Ceausescu calls someone, he never gives his name. Nor, like now, does he say where he is. You are on your own.

From General Nicolae Stan, chief of Ceausescu's protective service, I learned that he was at his residence in Snagov.

Paraschiv covered the 20-plus miles from my office to Snagov as fast as he could. The access road from the national highway to Ceausescu's residence, entirely closed to the public and usually empty, proved to be very busy on this morning. Inside the woods, around the first bend, there were two Soviet-built GAZ jeeps blocking the road. A colonel from the security troops came over to my car.

SECURITATE TROOPS IN SITUATION C

"Long life to the general," said he, respectfully touching his hand to his helmet in salute. Armed with a submachine gun, he was decked out in complete battle gear, including gas mask. Several yards farther, on both sides of the road, two armored vehicles trained their machine guns on my car. "The general will forgive me, but my orders say that no one may pass this point without the express confirmation of the commander-in-chief." Then he spoke into a portable radio telephone: "This is checkpoint zero zero one five. Checkpoint zero zero fifteen calling zero zero ten."

In the Warsaw Pact system, a zero in front of a military unit's

210

numerical designation means that it is secret. Two zeros mean that it is top secret.

"This is zero zero ten. This is zero zero ten," came back a voice I knew very well. It was that of General Luigi Martis, the commander of the security troops, a special command within the Ministry of Interior.

Copied after the Soviet model, the Romanian Securitate Troops have since 1950 been a special service branch beyond the traditional army, navy, and air force, with its own uniform and regulations and subordinate only to the general secretary of the Communist Party, through his minister of interior. The troops constitute an elite Communist military force, strongly indoctrinated—the ratio of political commissars is five times that of the Ministry of Defense—with substantially better equipment and standard of living, and more severe discipline than any other Romanian military unit. Their main task is to protect the Communist Party's central and regional headquarters and the central government, and to prevent the takeover of the national radio and television stations by hostile forces wanting to communicate with the population. After the Soviet invasion of Czechoslovakia, however, their actual duty became the physical protection of Ceausescu and his family against any foreign or domestic *coup d'etat*, including one originating with the Romanian military forces themselves. Over the course of time, their light arms were supplemented with artillery and armored vehicles, and an ultra-secret chemical and bacteriological unit was added in 1976. The bulk of the Securitate Troops forces were no longer kept around the Communist Party headquarters but around Ceausescu himself. They were in Baneasa during the season when Ceausescu had his headquarters in Bucharest or in Snagov, on the Black Sea during the summer months when he moved to Neptun, and in the Carpathian Mountains in the wintertime when Ceausescu's residence and office were in Predeal and Sinaia.

"Zero zero sixty-two is at zero zero fifteen. With car and driver," reported the colonel.

"This is zero zero ten. Zero zero sixty-two is approved by zero zero one. Allow his transit according to procedure C. Over."

"Roger from zero zero fifteen."

"Once more, Comrade General, please excuse the delay," said the colonel, "and the procedure. We are in Situation C, and you know that means combat alert."

"That's all right, Colonel. Do your duty."

Soviet-made armored vehicles, parked every hundred yards along the edge of the woods, kept my car under the constant watch of their machine guns. Uniformed troops with specially trained dogs were patrolling everywhere. All that completely disappeared from sight after I passed through the main gate, entering the fenced area of the residence.

Ceausescu's imposing Snagov residence was used mostly in the spring and fall. It looks out on the large Snagov Lake, the only significant body of water near Bucharest, in an area now restricted to the top *nomenclatura*. Constructed in modern but typically Romanian style, the residence has several additional apartments for his children, his mother, and other relatives. In a separate building there is a huge wine cellar with tables and chairs to accommodate more than twenty people, a movie theater, and a bowling alley. The court for volleyball, Ceausescu's favorite sport, is kept under constant maintenance, ready any time Ceausescu wants to humiliate his adversary team, which was usually headed by the prime minister. In front, moored at a long dock made entirely of marble, there used to be a Riva express cruiser, which I had purchased for Ceausescu a couple of years earlier in Italy, and which was mostly used by his son Nicu. The whole residence, except for the lakefront side, is surrounded by a high wooden fence, which is patrolled from the outside by uniformed security troops and militiamen with dogs.

Constantin Manea was waiting for me in front of the main building. "Hi, Boss. Sorry for the discomfort," rang out in his usual steady, monotonous voice, which neither fire nor earthquake could disturb. "I've got a cup of coffee for us in the gazebo. You still have to wait for Stefan Andrei. The Comrade ordered that you both go in together," he explained, crossing the garden to the wooden gazebo covered with climbing roses.

"After the Comrade left you so unexpectedly in his office yesterday, he came directly here," said the pale, tired Manea. "At around sixteen hundred hours," he went on, military-style, "the Comrade phoned me. Himself. That happens very rarely. 'Come here and bring the "M" file with you,' he said. I could hardly recognize his voice. I got here in less than an hour, bringing the Mobilization files I took out of the Comrade's own vault.

"Comrade Elena got here in the afternoon. Shortly after she came, the Comrade ordered me to call General Luigi Martis. 'Get him on the phone in person, and tell him to come here without telling anybody, not even the minister of interior,' was the Comrade's firm order. Martis spent more than an hour with the Comrade and Comrade Elena in this gazebo yesterday afternoon. A couple of hours after Martis left, we were surrounded by his troops. The Comrade gave me the order that no one, including the prime minister, should come here unless approved by himself." Manea paused, sipping his coffee.

"During the night Comrade Elena asked me to call the doctor. The Comrade had heart and respiratory problems. I don't think he has slept a wink. He looks terribly tired." A twitch of his hands betrayed Manea's weariness and inner tension. "All that happened after the Comrade tore up the presidential decree about Militaru."

Colonel Bajenaru, Ceausescu's main bodyguard, stepped out onto the walk, a few yards from the gazebo. "Stefan Andrei is here. What should I do?"

"Keep him outside. We'll be there in a second."

The son of a very poor family in a little pastoral village in Ceausescu's native Oltenia, Stefan Andrei early showed a quick mind and unusual spontaneity, and he was encouraged to continue his education. On the basis of his dynamic mind and fantastic memory, he made his way from shepherd, to student, to secretary of the Party's Central Committee, and since March 8, 1978, to minister of foreign affairs.

Andrei's doctoral thesis on international Communist movements has become a reference work for the Central Committee of the Romanian Communist Party. Noticed by Ceausescu soon after he came to power, Andrei was apppointed deputy chief of the International Section of the Central Committee and put in charge of relations with foreign Communist Parties and movements. In April 1972 he was appointed secretary for foreign relations of the Party's Central Committee, and in November 1974, member of the Permanent Bureau of the Political Executive Committee. Andrei always considered his positions within the Central Committee nothing more than stepping stones to becoming minister of foreign affairs, his life-long dream. In March 1978 his dream finally came true.

Andrei was already inside the gazebo, having tagged along behind Bajenaru. "What's going on here, Mike? Why all this commotion, Manea?" asked the tall Andrei, gesticulating as usual.

"Fix your necktie, Andrei," said Manea. "And comb your hair." Constantly agitated all the time that he was not asleep, Andrei's shirt collar was always unbuttoned, his tie askew, and his sparse hair flying in all directions.

"Is anything wrong with the Comrade?" asked Andrei, while going through the motions of straightening his tie and smoothing down his hair with the flat of his hand.

A WORRIED CEAUSESCU

"You should never be in a hurry to hear bad news, Andrei," said Manea philosophically. "Come join us for a cup of coffee." Looking at Bajenaru, he went on. "Tell the Comrade that Andrei and Pacepa are here. But give us ten minutes or so first to finish our coffee."

We were at the front of the residence when, fifteen minutes later, Ceausescu himself came to the door. "You are here," he said, for lack of anything better to say. "Let's go over to the gazebo. The air is better out there than inside."

Ceausescu was wearing a new white turtleneck sweater, but he still had on yesterday's wrinkled, dark gray pants, and the slippers on his feet made the usually quick-moving Ceausescu look old and tired. His face was very pale, his eyes underlined by dark rings.

"My tea," he ordered Bajenaru. Ceausescu chewed his upper lip and sucked in the air between his teeth with a loud wheeze. He always does that when he is tense or nervous. "I h-have unquestionable information t-that Brezhnev is p-plotting against me," he began, giving me a withering glance as if to seal my lips. "W-What have I ever done to b-bother Brezhnev?" he continued, now looking at Andrei. "Just because I didn't break off d-diplomatic relations with Israel after the Six Day War, as he wanted?"

"That's an old story, Comrade Ceausescu," temporized a totally puzzled Andrei, looking from one to the other of us with the despair of a fellow who has just fallen from the moon.

"O-Old or n-new, the Bear hasn't forgotten it and won't ever f-forgive it."

"You just had an exchange with Menachem Begin. There's almost nobody in the Romanian Party or government who knows anything about it, but Pungan is by now already in Moscow to report on it," said Andrei, intuitively trying to chase away Ceausescu's black clouds of doubt, even though he did not yet really understand what the problem was. "The Kremlin has nothing but profit from your relations with Israel. Isn't it true that you, a Communist leader, are trying to bring peace to the Middle East? Aren't you trying to get the Soviets to the conference table?"

Ceausescu's head bobbed up, his small, badger-like eyes darting from one of us to the other. Peace in the Middle East that would bring him a Nobel Prize was his fondest dream.

"Because I was the first in the Warsaw Pact to establish diplomatic relations with West Germany?"

"That's obsolete, Comrade Ceausescu. Everyone in the Warsaw Pact has done that by now."

"Because I withdrew Nadia from the World Gymnastics Championship in Moscow in protest against the Soviet and East German judges?"

"That's not Communist fundamentals. That's sports. That was nothing but public relations to gain popularity with the capitalist media. Nobody got hurt."

This dialogue between Andrei and Ceausescu went on and on. As usual, Andrei's superb logic and his optimistic nature started to raise Ceausescu's spirits. There was no doubt that this was why he had called Andrei there. Ceausescu needed to hear from his new foreign minister that he had been right.

"You know, comrades, I am not some swell-headed Tito out to befoul the basic tenets of Communism. Except for Moscow, Bucharest is the only Communist government to make private property not only taboo, but also something to be ashamed of. Isn't that so, Andrei?"

"Of course it is, Comrade Ceausescu."

"I'm not some idiot Dubcek, to tolerate chaos and provoke counterrevolution. Nowhere in the Warsaw Pact is the population covered better than in Romania. Who else in the whole Pact has one security officer for every fifteen people? Tell me, Pacepa."

"There isn't anyone else."

"You know, comrades, I've been a Communist since I was fifteen. Communism is everything to me. I never did, and I never will make ideological compromises. When it comes to Marxism, I don't go just half-way."

Elena came shuffling up to us in her slippers. Her dressing gown was only partly buttoned, and her long, tired, ashen face wore a sour expression.

"There you are, comrade," Elena began with irritation. "I've been looking everywhere for you. What's going on here? Is this a Party Congress or what?"

No one made any move to answer her.

"Who do you think you are, comrades?" she asked, measuring Andrei and me from head to toe. "Do you think the Comrade hasn't got anything better to do than to listen to your drivel? For shame!"

"I want to make a visit to Peking as soon as possible," Ceausescu intervened. "That's why I called you both over."

"You're a genius," Andrei cried, leaping to his feet. "April in Washington with the American president, May in Peking with the new Chinese general secretary, and June in London with the queen. We'll saturate the press all around the whole world with pictures of you with Jimmy Carter, with the Chinese, and with the queen. I'd give my eyeteeth to see Brezhnev's face when he hears."

A LESSON IN COMMUNISM

"If so, let's get going. Start moving on it today, Andrei. I want to go to Peking between my visits to Washington and London."

"Wouldn't it be better to wait and have the visit approved by the Political Executive Committee?" Andrei suggested bureaucratically. At that time this body had a regular session once a week, chaired by Ceausescu and followed by a short press release.

"Approved by whom?" squawked Elena.

"By the Political Executive Committee, Comrade Elena."

"Aren't you sweet! Who do you think you are, comrade?" Elena exploded, grabbing at Andrei's lapels so hard I thought she would rip his jacket right off his back.

"Listen to him, Nick. The Po-li-ti-cal Ex-e-cu-tive Com-mit-tee," she tried to imitate Andrei, gesturing broadly. "Maybe you think you were made in a test tube, not created by the Comrade and me. You were nothing but a miserable shepherd until the Party sent you off to get an education. Have you forgotten who the Party is? I'm asking you a question. Can't you hear me?"

"Of course I can, Comrade Elena."

"As far as you're concerned, the Party is the Comrade and me. Yesterday we made you a minister, tomorrow we can make you nothing but a damned shit. Believe me.

"I believe you, Comrade Elena."

"Don't you make fun of me, you miserable scum. I'll make you curse your mother for ever having brought you into this world, if you can't learn who your betters are."

Ceausescu tried to conciliate. "Enough, Elena. Let him go. He has enough to do."

"No, comrade. That was too much. If he doesn't know that, as far as he's concerned, the Political Executive Committee is you and me, then he doesn't have to go anywhere. He should be fired, here and now."

"All right, Elena. We'll decide that later. Now let him go."

"I'll tell you who the Political Executive Committee is, *Monsieur,*" Elena went at Andrei again, yanking at his tie. "It's a bunch of miserable creatures who yesterday were shit and today have limousines. That's all they are. The Comrade and I cleaned them up and put them there. When we don't need them any more, they'll be shit again. Don't you understand?"

"I do, Comrade Elena."

"What would you be, *Monsieur,* if we should fire you today? A miserable shit again. The house you enjoy with your precious wife isn't yours. It belongs to the Party. So does your car, and everything else you have. That's Communism, *Monsieur,* in case you haven't learned. In Communism no one has anything for himself. You are rewarded only as long as you are useful to the Party."

Ceausescu took Elena's hand and started to pull her away from the gazebo. "Come, dear. Let's have lunch." They had just begun walking toward the residence, when Elena turned her head back for a final salvo.

"Just look at that miserable Maurer. As long as he was loyal to the Comrade and me, he was prime minister. He could enjoy traveling all around the world. Who met Chou En Lai? Maurer. Who met the Pope? Maurer. When he started to forget who he was working for, he got fired. F-I-R-E-D, comrade. You don't believe that fairy tale about his poor health and resignation, do you?"

After the Ceausescus had left, Andrei and I sat down, drained of all emotion.

"I would give ten years of my life to see the Comrade married to someone else," said Andrei, wiping the perspiration from his forehead.

"You may have to give up your empire, Andrei," said Manea, who had come out to the gazebo, "if you can't learn to control your mouth." His eyes showed he meant it. "Comrade Elena wants the Comrade to fire you and appoint her brother-in-law in your place." Manea held up a small, gold-plated pillbox I had once brought him from Paris. "You ought to have a little box like this, Andrei. Fill it with shit and eat a little bit of it every time your tongue itches. Especially when you're with Comrade Elena. She's deadly serious."

XIV

"I'VE got two bags of documents here, and I'll need a couple of tables in the conference room to spread them out on," I told Manea as soon as I arrived at Snagov.

"The Comrade and Elena just came back from Bucharest. Their mood is still black. The Comrade has already asked for you three times, Boss."

"Can you put this out for me, Professor? The bags are numbered, and the files inside are marked with letters. Just set out the contents of each bag in alphabetical order."

"I'll take care of it, Boss. See what you can do for the Comrade. If you can maneuver him over to the bowling alley, we may all make it through another day."

Ceausescu was walking alone, with Bajenaru trotting like a dog a few steps behind him.

"What's new, Pacepa" I heard, even before I could fall into step with him. From the back, he looked much older than usual.

"BAPTIST" DISINFORMATION FOR CARTER

"I have a telegram from Washington that has just been decoded."

"About Carter?"

"Sort of. The station reports that 'Arsene,' a devoted and long-time agent who is now a high-ranking clergyman in the Baptist Church of the United States, was able to speak to Carter's personal minister on several occasions."

"Religion is Carter's weakness. That's where we've got to hit him."

"The station reports that, at their last meeting, the agent gave Carter's minister a letter from a 'group of Baptist ministers' describing the freedom of worship enjoyed in Romania, as opposed to the situation in all other Communist countries, and stressing the genuine human rights of the Romanian people."

"That's my letter."

"Yes, comrade. That's the letter you dictated to me. The Disinformation Service just put the clergymen's signatures on it."

"That's good news," Ceausescu exclaimed, looking up at me. "Give me the telegram." He snapped his fingers, and Bajenaru immediately brought him a pair of reading glasses.

When Ceausescu finished the telegram, his eyes were glistening for the first time in three days. "We should cultivate this channel to put the notion into Carter's head that Romania is different. That our Communism is not Soviet-style but Western. That we don't deny Western values—we respect them. If he wants human rights, let's give him human rights. We have to let that message keep dripping down onto his head." Ceausescu's mood of mourning started to change, and his step became sprightlier. "Speaking of religion. Last week Coman told me about some Bibles on cassettes. I didn't really understand. What's the story?"

"Our station in New York reported that by the end of last year ten thousand copies of the Bible had been put on cassettes, because it was believed that cassettes would be easier to smuggle into Romania than actual Bibles. The station provided a copy of the smuggling plan. Last week the first cassettes were confiscated at the border and at the mail censorship center.

"That's interesting. How many Bibles did you say?"

"Ten thousand."

"If each Bible is on only ten cassettes, which isn't even possible, that makes one hundred thousand. Give them all to the Securitate, to be erased and used in their monitoring work. That holds good from now on, up to the end of that stupid American operation. That's not the church. That's the CIA. What else is new?"

"There's a case in West Germany . . ."

"Don't you have any good news about America?" Ceausescu

interrupted. "I'm about to go there to face the number one enemy in his own den."

"This is an American story. It just happened to take place in West Germany."

"Go on."

"In the late 1950s, when I was chief of station there, a German born in Romania was recruited as an agent. 'Balthazar' is his code name. He was a janitor at an American military unit near Munich."

"Has he helped recruit any American officers?"

"Not yet. But some time after he had been recruited, he suddenly started turning over bags of classified military documents, as many as his car would hold."

"American documents?"

"Yes. He had been put in charge of burning the classified military documents marked for destruction."

"That's good." A shy smile made an effort to creep onto Ceausescu's lips.

"The documents were immediately sent to Moscow by the KGB advisors, and soon afterwards two KGB generals came to Bucharest. Moscow decided that, if well managed, the case could be of great value. 'Balthazar' became a joint effort. He was clandestinely brought to a safehouse in Austria and trained in how to secretly photograph the military documents and how to use deaddrops to pass the rolls of film."

AGENTS AT RADIO FREE EUROPE

"Was he tame?"

"Yes, comrade. He was so tame that he recruited his wife, who was a secretary at the Munich headquarters of Radio Free Europe."

"Do I know her?" Ceausescu interrupted. He is always interested in Radio Free Europe.

"I don't think so. She hasn't been in direct contact, only through her husband. She would bring home documents, and he would photograph them and pass them to us, together with the military documents. Now comes the news."

"Good news, I hope."

"Basically, yes. But also some bad news."

"I don't need any more bad news," he said with a wink, in a much better mood now.

"The good news is that last week 'Balthazar' came to his meeting in Salzburg and reported that there was still no suspicion of him. But he brought his wife with him, although it was against the rules we had with him. During the meeting poor, quiet 'Balthazar' could hardly open his mouth. She did all the talking."

"What a shrew."

"She said she had two important pieces of news for us. For one thing, her husband's military unit had been given new military equipment, and he could photograph the documentation for it. Secondly, she had become the personal secretary of the central news division director for both Radio Free Europe and Radio Liberty, with access to their most confidential files. She said she could now provide their documents on not only Romania but also the Soviet Union and other bloc countries."

"Put the case officer in for a medal."

"Her huge handbag was full of film cassettes. 'Here's a modest sample of what we can now bring you,' she said, according to the station report."

"Give them a bonus."

"Now the bad news," I went on, starting to read from the station report. " 'Balthazar's' wife stressed that they had spent over twenty years working for Romanian intelligence, risking their freedom at every one of the many hundreds of meetings her husband had held with us. She added that, despite this, they were as poor as they had been twenty years before." I put the report back in my briefcase. "The bottom line, Comrade Ceausescu, is that she threatened to break off contact unless we agreed to pay each of them a monthly salary, additional money for each document supplied, and a pension after their retirement."

"We do pay some of our agents that way, don't we?"

"Yes. But the catch, the station says, is that she wants a written commitment from us."

"In writing?"

"Yes, comrade. That's why I'm reporting the case to you."

"What's in the films she gave us?"

"Photographs of several American training and maintenance

manuals from the new military equipment they just got. From Radio Free Europe she turned over some photocopies of letters received from Romania. She claimed she could provide the whole archive containing many thousands of letters, as well as the ones received in the future."

"That's exactly what I want, to identify all those criminals who write to Free Europe and put them behind bars." Ceausescu paused, minutely studying his shoes. "Could she plant a plastic bomb in her director's office?"

"We'll have to check out her courage, comrade."

"She wouldn't need to know it was an explosive. She could very well think that it was just a file or a briefcase that we were asking her to plant." By now he had stopped walking and was looking deep into my eyes. "Have several remote-controlled plastic bombs made up. Plastic explosives disguised as thick file folders and books. That CIA wasp's nest has long since surpassed the limits of Elena's and my patience. Clear?"

"Yes, comrade."

Radio Free Europe has always been a top priority for Ceausescu because of its strong criticism of his government's human rights record. The ridiculous idea of using powerful bombs to scare the Romanian Department had, however, become an obsession with him only since the radio had begun making caustic remarks about his and Elena's personality cult.

Radio Liberty/Radio Free Europe has long been a thorn in the flesh not only of Ceausescu but also of all the other Soviet bloc leaders. Soviet leader Mikhail Gorbachev is certainly no exception. In June 1986, for example, in an article attributed to F. Bobkov, first deputy chairman of the KGB, Soviet citizens are warned that: "The secret services of imperialist states . . . are conducting subversive work against socialism in all directions, including the sphere of ideology. . . . The U.S. Congress has earmarked $250 million for the 'Liberty-Free Europe' radio corporation for 1986–87. . . . This radio corporation, which has operated under the guidance of the CIA for more than 3 decades, is the main center for subversive propaganda against the USSR and European socialist countries. . . . 'Radio Liberty-Radio Free Europe' is also an important center for political intelligence against the USSR. The activities of this radio station's leadership *are aimed at organizing various hostile acts, including illegal infiltration of the country, at collecting biased information, and at coordinating subversive work against the USSR.*[1]

"When can I take a look at 'Balthazar's' materials, Pacepa."

"I brought them with me. They're in your conference room."

Ceausescu wheeled around and began walking briskly toward the house. Manea had carefully laid out the files on several tables in the conference room. We started with the military section.

"Very interesting. We should set up a special, very secret task force at the Ministry of Defense to work with them."

The letters addressed to Radio Free Europe were written in Romanian, and Ceausescu read them himself, nervously turning over page after page.

"Some of these writers should be executed. The rest can end up in the salt mines. I want Coman to identify every single author. And I want to get the rest of the letters received by Free Europe. All of them."

When we were outside in the garden, he resumed his tirade. "I don't care how much we have to pay. But I want every, I repeat, every single letter Free Europe has received or will receive from Romania. I want the names of all those rats writing them. I intend to put order into this country, once and for all."

Ceausescu walked in silence for a long time. As far as he is concerned, Radio Free Europe's Romanian broadcasts are CIA operations designed to damage his personal credibility and prestige. They are his worst nightmare.

Finally he spoke. "We must make a deal with the 'Balthazars.' If they won't keep going without a written commitment, you'll have to find some way to give it to them. Stamp it top secret and tell them that we have to hold onto papers that are top secret. If they don't swallow that, tell them you'll put it into a safe deposit box with two different keys, one for us, one for them, so that neither party can open it alone. Be sure to make a copy of their key. Will that work?"

"I hope so, comrade."

[1] F. Bobkov, "Political Vigilance—A Requirement of the Times," Moscow: *Politicheskoye Samoobrazovaniye*, June 1986, No. 6 (May 22, 1986), pp. 25–33.

"Let's roll a few balls," concluded Ceausescu, leading the way to the bowling alley.

I was an easy mark for him that day. If his ball rolled into the gutter, he accused Bajenaru or one of his other bodyguards of having made some imaginary noise, and he would take his turn over. When by chance I got a strike, he claimed that it was somehow irregular and made me bowl another ball. The victorious Ceausescu finally stopped only because he became tired. "Let's go to the cellar," he proposed.

THE BEAR WANTS AMERICAN TECHNOLOGY

Romanian folk music, Ceausescu's favorite, was flooding through the whole wine cellar as we entered. Before we were able to reach a table, a waiter in black-tie materialized out of nowhere holding a tray with a newly opened bottle of wine and one large glass. Known as "Odobesti Yellow," it is Ceausescu's favorite, a flavorful wine of the same color and consistency as sunflower oil, which is made in very limited quantities in Odobesti, a Moldavian village renowned for its wines. Ceausescu downed two glasses on his feet, then sat down in his favorite easy chair beside a heavy, round oak table. The waiter refilled Ceausescu's glass and set the bottle down beside him in an ice bucket containing no ice—Ceausescu does not want his drinks cold, in order to protect his vocal chords. A few minutes later the waiter came out with another ice bucket, this one with ice, containing a bottle of good domestic wine. This one was for me.

When Ceausescu has a glass of wine sitting in front of him, he likes to tell stories. "When I met Brezhnev last month," he started out, after emptying one more glass, "he went out of his way to persuade me to double our intelligence effort in America. Except for a couple of hours at the KGB's electronics city, I spent the whole time talking with the Bear at the Kremlin. Sunday evening, before I left, he hosted a candlelight dinner in his private Kremlin dining room. Two white-tie waiters, one for me and one for him, came in just to serve us. Mine spoke Romanian. There was Romanian food for me, Russian for him. Everything was suspiciously delicious and subdued. The Bear launched into his lecture immediately after the soup. He quoted Lenin on

American capitalism, the number one enemy of the proletariat. In his fat head he believes he is the only one who hates American capitalism. It was on the tip of my tongue to say that I hated capitalism ten times more than he did; that I was being exploited by capitalism, while he wasn't; that he'd spent his whole life under Communism and didn't know what it was like to be tortured in a capitalist jail."

Ceausescu emptied two more glasses, then snapped his fingers for a new bottle.

"After the main course," he went on, "the Bear started massaging my brain again. 'American science and technology are not the property of the American capitalists but of the American proletariat and intellectuals who developed it, and through them they therefore belong to the world revolution of the proletariat.' As if I needed an ideological indoctrination. I couldn't stand it any more. I told him that if he wanted more American technology, then he should have more intelligence officers over there. That I had abandoned Moscow's principle of fifty-fifty diplomats and intelligence officers in the West. That I couldn't afford the luxury of sending one man to the West for official duties—as a diplomat, journalist, professor, or whatever—and another to perform intelligence tasks. That every Romanian representative abroad had to be an intelligence officer under deep cover. That in America even our ambassador was a colonel under deep cover, known as such by only two or three people in all of Romania. And do you know what the Bear said?"

"No, comrade."

"'All an ambassador can do is influence,' the Bear said, 'but the first thing I want from America is their military codes and their new military technology. Influence comes next.' That's the difference between us. For me, influence comes first. I firmly believe it can open the tightest doors, including technological ones. If Moscow gets a younger man in the Kremlin after the Bear croaks, he'll do exactly as I do. I'll lay you a hundred to one on that."

After draining his glass, Ceausescu nervously snapped his fingers for yet another, then went on with his story. "Only when the coffee and cognac were served did the Bear get to the point. 'In the life and death struggle against capitalism,' he said, 'whoever controls space controls the earth.' Then he finally asked me for more help in acquiring new space technology. Anti-ballistic missile systems, space lasers and radars are what he especially wants. 'You,' said the Bear, 'have a much better position in Washington than I do.' I liked that."

Snapping his fingers again, Ceausescu ordered bread with tomatoes, onions, and feta cheese. "How is Nicolae doing?" he asked me, referring to Nicolae Nicolae, the Romanian ambassador in Washington.

"He's now working on recruiting two State Department officers."

"Go-o-od! Push him toward the Congress and White House, too." Ceausescu started to eat, using his fingers. "We have over 300,000 Romanian emigres of the first and second generation in the United States. We should recruit as many as we can and give them financial support to help get jobs in the White House, Congress, State Department, Pentagon, everywhere. My greatest dream is to have the descendant of a Romanian emigre become American president and then to make another official visit there."

The door slammed noisily, and Elena appeared. "Is that fair, comrades? One of us working, while the others here drinking?" she said with a large smile, showing off her dull, yellow teeth. "What's going on here?"

"Pacepa has just been showing me some of his documents."

"It must have been more than that," she teased, looking pointedly at our glasses. "What are you keeping from me, dear?" she asked, using her sweetest voice.

The waiter appeared from nowhere with a bottle of Cordon Rouge champagne in an ice bucket. That is what Elena always drinks.

"Tell her about 'Balthazar,' Pacepa," Ceausescu ordered me, trying to preserve Elena's sudden good mood. "Explain how a simple janitor, without any clearances, was given secret military documents to burn in his furnace and instead passed them on to us."

I summarized the case, without saying anything about the wife and her job at Radio Free Europe.

Elena was not impressed. "What's so new about that, Nick? The Yankees have never been known for being able to keep secrets."

"As far as political information goes, you are probably right. But we're talking about military data."

"They're even careless with their nuclear secrets. If that weren't true, and if the Rosenbergs hadn't been able to arm Communism with the nuclear bomb, we probably wouldn't be here today. Nor would Brezhnev be in Moscow. And don't forget, half of the job was done by a woman. We ought to make Ethel Rosenberg an international heroine."

"Tell her about 'Balthazar's' wife, Pacepa."

I did as I was told and reported the rest of the case.

"Now that's a woman! What of it, if she wants to make a buck or two off us? Can we identify the writers if we get the letters sent to Free Europe?"

"Of course we can. That's what I was talking over with Pacepa."

"So we'll go ahead with it, won't we? And you, Pacepa, you'll give me the names of the scum who are raking the Comrade and me over the coals. You'll see, in only a couple of months those *messieurs* at Free Europe won't be getting any more anonymous letters."

After Elena had emptied her second bottle of Cordon Rouge, she moved affectionately onto Ceausescu's lap. "I want you, Nick," she purred sweetly, rubbing one of his legs with hers.

He was not yet finished with me. "Be back here by nine—with Andrei."

The Ceausescus left hand in hand. "Take care of the 'Balthazars,' Pacepa," he said as his last word, going toward his residence.

A few years ago the American press reported: "On May 8, 1981 Bavarian state police showed up at the headquarters of Radio Free Europe-Radio Liberty in Munich and arrested a German employee on charges of spying for the Romanian intelligence service. What was particularly shocking was that the suspected espionage agent . . . was the personal secretary of the central news division director of the U.S. government-owned radio stations. She had been working at RFE since 1952. . . . The woman's husband was also arrested as a spy."[2]

[2]Jack Anderson, "The Ante Rises Over Radio Free Europe," *The Washington Post*, July 25, 1981, p. B7.

Getting Ready for America

When I got back to Snagov in the afternoon, Stefan Andrei was there drinking coffee with Manea. At nine sharp, Bajenaru came out. "The Comrade is waiting for you."

"Is Comrade Elena there, too?" cautiously asked Andrei.

"No. She is with her photographers."

Ceausescu was in his private study. "I've been thinking that Arafat's recognition by Willy Brandt's Socialist International might be a good first step." After giving me a wink, Ceausescu looked straight at Andrei. "I want you to go to Bonn with Pacepa and give Brandt a personal message from me." Standing behind his desk, Ceausescu developed his thought further. Brandt had good relations with Kreisky. Despite the fact that he was a Jew, Kreisky seemed to be responding favorably to Romania's attempt to have him give Arafat official recognition. "You know how to ask Brandt for a friendly hand, comrades. And invite him to come visit Romania as my personal guest. I want to work on him, too. That's all."

"May I go?" asked Andrei.

Ceausescu nodded, at the same time making a sign with one hand that I should remain behind. "Are you ready for America?"

"I think so."

"I just want to go over a few points. First, I don't want *any* emigré demonstrations when I'm there. None."

"I've instructed Nicolae and the chief of station."

"Second, I want a good book exhibit."

"The ambassador is personally taking care of it."

"And the books about me?"

"It will include not only books about you but also the books you yourself have written."

"With portraits of me and Elena?"

"Yes, comrade."

"Do you have the new ones, in color?"

"Dumitru Popescu gave them to me yesterday." He was the Party secretary for propaganda.

"Is my television interview all set?"

"In principle, yes, with ABC."

"Be careful. That may be a two-edged sword. Have we forgotten anything? Yes, the Hungarians. No Kiraly stories in Congress. No critical articles in the press. That's an order."

"The New York station is in charge of that. Most of the Hungarian emigrés are concentrated there."

"The ambassador there is not an intelligence officer, is he?" The ambassador in New York at that time was Ion Datcu.

"No, comrade, only an agent. But he does his job."

"Remind me when we're there. I'll make him a colonel. That's a high enough rank to make him do something for it."

"Understood, comrade."

Ceausescu suddenly turned his back and left the office.

ATHENEE PALACE AS INTELLIGENCE FACTORY

For that evening, Oprea had organized a dinner party in a private salon of the Athenee Palace Hotel, to which he had invited his best friends. It was paid for by the DIE as a "reward" for the members of the government who had most actively supported its technological intelligence operations.

The Athenee Palace was built shortly before World War II, when it was one of the most luxurious hotels in the Balkans. In 1948, it was nationalized, and in the early 1950s a KGB advisor spent three years transforming it into a special hotel for Western visitors.

Over the years the Athenee Palace had become a joint Securitate-DIE project and a masterful, Soviet-style intelligence operation. Every one of its over 300 employees, from the top manager to the lowliest scrubwoman, was either an intelligence officer or a recruited agent. The hotel's general director, Vintila, was an undercover colonel in the Securitate's Counterespionage Directorate. His deputy, Rebegila, was an undercover DIE colonel who had previously served in several stations abroad. The receptionists were technical officers responsible for photographing the passports and informing the Counterespionage Directorate or the DIE about the guests' every important move. The doormen were surveillance officers. The housekeeping personnel belonged to a DIE unit responsible for surreptitiously photographing every scrap of paper in the guests' rooms and in their luggage. The telephone operators and most of the restaurant and nightclub personnel were officers of the DGTO's electronic monitoring directorate. Most of the waitresses and bartenders were surveillance officers responsible for clandestine photography. Several dozen elegant young women who hung around the lobbies and restaurants were part of an army of semi-prostitutes recruited and run on a tight leash by the Counterespionage Directorate. Some of the "foreigners" staying at the hotel were actually DIE illegal officers documented as Western visitors. A dozen or so "writers and artists" picturesquely wearing four-in-hand ties and French berets, who could be found sitting in the lobbies with a cup of Turkish coffee or a glass of cognac and avidly discussing politics, were paid Securitate agents.

Electronic monitoring devices were concealed in every room, as well as in the lobbies, at every table in the two restaurants and nightclub, and in all the private salons and conference rooms. All inside telephones were tapped, as well as the public ones within a half-mile radius. Still and television cameras were either permanently installed or disguised in portable concealment devices, ready to be deployed elsewhere. Regular and light-amplifier television cameras outside the hotel were permanently connected with the Securitate's Surveillance Directorate, which also ran the more than 30 cabs assigned to the three taxi stands located near the hotel.

With its beribboned doormen, smartly uniformed bellhops, and black-tie waiters swarming around in its charmingly nostalgic public areas, the Athenee Palace had everything you could find in a grand old Viennese hotel. In reality, however, it was a factory working around the clock to produce intelligence. So successful was the hotel that its model was copied, although never perfectly, in other luxury tourist hotels throughout Romania, especially in the Black Sea resort area. The most faithful replica, however, was to be the Intercontinental Hotel, an American-Romanian joint venture recently built in the heart of Bucharest next to DIE headquarters.

When I arrived at the Athenee Palace, both Vintila and Rebegila welcomed me obsequiously in the lobby.

"Our new psychologist is a gem, General," Rebegila remarked.

"His new girls are not only younger, livelier, and better in bed, they are also able to talk about anything with anybody. I've tried them out myself. That's part of the job," Vintila added, speaking rapidly with his usual lisp.

COMRADE NICU, THE LIFE OF THE PARTY

The dinner was in the hotel's main private salons. On the other side of the mahogany doors that Vintila threw open was a large, luxurious lounge furnished with low mahogany tables surrounded by overstuffed sofas and easy chairs upholstered in burgundy velvet. The dining table, decorated with napkins folded like fans and lavish floral arrangements, was in an adjacent room.

General Sirbu was holding court in the lounge, surrounded by the people he worked most closely with: Ion Ursu, chairman of the National Council for Science and Technology; Cornel Mihulecea, chairman of the State Committee for Nuclear Energy; and Gheorghe Boldur, deputy minister of machine building, who was responsible for the electronics industry. Waiters in short white jackets and white gloves were passing around trays of cocktails and sandwiches of fresh, black Romanian and salty, red Manchurian caviar. In one corner, a chamber ensemble was playing in low, muted tones. Before I could finish shaking hands with everyone, Oprea burst in, accompanied by Avram and Luchian and escorted by the hotel's chief of protocol. They were with their wives, and all were talking at the same time.

"Good evening to everybody!" Oprea sang out, a little pompously but trying to sound chummy. After looking around, he remarked: "It looks as though some of us don't pay enough respect to our life companions, do we, Mihulecea?"

"Self-contained in her home reactor with two children, Oprea," Mihulecea shot back, showing off almost all of his nuclear knowledge. The fact that he was from Elena's home region had made him Romania's atomic tsar.

"I really couldn't find the time to tell my better half what was going on this evening," Ursu began. "You know, I don't want to talk about sensitive matters on the telephone, Oprea. You know how she is, but I hope that tomorrow evening I'll get to go home earlier and tell her, although I'm not sure I'll do that, because then she'll be sorry she wasn't here today," he rattled on. Ursu could not even say *yes* or *no* in less than fifteen minutes. A nuclear physicist of modest accomplishments, he was, however, clever enough to back Elena to the hilt. That had moved him rapidly to the very pinnacle of Romanian science and technology.

The Burticas arrived a half hour later. His invariably late arrival at any function resulted from his close ties with the Ceausescus and from the years he spent as ambassador to Italy. "The Comrade called us over to his home. A glass of wine and some chitchat," Burtica let drop, typically.

As he usually does, Oprea raised his first glass of wine "to the Comrade."

"And to Romania's most esteemed scholar, the one who . . . " Ursu tried to add, getting to his feet.

Oprea beat him to it, however: "and to Comrade Elena."

After the second course, a group of dancers dressed in colorful folk costumes presented a short show, to the strains coming from a large orchestra set up in the lounge. The waiters were pouring champagne when Vintila opened the door to the lounge and Nicu appeared, dragging a scared-looking, cute young thing along behind him. "*Salve!*" he yelled, looking around the room. "I come in here just so I can lay this chick, and what do I stumble across but a fucking counterrevolution! Half of the government, top spy included. Slumming in the cesspools of capitalism," Nicu screamed, barely managing to make himself intelligible and bursting into an insane peal of laughter. "You wait for me outside, you dirty little brat. I've got matters of state to attend to here," he continued, shoving his girlfriend toward the door.

"I'll take care of *mademoiselle,* Comrade Nicu," Vintila broke in, happy to find a pretext for leaving.

"Who cares? Send her to hell! If I don't fuck her, I'll fuck somebody else. We've got over ten million women in this country," Nicu yelled after Vintila.

"Sit down, Comrade Nicu," said Oprea, leaping up to offer him his own chair. "A plate and a glass for Comrade Nicu," Oprea ordered a waiter, as Nicu navigated unsteadily over to the chair and sat down between Mioara Avram and Silvia Luchian.

"How about something to eat, Comrade Nicu?" Oprea asked solicitously.

"Oysters! I want oysters!" Nicu decided, his head hanging down and bobbing from one side to the other. "When my old man croaks, I'll make you my prime minister, Oprea."

"Oysters for Comrade Nicu Ceausescu," Oprea ordered the waiter, making it clear to all just who had come to honor his dinner.

"Oy-what?" the young waiter asked naively. Good Communists do not eat oysters, and the word had long ago disappeared from the menus of Romanian restaurants.

"You shitty kid! Get out of my sight. I want Vintila. Where is that idiot?" Nicu screamed.

Oprea and Avram ran out to find the director. Nicu screamed after them: "Tell the idiot he ought to be on duty here with the government. Not out there fawning on his capitalist shits."

Vintila, however, was already back in the lounge, bringing with him a small army of waiters carrying crepes suzette. Snapping his fingers for the lights to be turned off, he led the parade of flames, circling the table several times. Everyone applauded. When a sharp feminine cry pierced the semi-darkness, someone quickly turned the lights back on and I saw that Mioara Avram's face had turned beet-red, and her whole body was petrified. It took me a few seconds to realize that Nicu's hands were working busily under her skirt. I glanced toward Avram, who was standing nearby. His eyes bulged in Nicu's direction. "Let's have a glass together," said Avram, catching at Nicu's right hand and putting a glass of champagne into it.

"I don't drink piss. Give me a Scotch," said Nicu, emptying the glass into Mioara's lap.

"Scotch for Comrade Nicu," Oprea ordered Vintila.

A waiter, coming over instantly with a glass on a silver tray, tried to put it down ceremoniously on the table in front of Nicu, who slammed it across the table, splashing Scotch all over Mary and me. "I told you I don't drink piss. I want one on the rocks. Black Label on the rocks for everybody."

When the Scotch arrived, Nicu snatched two glasses from a tray and drained them. Oprea opened the new round with a toast: "I want to ask Comrade Nicu to be our messenger and to convey to Comrade Ceausescu our boundless devotion to the Communist Party and its supreme leader, our undying. . . . "

"Get out, you rat!" Silvia cried, interrupting the toast. With a firm gesture she pulled Nicu's hand out of her blouse. Like her husband, Silvia is sturdy and strong.

Nicu squeezed the last drops from his glass, asked for a refill, and reached over to empty Mioara's glass. Then, quick as a flash, he turned toward Silvia, grabbed the edges of her blouse with both hands and ripped it open, popping off all the buttons. After a moment of shock, Silvia retaliated. She started beating Nicu with her fists, trying to push away his hands, which were now tearing at her bra.

Out of the corner of my eye I saw Luchian get up and march slowly around the table, a siphon bottle in his left hand and a black look on his face. Once behind Nicu, he stretched out his enormous bear paw and pulled Nicu up by the nape of the neck like a kitten. When he had Nicu dangling a few inches off the floor, Luchian began squirting his face with the siphon, telling him to cool down. Then, with Nicu kicking him in the shins with the tip of one shoe and grinding a knee into his groin, Luchian slowly and deliberately strode over to the door, opened it, deposited Nicu outside, carefully closed the door again, and came back to his chair. A few minutes later, the dinner broke up.

CHAPTER

XV

DANA came with me to the airport. Although I had done a lot of traveling outside of Romania over the past twenty years, I had not yet been able to take her with me, or to meet her abroad. By coming with me to the airport, Dana and I could cheat a little emotionally and at least imagine that we were about to leave together for a trip abroad.

The Bucharest international airport is relatively new. After it had been half built, Ceausescu decided that the terminal building was too large. "The number of Romanians traveling abroad should be constantly declining, not increasing," he reasoned. Therefore, one third of the building was transformed into a "presidential pavilion." Finished in light brown marble inside, it is used only a few times a year, for Ceausescu's trips abroad. The rest of the time it is sealed off and kept under guard. In spite of the serious overcrowding during the tourist season, Ceausescu later decided that another section should be taken out of daily use and turned into a VIP lounge for high-level foreign visitors. This is where Dana and I were, separated from the crush of the crowd and spared the unpleasant attentions the border and customs officers inflict on everybody not fortunate enough to be accompanied by someone from the protocol service or to have some other sign of VIP status.

Stefan Andrei came running into the terminal at the last minute, when all the other passengers were already on the airplane. "I love you, Dana," he said, his sparse hair flying in all directions.

"Congratulations, Andrei." This was the first time Dana had seen him since he had been appointed foreign minister.

"Thanks, youngster. I need one more minute, Mike. I'm still

236

wearing the suit I put on for the Comrade. I'll be right back," he threw out over his shoulder, as he strode toward the restroom. I was used to Andrei, from our many trips abroad accompanying Ceausescu. Changing his clothes several times a day is part of his daily routine, and getting dressed is a matter of a few minutes for him. When we were traveling, Andrei would always arrive at Ceausescu's morning meetings still buttoning his pants with one hand and shaving with the other. Just before going in he would then find someplace like a windowsill to jettison his one-time razor, ordered in bulk from abroad. This day he was no different. When he came back, buttoning up the pants of his brand new suit, we started to walk toward the exit. "Would you paint something for me, Dana?" he said, stroking her hair as he went along.

On Romanian airplanes, which have no first class sections and contain the maximum number of seats allowed by the manufacturer, the first row is considered the VIP section and is always reserved. The last row on the left is kept for plainclothes anti-hijacking officers, who are armed with special, low caliber pistols and powerful narcotic gas sprays. A concealed buzzer connects them with the pilots, who are locked in their cockpit and separated from the rest of the airplane by a bullet-proof door.

"Coffee, please. A big, strong cup of coffee. And a glass of cognac," begged Andrei from one of the stewardesses, who recognized him. A glass of cognac has always been his cure for a hangover.

A Foreign Minister's Survival Tactics

"How was Elena last night?" Andrei asked.

"She slept through most of the movie."

"The witch tried to hit me on Sunday, but she doesn't know how tough my hide is. What time do we meet Brandt today?" His quick mind is always one jump ahead of his tongue.

"Four this afternoon."

"Bonn? The barracks?"

"Yes." For image reasons, the headquarters of the West German Social Democratic Party has, since the war, been located in very plain, barracks-like buildings.

"How about another coffee and cognac?" Andrei wheedled his

young stewardess, catching hold of her and pulling her down onto his lap. "Those beautiful blue eyes could do a lot more for me. I can read it in them." He stroked her legs, left bare by her miniskirt uniform. "What about a tasty lunch?"

The stewardess extracted herself from Andrei's arms with feline grace. "Comrade Minister's desires are very modest today."

Andrei has invariably been in a better mood with food under his belt. He is a good trencherman, a holdover from the poverty of his childhood. He wolfs down everything in sight, without discrimination. His recent taste for exotic foods was nothing but show, a way of parading his power.

"The witch is like the bubonic plague. Everybody hopes the Comrade will outlive her. I trust there aren't any microphones here, are there?"

Andrei has always been deathly afraid of microphones, particularly ones installed by Elena. It was a constant exercise of mental gymnastics for him to hunt out places to talk that would not be likely to have microphone coverage.

"Not yet, Andrei."

"You know, it was my job to make a political leader out of Nicu. The Comrade gave him to me and to Pacoste ten years ago. Haven't we done a fantastic job? Nicu will be mankind's most patrician Communist leader. That's what we've accomplished in ten years. Good raw material, too. Like the Comrade. May we have two glasses of rocks, Blue Eyes?"

"Just ice?" asked the stewardess.

"Just ice. I have the sauce." Andrei always travels with a large, accordion-like, red leather briefcase full of bottles of Scotch. "She has her eye on you," he said to me. "Her good one. No doubt about it."

"Who?"

"The witch. It feels so good to be a thousand miles away from her. May I have a cup of coffee, Jeannette?"

"Diane, Comrade Minister."

"Yes, darling. In the U.N.'s demographic statistics, Romania has the highest suicide rate, over 66 for every 100,000 people. The next is Hungary, with only 43, and the third East Germany, with just 30. If the witch takes over, we'll have 60 suicides for every 100. How long do you think it'd be before somebody poisoned her off? Two years? Three? We'll survive, Mike. When

Nicu takes over the scepter I'm going to stay plastered for a whole week. For a month. Some more ice cubes, Jeannette."

"Diane, Comrade Minister."

"Yes, darling. This is my little black book, Mike," he remarked confidentially, patting a small notebook bound in black leather with his large hand. "It contains some of the witch's malapropisms and pearls of wisdom. She'll never get her hands on it. I even sleep with it. Here, listen to this: 'December 19, 1976. *A* reported to *E* on preparations for a visit to Angola, *A* suggested that *E* accompany the Comrade. Why not in the spring, darling? It's too cold now.' Or this: 'December 22, 1977. *A* reported to *E* that among the valuable effects recovered by the DIE from a Romanian emigre who died in Holland were several Titians and Tintorettos. Are they historical documents or books? asked *E*.'"

"You're carrying dynamite in your pocket, Andrei."

"It's my survival kit."

"What's your secret with the Comrade?" I asked, trying to change the subject.

"With the Comrade? It's not a secret but an art. I've made hundreds of first-rate proposals to the Comrade, but I've never presented them as *my* ideas. For example, I'll put a file on his desk: 'Here's the telegram, Comrade Ceausescu.' 'What telegram, Andrei?' he says. I say, 'I thought you suggested that we send a fraternal greeting to Hua Guofeng at the end of China's 11th Communist Congress.' He reads it and asks for his fountain pen. 'Yes, I remember. Independence from Moscow. It was a good idea, wasn't it?' he asks. 'Inspired, Comrade Ceausescu,' I say. That's my art, Mike. Have you got any more ice cubes, Jeannette? It evaporates a lot faster at 30,000 feet." Andrei refilled his glass. "Where are we anyway, Mike?"

"We should be over Vienna."

"Look, listen, but don't ask. That's another of my rules for survival. The Comrade wants to be the only one to know everything. When I was Party secretary for international affairs, I saw him hundreds of times calling my deputy, Ghizella Vass, and giving her orders without telling me anything about it. It's no secret to me that Ghizella is responsible for assisting the subversive activities of Western Communist parties, and that she's connected with the DIE and the military intelligence people. I know we have training centers in Romania where Western Communists are taught sabotage and diversion and guerrilla operations for future use in their own countries, even though the Comrade tries to keep it a big, dark secret. I know his favorites are the Spanish and Greek and Israeli Communist parties. I also know that your DIE has a secret diplomatic pouch system besides the official one. You secretly use it to send Western Communist parties money and false passports and other IDs, for their subversive groups. I also know that the Comrade has a secret channel in France and Spain to communicate with Santiago Carrillo, that he sends him false IDs to use with his second and third identities. I know all this and many other things, but I've never asked the Comrade about them. Or Ghizella. Or even you." Andrei paused to empty his glass. "It was a long and hard road for me, to go from shepherd to foreign minister, and I won't give all this up easily. I know how to survive with the Comrade. Let's finish the bottle, Mike. Jeannette! Jeannette!"

"Diane, Comrade Minister. At your service."

"May I have some more ice cubes?"

Stefan Andrei's survival tactics seem to have stood him in good stead. He managed to remain Romanian foreign minister until the fall of 1985, when Ceausescu reappointed him secretary of the Party's Central Committee, this time responsible for rescuing Romania's bankrupt economy.

To Secure an Embassy

When the TAROM airliner started its descent for landing in Frankfurt/Main, it took me a little while to wake Andrei up. The ambassador, Ion Morega, and the DIE chief of station, General Stefan Constantin, under cover as an embassy counselor, were waiting to take us by car to Cologne, where the Romanian embassy is. Andrei sat with the ambassador on the back seat of his Mercedes, which displayed a large Romanian flag. I left the airport with Constantin in the station's fast, eight-cylinder BMW. "Floorboard it," I ordered the driver, anxious to get to the embassy and talk with Constantin about the upcoming meeting with Willy Brandt.

There is a strict rule in the Soviet bloc intelligence community forbidding the discusssion of classified matters in any car in the West, whether it be an embassy or station car or even a taxicab. To enforce compliance, the KGB was always telling stories about cars belonging to their embassies in which they had discovered American-made monitoring devices, although they never actually showed any of them. I had my own anecdote on the subject, which I used to tell in my lectures at the DIE school. It had taken place in West Germany, with the previous chief of station, Domitian Baltei. I was ordered by Ceausescu to participate, as his representative, in a meeting with a West German businessman targeted by Baltei for recruitment as an agent of influence. In order to mislead any West German surveillance, the scrupulous Baltei took me from the airport to Cologne and then began a long, winding drive through the most crowded areas of the old town, frequently crossing intersections on yellow or even red lights. After four hours, the driver, a professional surveillance officer, was convinced that we were not being followed, and he stopped the car on a dark sidestreet. A few minutes later, Baltei hailed a cab that happened to be passing by. "Now I can finally talk with you, General," he said in the cab, and he started telling me what his plans were for the meeting with the agent-target scheduled for that same evening. At the end of our ride, as Baltei was paying the fare, the driver turned around to me and said in fluent Romanian: "General, it was a real pleasure for me to hear my native language again." That was why on our trip from Frankfurt to Cologne Constantin told me nothing but juicy gossip about West German political life and, of course, some jokes about ambassadors.

Facing the Rhine River, the embassy, a modern building of concrete, steel, and glass, had been designed by Bucharest for the complex activities conducted in a country as important as West Germany. The doorman, a DIE officer with special anti-terrorist training, electronically unlocked the large glass door at the entrance and respectfully got to his feet. Several diplomats who happened to be in the lobby came almost imperceptibly to spontaneous attention with military stiffness. Except for three diplomats, everybody assigned there was an intelligence officer. Constantin and I walked up the stairs to the third floor, where the Cipher Service offices were. Abroad, the Romanian cipher system is based on the KGB's code rules. Two of these are the most strictly enforced. The first is that the materials used for enciphering and deciphering telegrams must be physically guarded by code clerks 24 hours a day, in addition to any alarm system used. The second is that the code clerks themselves must be monitored around the clock and not allowed to leave the embassy without being accompanied by another official.

The third floor was specially designed to accommodate these rules. It is a self-contained unit where the code clerks live and work, keeping each other under surveillance. The entrance is protected by a steel door that can be unlocked only from inside. Access to the area is prohibited to all other members of the embassy, including the ambassador. Only Constantin, as the DIE chief of station, was allowed in. He rang the buzzer, and—after the code clerk on duty had seen us on his television screen—the steel door was unlocked. As supervisor of the National Center for Enciphered Communications, I was of course allowed into all its areas abroad, and it was in fact part of my job to check them out. Once inside, Constantin went directly to another steel door, unlocked it, and then relocked it with us inside. The room was full of sound-activated reel-to-reel tape recorders monitoring every telephone and the microphones in every room at the embassy. The tapes were briefly reviewed on the spot and then forwarded to Bucharest in the diplomatic pouch. The electronic monitoring of every Romanian official abroad, from the ambassador on down, is one of the DIE's most meticulously performed functions. Constantin wanted to see if anyone from the embassy had learned anything about our meeting with Brandt. "Dillinger," the German agent who had set it up, wanted to keep the meeting a secret, unadvertised at the Romanian embassy and unrecorded in Brandt's appointment calendar. We listened to the tapes of the ambassador's and political officers' telephone conversations and found no reference.

From there we went down to the second floor, where the DIE secure area complex, off limits to all but DIE officials, occupies half the floor. Protected by steel doors and closed circuit television and guarded around the clock, the DIE complex contains offices with two or three desks in each, where the station members come after having finished their cover duties and read instructions from headquarters or write their intelligence reports. It also has photographic and chemical laboratories, secure vaults, and an accoustically controlled room, the only place classified discussions are allowed. We entered Constantin's office only long enough for him to turn on a jamming system installed within the walls, producing an inaudible "white noise," and to unlock a barely visible door behind his desk. It opened onto the accoustically secure room—the "bubble." The walls of the windowless room were not only accoustically insulated but also electronically shielded to prevent penetration from outside and radio emissions from inside.

Once we were inside the bubble, Constantin closed the door and started his report. The meeting for that afternoon had been set up with the help of one of Willy Brandt's closest collaborators, a DIE agent of influence. The agent, whose code name was "Dillinger," had been rewarded with gold watches for himself and other members of his family. According to Constantin, our meeting with Brandt should bring about the results desired by Ceausescu.

After finishing his report on the "Dillinger"-Brandt matter, Constantin opened a notebook and began discussing "OV," or currency operations. Standing for its Romanian name, *operatiuni valutare,* OV was at the time all the rage in DIE operations, as producing Western cash was Ceausescu's most insistent order. Constantin reported that in the first quarter of 1978 the station had made a little over $460,000 in cash and had smuggled an additional $600,000 worth of arms into West Germany. Furthermore, the station had sent two agents who were professional smugglers to Bucharest, for the purpose of smuggling over 150 pounds of cocaine out to West Germany. Then he presented the station's plans for the second quarter of the year. We had been in the bubble for almost one hour, when a code clerk opened its door and reported that the ambassador and Andrei had just arrived.

MEETING BRANDT OVER "TEA"

It was shortly before four o'clock when Andrei and I got to the SPD barracks in Bonn. When we were announced, Willy Brandt did not get up from his desk. He merely raised his head a fraction and mumbled something that might have been *"Guten Tag."*

With a gray pallor and dark rings under his eyes, he looked tired and mentally absent. One of his secretaries came in and put down a carafe of coffee and two empty cups, then discreetly left.

"I've got a cold. I'll stick to my tea," Brandt muttered, refilling his teacup from a thermos he took from under his desk. "How's my friend Ceausescu?"

After the usual amenities, I gave him the envelope containing Ceausescu's personal letter. While Brandt was reading through it, Andrei's nostrils started to twitch. Suddenly he said in English, which he speaks much better than German: "Excuse me, Chancellor. May we also have a cup of your tea?"

Brandt finally raised his head and looked at his old friend Andrei with a mixture of reproach and admiration, then buzzed for his secretary. "Two Scotches for my guests. I'll stick to my tea," he growled, reaching down for the thermos again to refill his cup.

"Double. And on the rocks," Andrei added. He was visibly excited by the familiar aroma emanating from Brandt's teacup.

The rest of the meeting went as expected. Brandt murmured something about being very optimistic over Ceausescu's message and accepted the invitation to meet in Bucharest. "By then I'll certainly have concrete news from Kreisky." Contrary to his usual cordiality, Brandt did not move from his desk when we left some two hours later.

"That was evidently just a rumor that Brandt had stopped drinking," Andrei said when we were back in our car. He took out a piece of paper and started drafting a telegram for Ceausescu about the meeting, which we both would sign. In essence it said that Willy Brandt would help.

The Western press reported that, on July 8, 1979, Yasser Arafat was received in Vienna by Austrian Chancellor Bruno Kreisky, who was accompanied by Willy Brandt. [1] *This was the first official visit by a PLO representative to a West European nation and implied recognition of the PLO by both the Austrian government and the Socialist International.*

The embassy's reception areas and dining room were brightly lighted when we got back. Waiters wearing white jackets, black

[1] *The New York Times,* July 9, 1979, p. A3.

trousers, and white gloves were milling around with platters, bottles, and food. They were all DIE officers who had also been trained as high-society waiters at the DIE school. Morega and Constantin were again trying to make a good impression on Andrei and me. The dinner was sumptuous, in keeping with the embassy's reputation for giving elegant, intimate luncheons and dinners, aggressively used by the DIE to develop and cement contacts of all kinds.

CHAPTER

XVI

I had spent the last few days with Ambassador Nicolae Ecobescu, a DIE collaborator and the chief of the Romanian protocol
office, flying between Washington, D.C., and Chattanooga, Dallas, Houston, New Orleans, and New York with representatives
of the State Department and the Secret Service, putting the
final touches on the plans for Ceausescu's official visit. Now
back in Washington, I spent the morning with Ambassador
Nicolae and Minister Counselor Ionita at the State Department,
where we took care of the photographic exhibit Ceausescu had
asked for. Before noon, we attended the opening of the book
exhibit in the languages of Romanian ethnic groups, which
Ceausescu had demanded to blunt American criticism of his
abusive human rights policies. It was displayed at the Martin
Luther King Library in downtown Washington and contained
all the books found in Romania that were printed in the various
languages. Like everything organized by Bucharest, the exhibit
did not neglect the opportunity to contribute to Ceausescu's
personality cult: A special display case held all the works ever
written by or about Ceausescu. Romanian embassy contacts and
DIE station agents of influence were mobilized to form a small
crowd, so the Romanian press could later report: "Already since
the first hours after its opening, the Romanian book exhibition
has enjoyed much success."[1]

---

[1] *Ceausescu's 1978 State Visit to the U.S.A.*, p. 64.

SETTLING IN AT BLAIR HOUSE

By five o'clock on the afternoon of April 11, Ecobescu and I were at Andrews Air Force Base outside Washington. There, together with the base commander, General Benjamin F. Starr, Jr., and State Department and Secret Service officials, we took care of the last-minute details. Promptly at six the presidential Boeing 707 landed at Andrews. A few minutes later, Protocol Chief Evan Dobolle went on board and invited the Romanian guests onto American soil. At the airplane's steps, Ceausescu and his wife were greeted by Secretary of State Cyrus Vance and his wife, Grace, as well as by other American and Romanian representatives. From the airport the Ceausescus rode with the Vances to their official residence, Blair House, across the street from the White House.

Blair House was already familiar to me from Ceausescu's earlier visits to Washington. So were Elena's traditional scenes over not yet having her luggage—which never came with the motorcade—when she arrived at Blair House. To avoid another crisis, I asked one of the people in charge of the house to show her around. The tour began in the drawing room with its beautiful Queen Anne desk and magnificent Sully portrait of Montgomery Blair, then continued to the Abraham Lincoln room. "It was in this room full of memorabilia that Mr. Lincoln signed the Emancipation Proclamation," the guide intoned, pointing to a pen-and-ink drawing of President Lincoln. In the dining room, the table was set with heavy linen damask for the Ceausescus' private dinner later that evening. "These beautiful Lowestoft plates on the table belonged to the Blair family," said the guide. On the second floor, Elena was shown Ceausescu's large bedroom, adjoining a spacious library, both decorated with fresh flowers. "This is your bedroom suite, Madam," said the guide, pointing to a room with a lovely, canopied four-poster bed. "Although it could not be refurbished in time for the 1957 visit of Queen Elizabeth, it is still called the Queen's Suite to this day," finished the guide, wishing Elena an enjoyable stay.

"Close the door, Pacepa," an acid voice suddenly rasped out. After I had executed the order, Elena exploded. "Just look at the harpy. She has never seen me before in her life, and she decides I should sleep here, not with the Comrade. Make this the ironing room!" Imitating the guide's voice, she went on, "'We have an Emancipation Proclamation.' These idiots have a long way to go before they'll really be emancipated." Then, looking disapprovingly at several spots on the walls: "This is the fourth time I have been put up in this miserable old house. Couldn't you have found a newer one, or a Sheraton? At least I hope that we won't be tormented by their stupid air conditioning again."

Air conditioning was one of my greatest headaches during the presidential visits I prepared. Shortly after he had taken over upon the death of his predecessor, Gheorghe Gheorghiu-Dej, Ceausescu returned from a secret visit to Moscow with a lingering pain in his throat. Gheorghiu-Dej had died from an exceedingly fast-developing form of cancer, its first symptoms having appeared as throat pains not long after his return from a vacation in the USSR. Although he had never made it public, in his circle of intimates Ceausescu always claimed to have unimpeachable evidence that the Kremlin had secretly assassinated Dej by radiation because of his insubordination. Ceausescu's first throat pains therefore panicked him. Doctors from all around the world were secretly brought to Bucharest over an anguishing period of weeks. Finally an old, very conservative West German doctor put it to him bluntly: "Sir, you talk too much and too loudly, and your vocal chords are terribly irritated." The doctor's prescriptions were old-fashioned: camomile tea and avoidance of all drafts, including fans and air conditioners. After that, all fans were removed from his residences, and the central air conditioning system installed at the Central Committee of the Communist Party was dismantled. During his foreign visits, especially to North and South America, I encountered unspeakable difficulties getting the air conditioning turned off in every building he was to visit. It repeatedly happened that the minister of foreign affairs and other dignitaries accompanying Ceausescu abroad had to spend their nights sealing off air vents and leaky windows, after Ceausescu had detected an imaginary draft in his bedroom.

Today I reported to Elena that everything was taken care of, although I was personally convinced that the air conditioning would not be turned off at such places as the NASA Space Center in Houston or Texas Instruments in Dallas.

Leaving Elena, I went to find the electronics team that immediately upon our arrival had started checking for monitoring devices. They had to "sweep" all the walls, floors, ceilings, and furniture in the rooms that Ceausescu and Elena would use. I found them on the second floor checking out Ceausescu's bedroom and the adjoining library, where he would be meeting with the foreign minister and other members of his entourage early the next morning. These rooms had already been swept for microphones earlier that day, after Blair House had been turned over to the Romanians, by two DIE technical experts who had arrived in Washington under cover as diplomatic couriers, but Ceausescu always wanted to have his own protective service recheck at least his bedroom, office, and dining room.

THE COMRADES' SPECIAL CLOTHES

The Ceausescus' luggage arrived one hour later in two escorted Secret Service trucks, accompanied by Ceausescu's tailor, two Romanian bodyguards, and Major Nicolae Popa, who was a kind of glorified valet. The Ceausescus' clothes have for many years been a priority matter of state in Romania. It all goes back to 1972. I was with Ceausescu in Cuba, when Fidel Castro told him he had uncovered a CIA plot to smear the insides of his shoes with a poison that would make his hair fall out—and a Castro without his beard was unthinkable! A few days later Ceausescu decided that he would never wear any of his clothes more than once. That same year, special clothes manufacturing sections were created within the Securitate's Directorate V, which was his protective security service. As Ceausescu earns no salary, all of his expenses are paid out of two secret accounts, one belonging to the Party's Central Committee and the other to the Securitate. In general, the Party pays for his housing, and the Securitate for everything that could be construed as related to his security, including food and clothing. The new Securitate sections designed and produced everything Ceausescu might ever contemplate wearing: blocked fedoras for the office and Lenin-style caps for visits to factories; tailored tweed overcoats and Soviet-style padded winter jackets; everyday suits of imported British material and German-style hunting outfits; for his feet, silk socks, suede slippers, black wing-tip Oxfords, smooth calfskin boots, and sturdy hunting boots with electric warmers in them, to name just a few of the products.

All Ceausescu's clothes are packaged in heavy, transparent plastic bags sealed with high frequency electrical equipment. They are then deposited in a climate-controlled warehouse next to his Bucharest residence, where the rule is to keep a one-year's supply in stock: 365 suits, 365 pairs of shoes, and so forth. Everything he has worn once is stamped with colored ink, so as not to be reused by mistake, and then burned in a furnace. When he is traveling, his used clothes are stamped at the end of the day as usual but then stored in special trunks to be taken back to Bucharest for burning. Ceausescu is not sentimental in any way. He does not have pet animals, clothes, or people that he wants to keep around him.

In 1974, special women's clothing sections were created for Elena, and soon she also had a one-year's reserve on hand. Soon, however, Elena became bored with the stringent security regulations and began to cheat by adding to her Romanian-made clothes a supplementary supply imported from Paris and London. She also cheated by instructing that some of her favorite clothes not be stamped and burned. Elena is both sentimental and superstitious about her clothing. If she feels that one dress has brought her bad luck, she will rip it up herself, even before it is stamped and burned; and if another seems to have brought her good luck, she will keep it to wear over and over. By the summer of 1978, the warehouse for her clothing was already about three times larger than Ceausescu's.

For many years Nicolae Popa, a chemical engineer, had been in charge of protecting Ceausescu's clothing and person from chemical, radioactive, and bacteriological contamination. His main tasks were to ensure the secure transportation of the Ceausescus' luggage, to disinfect everything, to install radiation detectors everywhere, and to make chemical analyses of their food, using a portable laboratory. Popa also was responsible for bringing all the food along that the Ceausescus would be eating during trips, carrying it in special, sealed coolers containing everything from staples like butter, flour, salt, sugar, oil, and vinegar down to Ceausescu's favorite steaks. After arriving at Blair House, Popa first deposited his food containers in a room close to the kitchen and put one of his subordinates on around-the-clock guard duty.

Then Popa and a bodyguard moved several large steamer trunks to the second floor. They were filled with sterilized pillows, bed linens, towels, and bathrobes, as well as bath mats and bedside rugs. Before doing anything, Popa and his sidekick, using a disinfectant, washed down the floors, rugs, and every piece of furniture in the bedroom, bathroom, and library, drying them with a portable blower. They removed all the bed and bath linens, replacing them with the linens from the trunks, of which there was enough to last for the whole length of the visit. All of these operations were supposed to be religiously repeated every morning, the foreign housekeeping personnel being no longer allowed to set foot in these rooms or to supply any new linens. Then Popa installed concealed nuclear radiation detectors in each room of the presidential suite. When everything was ready, General Nicolae Stan, the chief of Ceausescu's protective service and his aide-de-camp, posted bodyguards at the door to the bedroom and at each entry to the presidential suite. Only when all of this had been accomplished did Popa move the clothing trunks inside Blair House.

Years later, I came across the book Inside Blair House *by Mary Edith Wilroy, who was the manager there from 1961 to 1975. She lived through two earlier Ceausescu visits to the United States, in 1973 and 1975, both of which I also prepared. She writes: "All through the house, the Romanian security people kept watch. One security man was stationed on each stairway landing, and there was a guard on duty twenty-four hours a day in front of the President's bedroom door. It was the most security we had ever seen. . . . The Ceausescus took all their meals in their rooms, served by their personal waiter. The chambermaids had been told that they were not to enter the Head of State's suite. When they came up the morning of the second day of the visit to change the sheets, they were told that would not be necessary. One chambermaid did manage to get in with a tray one morning. Everyone was intrigued by the atmosphere of mystery that surrounded the room. She reported that the Ceausescus had brought along their own bed linens, which they had put on the beds. . . . I gathered that they sent whatever laundry they had over to their embassy, because we never saw any in our laundry room.*"[2]

A SPY AS AMBASSADOR

I was in the Lincoln room, admiring memorabilia of Francis Preston Blair, when I was informed that Ceausescu had invited me for dinner. During his visits abroad, it was not unusual for me to be seated at his table for lunch or dinner or to be asked to play chess with him. On this particular evening, I dined with just Ceausescu and Elena, and it was clear from the very beginning that their interest was in being briefed on the latest information concerning their visit to the United States. As soon as his waiter had left the room, Ceausescu turned on a portable stereo and asked his usual, "What's new?"

"The ambassador and the chief of station have prepared a confidential report for you," I replied, taking a file out of my briefcase.

"Who else knows that Nicolae belongs to you?" He always asked the same question every time I mentioned Ambassador Nicolae's name. Although it had been his own decision that the ambassador to Washington should be an intelligence officer under deep cover, Ceausescu was always afraid that a leak could anger the White House and damage the liberal, Westernized image he was trying to give himself in Washington.

"Only three other people, comrade: Minister of Interior Teodor Coman, DIE Chief of Personnel General Nicolae Ceausescu, and myself."

"I have been told that you and Nicolae are friends of Ion Voicu's, and that you play the violin together. Is that true?"

"Yes, comrade."

"Is Nicolae solid enough to keep his military rank and intelligence assignment a secret?"

"I consider that he is."

Elena, seated next to me on the other side of the table, broke in. "How can anyone who plays the violin be reliable?" After

[2]Mary Edith Wilroy and Lucie Prinz, *Inside Blair House*, Garden City, New York: Doubleday & Company, 1982, pp. 146, 252.

a pause, she went on. "I heard a rumor that he had a terribly expensive violin." She looked at me with a question in her eyes.

"He has an eighteenth century Guarnieri del Gesu, which was a present from a West German company while he was minister of foreign trade."

"If it's an antique, it ought to be taken into government custody."

"The prime minister approved allowing Nicolae to keep it."

"Who does the prime minister think he is? An idiot, that's all he is. How many times have I told you, Nick, that we don't need a prime minister any more?"

READY FOR THE AMERICAN MEDIA

"What about the book exhibit I ordered?" Ceausescu asked me.

"It opened today at the Martin Luther King Library in Washington. Included is a special display case with books written by and about you."

"Listen to him, Nick. In all of America they couldn't find any better place than a library for black people!"

"The director of the library opened the exhibit with an address presenting you as a brilliant thinker and political personality, whose love of books has favorably influenced the whole course of publishing in Romania."

"Did he say 'brilliant thinker and political personality'?"

"That's what he said, Comrade Ceausescu. I was there."

"Nothing about me?"

"Yes, Comrade Elena," I lied. "He spoke of you, too. And your portrait is there next to the Comrade's."

"Anything new on the television interview?" Ceausescu calmly continued.

"Yes. ABC insists on taping the interview tomorrow afternoon, so they can put parts of it on the air during the prime-time news tomorrow evening, the first day of the official visit, and broadcast the entire interview on Sunday, April 16th, on the 'Issues and Answers' show."

"Is the interviewer somebody?"

"Yes, comrade, Barbara Walters. She is one of ABC's best."

"A woman? A woman to interview you, Nick? That's ridiculous! What's her name again?"

"Barbara Walters."

"Isn't she the harpy who interviewed Fidel Castro and made a circus out of his personal life, with his estranged wife and his love affairs? Isn't she that one?"

"I don't remember, Comrade Elena."

"Fiddlers! That's all they are, nothing but fiddlers. I told you so. It's all a plot against you, Nick, no question about it. Why else, out of two hundred million Americans, could they find only that harpy to interview you? It's a plot to compromise you, comrade. Can't you see that?" After reaching this decision, Elena furiously and ostentatiously left her half-eaten steak on the table and marched out of the dining area.

"Who is in charge of the interview?" asked Ceausescu.

"Ionita. He's a man of tact and has had many years of experience in the United States."

"Fit the interview into tomorrow's schedule. And don't forget, you and Nicolae will be responsible with your heads if Walters asks anything about Comrade Elena or the family."

The discussion continued for almost two more hours, Ceausescu being interested in everything, from White House protocol rules down to the names of the American officials designated to welcome him at the airport in New York on the last day of the visit. He is very serious, systematic, and meticulous in preparing his visits abroad.

KING'S GAMBIT VS. KHRUSHCHEV

After dinner I excused myself, but soon a bodyguard came and said, "Comrade Ceausescu invites you for a game of chess." Every time he summoned me to play chess, I remembered the description of him drawn by the Spanish Communist leader Santiago Carrillo shortly after Ceausescu's nomination.

Carrillo had come to Bucharest as Ceausescu's personal guest to inspect a secret paramilitary training center for Spanish Communists, set up by the Romanian Communist Party with the professional help of the DIE. After a long day of shooting practice, Carrillo, a subtle connoisseur of Communist psychology, launched into a discussion with one of his Spanish comrades, evidently not imagining he was being taped. He described Ceausescu as uneducated but possessing native intelligence and a solid Marxist background; a man of peasant prudery and apparent modesty, but bursting with unlimited personal ambition; a leader who would give new international dimensions to the concept of the personality cult. "Up to now, however," Carrillo concluded, "he looks more like a chess player who has not yet learned how to lose." Now, some ten years later, Ceausescu still had not learned how to lose, either at politics or at chess.

Ceausescu ordered his favorite "Odobesti Yellow" wine and turned the portable stereo up loud, and even before he had finished his first bottle he became garrulous. When away from home, without his favorite movies, he loves to finish the day with wine or cognac, reminiscing about old times. I knew all these stories by heart. Except that every time he told them, his personal role at that period became increasingly important.

On this evening Ceausescu started with his usual King's Gambit and with Stalin's heavy drinking. He recalled the cynical pleasure Stalin used to take in forcing his guests to drink, until he got them into embarrassing or even disgraceful situations. Then he recalled a visit to Moscow, where, during the farewell dinner, Stalin secretly ordered that the wine served to the Romanian guests be mixed with vodka instead of mineral water. He went on to say that the same wine with vodka had been served to the Romanian plane crew members, and that this was the real reason why the presidential airplane had hit a tree on its return from Moscow, killing the minister of foreign affairs, Grigore Preoteasa, and three crew members and wounding the president, Chivu Stoica. "I barely got out of it alive," was Ceausescu's dramatic ending. His story was factually correct, except that it had been his predecessor, Gheorghiu-Dej, not himself, on that airplane, and the Kremlin leader had been Krushchev.

Changing the subject, Ceausescu recalled the Western propaganda, especially after Stalin's death, proclaiming that the East European governments were being kept in power only by Soviet occupation troops. "If I had done it differently," said Ceausescu, "Romania might now be a Soviet republic. But I never asked for any Soviet withdrawal. Not I. I got an 'Old Bolshevik' to do the job. I got Bodnaras." Emil Bodnaras was a Romanian bourgeois army officer, who defected to the Soviet Union in the early 1930s. There he became a member of the Soviet Communist Party and officer in the Red Army, and in 1944 he came to Romania with the first Soviet troops, becoming Romania's minister of national defense. "Bodnaras was perfect for the job I had in mind," Ceausescu went on, as he ordered a new bottle of wine and a plate with his favorite tomatoes, onions and feta cheese.

"During one of Khrushchev's secret visits to Romania, I pushed Bodnaras out in front. He asked for the withdrawal of the Soviet troops from Romania, saying that it would help neutralize Western propaganda claims that the Romanian government would not be able to remain in power without Soviet bayonets. Only Bodnaras, as an 'Old Bolshevik,' could raise such a terribly delicate matter, and I was happy to have him there to do it. And Khrushchev bit. I don't care what other people say about him, Khrushchev was brilliant, and I am very proud that I was able to fool him. Although it was not until somewhat later that Khrushchev actually decided to withdraw the Red Army,[3] and only after I had given him some fantastic military intelligence, still I determined that, as a sign of my gratitude, I would build Bodnaras the most luxurious residence ever. Have you seen his marble indoor swimming pool and his movie theater?"

While basically true, Ceausescu's story had a few inaccuracies. Not Ceausescu but Gheorghiu-Dej handled the discussions with Khrushchev. Not Ceausescu but Gheorghiu-Dej instructed Bodnaras on how to appeal to Khrushchev, Ceausescu at that time being lower in rank than Bodnaras. Not Ceausescu but Gheorghiu-Dej had Bodnaras's famous residence constructed just across from his own. A respect for historical accuracy has never been among Ceausescu's priorities, and he has always manipulated the past to suit his image of himself.

"Do you remember that time during a visit to Romania when Khrushchev began giving us lessons in how to seed hybrid corn?" Ceausescu went on, roaring with laughter. I had been there that time, when Khrushchev was secretly shown an immense collection of genetic materials for hybrid corn stolen by the Romanians from the U.S. government and from private American farms.

---

[3]The decision to pull the Soviet troops out of Romania was announced at the May 1958 meeting of the Warsaw Pact Political Consultative Committee in Moscow.

Following several years of disastrous drought and famine after the end of the war, Bucharest pinned its hopes on the hybrid corn made famous by American farmers. Under bilateral agreements, dozens of Romanian agricultural engineers, who were actually intelligence officers or agents, were sent to the United States. Dispersed to federal or state research institutes and to private organizations and farms, over the years they secretly collected thousands of pounds of the genetic materials for reproducing American hybrid corn in Romania. A special diplomatic pouch regularly transported these materials to Bucharest without biological deterioration. Several valuable American specialists were also recruited, including a scientist working at the United States Department of Agriculture's Research Center in Beltsville, Maryland. The latter alone supplied the whole United States national hybrid collection, containing over 14,000 assortments and species, which became the standard basis for later research work in Romania.

These genetic materials were presented to Khrushchev in 1962. He promptly asked that the collection be shared with the Soviet Union, and this was done a few days later. But before leaving, Khrushchev could not resist lecturing the Romanians, in his famous peasant way, on just how he thought they should seed the hybrid corn, how they should handle it, and how harvest it.

It was not until ten years later that Romania, using these materials, became one of the largest producers of hybrid corn in Europe. American brands, such as Pioneer and Wyoming, created in the United States after many years of research and great effort, are now produced in Romania and exported as Romanian hybrids—RH brand.

Ceausescu won that chess game, started another, and had just ordered a new bottle of wine, when Elena came in, holding up two pieces of Wedgewood china. "Look, Nick. Aren't they awful? I bought them during our stopover at Shannon. They don't have any nice glaze, and I had to pay American dollars for them. I told our ambassador's wife that our Romanian porcelain was much shinier, and that we should be exporting it to Great Britain, but guess what she said? That English and Irish porcelain was more famous! She's a stupid old fuddyduddy."

The chess game was almost a draw, but I decided it would be

wise for me to lose it. When I left, Elena, her dressing gown flopping open, was leafing through a briefing file on the visit. "Look here, Nick," she said, pointing to a page of biographic data on Jimmy Carter. "He's a peanut farmer. Farmer means peasant, doesn't it?"

CHAPTER

XVII

THE travel clock on my bedside table showed a few minutes before five when I heard a knock at the door of my room in Blair House. I was sure it would be Aurel Florea, the first counselor of the Romanian embassy. A tractor mechanic by training, Florea was not brilliant, but he was pragmatic enough always to be punctual and respectful with his superiors. His common sense and an enviable ability to simplify even the most complicated situation, together with a good feel for human psychology, were the keys to his successful career. From having been an intelligence captain in London, where he learned good English and recruited valuable, long-standing sources in both major British political parties, Florea rose to the position of chief of the DIE's North American Division. Now, when Ceausescu had made the United States his first priority, Florea had just been appointed chief of station in Washington.

LAVISH PRAISE FOR THE LEADER

Florea put several folders on my table containing materials I had to present to Ceausescu and Elena that morning. The first folder contained telegrams from Bucharest. On top was one signed by Manea Manescu, the prime minister, reporting in two full pages that all was well in Romania. The telegram ended fulsomely: "We who have remained behind in Romania, the members of the Political Executive Committee, Council of State and Council of Ministers, learning with vibrating patriotic pride about your arrival in Washington, want to express to you and to Comrade Elena our admiration for the brilliant way you are going to show to the U.S. people and to the whole world the principled stand and contribution of Romania and your own contribution to the complex issues of the contemporary world. The whole Romanian people, approving with pride, enthusiasm, and great expectation your mission of peace to the U.S., is anxious to see the most beloved and esteemed son of the Romanian people and our beloved Comrade Elena back on Romanian soil. We respectfully ask you to take care of your health and to come back to the helm of our country more vigorous than ever." Eulogies are as important to Ceausescu as the air he breathes. Underneath this telegram was a pile of similar ones from other Romanian organizations, all eloquently praising Ceausescu and Elena. Most of them would have been drafted by Popescu the Lord, as usual.

In the second folder there was a joint report from the ambassador and the DIE chief of station describing preparations being made for Ceausescu's visit. It was written in the same bombastic style Ceausescu liked to hear. "The United States visit of the President of the Socialist Republic of Romania, Nicolae Ceausescu, and of his esteemed wife is awaited with legitimate interest by political, diplomatic, industrial, business, and journalist circles—by U.S. citizens—as an expression of the profound esteem and respect enjoyed in the public opinion of the United States by the forceful personality of the head of the Romanian state." Ceausescu will not read any report that is not lavish in its praise of him.

In the third folder there was another joint report containing laudatory remarks made by American personalities about Ceausescu's visit. Another folder contained eulogies to Ceausescu made by a number of Romanian emigrés living in the United States. "They're all our agents," Florea whispered in my ear. "All of them will give speeches during tomorrow's meeting between the Comrade and the Romanian emigres. It will be perfect. We wrote every word for them."

The rest of the papers were of the same nature. All of them had been typed on the special IBM typewriters with large characters used for Ceausescu alone, which had earlier been shipped from Romania for the visit. Only the DIE special report containing intelligence from all around the world was handwritten in easily readable black ink. After Ceausescu learned in Moscow that a typewritten text could be reconstituted by monitoring the impulses from an electric typewriter, he ordered that all intelligence reports given to him abroad be handwritten.

"What's new" asked Ceausescu, when he received me at seven o'clock. The rules for his mornings abroad are very strict. He always starts at seven with his chief of intelligence, followed by the foreign minister. Only after that will he receive other members of his party, no matter what their rank, even if the prime minister is there on the trip with him.

Glasses on his nose, Ceausescu leafed with his usual pleasure through the telegrams from the prime minister and the various Romanian organizations and then carefully read the report on the Americans' preparations for his visit and on favorable remarks about him made by American personalities. "Put them into proper form and have them published in Romania.[1] In the West, too, if you can," Ceausescu ordered me. "And give Comrade Elena the telegrams from Romania." Over the last couple of years the division of labor between them had become more and more evident. Ceausescu let Elena have the domestic authority, while he himself concentrated on international matters. My meeting with Ceausescu that morning was completely without incident, all the way to the end. Despite the six-hour time difference between Bucharest and Washington, Ceausescu was in good physical and mental shape. He has a remarkable resilience, although he is very short in stature and does not have an athletic constitution.

As I left Ceausescu, Andrei was just arriving at the door, throwaway razor still in hand. "How's the weather inside?"

"Like outside." It was a beautiful, sunny spring morning in Washington. Andrei ditched his razor on a window sill, knocked at Ceausescu's door and entered the library without waiting for an answer.

"Comrade Elena is asking for you," the bodyguard on duty told me. "She's in the garden, with the photographers."

When Elena had finished posing for the photographers as-

---

[1]They were published in English in the book *Ceausescu's 1978 State Visit to the U.S.A.*, pp. 49–63.

signed to take daily pictures for her collection, she started walking toward me, wearing a sugary smile over her shabby yellow teeth. "What do you have for me today, Pacepa," she mewed, looking hopefully at the folder I was holding in my hand.

"Some telegrams from Bucharest."

"Read them to me, darling."

Once that was over, Elena made her way back to the house, holding onto my arm and waddling from side to side.

"Listen to me, Nick," she burst in on Ceausescu, slamming the door behind her. "I want all these telegrams published. Every one of them." She grabbed the folder out of my hands and plopped it down on Ceausescu's desk.

"Just give Pacepa whatever you want published. He'll take care of it."

"Make sure they all get published, Pacepa." Turning to Andrei, she looked him up and down: "Are you going to natter at the Comrade's head all day long?"

"I've just finished, Comrade Elena," said Andrei, happy to leave.

"If so, let's go outside, Nick. The rest of your idiots can wait. It's such a beautiful morning."

After they had left, I was notified that the chief of the U.S. Secret Service team in charge of Ceausescu's visit was downstairs asking for an immediate meeting with me. He got straight to the point: "We have a demonstration against President Ceausescu going on between Blair House and the White House. To prevent the president from seeing it, we will need to take a different route."

There is nothing more calamitous for Ceausescu than to see a demonstration against himself; it can put him into a violent, towering rage. That had happened a few times, and just the thought of it had become a nightmare for me. The first time I accompanied Ceausescu abroad was in 1970, on a visit to New York. Just as he was returning to the Romanian Permanent Mission from his first visit to the United Nations, he caught sight of a fellow wearing placards around his neck asking Ceausescu for more human rights in Romania. When Ceausescu called me on the carpet, he was completely deformed with fury, as he paced from one side of the room to the other. "Make the miserable swine disappear from the face of the earth," he ordered. The protester turned out to be a Romanian emigre named George Boian, who had a permit to demonstrate valid for the whole period of the visit, and he stubbornly kept on, in spite of both promises and threats from Romanian diplomats. A helpful Secret Service did carefully change the daily routes so that Ceausescu would not see the demonstrator, but every day Ceausescu sent one of his personal bodyguards over to see if the man was still on the street. Upon learning that he was, he would make a dreadful scene. Because of the rage he provoked in Ceausescu, Boian entered into contemporary Romanian history. For many years the code name used in DIE correspondence for anti-Ceausescu demonstrations was "Boian."

One of Ceausescu's stormiest reactions took place several years later, when he learned from a Radio Free Europe broadcast that a recent Romanian emigre, Sergiu Manoliu, and his mother, Carmen Manoliu, had organized a demonstration across from UNESCO's headquarters in Paris. Calling for human and emigration rights in Romania, they hoisted a Ceausescu portrait swathed in mourning for several days. Livid with rage, Ceausescu ordered that Sergiu Manoliu be "beaten to death," so that "no other person will ever desecrate the portrait of the Romanian president." Subsequently, Sergiu Manoliu barely escaped with his life from a DIE operation using French professional terrorists who had been given asylum in Romania and were regularly used by the DIE for drug smuggling and terrorism.

"Let's both go outside," the chief of the Secret Service team suggested, and we immediately left to have a look at the demonstrators and to establish alternate routes. Then I went to the White House and checked on the preparations for the official arrival of the Ceausescus, scheduled to take place on the White House lawn. The members of the welcoming committee were already there: Vice President Walter Mondale, Secretary of State Cyrus Vance and his wife, the deputy commander of the Joint Chiefs of Staff Admiral James Holloway and his wife, U.S. Ambassador to Bucharest Rudolph Aggrey, and other State Department officials, together with the dean of the diplomatic corps, Dr. Guillermo Sevilla-Sacasa. At ten-thirty the Ceausescus arrived, and his broad smile showed that he had not seen any demonstration against him. Unfortunately, the good mood did not last.

WRONG ANTHEM AT THE WHITE HOUSE

President Carter introduced Ceausescu to his welcoming committee, the military guard presented arms, and the band started to play the Romanian national anthem. The Americans all stood at respectful attention. I was dumbfounded, however. They were playing the old "Fatherland Romania" from capitalist days, not the new anthem Ceausescu had personally introduced. I cast an eye toward the platform of honor. Carter was smiling broadly, as if attesting to his enjoyment of the melodic Romanian anthem. Ceausescu's fingers were furiously agitated, his face black, his ferocious eyes trying to catch mine. I maneuvered to have Secretary Vance informed of the *faux pas*, and in an instant the whole welcoming committee was discreetly abuzz. The news reached the deputy chairman of the Joint Chiefs, who, while passing it on to Vice President Mondale, made a gesture indicating he would take care of it and then strode off importantly. The band, however, played relentlessly on, down to the very last note, and I knew that it was only a matter of time before Ceausescu would accuse me of being a CIA agent.

The rest of the ceremony proceeded as if nothing had happened. In his welcoming speech, Carter said: "It is also of great benefit to me as President to have a chance to consult with a national and international leader like our guest today," and he emphasized that the influence of Ceausescu and Elena "throughout the international world is exceptional." Somewhat calmed down, Ceausescu winked at Elena, who was showing off her sweetest smile and her stumpy yellow teeth. In his reply, Ceausescu made only a few of his favorite points: equality between the large and the small, the developed and the underdeveloped countries, including equality between Romania and the United States; himself as the father of human rights and a fundamental supporter of the Helsinki accords and as the creator of a new international economic order.

After the first official meeting between the two presidents, Ceausescu and his party went to the State Department for a luncheon given in his honor by Vance. I accompanied Elena to a luncheon given in her honor by Mrs. Vance at the historic Woodlawn Plantation in Mount Vernon, Virginia. Throughout the whole drive Elena did nothing but complain. First of all, she should really be at the same luncheon as her husband, not shunted off to some sideshow with American wives. "I'm a political leader and an internationally renowned scientist." Second, it was unfair for her to be escorted by the State Department's protective service and not by the Secret Service, as her husband was. "I'm not a president's wife. I am the next in line after the Romanian leader. Is that clear, you fiddler?" Third, the national anthem. "For that alone you should be fired and sent back to Romania on foot." When the car arrived at Woodlawn Plantation, I braced myself: "Just look at it. What a ghastly, stinking old house out here in the middle of nowhere. And sand everywhere. You should have warned me to wear boots, you imbecile."

We got back to Blair House just in time to receive the key to the city of Washington from Mayor Walter Washington and his wife. After the routine ceremony, photographed from all angles by Romanian newsmen, Elena pushed me into a corner. "You idiot, why didn't you tell us that the mayor was a descendant of his?" To Elena anyone named Washington had to be related to George Washington.

In the center of the room Ceausescu was dictating the communiqué for the Romanian press: "The Golden Key of Washington was offered to President Nicolae Ceausescu . . . as a symbol of the valuation given to the tireless political activity of the Romanian President, dedicated to his country's welfare and progress, to the cause of peace and understanding in the world . . ."[2]

Elena, who was holding the box with the key, gave it to me. "Find out if it's real gold. If it is, give it to me; if not, put it away with the rest of our trophies."

Barbara Walters was now there with her team. She was Elena's nightmare, the "harpy," the "viper," the "vampire," who wanted to suck dirty stories out of the private lives of Communist leaders. While waiting for Ceausescu to reappear, I had the unexpected pleasure of a long talk with her. She was incredibly human, friendly. We talked about anything and everything, from her previous interviews with other leaders, to her private life, her beloved daughter, her phobia of darkness.

[2]*Ibid,* p. 87.

In the evening, the dinner given at the White House in Ceausescu's honor started with the Romanian anthem. "This is the good one," Carter said, apologizing obliquely for that morning. Then both presidents gave speeches, and after the dinner the guests were invited to attend a recital in the reception hall. "Our program is entitled 'In Memory of Gershwin,' " Carter gushed, leading the two artists over to the piano.

SUMMING UP A SUCCESSFUL FIRST DAY

Back at Blair House, Ceausescu invited his officials in for a glass of wine. Elena caught me at the door and was about to buzz something into my ear, when Ceausescu remarked: "Farmer he may be, but he's not a peasant. Isn't that so, Elena?" He had evidently been won over by Carter's eulogies and his smile.

"But he's not a gentleman, either, Nick. No folk ensemble, no ballet, no symphony in his artistic program. Nothing but two handicapped people—one blind and one a Negro." After a short pause she went on. "What did he say about me, Nick? There were so many people there, I just can't remember."

"Nice things, Elena. Something about you as a scientist."

"What, exactly, Nick?"

Ceausescu asked that his interpreter, Sergiu Celac, be called in with his stenographic transcript of Carter's speech. "Read us what the farmer said about Comrade Elena."

"Yes. He said: 'I was particularly eager to impress the President's wife tonight because she, on her own, is a distinguished scientist, a chemist, and has done great research work.'"[3]

"How lovely. And what did he say about Palade, dear?" she mewed further. "I heard him saying his name."

"I have it," said Celac. "President Carter continued as follows. 'And I was very careful to place on her left someone who could speak her language about science and about whom I could brag that he is a distinguished American to show how superior our country was. As a matter of fact, Dr. Palade is a Nobel laureate, and I wanted to let Mrs. Ceausescu know how advanced we were

[3]*Ibid*, p. 98.

in training Americans to win the foremost prize in all the world. So I was explaining it to her very carefully and in the middle of my dissertation he'—that means Palade," the interpreter filled in—"'pointed out to me he was born, raised, and trained in Romania.'⁴ I think that's all," Celac ended.

"That's sweet," Elena smirked. "They finally get a Nobel Prize winner, and he turns out to be a Romanian. Isn't it true what the Comrade always says? There's no other country greater than Romania and no other people cleverer than we are."

"There is always much truth in what the Comrade says," approved Oprea. "He's so sensitive. Celac, would you read the part where Carter talked about the Comrade?"

"Here it is. 'I have had a delightful day with the president of this great country. I think it is accurate to point out that as the leader of his great nation, he has not only brought tremendous progress to Romania, but also has taken on a role of leadership in the entire international community that is notable.'"⁵

"That's marvelous. I couldn't have said it better myself," Oprea lied.

"It was delightful the way you hit Carter below the belt," said Vasile Pungan. "When you called Abraham Lincoln a Marxist. Can you find it, Celac?"

"I know what I said; I don't need Celac for that," Ceausescu interrupted. "I quoted from Marx, who called Abraham Lincoln 'this honest son of the working class.'"

"During the Spanish Civil War there was a volunteer brigade named for Abraham Lincoln. He became a symbol for the American Communists, and he still is," filled in Andrei, who had given Ceausescu the Lincoln vignette for his speech.

"There was another blow for Carter," Pungan boomed in his loud voice. "He began praising the audience, commenting that America was two hundred years old and its population came from almost every European country. Big deal! And then you made your point, Comrade Ceausescu. You said that in 1980 Romania would celebrate two thousand and fifty years since its creation, and that the Romanian people had been there forever and would stay there forever. That was marvelous."

⁴*Ibid.*
⁵*Ibid*, pp. 98–9.

"Celac, would you like to read what Carter said about the Helsinki Conference?" asked Andrei, who usually has little to say when Elena is present.

"He said that Romania was 'one of those countries instrumental in evolving the Conference on Security and Cooperation in Europe.'"[6]

"That's the work of our embassy here," said Andrei. "It kept whispering this idea over and over all around Washington, until even Carter learned it."

"Just look at him, comrades," Elena lashed out. "He— did—it. He—does—everything. It's less than a month since the Comrade appointed you foreign minister, and now everything's been done by you. In our country it's the Comrade who does everything. The Comrade, not you, you *mascalzone.*"

Andrei was sinking down lower and lower in his chair. Only a few days earlier, during our flight to West Germany, he had told me how careful he was not to take credit for anything in his relations with Ceausescu. Pungan broke in, trying to keep the evening from taking a bad turn, and suggested watching the videotape of that part of the Barbara Walters interview shown on the news that evening.

"At least the harpy didn't sting," said Elena when the short tape came to an end. "She understood that if she did, she would have to fight me."

"The interview was much longer, Comrade Elena," said Oprea. "I was there the whole time. It was just incredible, unique. The Comrade was so sensitive. Would you like Celac to read the Comrade's answer when Barbara Walters asked him about the present relations between Romania and the United States?"

"Yes, I have it right here," said Celac, taking out another notebook. "The Comrade said: 'Naturally, there are still problems to be solved . . . among which are the most-favored nation clause and the granting of more freedom by the United States to U.S. companies . . . I mean, the granting of up-to-date technologies. Under a U.S. law, American companies cannot give some technologies without relevant approvals. That is why it is

[6]*Ibid.*, p. 100.

necessary for the American companies and firms to have more freedom of action.' Is that what you are looking for, Comrade Oprea?"[7]

No Dollars for Color Television

"Yes, Celac. Isn't that extraordinary? It is exactly what Brezhnev just asked the Comrade. To obtain prohibited technology that Moscow cannot get. I couldn't believe that the Comrade would attack so frontally. He is so aggressive."

"Harum-umpf." Ceausescu coughed, trying to catch Oprea's attention. He pointed to the wall with one hand and to one of his ears with the other.

"Oh, I understand. The walls could have ears," Oprea said loudly. Ceausescu gave him an acid look.

"Isn't he an idiot, Nick? Why do you keep saying that Oprea is the best man you have?"

"Your interview was marvelous," threw out Ion Avram, the minister of heavy industry, giving his friend Oprea a hand. "I wish we could show you in color on Romanian television, too. We'll have to do it someday, Comrade Ceausescu."

"I've told you many times, Avram, there is a political consideration that's holding us up. We have to decide which color television system to adopt: the Soviet, the American-Japanese, the French, or the West German. Any one we select will make somebody else unhappy, and I don't want to annoy anybody now. I need friends, not enemies."

"The Comrade is so profound," chimed in Oprea, trying to repair the bad impression he had just made.

"It is also a matter of money, comrades," continued Ceausescu, extending his dialogue with Avram to the rest of those present. "We just don't have the dollars now for color television." Lowering his voice, he added: "The military industry is the one we have to invest in now, not the food or shoe industry. Our people are docile enough; they know how to tighten their belts. They can live without color television for now."

[7]*Ibid,* p. 89.

"Why should we think about color television, Avram?" asked Elena. "Isn't it enough that we've given them one television set for each house? Isn't that true, Oprea?"

"Almost, Comrade Elena. One for every fifty houses."

"Whatever. The idiots ought to be happy enough with what they've got. Why should we put ideas in their heads about color television, Avram? Are you crazy?"

In 1978, Romania and Albania were the only European countries without any color television broadcasting. In Bucharest, however, a small color television broadcasting system had recently been installed, imported for the use of Ceausescu's family only. When a rumor, stemming from one of Nicu's drunken sprees, started about an alleged color television broadcasting system for Ceausescu only, he ordered me to mount a disinformation operation spreading the word that there had only been demonstrations by foreign companies eager to sell their systems to Romania.

On Ceausescu's personal order, the DIE was deeply involved in obtaining complete technological intelligence for the two color television systems favored by him—the French SECAM, in which the Soviets were interested, and the West German PAL. "When you have the complete technology on either of them, it will be much easier for me to make my political decision," he said with a wink, shortly before our visit to Washington.

"Who Were Those Elegant Ladies at Your Table?"

"That's all for tonight," said Ceausescu, draining his glass. Even before the last person had left the room, Elena jumped on me. "All day I've been meaning to ask you: Who were those three elegant ladies at your table tonight? Americans?"

"Yes, comrade."

"Wives?"

"Yes, comrade."

"American wives! I was sure I recognized the amusing one you spent the whole evening cheek to cheek with. Wasn't she the ambassadress?"

"Yes, comrade, it was 'Bertha.'"

"Fantastic! Fan-tas-tic! That floozie in the White House! So she hadn't invented all those stories about having an open entree to the White House. That's marvelous. We've got to get busy right away and have her stud come over here with his big dick for her, darling, to ask her all about the White House during a good fuck. The ambassadress has to learn that nothing is for nothing in today's world."

"What stud? What floozie?" Ceausescu broke in. Before he could finish, Elena was on his lap, whispering about the ambassadress.

"Wouldn't it be fabulous to have an influence agent at the pinnacle of American society?" I heard Elena finishing her recital.

"We'll have to think about that."

"We ought to send her boyfriend over here, Nick. At first just for a visit, then for good."

"We'll decide on that as soon as we get back to Bucharest," Ceausescu declared.

"She has to do whatever we want, Nick."

"Now or later, Elena. Anyway, if she should ever start thinking about not doing what we want, then all we need to do is have somebody show her the pictures and suggest that a newspaper correspondent might find them in some hotel lobby."

The same day I arrived in the United States after having been granted political asylum, I reported on this hostile operation against the United States government. I later learned that on the basis of my reporting an investigation had been conducted and "Bertha's" affair with the Romanian driver had been confirmed. [8]

CREATING A SON FOR AN AMERICAN NOBEL PRIZE WINNER

Abruptly Ceausescu changed the subject. "Today I saw Brzezinski at work." Zbigniew Brzezinski was President Carter's national security advisor at the time. "The Poles have managed to get a nice penetration into the White House." Ceausescu considers all Romanian emigrés, no matter what their current citizen-

[8] *The Washington Times*, May 4, 1987, p. 6A.

ship, as still Romanians who should obey Bucharest's orders. This is the common view throughout the Soviet bloc.

Ceausescu pursued his thought. "How many Romanian emigrés do we have in America, Pacepa?"

"Something over 300,000, according to DIE records."

"That's quite a talent pool. To get a Romanian in as the right-hand man of the American president should be our most important goal for the future. We ought to have our Brzezinskis in here, not only in the White House but also in Congress and in the State Department."

"Come on, Nick! They haven't even been able to recruit Palade, no matter how much you and I insisted. Did you hear in Carter's toast how nicely he talked about Palade and his Nobel Prize, and about how close he was to the president of the United States?"

Dr. George Palade was born in Romania, studied there and married the daughter of Nicolae Malaxa, one of the wealthiest Romanian businessmen before the Communist era. In 1944 the Soviet Army occupied Romania, and Palade soon left with his wife and father-in-law for the United States. When he later became the director of a microbiology institute in the United States and won a Nobel prize, Elena ordered that he be recruited "immediately."

Palade was a DIE recruitment target for many years, but, when it was finally realized that his loyalty to his adopted country was unshakable, Elena ordered a new tactic. She told the DIE to create a fictitious illegitimate child for Palade, the supposed fruit of some love affair he had before his marriage, while still a medical student in Romania. The DIE invented this child, a son, out of whole cloth, registered him in all the necessary public records, and then gave his identity to an illegal intelligence officer who had good credentials as an engineer. At the time I had left Bucharest for this trip, the DIE had been working out a complicated operation to have Palade "discover" his "son," who would be the illegal officer. The DIE was confident that the "son's" romantic story and early photographs of his "father," together with his personal charm and professional competence, would induce Palade, once in contact with him, to do everything he could to get the "son" an exit visa from Romania. Ceausescu had long since prepared himself for the meeting with Palade at which he would generously agree to this act of clemency.

"Champagne," Ceausescu suddenly ordered. "And get Celac for me."

The waiter came over with Cordon Rouge, and Ceausescu downed two glasses, then asked his interpreter: "Find what Carter said about me and his Georgia."

"Yes, comrade." Celac has always been prepared when called by Ceausescu. "He said, referring to you: 'This is the president's fourth trip to our country, and after he leaves Washington shortly, he will be going to Chattanooga, to Dallas, to Houston. He will also be visiting New York. Unfortunately he won't get to Georgia *(laughter)* on this trip. He is going to save that for dessert when he comes back on his next trip.'"[9]

"Exactly. Dessert, that's what he said. Dessert. Thank you, Celac," said Ceausescu, dismissing the interpreter with a wave of the hand.

"Well, let's now have the dessert, Pacepa," he whispered as softly as he could, after Celac had left. "I want you to start immediately feeding Billy money through your Liberian agent and his brother in London. The Billy operation shouldn't take place here, under American eyes. Use London and Liberia. In the meantime, send one of your best officers to the office we opened in Atlanta. He should provide future logistical support. By the time I make my next visit here, Billy should be a long-standing and productive agent. And then I'll go to Georgia for dessert!"

As Ceausescu was leaving the library, he ordered me to find a way for Elena to participate in the ceremony of signing the joint declaration, scheduled for the next afternoon at the White House. I attempted to point out that as far as I knew there was no such precedent at the White House, and that she was supposed to go with Rosalynn Carter to visit the National Museum of History and Technology and attend an official luncheon there. A suddenly tired Ceausescu cut me off: "Change it. Make Rosalynn understand that this is Comrade Elena's most ardent desire."

[9]*Ceausescu's 1978 State Visit to the U.S.A.*, p. 100.

XVIII

SINCE Watergate, Ceausescu has hated the United States Congress, holding it responsible for the resignation of Richard Nixon, in whom he had made long-term investments. With Ceausescu, however, his political goals have always taken precedence over his personal feelings. In preparing for the current visit, he asked me to put as many congressmen as possible into his schedule. Numbers are what count for Ceausescu, more than anything else. Especially numbers of people. "Not too many Republicans. They are reactionary." That is Ceausescu's favorite word for anti-Communist. He also prefers members of the Senate over those of the House. "Their terms are too short."

SENATOR JACKSON TAKES A HARD LINE

This morning Ceausescu was joined for breakfast at Blair House by Senators Alan Cranston, Edward Kennedy, Ted Stevens, Adlai Stevenson, Abraham Ribicoff, Harrison Williams, and Jacob Javits. Just before they came, Ceausescu ordered me to entertain Senator Henry Jackson, scheduled for his next meeting, in case the breakfast lasted longer than foreseen. "Warm him up. Jackson is not only the chairman of the Senate's Energy and Natural Resources Committee, he is also a Jew. You do remember our most valuable national resources, don't you?" he asked. "Oil, Jews, and Germans!" he added, without waiting for my reply. "We should extract as much money as possible from them."

In 1975, the United States granted Romania most favored nation status, but the Jackson-Vanik Amendment to the 1974 Trade

274

Act ties its annual renewal to free emigration rights. I became one of the few people responsible for keeping this status alive for Romania, and my earlier meetings with Senator Jackson had been in this capacity.

In his discussion with Ceausescu that day, Jackson was polite but very firm, his main concern being over human rights and freedom of emigration. He stated flatly that, based on his experience, Bucharest had repeatedly tried to cheat on emigration; that the current situation, according to verifiable figures he had, was far from satisfactory; that emigration and human rights were systematically being violated by Bucharest; that emgires from Romania were being forced into intelligence operations in the West; and that substantial corrections would have to be made if Romania wanted to preserve its most favored nation status. I always admired Senator Jackson's firmness.

After the meeting Ceausescu erupted in fury. "That son of a bitch," he muttered through clenched teeth, racing upstairs to the library, which had become his temporary lair. Once there, however, he had second thoughts, demonstrating again that Communist leaders respect only force. Turning the stereo up loud, Ceausescu ordered me to send a telegram to Bucharest asking that DIE attempts to recruit Jews filing emigration requests be temporarily halted. Then, walking agitatedly around the room, he dictated the text of the Romanian press communiqué about his meeting with Senator Jackson: "During the talk, which took place in a cordial atmosphere, they tackled problems pertaining to the development of the Romanian-American collaboration, based on equality, mutual respect and advantage, especially in the economic field, and views were exchanged on certain aspects of the present-day international situation."[1]

At noon, following a short meeting between Carter and Ceausescu and a formal meeting of the American and Romanian delegations, the two presidents signed their joint declaration. Seated next to their husbands at the official table were both Elena Ceausescu and Rosalynn Carter. Rumor had it that this was a first in White House history. Ceausescu had once again proved to be an astute judge of human nature. Elena's wish to participate in the signing had been whispered into Rosalynn's ear.

[1]*Ibid*, p. 109.

After this ceremony, Ceausescu left for a working luncheon at the National Press Club. I accompanied Elena to an official luncheon given for her by Rosalynn Carter. Evidently convinced that Elena really was a scientist, Rosalynn had scheduled the luncheon to take place at the National Museum of History and Technology. "Just look at the peanut head," Elena exploded during our drive. "She thinks I've never seen a museum before. Idiotic, darling. A presidential luncheon in a museum! I hope she's not going to serve us fried dinosaur."

After the luncheon, attended by renowned scientists carefully selected by the White House, Rosalynn took Elena on a short tour of several museum rooms temporarily closed to the public. Romanian photographers and television crews busily took many pictures, but the Western news media showed little interest. Waiting at the exit, however, was a man who had evidently been told that Rosalynn was with a foreign visitor, and he asked Elena what country she was from.

"Romania, darling!" said Elena, turning toward the anonymous questioner.

On our drive back to Blair House, Elena ordered that the Romanian press communiqué about her luncheon with Rosalynn include the following: "On their way numerous citizens welcomed them with consideration and respect. A great number of radio and television reporters were present. Mrs. Elena Ceausescu answered questions of press correspondents."[2]

We got back only a few minutes after Ceausescu had returned from the National Press Club. "The Comrade was asking for you," one of his bodyguards told me. "He was furious."

"RAUTA SHOULD DIE!"

Ceausescu was in the library, pacing from one end to the other and clenching his fists. "Where were you?" he asked nervously. "Why is Rauta still alive?" Constantin Rauta was the DIE engineer who had defected to the United States in 1973. "Who canceled my order to have him executed?" Ceausescu went on, glaring at me. "Rauta should die the moment I get back to Bu-

2*Ibid.*, p. 127.

charest. Killed by the Mafia, as I have ordered many times." He continued his nervous pacing, without looking in my direction. "He should also be compromised in the West as a drug smuggler. Just in case. Some foolish minds may try to connect his death with his defection."

Suddenly Ceausescu stopped in front of me. "His wife has got to have a lover in Bucharest. Can you understand me? A lover!" Now he was yelling. "A lover who's good at sex. One who'll keep her tied down there with his dick for the rest of her life. She has to refuse to leave Romania, and that'll put an end to Rauta's case. And he should be killed! Killed! Killed!"

It was only later that I learned what had happened at the National Press Club. Ceausescu had been given a hard time by Nestor Ratesh of Radio Free Europe and other American journalists, who had asked for Rauta's family to be released from Romania.

Since 1965, Ceausescu has been the absolute proprietor of Romania. His portrait is on display everywhere, more than those of Hitler and Stalin in their day. Ceausescu's will becomes law at the mere scrawl of his pen. His army and security forces are more repressive than Idi Amin's ever were. All the domestic media, from children's magazines to television stations, belong to Ceausescu more than the Hearst newspapers ever belonged to William Randolph Hearst. *Scinteia,* the official voice of the Communist Party, always devotes the two righthand columns of its front page to what Ceausescu did the day before, whom he met and what he talked about; the rest of the paper consists mainly of articles praising Ceausescu's leadership in every facet of life. Each day's radio and television broadcasting program starts and ends with praise to "the most adored and esteemed son of the Romanian people." During his current visit to Washington, Ceausescu had been preening around and showing off his power, and now he had been humiliated in front of 200 American journalists and foreign press correspondents. It was all Rauta's fault. He had committed the unforgiveable crime of *lèse majesté.*

Ever since his defection in 1973, Rauta had been a thorn in Ceausescu's side. At first it was because he defected taking a whole diplomatic pouch with him and turning it over to the

American authorities. Then it was because Rauta made all kinds of interventions on Capitol Hill and staged demonstrations in front of the Romanian embassy in Washington, asking for his wife and daughter. Now Rauta's actions had started to bear fruit. There had been almost no single week over the past two years without some kind of appeal, request, pressure, or condemnation from a member of the U.S. Congress in connection with Ceausescu's refusal to allow Rauta's family to emigrate. In 1976, when—under pressure from Congress—the State Department had officially asked that the American consul in Bucharest be allowed to speak privately with Rauta's wife, Ceausescu had exploded: "I am president here!" He immediately called the minister of interior and directed him to provide "evidence" that the consul was an active CIA officer.

"Why are you gasping like a fish? If you don't have the evidence today, you'd better make it for tomorrow. If the Americans ask once more to have their consul talk to Rauta's wife, I'll expel him as a spy and plaster it all over the press, around the whole world."

The next day, as usual, Ceausescu had second thoughts. "Our proletarian arm should be long enough to reach criminals wherever they are hiding," he said, again ordering that Rauta be secretly killed in the United States without any trace of Bucharest's involvement. "Use the American Mafia to do it. Today we need them; tomorrow they may need us, and we won't forget their help."

At that time, 1976, the DIE had no contacts with the American Mafia. Soon afterwards, however, an American from New York City was arrested at the Bulgarian border for the possession of undeclared merchandise, including drugs and monitoring devices. Under a bilateral agreement, as soon as the Bulgarians learned that the man's wife was a native Romanian, his case was turned over to the Romanian Securitate. During his interrogation by the Romanians, he admitted to being an important member of the American Mafia, and his case was given to the DIE.

The DIE recruited "Leman" and gave him secure living conditions in Romania, including the luxury of a personally owned apartment and a firm commitment for political asylum, if needed. "Leman" moved his wife and his drug smuggling business to Bucharest. Given the task of locating and assassinating

Rauta, "Leman" came up with reliable information, photographs of Rauta secretly taken in the United States, and an operational plan to kill him in an "unfortunate accident" in which he would end up at the bottom of a river. Ceausescu personally approved the assassination plan. By the end of March 1978, however, when "Leman" was in Washington to do the deed, Ceausescu had second thoughts. He postponed Rauta's assassination until the end of his official visit to the United States.

BIBLES INTO TOILET PAPER

Around three o'clock, when I informed Elena that Professor Emanuel Merdinger was there, she was practicing an acceptance speech for her honorary diploma.

"I don't care who is waiting for me. Is my diploma there or not?" Elena was all smiles in anticipation. Two seconds later, however, she pounced on me. "It's still a mystery to me why you decided to punish me with this awful university, and to make a martyr out of me with this filthy Jew. In Romania we're giving all the Jews the sack, but here I have to flirt with one in front of the press."

"I should respectfully report to you, Comrade Elena, that the University of Illinois has the third largest university library in the United States, with over five million books." I had come prepared for this and was determined to avoid any discussion about Professor Merdinger.

"Is that true? If so, darling, why don't you give them my book? Why do you always wait for me to think of things? Your mind is off playing the violin, you fiddler!"

"I was waiting to have it translated into English, like the one just printed in German."

"Big deal. If they want science, they should learn Romanian. Have you called the photographers?"

"Yes."

"Idiots that they are, they may miss the ceremony." Elena is always interested only in the photographers, never in the journalists. The latter are told what to write anyway.

As General Aurel Florea had just reported to me, Professor Merdinger had been briefed in minute detail on the degree of deference and flattery to use with Elena. When she entered the room, Merdinger was humbly bent over at the waist. Keeping his eyes glued to his shoes, he sang out a flowery hymn of praise.

Clutching the diploma with both hands, Elena cleared her throat, coughed a couple of times, looked helplessly at Merdinger and at me, and all at once burst out in a very loud voice: "I would like to express my special gratitude for the distinction I have been awarded." That was the last sentence of the acceptance speech Ceausescu had composed for her, the rest of which was a eulogy on the Romanian contribution to the development of science and technology throughout the world. Forgetting the rest, she hastily left the room and did not stop until she had reached the library. When I caught up with her there, Ceausescu, Pungan, Oprea, and Andrei were admiring her diploma.

"I know Merdinger. Was he nice today?" Pungan asked Elena.

"Very nice. We should use him for promoting our interests in America, Nick. He is such a good friend of Romania."

"What a marvelous story," Oprea chimed in.

In mid-1985, Bucharest once again came under attack on Capitol Hill and in the American press for human rights abuses, following a Wall Street Journal *disclosure that 20,000 Bibles donated by the World Reformed Alliance to the Reformed Church in Romania had been intercepted by the Romanian government and recycled into toilet paper.*[3] *A month later this matter was the subject of four letters to the* Journal's *editor:*

"Where are the human rights of the Christians whose shipment of 20,000 Bibles was intercepted by the Romanian government and sent to a pulp mill to be turned into toilet paper?" wrote Congressman Mark D. Siljander, asking for cancellation of Romania's most favored nation status. Another letter writer also expressed revulsion. A third letter was written by a Romanian bishop and, it goes without saying, defended Bucharest.

The fourth letter was from Professor Emanuel Merdinger, who wrote: "I cannot and will not believe that Bibles were recycled in Romania for toilet paper. Laszlo Hamos, who is quoted in the article, is a Hungarian by origin and has carried out this campaign of hate against Romania for many years and for one pur-

---

[3]Peter K. Keresztes, "The Bible as Romanian Toilet Paper," *The Wall Street Journal*, June 14, 1985, p. 24.

pose: He wants Transylvania ceded to Hungary. This would be impossible without a war. In World War I and II the Romanians occupied Budapest and will do it again if there is another war."[4] This is, word for word, exactly what Ceausescu used to say in his rages against Budapest. It is precisely what he said to me in March 1978, when he ordered the savage reprisals against Carol Kiraly, the Romanian dissident of Hungarian descent. Furthermore, Laszlo Hamos was one of the main organizers of an immense anti-Ceausescu demonstration that took place on April 16, 1978, outside the Waldorf Astoria Hotel in New York, where Ceausescu was staying. That same evening a furious Ceausescu ordered Ambassador Nicolae and me to pay professional criminals to kill Hamos and another two organizers of the demonstration whose names he had been told.

HIS OWN FIFTH COLUMN

In the evening, Ceausescu went to the Romanian embassy for his long-awaited meeting with Romanian emigres from the United States and Canada.

In the early 1970s, when Ceausescu learned that Romania had over 600,000 emigres abroad, he became very interested in Adolf Hitler's Fifth Column. That was not too surprising, as Ceausescu had always studied Hitler's "charisma" and had repeatedly analysed the original Nazi films of Hitler's speeches. Some of the films, such as the one of his speech opening the 1936 Olympics, became part of the permanent collection at Ceausescu's residence.

Hitler's style fully rubbed off onto Ceausescu. The latter's speeches are loaded with the same kind of *wir muessen*. We must do thus and so, screamed at his listeners and emphasized by arms flailing and fists pounding the table. The most startling similarity, however, is in the way Ceausescu strikes a nationalistic chord with his listeners. In almost every speech he recalls the Romanian people's origins in proud Roman and Dacian warriors and their 2,000-year continuity, just as Hitler harped on the Aryans and Niebelungen and proclaimed a Thousand-Year Reich.

[4]"Letters to the Editor: Stop Pampering Romania," *The Wall Street Journal*, July 11, 1985.

The words *sovereignty, independence,* and *freedom* appear regularly in Ceausescu's propaganda and appeal to the same sort of wounded national pride that the Germans felt after World War I, enabling Hitler to come to power screaming about freedom for the fatherland. Ceausescu is always exhorting Romanians that only through more hard work can the country's freedom be attained, much as Hitler proclaimed that *Arbeit macht frei*—work makes you free—and cynically posted it over the gates of Auschwitz and Dachau. Ceausescu's propagandistic vocabulary is so ingrained that even in his toast to Jimmy Carter at the White House on Wednesday he boasted that "for almost 2050 years . . . since the setting up of the first Dacian state, the Romanians have . . . fought to be free and will always be free."[5]

In Ceausescu's view, the Fifth Column played an important role in portraying Hitler worldwide as a charismatic leader. That was why Ceausescu wanted to have his own Fifth Column, an army of emigré sympathizers in Western countries. He considers all emigrés Romanian citizens falling under Romanian law and obliged to promote, defend and support Bucharest's policies, exactly as Hitler did. In Ceausescu's concept, the Romanian Orthodox Church should penetrate into emigrés' souls and thoughts, just as microphones, mail censorship, and Securitate agents do with his domestic population. He therefore ordered that priests who were either deep cover DIE officers or agents be sent abroad to take over the emigré churches and their congregations, indoctrinate the emigrés, and silently bring their organizations under Bucharest's control.

In the new Romanian Fifth Column that began to be created in the early 1970s, Ceausescu envisioned not only a useful instrument for plotting against the West or for spreading rumors and disinformation. For him and for Elena, it was also supposed to be the showcase presenting their smiling faces to the West. When Ceausescu gave me instructions for his meeting with the Romanian Americans, he ordered that no effort or cost be spared to make it a "grandiose" occasion. "Get all your agents there, especially the priests! Write their speeches for them, and teach them how to read them. A festive Party Congress in America,

[5]*Ceausescu's 1978 State Visit to the U.S.A.,* p. 101.

that's what it should be." The DIE stations in Washington, New York, and Ottawa spent weeks selecting the participants, paying the expenses for some of them, briefing the speakers, and preparing most of their speeches. This morning I had presented Ceausescu with a handwritten report describing the participants, with biographical summaries of all the speakers, including their contribution as agents, and giving the gist of their speeches, in which he made only a few changes.

That evening, more than 250 Romanian emigrés had been "invited" to meet Ceausescu at the Romanian embassy. A few hours earlier, I had given the United States Secret Service a list of their names. This list was a unique bouquet of DIE agents gathered together from the United States and Canada. Among them were members of various churches, representatives of emigré organizations taken over by the DIE, and the chairmen of emigré organizations created and funded by the DIE. Twelve people gave speeches of praise or flattery, and four of them were churchmen. According to Florea, only one of the eulogists was not a DIE agent.

The meeting, which was continuously and abundantly nourished with traditional Romanian food and drink, became warmer and warmer as time went on. Flattery was the evening's keynote, and the carefully selected participants outdid themselves. Ceausescu, in seventh heaven, made a rousing, patriotic speech, playing for all he was worth on the nationalistic heartstrings of his listeners. He wound up with a vibrant appeal for his audience to help their homeland and the Romanian Communist Party.

In an unusual departure, Ceausescu did not leave until the last emigré participant at the meeting had gone. He and Elena then enjoyed a glass of champagne with the embassy staff, asking them to work harder and better to make all Romanian emigrés in the United States as loyal to the homeland as those who had been at the meeting.

On the way back to Blair House I was sitting in Ceausescu's car. He and Elena, glowing warmly from the champagne and the flattery, were each nestled into a corner of the limousine. "It really was just like a Party Congress," said a delighted Ceausescu. "Your boys did a good job, Pacepa."

"Go on!" disagreed Elena. "Are you trying to say that the Party

Congresses are staged by Pacepa's spooks working behind the scenes? *You* are the magic attraction. People travel from all over, just to be able to shake your hand. And mine."

VENDETTA AGAINST THE ARCHBISHOP

Back at Blair House, Ceausescu went to the library, turned on the stereo, and asked for the chess set.

"The dominie looks good in his monkey suit. What kind of a job is he doing?" Ceausescu started out, opening the game.

He was referring to the archbishop of the Romanian Orthodox Church in the United States and Canada, who had been dispatched from Romania to take over control of the emigré churches in the United States and Canada. In the Washington station's handwritten report that I had passed Ceausescu that morning there was a substantial chapter on the archbishop's prolific contact with the DIE as a long-standing agent who had been successfully used during the years he had lived at the Romanian Mission in Jerusalem and at St. Tikhon's Monastery in South Canaan, Pennsylvania.

"Active and productive, according to Florea."

"We need to make him a deep cover officer, the way we did his predecessor. Understood?"

"Yes, comrade."

The "predecessor" was Archimandrite Bartolomeu Anania, an old DIE hand who had been sent to the United States years ago to take over an emigré religious newspaper called *Credinta* (*Faith*) and use it for influence. The DIE recalled him in 1974 because of reports that he intended to defect to the United States. If that had happened, it could have compromised the use of high-level clergymen as a cover for DIE officers, something Ceausescu wanted to keep a dark secret.

"We ought to make the dominie a colonel, or even a general. And pump as much money into him as we can. With money you can buy anything in America, churches included. How many emigrés have we got here?"

"Over 300,000." Ceausescu loves to hear this figure, which is impressive by Romanian standards.

"How many in the computer so far?"

"Around 100,000."

"When will all 300,000 be included?" he went on, further trying to distract me from the game.

"Sixteen to eighteen months. It took some time for the project to get off the ground. Now it's just a matter of feeding in the data."

In 1975, Ceausescu had ordered the DIE to set up a complete, computerized inventory of all emigrés who were native or second generation Romanians, arranged by country of residence, profession, and place of employment. It was an ambitious project, to be constructed from consular records, mail censorship data, and intelligence sources. Ceausescu considered it to be the most important step toward creating his Fifth Column, and he ordered that it be completed in the space of no more than one five-year plan.

"Three hundred thousand is a whole army," Ceausescu remarked, after he had discreetly pushed one of his pieces forward, although it was not his turn. "If only ten percent worked in industry, and each one of them could solve only one technological problem a year, it would give us 30,000 new technologies. At $50,000 for each technology—and that's an impossibly low figure—we would be saving one and a half billion dollars a year. And if only one percent would go into American politics, that would give us 3,000 political activists in America. What about that?"

Ceausescu ordered wine and a plate of his favorite tomatoes, onions, and feta cheese.

"What's new with that priest you sent here via Italy a few years ago?"

"'Avram'?"

"The one who had such a touching story about the persecution of his family in Romania under Communism. The fat little shrimp who hasn't been able to learn English yet. He gave a nice speech today."

"'Avram,' comrade. Florea reports that he's taken over a church in Detroit and is now one of the station's most active influence agents among emigrés."

"I told you so when I met him on my other visit here. He has the wiliness of a Romanian peasant. And he's very devoted, won't ever forget who's boss. Take care of him."

"Yes, comrade."

"He should also be used against Trifa. Every single agent has to be put on the job of destroying that filthy reactionary swine," Ceausescu erupted. "I won't be able to sleep until I see him thrown out of America, tossed away like trash."

When a bodyguard came in to report that Elena had finished her massage and was waiting for Ceausescu, he was still cursing Trifa. "We have to crush him like a worm," Ceausescu said, grinding his foot into the floor, before he left the library. "Like a worm!"

Valerian Trifa, a naturalized American citizen, was the archbishop of the Romanian Orthodox Episcopate of America, embracing most of the emigré churches in the United States and Canada. There was also another—much smaller—Romanian episcopate in the United States, which was taken over by the DIE. It was now headed by a trusted agent from Bucharest and given the grand name of Romanian Orthodox Missionary Archbishopric in the United States and Canada. Ceausescu intended for the latter to take over Trifa's parishes and congregations. Despite all the pressure exerted on him over the years, Trifa refused to be subordinated to Bucharest's canonical and political rule.

Trifa had personally come to Ceausescu's attention in February 1972, during the first day Ceausescu took over the DIE. General Gheorghe Bolanu, then in charge of DIE operations against emigrés, vehemently complained about the inability of the Romanian authorities to subordinate him canonically.

"Recruit him as an agent!" Ceausescu interrupted Bolanu's report.

"We've tried. He's stubborn as a mule."

"Don't you have anything compromising on him?"

"We do, Comrade Ceausescu. When Trifa immigrated to the United States in 1955, he did not disclose that as a student he had been a member of the Iron Guard fascist organization. We have hard evidence of that."

"Blackmail him! Threaten that you will inform the American authorities, if he doesn't cooperate with us," said Ceausescu.

"We did, but Trifa obstinately refused," replied Bolanu, who is obstinate enough himself.

"What kind of DIE have we got? If we can't recruit a wretched priest, how can we ever hope to recruit a prime minister?" Ceausescu cried out.

The next day, Ceausescu called Bolanu and me in and asked us to report back to him on what was known about Trifa's activity as an Iron Guard member. DIE investigations determined that Trifa had joined the Iron Guard in the mid-1930s, becoming a *legionnaire,* as its members were called, at a very young age. It was also learned that, as he was an old and trusted member, the Iron Guard had supported him to become chairman of two student organizations, with the goal of changing them into legionnaire branches, and that in 1940 he had become the editor of the Iron Guard newspaper for a short time. A Securitate source reported that, on the evening of January 20, 1940, Trifa had delivered an inflammatory speech to several thousand students gathered in front of the Bucharest university, and that the next morning the Iron Guard had started an armed rebellion to take over political power in Romania. Archive reports on this rebellion, which had a strongly anti-Semitic bias, gave details on: the pogrom organized by Iron Guard "death detachments" in the Jewish section of Bucharest; the crushing of the rebellion by the government; and the support given to the government by Berlin, which considered the Iron Guard—although a Nazi organization—to be too anarchistic. The archives also showed that the government had arrested most of the Iron Guard members and sentenced them, though some of its leaders had escaped to Germany, which had given them asylum. This group, Trifa among them, had been condemned *in absentia* by Bucharest. More recent DIE reports showed that after World War II Trifa broke contact with the Iron Guard and that after 1955, when he came to the United States, he dedicated his life to the priesthood. They also showed that his hatred for Communism had caused him obstinately to refuse any form of cooperation with Bucharest.

"Was he involved in the Iron Guard pogrom against the Jews?" Ceausescu interrupted Bolanu's report, evidently displeased with its last part.

"Not according to the file."

"We can't get Trifa expelled from America just because he was an Iron Guard member. We've got to make him a Nazi criminal. Keep digging," he said in dismissing us.

Extensive DIE investigation resulted in the unequivocal conclusion that Trifa had not been personally involved in crimes or
assassination attempts. Refusing to accept this, Ceausescu told
the internal Securitate to conduct a new investigation, but the
result was the same.

At this point, Ceausescu personally stepped in and ordered
Bolanu to mount an operation aimed at getting Trifa denatural-
ized and deported from the United States as a Nazi war criminal.
Ceausescu also ordered that intelligence officers and agents
under cover as priests and religious be sent to the United States
and Canada in preparation for the gradual takeover of Trifa's
episcopate.

The framing of Trifa as a war criminal was a long process that
followed to the letter the guidelines received from the KGB on
how to go about such an operation. First, the general horror
scene of crimes actually committed by others should be set, to
bring back heart-breaking memories in the minds of survivors.
Next, one of the real butchers of that time and place should be
selected—one now dead, whose style of killing had been peculiar
to him so that it would be remembered by the survivors—and
then his crimes should be attributed to the target.

In the Trifa case, the Romanian service chose an Iron Guard
assassin who had customarily shot his victims while riding in the
sidecar of a motorcycle. In an elaborate photomontage, Trifa's
head was substituted for this man's in a photograph destined for
publication in the West and for use as the most suggestive evidence against Trifa. Letters and other written statements were
composed under the supervision of a psychologist and attributed
to people by then long dead—some having died in Communist
jails—and to a few agents living in Romania, some of whom were
later allowed to "emigrate." All of these statements depicted
Trifa as a vicious monster, giving convincing details about how
he had ordered Jewish homes, stores, and synagogues to be set
on fire and Jews to be tortured and killed, and about how he
himself had been seen killing Jews. The wording was designed to
persuade survivors living in the West to recognize some of the
details of these scenes from over 30 years earlier and to point to
Trifa as the author of the deeds.

At the end of 1972, the DIE indirectly informed Trifa that the
United States and Israel had secretly asked the Romanian gov-

ernment for evidence relating to his Nazi activity. He was offered protection in return for cooperation with Bucharest. The new recruitment attempt failed, just as the old ones had.

In early 1973, Ceausescu decided to start his operation to compromise Trifa indirectly, making it seem the work of Jewish organizations and the United States government. "I don't want to be caught red-handed," he said, "in case the American government takes too close a look at the evidence."

A DIE agent, an American Jew, who was familiar with Trifa's case from having previously been used against him by the DIE, was selected to start the ball rolling in the United States. He was given a substantial number of falsified documents accusing Trifa of being a Nazi criminal, and the counterfeited photograph.

Another DIE agent, who was living in Western Europe and was also a Jew, was soon introduced into the operation, providing some international Jewish organizations with "evidence" of Trifa's personal role in assassinating Jews. This agent was conceived as being a second, independent source of confirmation for the information from the first.

In 1974, Ceausescu ordered that the "Marcu-Yesahanu" connection be used to involve the Israeli intelligence service in the operation. At a meeting in Bucharest, Marcu informed Yesahanu that the DIE had gathered spectacular evidence against a Nazi criminal hiding out in the United States as a high-ranking clergyman. In Marcu's story, the Romanian government had, however, decided not to act against the man, lest its direct intervention against an Orthodox bishop be interpreted as another Communist attack on religion. Yesahanu became extremely interested in the case, since the discovery of Nazi criminals had always been one of the main tasks of the Israeli intelligence service. Following Yesahanu's repeated requests and firm commitment not to involve Romania, Marcu finally let himself be persuaded to give him copies of the "documents," but only as a personal gesture, not with his government's approval.

Toward the mid-1970s, the wife of Romania's chief rabbi, Moses Rosen, had been arrested in London for shoplifting in a department store. She was, in fact, a kleptomaniac. Ceausescu immediately ordered that Rabbi Rosen be used against Trifa, in exchange for help in solving his wife's problem and keeping the incident a secret. The then chief of the DIE, Nicolae Doicaru, was personally charged by Ceausescu with manipulating Rosen. According to Doicaru, Rosen agreed to cooperate, was immediately sent to the United States to create a public climate against Trifa, and later was repeatedly used to help Bucharest in other influence operations in the West.

Ceausescu's efforts bore fruit in 1975, when a denaturalization suit against Trifa was started in the United States District Court in Detroit. Washington asked Bucharest to cooperate in the trial, but Ceausescu remained faithful to his original decision. He approved that the American authorities be given only a few items of evidence, basically ones dating from before the Communist takeover of Romania, and decided to avoid any deeper, more direct involvement.

In 1976, Ceausescu ordered that new attempts be made for Trifa's recruitment, this time under the pressure of the trial against him and an official U.S. request to Bucharest for cooperation in the trial. The chief of the DIE's Emigré Brigade, Colonel Constantin Afrim, a former undercover consul in the United States, and his deputy, Colonel Nicolae Sporis, alias Spataru, were directly involved. Their discussions with Trifa were unsuccessful, and Ceausescu finally decided to put into motion the full operation for having Trifa expelled from the United States.

After receiving asylum in the United States, I reported to the American authorities about Ceausescu's vendetta against Valerian Trifa for refusing to subordinate his episcopate to Bucharest, as well as about the false evidence against him fabricated by the DIE. The photomontage was soon located and seen to have been fabricated. In 1979, however, the Justice Department's newly created Office of Special Investigations believed it had evidence that Trifa had indeed been a Nazi war criminal and took the case to court a year later. In the end, Trifa voluntarily surrendered his naturalization papers, and, in August 1984, he was deported from the United States. In January 1987, he died of a heart attack in Cascais, Portugal, where he had taken refuge.

CHAPTER

XIX

On Friday morning we flew on Air Force One to Chattanooga, Tennessee, to visit the 2.4 million kilowatt Sequoia Atomic Power Plant, scheduled to start production in 1979, and the Combustion Engineering Works, which produced pressurized boilers and other components for nuclear power plants. This visit had been set up at Ceausescu's specific request. His dream was to make Romania a major producer and exporter of nuclear power plants, using its large and relatively untrumpeted uranium reserves.

GETTING THE CANDU FOR ROMANIA

It was in 1967 that the DIE had first learned the Canadian government was developing a new type of nuclear reactor operating on natural uranium, which Romania had in abundance, rather than on enriched uranium, which only the United States, the Soviet Union, Great Britain, and France could produce and provide. One year later, two Romanian nuclear specialists "defected" to the West and found employment in Canadian nuclear facilities. Both were undercover DIE officers. In 1969, two DIE illegal officers documented as Western citizens were also among the employees of the Atomic Energy of Canada, Limited—AECL. In the uniqueness of the Canadian reactor, called CANDU, Ceausescu saw the perfect solution for making Romania an exporter of atomic power plants, uranium, and heavy water—used by CANDU as a moderator—throughout the Third World, where he judged countries reluctant to have their future industrial development depend on either American or Soviet technology.

In January 1970, Ceausescu created a State Committee for Nuclear Energy to deal with his plan, but it proved incapable of producing anything but bureaucrats and paperwork. In 1972, he put the nuclear program under his personal supervision, with me as its national coordinator. Then was when he made me his personal advisor, in addition to the other positions I already had. He also appointed the deputy director of the DIE's Illegal Brigade, Colonel Constantin Stanciu, as deputy minister of foreign trade and made him my assistant for the nuclear program. A secret staff of research scholars and undercover intelligence officers was set up outside Bucharest in a large DIE safehouse, to coordinate the intelligence effort for obtaining the technology for the CANDU reactor and for the industrial production of the heavy water it used as a moderator. Soon this staff expanded its activity to the United States, France, Italy, and West Germany to obtain intelligence on the steam turbines needed by the CANDU reactor to generate electricity, as well as on the construction of nuclear power plants able to withstand earthquakes, floods, and high winds.

Ceausescu conceived the heart of the whole operation to be a new generation of DIE illegal officers with technical backgrounds. They were to be dispatched to the West as Western citizens to gain access to the needed nuclear technologies. Up to a point, these illegals were similar to the famous KGB illegal officer, Colonel Rudolf Ivanovich Abel. A fluent English speaker, Abel was transformed by the KGB into a native American named Emil Goldfus, born in New York in 1903, as New York City birth records showed. Secretly infiltrated into the United States, Abel (alias Goldfus) spent many years in New York as an American who had supposedly never heard of the Soviet Union or Communism. He was caught by the Federal Bureau of Investigation only when another KGB illegal officer, Reino Hayhanen, who knew him, defected to the United States.

Romania's new breed of illegals were recruited from among scholars and highly qualified engineers. They were taught to become fluent in Western languages and were given intensive individual intelligence training. Finally, they were documented as Western citizens with good academic credentials and secretly dispatched to the West. Among the DIE's main nuclear targets in which such illegals have eventually been employed in significant positions were: in Canada, the AECL, General Electric of Canada, Combustion Engineering of Ottawa, and Donlee Manufacturing of Toronto; in the United States, General Electric and Combustion Engineering; in West Germany, Siemens, AEG, ITT, and Kraftwerke Union; and in Italy, Ansaldo Nucleari Impianti. A corps of illegal couriers especially set up for the nuclear operation started unloading dead drops in the West and picking up significant quantities of undeveloped film.

As he usually does before meeting an international leader or making other important foreign policy decisions, Ceausescu ordered the DIE to prepare a detailed study of the AECL, the Canadian Export Development Corporation—EDC—and their conditions for exporting their CANDU-600 reactor. The DIE study showed that the Canadians were having serious problems with it. Firstly, the furor provoked by the 1974 Indian atomic bomb caused the Canadian government to pass laws requiring foreign customers for CANDU reactors to be signatories of the Nuclear Non-Proliferation Treaty. They also had to permit Canada to inspect the nuclear equipment it sold. This excluded the Communist bloc and numerous Third World countries from even considering the import of CANDU reactors. Secondly, a reactor sold to Argentina had produced a $130 million loss for AECL, because it had not allowed for inflation in the contract. Thirdly, Canada would have to sell at least 20 more reactors to recover its huge investment made for developing the CANDU. And fourthly, the Canadian government was so desperately in need of exporting the CANDU that it had used a $5 million bribe to grease its sale to South Korea.

A few days after Ceausescu had gotten the DIE study, I was called into his rose garden. "We should use Pavlov's conditioned reflex," he started off. "We should make the Canadians' mouth water, just as Pavlov did with his dog." He ordered me to mount a disinformation campaign spreading the idea that Bucharest not only was willing to agree to Canadian inspection but was also interested in buying as many as 20 CANDUs, together with the uranium and heavy water needed to run them—on the condition that the Canadian government transfer the CANDU technology to Romania and show the Romanians how to build the reactors for later export to the Third World.

During that walk, Ceausescu decided the future of Romania's nuclear program: Canada should be kept "drooling" until Romania learned to produce CANDU reactors; together with natural uranium and heavy water, they would become a valuable source of foreign currency for keeping Romanian Communism alive; Bucharest could make all kinds of non-binding promises to the Canadians, but under no circumstances should it agree to any limitation or precondition for the export of CANDU reactors; on the pretext of purchasing CANDU reactors, Bucharest should obtain a Canadian credit of $1 billion or more, as well as the right to pay not in cash, but in merchandise difficult to export to the West; eventually Romania would buy from Canada only enough parts for one or two nuclear reactors to be built in Cernavoda, as a model for promoting Romanian export of nuclear power plants to the Third World; the rest of Romania's CANDU nuclear reactors as well as the installations for producing heavy water were to be built on the basis of intelligence materials.

In line with this strategy, on October 27, 1977, Romania signed a nuclear cooperation treaty with Ottawa, which believed Bucharest wanted to import 20 CANDU reactors. Four were supposed to be entirely built by AECL, and the rest in cooperation with the Romanians. On November 19, Romania also signed a license agreement by which AECL would transfer CANDU technology to Romania. AECL thus threw open its doors to Romanian specialists, most of them DIE officers.

The results of Ceausescu's operation were significant. The DIE soon obtained intelligence covering approximately 75 percent of CANDU-600 technology, a modern security system for nuclear plants, technology and equipment for producing heavy water, and architectural and construction plans for nuclear plants built in Canada, West Germany, and France. With this intelligence, the State Committee for Nuclear Energy was in the final phase of redesigning and producing the CANDU-600. The Ministry of the Chemical Industry had already started producing heavy water at ICECHIM-Bucharest.

A spin-off result of this intelligence operation was a factory in Targoviste producing special valves for the nuclear and chemical industry. This factory was based entirely on technological intelligence provided by "VISAN," a DIE illegal officer in France who worked for a well-known French company that supplied most of the nuclear power plants in the West with safety valves. Besides eighteen volumes of technical documentation for these nuclear valves, "VISAN" also provided the DIE with intelligence about everything else produced by the company, as well as about its equipment and machinery. As with the Canadians, Bucharest invented the prospect of commercial cooperation to make the French company "drool," which of course never came to fruition. This pretext did, however, permit the Romanians to send their specialists to the French company to learn how to use the intelligence provided by "VISAN," so that the French company could be reproduced in Romania.

In 1981, "VISAN" defected to France. In a book he later published about his activity as a DIE illegal officer, he described this elaborate intelligence operation in detail. [1]

When Air Force One had reached its cruising altitude, Ceausescu invited Gheorghe Oprea, Stefan Andrei, Ion Avram, and me to join him for breakfast.

"What's new with our CANDU, Pacepa?" Ceausescu led off.

"Stanciu was just called back to Ottawa. The Canadians have finally decided to start with the transfer of technology." Colonel Constantin Stanciu, under cover as deputy minister of foreign trade, was the head of the Romanian team negotiating with AECL.

"Good. They've fallen for our story with France, have they?" Ceausescu asked, winking toward us. The previous December he had ordered me to launch another disinformation campaign to make the Canadians believe that, if they did not "hook" the Romanians by immediately delivering the technological documentation for the CANDU-600, Bucharest might turn to France as a supplier of nuclear reactors.

"Evidently, Comrade Ceausescu. They want Stanciu there before the end of this week," I answered.

"What a marvelous idea!" Oprea exclaimed, gazing into Ceausescu's eyes. He never eats in Ceausescu's presence.

[1]Matei Pavel Haiducu, *J'ai refuse de tuer*, pp. 99–101.

"And keep them salivating, but go down from 20 to 16 reactors, then to four, and finally to two CANDUs. The whole trick is to keep the bell dinging."

"And the dog salivating," Andrei broke in, while polishing his plate.

"CANDU, uranium, and heavy water should become one of our Uzis," said Ceausescu, "one of our main exports to the Third World. Independent nuclear power from an independent Romania!" he proclaimed, pounding the table.

"And we should get the billion dollar credit from the Canadians for buying their CANDU," Oprea intervened.

"After we get the billion from Ottawa," Ceausescu concluded, "then we give the Canadians our final word: one reactor, and that one to be built mostly in Romania and paid for only with countertrade."

"CANDUs for shoes," flattered Oprea.

"And for steel," added Avram. Shoes and steel were Ceausescu's very favorite countertrade merchandise items, as Romania had built enormous shoe and steel plants and now had terrible difficulties exporting these products for hard currency.

Canadian journalist Thad McIlroy, who spent three years researching the story of CANDU's sale to Romania, wrote a comprehensive investigative report that shows what happened after my July 1978 break with Bucharest. According to McIlroy's report, in October 1978 Bucharest resumed its nuclear negotiations with Ottawa, and soon significant numbers of Romanian engineers were all over the Canadian plants; however, the number of CANDU reactors to be imported by Romania became smaller every year. "Then in March 1982 the deal collapsed," states McIlroy's report. "In September 1982 the Soviet Union entered the fray. It announced that it had signed an agreement with Romania for the joint construction of three Soviet-designed VVER-1000 reactors."

McIlroy neatly sums up the results of the CANDU operation: "Romania obtained a $1 billion (U.S.) dollar loan package from Canada to finance the sale. $320 million of the loan was grabbed immediately. This money was to be used partly to place down payments with Canadian manufacturers. As [the Romanians] *have stopped placing orders in Canada, they have used the money on non-nuclear related projects—in other words these funds were obtained fraudulently and were misappropriated. . . . But countertraded goods from this deal have begun to come into Canada. In January 1985 nearly 200,000 tons of Romanian 96" carbon steel plate hit North America. . . . The Romanian steel was sold for a declared price of $317/ton. At the time Canadian firms were selling the same product for between $500-$550 a ton."*[2]

It was precisely 10:00 AM when the airplane landed at Lovell Airport in Chattanooga and the governor of Tennessee and his wife welcomed the Ceausescus with an honor guard and a 21-gun salute. Thirty-five minutes later we were inside the Sequoia Atomic Power Plant, the most modern unit of the Tennessee Valley Authority. This was an unfinished giant, whose reactors would eventually have 39,000 zirconium tubes containing some 110,000 tons of uranium dioxide. Soon after noon, the Ceausescus were greeted by the chairman of the Combustion Engineering Works, who stressed the good relations existing between his company and Romania.

It was past two in the afternoon before we were back on our airplane. As soon as we had taken off, Ceausescu called Oprea, Avram, and me into his temporary office.

"Th-they s-started at the same time as we did," Ceausescu sputtered. "Theirs is twice as big as our Cernavada power plant, and in 1979 theirs will have its second reactor in operation and working at full capacity. And ours still exists only on paper." Ceausescu had started out calmly enough, but his stuttering forecast bad weather ahead, and none of us made a move to say anything.

Elena jumped into the conversation, though up to then she had seemed to be staring vacantly out the window. "Look at them—a bunch of incompetents who came here to America just for the free trip."

"Don't you have anything to say, Oprea?" intervened Ceausescu.

[2]Thad McIlroy, *Canada's CANDU Sale to Romania: Dubious Customer/Doubtful Benefits: An Investigative Report,* sent to The Hungarian Human Rights Foundation, Mississauga, Ontario, on May 1, 1986, *passim.*

"What can he say, comrade?" Elena went on. "He got to be an engineer overnight. And now you expect him to have ideas!"

"Yes, Comrade Ceausescu, yes! You're certainly right," replied Oprea, deciding to take on only one of them at a time. "We are terribly late with our nuclear program. I will immediately draw up a plan to give it new impetus."

"You are certainly right! You are certainly right!" Elena mimicked Oprea. "Who do you think you are to decide if the Romanian president is right or wrong?"

Ceausescu calmly continued: "I don't think that a simple plan would be enough. We need more radical measures. Why don't you think about moving the whole State Committee for Nuclear Energy and all the other organizations involved in the nuclear program out of Bucharest entirely? Someplace where they wouldn't be distracted by anything and could concentrate solely on their work."

"Did you hear, Oprea?" Elena kept after him. "Don't you know how do anything but scribble out another plan on another piece of paper? Look at the Comrade! He has solutions! You may understand that what he has just said so nicely is not a suggestion. It's a presidential order!"

"I have already done a report for you proposing to move them to Slatina," Oprea lied.

"Yes, that's not a bad idea. Let's move them there," approved Ceausescu.

I had long known about Ceausescu's desire to concentrate the sexiest new economic developments around his and Elena's birthplace, but he always maneuvered it so that the proposal seemed to come from someone else. Not long before, the minister of the metallurgical industry had been selected to propose that the immense and modern aluminum rolling-mills designed with technological intelligence from the United States and West Germany be built in Ceausescu's Oltenia. Gheorghe Oprea was the mouthpiece to ask that the new automobile factory created with the French Citroën firm be called OLTET and situated in Ceausescu's native area. The chairman of the State Committee for Nuclear Energy had recently "suggested" that Oltenia be the host for the new heavy water factory. And Oprea had also successfully insisted that Romania's first highway be built between Bucharest and that same Oltenia.

"Avram, how far along are you with the construction of the steam generator?" asked Ceausescu, already calmed down after making the decision about Slatina.

"We are almost ready, Comrade Ceausescu. When we are back, I'll invite you over to see it!"

"To see what? To see that same old fake generator you made out of wood to show the media?" Elena chuckled. In her hand she was ostentatiously holding *The Wall Street Journal* of April 12, containing a paid advertisement showing large pictures of herself and her husband.

"To see the real one, Comrade Ceausescu. Now we have a lot more intelligence, we have learned a lot more, and we are ready to move forward. Our turbine will be finished before the end of the year."

"Too bad for you, if you're lying again," pronounced Elena in leaving. She had seen her hairdresser calling her from the doorway.

Ceausescu commanded his chess set and signaled for me to sit down. The other two men left quietly, since no one ever wanted to be with Ceausescu when he was playing chess.

"Did you hear what the manager said?" Ceausescu went on. "About how strong a wind the reactor could withstand?"

"He said it was designed to hold out against 300-mile-an-hour hurricanes."

"And the most devastating earthquakes and floods. We've got to have the blueprints. Recruit somebody there and pay him handsomely. Or slip an illegal into the place."

Ceausescu led off as usual with the King's Gambit and asked, "What's new?" He has always treated his airplanes like a secure "bubble" impervious to microphone attack and been careless about what he discusses during flights. From force of habit he was the same on Air Force One.

"Last night," I reported, "I received a telegram saying that one of our intelligence officers working in the Canadian heavy water factory transmitted over a hundred more cassettes of undeveloped film on the installation."

"Check! Are you sure we'll be able to finish the heavy water factory without having to buy the know-how and license?"

"Based on what the station reported, our agents have given us everything the Canadians have."

AGENT "235" FROM PAKISTAN

After a pause, Ceausescu asked in a very low voice: "Do you have any news from '235'?"

"Yes, comrade. Before we left Bucharest we received a post-card from him, sent to an accommodation address in Austria. Using an open code he reported that his interrogation was over, he was not under suspicion, and he had just been sent on a business trip to Western Europe. He asks for a meeting. He dated the postcard April 5, 1978, and it's a picture of Sacre Coeur in Montmartre. According to his accommodation plan, the meeting should take place 30 days after the date he wrote, in front of the cathedral, at 9:00 PM, with the alternate the next day."

"Are you serious?" Ceausescu's hand holding his queen was suspended in mid air.

"Our technical operations directorate analyzed the postcard and confirmed that it was written by him. They couldn't find any sign of stress indicating that he might have been forced to write it under pressure."

"Bajenaru-u-u!" Ceausescu yelled, calling for his favorite body-guard. "Bring me a glass of water."

The code name "235" was what Ceausescu had spontaneously dubbed one of his favorite agents, a Pakistani scientist and intelligence officer, known to him in person, who had previously furnished data on nuclear energy.

In 1975, I showed Ceausescu DIE information indicating that Pakistan was conducting ultra-secret operations to develop its own military nuclear capability. That was also Ceausescu's secret dream. When he ordered an "in-depth study" on Zulfikar Ali Bhutto, Pakistan's prime minister, I had no doubt that Ceausescu was going to make a frontal attack on him. A few days after I had presented Ceausescu with the study, he ordered the minister of foreign affairs to set up a meeting for him with Bhutto. A short stopover was arranged in Karachi, with Bhutto welcoming Ceausescu at the airport. When the Romanian plane landed, Bhutto was there, accompanied by numerous local dignitaries, and he invited Ceausescu to a nearby palace for lunch.

In comparison with his earlier cases, Bhutto was a relatively easy prize for the experienced and well prepared Ceausescu.

After lunch, he asked for a private discussion, accompanied only by a DIE interpreter and me, where he launched his frontal attack. "You and I share the same dream, to make a place in history for our countries," Ceausescu began, "and the best way to do that is to build up their power. In our day the only real power is nuclear power. We should build it secretly. Working independently, our intelligence services"—pointing toward me—"have obtained remarkable results. Together we might be able to realize our dreams. In this envelope is a sample of what we can do. If you agree, let me know. If not, you may forget the whole thing."

Bhutto carefully put the envelope into his pocket. It contained an inventory of the nuclear intelligence information Romania could secretly provide to Pakistan. Bhutto reacted almost exactly as Ceausescu had expected. Just before our departure, he gave Ceausescu an envelope. "Inside is a man's code name, a phone number, and a password. I think future contacts should be between two individuals, not two governments, my dear friend."

Two weeks later, the man who would become "235" had a private dinner with Ceausescu at his residence in Snagov. Radu Andreescu was the operational alias of a brilliant DIE engineer who became his regular contact. Ten days later, Andreescu left for Pakistan with a voluminous diplomatic pouch containing sensitive nuclear intelligence obtained from the West. He came back with the complete project for the Canadian CANDU reactor, containing much more data than the DIE had as yet been able to obtain. On further visits to Pakistan, Andreescu took with him technical intelligence on French nuclear security systems—highly desired by the Pakistanis—and he brought back to Romania supplementary intelligence on the Degussa centrifugal system for enriching uranium, on which Bucharest was already working, and significant data on the industrial production of uranium 235.

The postcard was the first sign of life we had gotten from "235" since the July 5, 1977, *coup d'etat*, when General Muhammed Zia ul-Haq arrested Bhutto and declared himself chief administrator of martial law.

"Checkmate! Bajenaru! A Cordon Rouge," commanded Ceausescu. "You must be terribly careful. We've got to hang on to our Rosenberg."

After a second glass, and without any apparent connection, Ceausescu suddenly asked me: "How big was the press?"

"The one in the metallurgical lab of Combustion Engineering?"

"Uh huh."

"Twenty million tons."

"When I visited the 'Star' plant, I was told that, the higher the pressure, the bigger and purer the diamonds. Is that true?"

"Yes, comrade. We tried to get that press, but it proved to be impossible. It's very tightly controlled American equipment."

"The chief of a Communist foreign intelligence service should never say something is impossible. We *must* have it."

"ANY AMERICAN CAN BE BOUGHT"

"Wasn't it there, darling, that we saw Traian Vuia's grandson?" broke in Elena, who had just come back.

The Romanian engineer Traian Vuia invented and constructed the first monoplane aircraft in 1906, although it failed to fly. The Frenchman Louis Bleriot had the first operative monoplane, which he flew across the English Channel in 1907. Years later, however, Vuia invented a pressurized steam generator, which proved to be so efficient that it soon became known as the "Vuia generator." His grandson, an American citizen, was now an expert on nuclear pressure boilers constructed on his grandfather's basic principles.

"What do you know about the young Vuia, Pacepa?" Ceausescu asked.

"Vuia's grandson is reported to be a loyal American engineer."

"A lo-yal A-me-ri-can! Have you ever seen a loyal American, *monsieur?* Any American can be bought, if you know how. Don't you know what money is, darling? Money, m-o-n-e-y," she intoned, rubbing her fingers together under my nose.

"Yes, Pacepa. Vuia may be an American, but don't forget that dollars are American, too."

"What do you mean 'American,' dear? Vuia is a Romanian. Anyone born a Romanian remains one forever. He and his children and his great grandchildren."

"Pacepa knows that, Elena," said Ceausescu, trying to clear the air.

"If that's the case, why don't you remember, *monsieur,* that we've named one of our biggest Communist factories for Traian Vuia?" Elena screamed at me. "Have you tried bringing the grandson to Bucharest and rubbing his nose in that? Have you tried to show him how the Comrade has honored his grandfather? Have you asked him what he's doing to honor the Comrade?"

"We certainly should use Vuia's grandson, Pacepa. Not just because of his name . . ."

"I've been told that Traian Vuia is in every single encyclopedia," interrupted Elena with annoyance. "More than you are, Nick."

" . . . but especially because of his nuclear specialty. Bring him to me in Bucharest. I'll recruit him."

"Tell this fiddler that recruiting agents is his job, not yours. That's for him and his stinking service to do. And tell him it's his job to make an agent out of every single Romanian living in America who has learned to wear shoes. Not just Vuia."

Elena went back to her picture in *The Wall Street Journal* just as suddenly as she had butted into Ceausescu's discussion. The silence of the chess game was now disturbed only by the hum of Air Force One, until abruptly broken by Ceausescu. "Who's going to welcome me at Texas Instruments?"

"Their vice president, Grant Dove. He was the highest level I could get."

"Since I have to go to Dallas, the least they could have done would have been to have their president open the door to that microelectronics empire for me."

The First Communist Leader at Texas Instruments

It was still terribly difficult for Ceausescu to face the idea of setting foot in Dallas, the "barbaric" town that meant nothing else to him but the place where President Kennedy had been assassinated. Only his boundless ambition to be able to do something Brezhnev could not, could make him overcome his deep, animal-like fear for his life and send him to Dallas.

When the captain announced that the presidential plane would shortly be landing at Dallas airport, I conceded the new chess game and asked for permission to leave.

"Yes, take care of the pilots and the Secret Service. Don't forget, we're in Dallas!"

At the airport, when he was welcomed by Robert Folsom, the mayor of Dallas, Ceausescu was white as a sheet. From there the motorcade took us directly to Texas Instruments, the first stop in Dallas. As Ceausescu stepped inside the company's building, his face and eyes lit up. He had accomplished his wish to be the first Communist president to set foot inside Texas Instruments. Ceausescu always wants to be the first. He was indeed able at last to step into that prohibited empire, but he could not even shake hands with one worker; he could only look at the equipment and the people producing the chips through a protective window wall.

That afternoon, the mayor of Dallas gave a reception for Ceausescu in the modern new city hall, pointing out that Ceausescu was the first foreign head of state to visit the new building. Less than an hour after our arrival, the head of the Secret Service team took me aside to say that an anonymous telephone caller had claimed there was a bomb planted in the city hall. He asked me to get Ceausescu immediately and to follow him on a preestablished escape route out of the building. Ceausescu was toasting with the guests when I caught his arm and told him that, for security reasons, we were being asked to leave the building right away. He turned white as a ghost and grabbed Elena, sputtering, "P-put y-your g-glass d-down, woman!" as he pulled her along, following me down an escalator. When he lost his balance and stumbled, I was not sure if it was because the rush of emotion had thrown him, or because it was the first time in his life that he had been on an escalator. It was not until the next day, after we had left Texas and were on our flight to New Orleans, that he asked me why he had so suddenly been evacuated from the Dallas city hall.

After the reception given by the Dallas mayor, Ceausescu attended a working dinner arranged by the Texas Chamber of Commerce. There, in his answering speech, Ceausescu unexpectedly pointed to the vice president of Texas Instruments: "Some of the products turned out by Texas Instruments also have a strategic character. We are not concerned with turning out such products, because we stand for disarmament, for the destruction of atomic armaments and of weapons in general. We

stand for a world without weapons, a world of peaceful cooperation. That is why we wish to achieve cooperation, not for electronics for military purposes, but for electronics for industrial,
economic purposes."[3]

Back at his hotel suite, Ceausescu called me in: "Give them any
kind of further assurance they want that we're not interested in
military electronics. Just use your imagination."

[3]*Ceausescu's 1978 State Visit to the U.S.A.*, pp. 154–5.

XX

OVER the many long years I spent with Ceausescu, I had watched his primitive fear for his life grow in geometrical proportion to his rise in power. I was sure that as long as he was still in Dallas he would not be able to sleep a wink, that the specter of President Kennedy's assassination would keep him awake all night. And when Ceausescu cannot sleep, he cannot stand to be alone. It was one-thirty in the morning when he called me in and asked for the briefing files on the NASA Space Center in Houston, as well as for the latest Radio Free Europe commentaries on his trip. At three o'clock he called me back again, to return the files I had given him.

OPERATION AGAINST RADIO FREE EUROPE

"We must compromise Free Europe once and for all," Ceausescu exploded, even before I could close the door. "The way Gierek did," he continued, leaving the desk to turn the television set up louder.

Polish First Secretary Edward Gierek had told Ceausescu about a successful operation against Radio Free Europe, and Ceausescu frequently exhorted me to set up something along the same lines. According to him, Gierek claimed that Polish intelligence had kept an illegal officer there for eight years, having him photograph everything he could get his hands on and send it back to Warsaw. When Gierek had enough evidence that Radio Free Europe was a "CIA wasp's nest," he recalled the man.

"How many times do I have to tell you the story before I get a similar Romanian case?" Ceausescu went on. "What about your 'Ionescu'?"

It was in 1977 that Ceausescu first ordered the DIE to work up a Gierek-style operation and then to explode it in the press, in order to shake up Radio Free Europe's Romanian department. The DIE selected "Ionescu," one of its agents inside the radio; he was a former colonel in the Romanian army who had defected to France in 1952 and become a Radio Free Europe employee in Paris. Ceausescu approved the case and signed a secret decree giving "Ionescu" the rank and pension of a retired general if he would repatriate to Romania. "Ionescu," who was by then 66 years old, was repeatedly contacted in France and Austria. He was reportedly flattered by the attention, but he made it clear that his final acceptance was contingent upon convincing his French girlfriend that they should finish out their days in Romania. Evidently that proved to be not an easy task.

"He hasn't yet given a final answer, Comrade Ceausescu."

"Push him. Force him. Blackmail him. Or get him to come to a meeting in Austria and kidnap him," said Ceausescu, making it very clear that these were now his orders for the case. "I want to see the bomb we have prepared for that wasp's nest explode in the Western press." He started walking around the room.

"In order to destroy our enemies," Ceausescu went on, "we first have to discredit them. That's what I want with Free Europe. I want it discredited as a CIA operation that has its spies inside Romania undermining our sovereignty and independence. But I don't want the words to come out of my own mouth. I don't want to say that the American Congress is lying about Radio Free Europe, because I need Congress for the most favored nation status. I don't want to say that Carter, Vance, and Brzezinski are lying, because I need their political support and money. Who should say that, Pacepa?" he finished rhetorically, stopping in front of me.

That was easy. "Radio Free Europe itself."

"'Ionescu.' He has to speak out, and I've already approved everything he will say, haven't I?"

"Yes, comrade. All his future declarations have been prepared. Service D has already put Ionescu's signature on all of them."

"We should show through the mouth of 'Ionescu' that Free Europe is nothing but a CIA espionage nest. Once that's done, it will just be a matter of technique to prove that the Voice of America, Radio Liberty, and the BBC are the same. Moscow and the rest of the Warsaw Pact will do the job."

Ceausescu went back over to the desk. "That's why I want 'Ionescu,' dead or alive. Understood?"

"Yes, comrade."

"What's new?"

"Over 100 members of the United States House of Representatives are going to raise the issue of whether to continue most favored nation trade status benefits for Romania," I started out. "This was prompted by the latest letter smuggled out from Carol Kiraly."

"That must not happen," Ceausescu replied. "Without that status we cannot export to the United States. We cannot have insured credits and open doors for technological intelligence."

"The emigrés plan to organize a hostile demonstration in New York on Sunday," I went on, "and they may have a lot of people there."

"F-Fascists! They should be exposed as fascists, all of them," Ceausescu cried. "As people who sent thousands of Jews to concentration camps—two hundred thousand of them. We should say that after the defeat of fascism these people ran away from the country and settled in various parts of the world, where they are trying to revive fascism." Ceausescu was warming up to his favorite propaganda subject. "And Nicolae"—he meant the Romanian ambassador—"should call the White House immediately and demand that the demonstration be stopped."

It was almost four o'clock when I left Ceausescu, but a half-hour later a bodyguard announced that I was to go back to him again. When Ceausescu spotted the chess board under my arm, his ashen face became faintly lit by a smile. As usual, he opened with the King's Gambit.

Ten minutes later I unexpectedly called out, "checkmate."

"You're better at night than you are during the day," he retorted.

Using the same King's Gambit, Ceausescu started a new game, determined to win. Although he has enormous powers of concentration, he is not usually able to do two or more things at the same time, except when he is playing chess. After he has constructed in his head the tactic and strategy of the game and his future moves, Ceausescu can use the most treacherous methods to divert his partner's attention. Asking his opponent questions was one of them.

A Technical Treasure for Khrushchev

"Who gave us the American hard-alloy technology that saved our independence?" Ceausescu discreetly moved a bishop out of turn.

"'Herbert.'"

"Tell me his story," Ceausescu commanded.

I related the story, as briefly as I could. In the early 1960s "Herbert," the chief representative of a West German consortium composed of Schloemann, AEG, and several other companies, which had an office in Bucharest, was observed having several affairs with married women. He was not blackmailed. Instead, an educated, intelligent, and attractive young Romanian woman, "Rodica," who was working for a foreign airline, became his mistress. She was, of course, a Securitate agent. In early 1963, "Herbert" himself became an agent. In exchange for a better life with "Rodica" in Romania, where he spent several years, and for priority treatment in his commercial deals, he furnished valuable technical documents. One of these exceeded all expectations. Upon returning from a routine trip to West Germany, "Herbert" presented the DIE with a complete project, with many thousands of blueprints and crates of technical documents, enough to allow the cloning of a brand new, very sophisticated rolling mill then under construction in the United States for producing the ultra-hard alloys needed for a new generation of military and space rockets.

"How much did you pay for the project, Pacepa?"

"What he asked: $64,000."

"And how much did Moscow pay us for it?"

"Four million."

"That wasn't even the payoff. Remember how I took the project, caught a plane, and put the whole thing on Khrushchev's desk? The next day, after he had been told by his experts what an incredible treasure I had given him, he hugged and kissed me on both cheeks. 'I don't think we need to keep any more Soviet troops in Romania, Comrade Ceausescu. It is enough that we have you there,' Khrushchev told me. That project accomplished the miracle. That and Bodnaras. Without them, we would probably still have Soviet troops in Romania."

"Is it really true, Comrade Ceausescu, that that project played such an important role in the withdrawal of the Red Army from Romania?" I asked, timidly moving into the offensive.

"It certainly is," replied Ceausescu, unobtrusively sliding his queen over one square. "Two years later Khrushchev said that the Soviet Union was going to produce a new generation of military and space rockets before America did. The hard-alloy installation was not put into operation as early as Khrushchev predicted, but it is still far and away the most modern rolling mill of its kind in the Soviet Union."

Ceausescu's story was basically correct. Only one minor point was inaccurate. It was not Ceausescu, but Gheorghiu-Dej who took the project to Moscow and traded it with Khrushchev for the withdrawal of the Red Army from Romania.

The sun was beginning to rise over Dallas when Ceausescu finally broke off the chess game. "Today I'll be putting my other foot into NASA!" he exulted, leaving to wake his wife.

When Air Force One landed at Hobby Airport in Houston, Ceausescu paid no attention to the fact that he was welcomed only by Texas Secretary of State Steven Oaks and Acting Mayor Judson Robinson. Elena noticed it, though. "Where's their wretched governor?" she complained. "He's probably never seen a head of state in all his life, but he couldn't come to meet us."

NASA's Building 30

From the airport, the official motorcade headed directly for the NASA Space Center. When Ceausescu got out of his limousine, his short silhouette looked smaller than ever against the backdrop of NASA's enormous steel and concrete buildings. Dr. Sigurd Sjoberg, the deputy director of the gigantic enterprise, welcomed the guests and introduced our guide, astronaut John Young, saying Young had made four journeys with the Gemini and Apollo space ships and two moon landings.

Young was polite but businesslike. When he explained that the center employed more than 3,600 graduate engineers, scientists, mathematicians, flight instructors, and, of course, astronauts, Ceausescu whispered into my ear, with a nuance of satisfaction: "We have more than that working in our shoe industry, don't we?" He was especially interested in the design and testing of space vehicles, and he kept me at hand to take notes. Elena made an effort to appear interested in the buildings devoted to manned space flights and scientific experiments conducted in space.

All prominent visitors see Building 30, the space flight control center, since it is the most spectacular, with its computers that control the space ships and the entire center. The Romanian journalists and photographers, overwhelmed by what they were seeing, scattered everywhere. When Ceausescu was invited to sit at the director's flight desk, Elena nudged me: "Get the photographers. It would be just like those idiots to miss the very moment when the Comrade was managing the whole space flight system."

Except for Elena, everybody in the Romanian party was impressed by this visit. "According to de Gaulle," Andrei said on our way out, trying to put his feelings into words without seeming to praise American capitalism, "the United States doesn't have a foreign policy; it has only foreign problems. Judging from what we've seen here, though, I would say that they have a tremendous space policy!"

"If they are as tremendous as you say," responded Elena severely, "then why, my dear comrade, was Gagarin the first man in space?" She looked fixedly at each of us in turn, until all our smiling faces turned guiltily solemn.

At noon, during the reception given by the mayor of Houston, the latter offered Ceausescu the key to the city. In his toast, Ceausescu said: "You know, we have a story in Romania, a story with an enchanted key, a key which helps one fulfill many wishes. . . . And, if by any chance, this key should be enchanted, you may rest assured that I would not use it but in the service of friendship, of peace and collaboration."[1] As we were leaving the River Oaks Country Club, where the luncheon had taken place, Ceausescu pushed me ahead into his limousine. "You must make use

[1]*Ibid.*, pp. 165–6.

of that key to recruit some agents here. At lunch I learned that they have the technology to drill down to 18,000 feet and more. That's what we need for our newly discovered deep oil reserves."

As Ceausescu drifted off into a light slumber, Elena put in her two cents worth: "If the key isn't real gold, don't bother with it though."

The next stop was New Orleans, where we landed in the afternoon and left almost immediately for the Royal Orleans Hotel in the old French Quarter. For weeks, ever since I had been in New Orleans to prepare for the visit, I had been worrying that Elena would not be happy with this venerable but old fashioned hotel. Sure enough, it was not long until she called me: "You idiot, why didn't you put us up at a Sheraton? It's not coming out of your pocket." Feeling a draft, she called in the whole Romanian group, and everyone, from minister to bodyguard, had to stuff newspapers into all the air conditioning vents in the presidential suite. "Let them work. Show me the downtown," she said to me, taking my arm.

I tried to introduce Elena to the unique charms of Bourbon Street. After no more than half an hour she decided: "It's dirty, noisy, and miserable. Let's go back to our hotel."

After a reception and dinner given by the mayor, Elena was in good spirits. Ordering her favorite Cordon Rouge champagne, she said: "You know, Nick, I had an interesting conversation with the 'mayoress.' She wants her people here to have lots of babies." Draining her glass at a gulp, Elena called for the translator, Sergiu Celac. "What was it that fellow said about the Comrade?" she asked.

"Which one?"

"The one who was talking about the Comrade and the centuries," Elena explained, in her own inimitable style.

"Mr. Basil Rusovich, Jr., the president of the International Trade Center," said Celac, pulling a notebook out of his pocket. "He said, 'I make bold to compare him to the great personalities that have lived throughout the centuries.'[2] That's what he said."

"See, Nick? A man like you comes along only once every five hundred years." Elena got another glass of champagne. "How do you feel being so big, so important, and yet the head of such a

[2]*Ibid.*, p. 170.

little country? The only one smaller is Albania. But if you sign that decree, in less than ten years we'll have forty million people."

"Hey, woman, be serious. Shut up," said Ceausescu laughing, but flattered nevertheless.

That was not the first time I had heard Elena fantasize about forcing every family in Romania to have a minimum of four children. Her most cherished dream is to become the president of Romania herself and to have her name go down in history as the only woman president who doubled her country's population during her presidency.

A few years later the American news media reported with both relish and bewilderment that President Nicolae Ceausescu had signed a decree obliging every family in Romania to have at least four children.

COVERING WASHINGTON WITH INFLUENCE

When Elena left for her evening massage, Ceausescu ordered wine, along with tomatoes, onions, and feta cheese, and his portable stereo. "With the proper cassette," he added.

A few minutes later, Ceausescu downed two glasses of his yellow wine at once, while Bajenaru was setting up the stereo and putting on a cassette containing Ceausescu's and my voices, so as to screen our conversation from possible concealed microphones.

"Turn it up louder," he ordered Bajenaru, as he began wolfing down his favorite snack. Pulling his chair closer to mine, Ceausescu continued in a low voice.

"We should have our influence agents all over Washington," he said, biting into a whole tomato. "Real influence agents, not any of your cloak-and-dagger spies skulking up to secret meetings at night with their coat collars turned up and their hat brims pulled down over their noses." He went on ruminating out loud, all the while continuing to stuff food into his mouth with his fingers. "We ought to be giving our agents their marching orders in broad daylight, so as not to raise any eyebrows. Is your agent in the White House or the State Department? Then go see him openly, in connection with my visit here, or with my invitation for Carter to visit Bucharest, or with some confidential message to the American president that I can give you anytime you like. Is your agent in Commerce? Ask him for some prohibited equipment or technology, saying it will help us preserve our independence from the Soviet Union. You might not get it, but that would be good cover for developing an influence agent and meeting with him in his own office. Even a journalist agent shouldn't be met secretly any more, but openly, on some official pretext. If you can't think of anything, I'll agree to an interview, and you could then stretch that out to provide cover for a dozen meetings, not just one. Doing it this way, you shield the agent from the FBI's prying eyes, and you don't have to worry about security when you get down to the real business at hand: influence." Ceausescu paused briefly, attentively cleaning his plate with a piece of bread. When he had finished, he drained his glass, made a sign for me to refill it, and ordered a fresh bottle. "That's the way I want our influence agents in America handled, including Billy Carter—officially, not suspiciously."

Ceausescu then started issuing a flood of orders about how Billy Carter should be recruited, how the payments should be made to him in Switzerland, not directly from Romania but through the two Libyan agents, and how he should be handled and used, until the door banged against the wall and stanched the flow. Elena stormed into the room, her dressing gown entirely unbuttoned.

"What's all this silly noise here, Nick?" she asked, looking balefully at the portable stereo.

"I've been talking with Pacepa about Carter's family."

"Americans don't have families. All they care about is money."

"Carter has an interesting brother, my dear. Very interesting. And I'm going to get him."

"Knock it off, Nick. Americans don't care about their relatives. You, fiddler, show me one single American president who made his brother prime minister, and I'll eat him. Buttons and all," she added, glaring at me.

"They don't have prime ministers, Elena."

"Whatever. Show me one who made his wife vice president. Just one. They don't care, Nick. They respect money, not family."

"Carter's different, Elena."

"No American is different. What does Carter's brother do?"

"Takes care of Carter's farm."

"A farmer! I told you American presidents don't look after their families," Elena said with disgust. Ceausescu, of course, had found nice government sinecures for all his and her relatives. "Don't waste your time. Come on, Nick, I need you." She was purring now and sliding her hand up under his sweater.

CHAPTER

XXI

THE Romanian news media afterwards would announce that on this Sunday morning President Nicolae Ceausescu and Comrade Elena Ceausescu were the "guests of the oilworkers"[1] on an offshore drilling rig along the coast of the state of Louisiana, in the Gulf of Mexico. Oil, Jews, and Germans are, according to Ceausescu, Romania's most valuable natural resources, and he tries to extract the maximum profit from each of them.

Soviet geological studies made in the 1950s discovered new oil fields on both sides of the Romanian Carpathian mountain chain, but most of them lay at a depth of four or more miles. That made drilling virtually impossible for the ill-equipped Romania, which was also unwilling to allow any other foreign finger to touch them. Confidential geological research indicated that there were also oil reserves under the Black Sea. At Ceausescu's personal direction, the DIE began getting deeply involved in intelligence operations to procure technical data on offshore drilling rigs. At the beginning of 1978, a Romanian offshore drilling rig constructed with illegally obtained technology was almost ready to be launched, and now Ceausescu wanted to see an American original with his own eyes.

When the helicopter landed on the *Ocean Queen* platform, Ceausescu was visibly impressed by its majestic construction. He was all ears when an engineer mentioned that the rig was equipped with a patented new system designed to withstand waves of 15 feet and more. "We must get it!" Ceausescu discreetly whispered to me, and I understood that he meant by

[1]*Ibid.*, p. 177.

means of industrial espionage, as usual. He always prefers stealing to buying from capitalists. At the end of the visit, despite the windy and noisy conditions on an offshore rig, Ceausescu was able to gather a dozen or so people around him for a few memorable words, expressing the hope that "specific steps would be taken for carrying out mutually advantageous cooperation actions."[2]

ON TO NEW YORK

Back at the New Orleans airport, a Romanian security officer guarding Air Force One reported that the counselor of the Romanian embassy in Washington had unexpectedly arrived on a commercial flight and urgently wanted to see me. It was Aurel Florea, who, as soon as Air Force One had taken off, immediately gave me a detailed written report on the anti-Ceausescu demonstration scheduled to take place that day at Ceausescu's hotel in New York, the Waldorf Astoria. According to Florea's report, Romanian emigrés were joining the Hungarians in what they intended to make the largest emigré action ever to take place in the United States.

As Air Force One cruised relentlessly toward New York, I presented Ceausescu with the report. "I don't want to read anything now," he said wearily. "Just tell me what it says."

"Please read it," I begged.

As Ceausescu read page after page of the report, he turned first white and then red. By the time he had finished it, he was in a towering rage. "Andre-e-ei!" he yelled. Suddenly awakened from a nap, Andrei came stumbling in, with a look of alarm in his swollen eyes. "Sleep, Andrei, sleep. That's the only thing you're good for. Why haven't you said anything about this filthy mess?" Ceausescu asked, trying to reach up high enough to smack the tall Andrei in the face with the report. "What are you, a foreign minister, or a shit?"

"Idiots, comrade, just idiots," chimed in Elena, who had just popped up from her nap and had no idea what was going on.

After Ceausescu had calmed down, he ordered Vasile Pungan

[2]*Ibid.*, p. 179.

to call the White House from Air Force One and inform it about the planned demonstration, qualifying it as a hostile act and firmly asking that it be prohibited.

At five o'clock in the afternoon, the plane landed at John F. Kennedy Airport in New York. As it was rolling down the runway, I informed Ceausescu that he would be welcomed by representatives of the mayor of New York City and of the governor of New York State. "Are the governor and the mayor Texans, darling?" Elena asked over her shoulder. "I thought it was only in Texas that the governor and the mayor of Houston were too snooty to welcome us in person!"

After the brass band had played the Romanian anthem—the right one—Elena pulled Ceausescu over toward a small group of young people and children waving Romanian and American flags. They both ploughed into the friendly crowd, shaking hands and embracing the children.

As I got off the airplane, the DIE station chief in New York, General Aurel Gheorghe, assigned under cover as counselor in the Romanian Permanent Mission to the United Nations, tried to catch my attention. As Ceausescu was still shaking hands, I went over to where the diplomatic corps was standing, grabbed Gheorghe and pulled him through to the other side of the security rope.

"Bad news, Boss," Gheorghe started off in his easy-going manner, which always made it hard to tell whether he was drunk or sober. "On the way to the airport I drove past the Waldorf, and I was horrified. There must have been five or six thousand there demonstrating against the Big Boss. Hungarians and Romanians together. I've never seen anything like it. The Big Boss, and especially *Madame*, are liable to have a heart attack!"

The head of the U.S. Secret Service team in charge of Ceausescu's security, who was in another corner talking with the chiefs of the FBI and Secret Service offices in New York, signaled that he also wanted to talk to me. He had the same information as Gheorghe, and he decided that it would be best to bring the guests into the Waldorf by an entrance in the underground garage. He asked me to go with him in an advance car, in order to make on-the-spot decisions, if needed.

Ceausescu and Elena were already in the armored limousine when I went to them. The chief of his bodyguards was slowly pouring alcohol on their hands, a ritual repeated with religious fanaticism every time Ceausescu shakes hands, whether with people on the street or with foreign heads of state. In a few words I informed him of the demonstrations and of the Secret Service's suggestion. Since there was nothing on the official schedule that Sunday evening, I proposed forgetting the Waldorf Astoria for that day and going straight to the Romanian Mission, spending the night there, and then picking up the schedule again the next morning at the Waldorf. "We have a special apartment for you inside the mission," I concluded.

"How can you even think about making the Comrade sleep in your dirty mission, after Blair House?" was Elena's furious reaction. "He's insane, dear. Somebody spotted three emigrés somewhere out there, and he has to build up a big horror story around them." She then turned on me: "Why would anyone want to demonstrate against the Comrade, you fiddler? Have you got cataracts on your eyes? Couldn't you see how the Comrade was welcomed with open arms at the White House and everywhere else?"

A RAIN OF EGGS

The chief of the Secret Service detail appeared at the car door. "How dangerous is it?" asked Ceausescu.

"It may be unpleasant, but it's not a life-threatening situation," was the reply.

"Let's go. I'm not going to let a dozen emigrés change my plans."

The motorcade took a roundabout route approaching the hotel, but, in order to get to the underground garage, it had to drive through masses of demonstrators, who booed, screamed deliriously, and held up huge posters saying "Ceausescu the Red Terror!," "Ceausescu the Criminal!," and "Ceausescu—Dracula!" A rain of eggs smashed against the Secret Service car I was riding in, turning the windshield opaque, so that the driver could not see and crashed into the side of the underground garage. It took him only a couple of seconds to straighten the wheels and continue on, but it was long enough to slow down Ceausescu's black Cadillac. It turned bright yellow and red under the heavy hailstorm of eggs and tomatoes. When the presidential limousine came to a halt, Ceausescu and Elena were immediately surrounded by a solid wall of Secret Service, FBI, and police officers, which moved as a body through the lobby. Small groups of emigrés, who had smuggled themselves inside earlier, unwrapped banners saying things like "Ceausescu—Idi Amin!" and "Ceausescu—Idi Aminescu!"

When Ceausescu finally got to the Presidential Suite, he was as pale as a ghost. Abruptly he ran into a bathroom and, without bothering to close the door, began vomiting convulsively. It was the same reaction as when I had reported to him about Moscow's attempt to recruit General Militaru—that same physical fear for his own skin. Elena arrived a few minutes later, accompanied by her female Secret Service bodyguard and surrounded by a protective squadron. In the crush, she had lost her purse, which had been picked up by a police officer.

Ever since Ceausescu had started his rise to Communist power, he had never been confronted with any *ad hominem* public reaction against himself. In 1944–1946, there had been anti-Communist demonstrations in Romania, but they were directed against the new Communist Party itself, not its leaders. November 8, 1945, was the first St. Michael's Day free of fascist occupation, and hundreds of thousands of Romanians gathered in front of the Royal Palace to express support for King Michael. I was among them, a high school student driven there by my antifascism and hunger for freedom. The crowd was full of young people like me, as well as professors, lawyers, doctors, businessmen, and even workers and peasants, who were trying to see a remnant symbol of democracy in the king.

Across from the Royal Palace in Bucharest there was a massive six-story, still partly unfinished building that had been constructed by the pro-Nazi government as the headquarters for the Ministry of Interior and its political police, including a Gestapo section and an interrogation center with hundreds of cells on three floors underground. This was the first institution taken over by the Soviet Army and Communist forces after the war. From there came the first volley of gunfire into the people, who were cheering, "Long live the king!" At that time I did not know that the Soviets and the Romanian Communists would not normally fire into the air. Only later did I learn that bullets, like other material possessions, are more valuable to them than human lives. When the second volley rang out I saw people falling, I heard cries of pain, and I understood. As if on command, the horror-stricken masses turned toward the Ministry of Interior with its heavy machine guns firing from the balconies. After the second burst of bullets, hundreds of trucks appeared from the nearby streets. They were loaded with several hundred workers well oiled with alcohol and armed with sticks, chains, and wrenches. They rushed headlong at us, creating a vacuum around themselves. "Killers! Criminals!" rang out from over a hundred thousand throats.

"Killer! Criminal!" came the muffled cries from outside the Waldorf Astoria—the same words as in November 1945. Those words seemed to have ominously pursued me all my life.

"Killer! Criminal! Ceausescu—Idi Amin!" The cries could now be clearly heard in the suite on the 29th floor, coming in from outside over powerful loudspeakers. White as a sheet, Ceausescu moved from one room to another, saying nothing.

There were Romanian bodyguards everywhere in the Presidential Suite busily using special antiseptics to wash down the floors, carpets, furniture, and even the doorknobs and light switches—anything Ceausescu might touch. In the bedroom, the valet and the hairdresser were taking off the hotel bedlinens and replacing them with the linens brought in sealed trunks from Bucharest. The study had been transformed into an ironing room, since every piece of underwear and table linen, although previously sterilized and kept in sealed plastic bags, now had to be ironed again to kill the germs.

I arranged for the Ceausescus to have a private dinner in their suite. As usual, a portable chemical laboratory was set up, and Major Popa first checked all the food to be sure it contained no poison, bacteria, or radioactive substances. Then he personally supervised its preparation by the Romanian chef in the hotel's kitchen. A special cart, built for Ceausescu's visits abroad, is always used to transport his food. In the kitchen Popa locks it with a cipher system that is changed daily. The cart is accompanied by Popa and one of the bodyguards, both armed, and unlocked when it gets to the dining area, where only Ceausescu's waiter is allowed to serve.

When I later returned to the Presidential Suite, the food was still on the table, untouched. The roar from the demonstration outside was getting worse. "Ceausescu— killer!" bounced back from the dining room windows, "Ceausescu—criminal!" from the salon and bedroom. There was a short pause, and then "Ceausescu—Idi Amin!" rang out from everywhere. This refrain was repeated for hours with mathematical precision.

RETREAT TO THE ROMANIAN MISSION

"The Comrade wants to visit the new building of the Romanian Mission," Elena finally said in capitulation, coming out of the bedroom.

"As soon as the Secret Service can clear a safe exit from the hotel and itinerary through the city," Ceausescu's strangled voice croaked from the bathroom.

Ceausescu and Elena left in the armored Cadillac, flying no flag, although that did not fool the crowd of demonstrators. Another hailstorm of eggs and tomatoes doused the limousine, accompanied by uninterrupted "boos" coming from thousands of throats and punctuated by shouts of "Dracula!" over the loudspeakers.

The New York headquarters of the Romanian Mission to the United Nations is located in a 17-story building at the corner of Third Avenue and 38th Street. The building, once a hotel, had been purchased by the Romanian government as the headquarters for all the Romanian organizations represented in New York and the living quarters for their employees. Like all Soviet bloc leaders, Ceausescu believes that having everything concentrated in the same building makes it easier to control people.

On paper, the building is managed by the Ministry of Foreign Affairs, but in fact it has been under the DIE from the day it was purchased. That is another general rule within the Soviet bloc. The first ten floors were turned into offices, the rest into apartments and rooms for the employees. One whole floor was occupied by an impressive suite designated for Ceausescu, which has never been used. He has a similar suite in most of the major Romanian embassies.

The only entrance to this fortress of a building is protected by heavy locks, iron grills, alarm systems, closed circuit television, a doorman armed with a submachine gun under his desk, and a duty officer carrying a pistol in his pocket. The whole building is equipped with an elaborate electronic monitoring system covering every nook and cranny. The number of concealed microphones in a given room depends on what it is used for, but none is exempt, except for Ceausescu's apartment. A nearby telephone intercept system has all the telephone outlets installed throughout the building wired into it. The flick of a switch is enough to start the monitoring of conversations in a room or over the telephone.

New York had the second largest DIE station in the world, after Cologne; in 1978, over 90 percent of the Romanian employees at the mission were intelligence officers. Three floors of the building are occupied by the New York station, with its security system, cipher service, monitoring centers, photo and chemical laboratories, "bubble," and work areas. The access doors and most of the rooms are controlled by a separate alarm system and closed circuit television. A special, accoustically secure room was built between the offices of the ambassador and the chief of station. Jointly designed by the KGB and the DIE, it was supposed to be the ultimate in its field.

When Ceausescu's limousine pulled up, the ambassador and the chief of station jostled each other to be the first to open the car door. Ceausescu and Elena went directly to the elevator, without responding to the cheering women and children in folk costumes or stopping to accept their proffered bread and salt—an old Romanian custom when welcoming guests to a new house. Not until he was in the large salon with his and Elena's portraits hanging on the wall was Ceausescu able to squeeze out his first articulate sound:

"Bajenaru, alcohol!"

Ceausescu washed his hands for a very long time, although he had not touched anyone else's hand since leaving his hotel suite. It was probably a reaction to the eggs and tomatoes that had been thrown at him. Ambassador Datcu unsuccessfully tried to slip in a few words about the work of his mission.

"Get Carter on the phone this minute," Ceausescu ordered Pungan, "and tell him to have the criminals arrested."

"Why the Peanut Head? This is New York, not a farm," hissed Elena. The gnashing of her teeth could be clearly heard all around the room.

"I am a president. A president, just like him. He's the one who should be looking after me, not the mayor!" screamed Ceausescu, standing in front of Pungan. Facing his hulking chief advisor, the five-foot-five Romanian president, with his arms now dangling down helplessly and longer than normal at his sides, looked positively wretched. When, a minute later, he confronted the tall, handsome Andrei, Ceausescu looked even more abject. "What did Vance say?" his metallic voice shrilled out.

"I couldn't find Vance, but I spoke with Nimetz." Matthew Nimetz was a counselor at the State Department whose name was familiar to Ceausescu.

"Why not with the doorman? He ought to be more on your level," Elena broke in acidly. "Listen to the sheep herder! The fascists are about to assassinate us, and you, you miserable worm, what are you doing? Nothing!"

"Get out! Out! You too! And you!" screamed Ceausescu at Andrei and Ambassadors Nicolae and Datcu. "And don't come back without Vance. What's happening here is more infamous than Sarajevo," he roared, referring to the 1914 assassination of Archduke Francis Ferdinand of Austria, which set off the First World War.

"And you? What do you have to say?" Ceausescu whispered to the New York chief of station.

"That you're letting these emigré sons of bitches ruin the only day you have in New York." General Aurel Gheorghe, the son of an activist who had been in the Communist Party for almost as many years as Ceausescu was old, has always been impertinent.

"Your father was also foul-mouthed," said Ceausescu.

"But he lived to be ninety. Call down a curse, and let's get on to something worthwhile. I want to show you the library. We have the only Romanian library abroad, and we've made it play an important role on the American cultural scene, and in our influence operations."

"Watch your language!" shouted Ceausescu. But he accepted the invitation.

A Useful Instrument of Influence

The Romanian Library had been created six years earlier, following a bilateral agreement that allowed an American library to open in Bucharest—located only a few yards from DIE headquarters. Since the American library cultivated contacts with Romanian dissidents and anti-regime writers, Ceausescu considered it a branch of the CIA and ordered the DIE to take over the Romanian Library in return.

It was located on the second floor, where Emilia Gheorghe, its manager, welcomed Ceausescu and Elena. A former public prosecutor who became a DIE colonel, Emilia was the wife of the station chief. With an iron hand she managed the library's affairs, the intelligence officers working for it, her husband, and her daughter—a young intelligence officer sent as a student to Columbia University so as to marry an American and become a U.S. citizen. Emilia was well known among the emigrés and feared within the large Romanian community living inside the mission building.

In a few well chosen words Emilia described the library as a useful instrument for conducting Ceausescu's influence policy inside the United States. Guiding the guests around the library rooms, she talked about the conferences, film galas, and exhibits organized in numerous centers of various American states as far away as Ohio, Oregon, Texas, and California; about the "Festival of Romanian Poetry and the Poetry of Other Nationalities Living in Romania," which she described as having been targeted against Zionist and Hungarian irredentist propaganda; about the symposium in New York called "The Latin Tradition of Romanian Culture and Civilization" and its conclusion that the Romanian language was closer to classical Latin than the languages spoken in ancient Gaul, Iberia, or even some regions of Italy; about the scientific session called "The History of Romania: Independence and Modernism," organized at the University of Wisconsin; about Romanian language courses organized in 20 American centers and the support granted to students and doctoral candidates who were preparing works on Romanian culture and history and were the station's prime recruitment targets;

about the successful lectures given by "your brother, General Dr. Ilie Ceausescu," at university centers in New York and Boston; and about a book exhibit soon to open containing books written in Romanian and English devoted to the life and work of the president of Romania, "an outstanding personality of international political life, widely known and appreciated in the United States of America and in the entire world."

"Don't you have any scientific books?" Elena asked, inspecting the bookshelves with a steely eye.

"Of course. We have a lot of scientific books on Romanian history, language, the continuity of the Romanian people—who became the owners of our lands long before they were tarnished by Hungarians, Germans, and Jews—about our Communist society, about. . . ."

"I mean science-science," said Elena, trying to make it clearer.

"We have the Comrade's books."

"Don't you have anything on chemistry?" Elena scrutinized the librarian suspiciously.

"Let's take a look," Emilia answered naively, touching Elena's arm to guide her over to the bookshelves.

"Don't you touch me!" Elena screamed.

"Comrade Elena is right, Pacepa," Ceausescu broke in. "We need a new section here on Romania's contribution to world science."

"That would be wonderful," exclaimed Emilia excitedly.

"Is she hysterical, darling?" Elena asked me, giving the librarian a clinical appraisal.

"Such as the Romanian contribution to chemistry," Ceausescu went on.

Elena gave Emilia one more malevolent glance, then grabbed her husband's arm and pulled him over toward the one wall of the library not covered with shelves but having only Ceausescu's portrait on it. "She's absolutely hopeless, dear, an old stick-in-the-mud. Imagine, she's never even heard about Romania's women scientists and their role in world science."

Gheorghe, who suddenly understood his wife's gaffe, moved in between Elena and Emilia, trying to change the subject. "We've done an exhibit on our influence operations inside the United States. Please!" He led the way over to a side door and broke the lead seal protecting it. "It's top secret. For the Comrade, but especially for you, Comrade Elena," he said, trying to clear the air.

"This is just a small sampling of what we have had published in the United States through our influence agents," Gheorghe began his presentation. Displayed on several tables were books and brochures published with DIE funds, American newspapers containing favorable articles on Romania and Ceausescu, and emigré newspapers and magazines in which articles written in Bucharest had been planted. On a separate table there was a display of several emigré newspapers entirely financed by the DIE and a cassette recorder that, when Gheorghe pushed the button, started "broadcasting" in English and Romanian. "This is a program of our radio station 'Doina.' It's supposedly run by Romanian emigrés, but it's funded by us," Gheorghe pointed out.

Captivated by the exposition, Ceausescu went from one table to the next, listening to the explanations, making suggestions, and giving orders.

"Let's see what the Peanut Head has accomplished," said Elena, cutting the visit short.

"THE ORGANIZERS SHOULD BE KILLED"

Pungan and Andrei were waiting in the salon, together with the two ambassadors. They all tried to explain that the White House and the State Department were doing their best, but that it was the mayor of New York City who really held the key to solving the problem. "City Hall authorized the demonstration." Pungan summed it up. "Now the mayor should de-authorize it."

"Who the hell is this mayor?" burst out Ceausescu.

"A Jew recruited by Budapest," reported Gheorghe. "I have incontrovertible evidence of his support to the Hungarian emigrés."

The newly elected mayor of New York was the colorful Edward Koch. "I've been trying to reach Mayor Koch," said Datcu, "but I haven't been able to get through yet."

"To reach him why?"

"To ask him to break up the demonstration, Comrade Ceausescu."

"I thought you'd learned he was a Jew and a Hungarian agent."

"Idiot, Nick, he's an idiot," Elena decided. Then turning toward Datcu, she said, in her sweetest voice: "You do play the violin, ambassador, don't you?"

Ceausescu decided that Mayor Koch should be ignored, and he ordered Pungan and Andrei to resume their pressure on the White House and State Department. "Tell them that my security is in great danger. That if they don't do something, I'm going to go directly to the airport and leave for Bucharest."

According to Ambassador Nicolae, the State Department took Ceausescu's threat seriously and asked the New York police commissioner, Robert McGuire, to assure the Romanian president that he was not in danger. At midnight, McGuire personally appeared at the Romanian Mission and told Ceausescu that he could return to the Waldorf without fear.

Finally Ceausescu agreed, but only if the commissioner would give him firm security guarantees and would ride in the same car with him. After midnight, under a reinforced police escort, Ceausescu left for the Waldorf, taking in his car not only Elena and McGuire but also General Stan, the chief of the Secret Service detail, and me. The motorcade proceeded without incident until it reached East 49th Street, where an egg struck Ceausescu's car.

"Where are your guarantees for my security, Commissioner?" Ceausescu asked menacingly. "It could easily have been a hand grenade."

"But it wasn't," replied McGuire with disarming logic.

In the Waldorf's lobby there were a few protesters still waiting. When they saw Ceausescu, they took signs out of their pockets reading "Ceausescu—Idi Amin" and "Ceausescu—Dracula."

Ceausescu went upstairs and threw up again, before coming back into the salon of his suite and starting to pace furiously around the room. He ordered the two chiefs of station and Ambassador Nicolae to be called in immediately.

"Turn on the stereo," he ordered me, after they had come in. "And the television set. Louder." He drew us closer to him with a nervous sign. "Do you know the names of the organizers?" he asked, looking at Gheorghe.

Gheorghe gave him two Hungarian names—Laszlo Kalman and Laszlo Hamos, who represented a Hungarian emigré organization for human rights in Transylvania—and one Romanian: Archbishop Valerian Trifa.

"They should be killed, this very night, as a clear warning to anybody else who might try an attempt on my security. They should be killed by professional criminals," Ceausescu ordered. "And have a note pinned to Trifa's body saying that's what will happen to every war criminal. Have it signed by 'Jews who suffered in Nazi concentration camps' or something like that. That's your job, Gheorghe. You'll do it tonight, or you'll be on your way out of New York tomorrow," Ceausescu snarled through clenched teeth.

"And you, Florea. You and Nicolae are to organize a demonstration of Romanian emigrés here at the Waldorf Astoria for tomorrow morning. If you can't find anyone else, get your agents. Tomorrow morning I want to receive a delegation of Romanian patriots protesting against the Hungarian demonstrators and the Romanian fascists." Ceausescu paused briefly. "That's for tomorrow morning. If not, you, and you"—pointing at Florea and Nicolae—"will leave tomorrow for Bucharest. On my airplane."

Ceausescu turned on his heel and left the room without saying another word. Four of his bodyguards kept watch in his bedroom all night long.

XXII

I spent the rest of the night at the Romanian Mission. It was eight o'clock in the morning when I arrived at the Waldorf Astoria, which was now surrounded by barricades and police officers in cars, on horseback, and on foot. Some 300 feet outside the barricades was a group of perhaps 20 people holding up Romanian flags and pictures of Ceausescu. According to Florea, these Romanian emigrés were all DIE agents who had been hauled out of their beds for the demonstration ordered by Ceausescu.

From General Stan I learned that Ceausescu had spent the whole night pacing around, and that all his bodyguards were now armed with submachine guns and hand grenades taken from the presidential airplane during the night. At the moment he was asleep in an easy chair.

MAYOR KOCH TO THE RESCUE

It was nine o'clock when Ceausescu called me in. A few minutes later, Andrei and Pungan asked to be received. They reported that the State Department had called Mayor Koch and asked him to cancel all his other appointments and go to the Waldorf to see the Romanian president.

"I don't want to talk with that dirty Jew," Ceausescu exploded. It was too late. General Stan came in and announced that U.S. Ambassador to Bucharest Aggrey, Mayor Koch, Police Commissioner McGuire, and some other people were outside waiting to see Ceausescu.

"Let the swine in," Ceausescu decided, after a moment's hesitation.

Followed by the others, the newly elected mayor noisily and jovially entered the suite, evidently determined to calm down his one-day visitor. "Every cloud has a silver lining," Koch led off boisterously, stopping in the middle of the room and trying to figure out which one of us was the president. "You may have had a few unpleasant moments, but it has given me the chance to welcome such a famous and distinguished guest to our city."

"This is an outrage. You should not permit this demonstration," Ceausescu started off, without answering Koch's greeting or even looking in his direction.

"Mister President, you should feel complimented," the mayor said. "They only picket very important people. They demonstrate against me all the time. I don't mind. I walk right through the picket lines. All it means is that you are important."

"I am p-president of a f-foreign c-country. Th-this should not be allowed."

"They demonstrate against President Carter when he comes here."

"If President Carter came to Romania, I would not permit any demonstration against him."

"Protests are as American as the First Amendment," the wise-cracking mayor retorted with a smile. "They're guaranteed by our Constitution."

"Wh-why are you Americans interfering in th-the internal affairs of our c-country? Th-there are international agreements p-prohibiting such interference. Th-these treaties s-supersede the C-Constitution," Ceausescu replied in a threatening tone.

"Don't let the problem get to you, Mister President. You've got to get to the problem," Koch came back with exuberant self-assurance.

"If your s-security c-can't t-take care of these crowds, then let my security h-handle it," Ceausescu replied nervously, looking at me.

"Thank you for the offer, Mister President. But that won't be necessary. Tell the president what we've done, McGuire."

Commissioner McGuire reported that several hundred police officers were now keeping order, and that there were no more demonstrators around the hotel.

"It's Monday morning, Mister President. Now they've all gone to work. They can't feed their children if they spend the day just shouting slogans outside the Waldorf," Koch offered in explanation.

"They were not slogans. Those people gravely insulted a foreign president and th-threatened his life on your territory, and you've got to answer for that," Ceausescu sputtered angrily.

Koch tried to downplay it. "A couple of tomatoes and a few eggs?"

"They could have been hand grenades."

"But they weren't. They don't want to kill you. It didn't have anything to do with you, Mister President. It's not you, it's your policies," Koch added sweetly.

"They are war criminals! They are fascists! I have hard evidence against those people who tried to kill me outside. They sent Jews to Nazi concentration camps. They killed them with their own hands."

"I'll take care of these Nazis, Mister President, and you take another look at your policies."

Stuttering badly again, Ceausescu launched into a long dissertation, trying to explain that the Romanian people enjoyed infinitely more human rights than the Americans.

Koch stood up. "Let's be friends, Mister President, and maybe one day we can eat together in a Romanian restaurant here." Muttering something about a meeting of his own cabinet he had skipped in order to come to the Waldorf, he took his leave, but not before finally being able to shake Ceausescu's hand and give him a hearty slap on the back.

"Alcohol!" screeched Ceausescu the minute the Americans had left. "And open the windows," he ordered Stan. "It smells like a pig sty. A Jewish swine, a New York cop, and a dirty nigger!" he went on, while wiping his hands.

"Write a press communiqué about the visit, Pungan, in case the swine makes it public. Just say, 'Problems of common interest were discussed,'" Ceausescu ordered.[1]

We were about to leave when Stan reported: "Counselor Aurel Gheorghe is asking to be received." Ceausescu signaled for me to remain.

Gheorghe drew himself up in a military posture I had never

---

[1] *Ibid.*, p. 183.

before seen him affect and reported without breathing: "Comrade President of the Romanian Socialist Republic, your order has been executed." From his briefcase he removed a newspaper clipping and its handwritten translation and gave them to Ceausescu.

"Read it."

"I shouldn't, Comrade President," said Gheorghe, pointing to indicate that the walls had ears.

Ceausescu called for his glasses. After reading the clipping through twice, he passed it to me. It was a short item stating that Laszlo Kalman, one of the organizers of the demonstration at the Waldorf Astoria against the Romanian president, had been in an automobile accident on his way home from the demonstration.

"Croaked?" Ceausescu asked monosyllabically, looking meaningfully at the walls.

"There's no report in yet. I'll have to get hold of my man."

"Don't lift a finger. No more involvement. The Western press will report the outcome. What about the other one?"

"Still in the works. Should I leave New York on your airplane?" Having known Gheorghe for over 20 years, I could easily read the irony in his voice.

Not Ceausescu. "You stay here. Take care of the other one, too." He suddenly seemed to perk up, as he shook Gheorghe's hand in a friendly manner. "You Pacepa," he turned to me, "you take care of Comrade Elena today. And have the plane ready. I want to leave for Bucharest in the afternoon."

Outside the salon, I cornered Gheorghe and asked for an explanation.

"That little news item came like manna from heaven. A good tranquilizer for the Big Boss," said Gheorghe, winking at me. I left him to go look for Elena.

ELENA CONSIDERS NEW JEWELS

"Don't you have any jewelry for me, darling?" Elena started off when I arrived at her boudoir, where her hairdresser was working on her.

"Everything is ready."

Several famous jewelery stores that had made good money off

Elena in the past had sent their new collections to the Waldorf Astoria. The cases were now locked up in a room next-door to the Presidential Suite, heavily guarded from outside.

"Let's see what you've gotten for me. Open up everything," Elena commanded eagerly, while settling back comfortably into an easy chair. She is not like Ceausescu, who is always on the move, walking around. She sits down whenever she sees a chair and stays put there. Nor is she like a poker player, peering into his hand as he slowly spreads out the cards. No, Elena wants to see everything at once, and to have everything at once.

After I had opened the cases, Elena directed me to place them all around her, and she started to weigh the jewelry in her hands. Her main criteria are the weight of the gold and the size of the diamonds. When she cannot make up her mind between two items, the price settles it: the more expensive, the better she likes it. I was watching Elena play with her toys when General Stan said through the locked door that the Comrade wanted to see me.

"Tape my discussion with Klutznik," Ceausescu whispered when he saw me. As usual, he considered his meeting with the president of the World Jewish Congress, Philip Klutznik, the most important after the ones with the president of the United States. "Romania has a proletarian dictatorship form of government. America has a Jewish dictatorship form of government," is what Ceausescu always says. Within his close circle of intimates, he always used to take particular pride in telling how he had recruited the former president of the World Jewish Congress, Nahum Goldmann, and the secretary of this prestigious international organization as Romanian agents of influence. Ceausescu also liked to impress his cronies by telling them he had the new president, Klutznik, in his pocket.

No third party was usually present at Ceausescu's meetings with these Jewish leaders, but I had the tapes. There was always a significant difference between what Ceausescu said about these "personal agents" and what was on the tapes. The tapes mostly revealed his attempts to gain advantages as mediator in the Middle East conflict, so as to lure Jewish money to Romania and obtain low-interest credits, and the efforts of his conversation partners to get more Jews out of Romania.

After Klutznik had left, I went back to Elena, who in the

meantime had set aside over a dozen sets of jewelry and was still working.

"The prices are ridiculous, darling. You should bargain them down," she burst out, happy to have someone to talk to again. As she has never actually purchased anything since 1965, when Ceausescu became the Romanian leader, she has not the slightest idea of the value of any merchandise. She has, however, two basic rules: Every price in Romania is too low, and every price abroad is too high. Whenever she picked out some jewelry or furs abroad, I had to swear that somebody would get the price drastically reduced, because "we shouldn't be fattening the capitalists with Communist money."

Sometimes she would put on a dramatic show when she was shopping. The last time was in Buenos Aires. We were together in a jewelry store, where she fell in love with a set of earrings, brooch, and ring, each shaped like a flower with movable petals covering the diamond center. Elena was fascinated by the idea of being able to wear them different ways, from wide open to tightly closed. When she asked for a 50 percent discount, the owner laughed in her face, and Elena walked out in a huff. Once back in Bucharest, however, she ordered me to telephone the store and ask for only 25 percent off. The answer was, "already sold," and Elena was sick for two weeks. When she finally directed that the store custom order the set for her, the price had doubled. Since then, she has not wanted to see any more salesmen, and she always wants to have the jewelry sent to her on visits abroad or in Bucharest. But she has kept her pride: "I've never paid a capitalist his asking price."

Elena can play at jewelry for days. That was why, when General Stan shouted through the door that Mrs. Frieda Rosenthal, the wife of a U.S.-Romanian Economic Council official, was there to take her to visit the Metropolitan Museum, she asked distrustfully, "Is there anything there worth seeing?"

Elena decided that one hour would be enough for the Metropolitan. She does not like museums, and if she did occasionally visit one it was only for the press. As we left the Metropolitan, the press was the only thing she cared about. "Tell the idiots to make a long communiqué, and to mention the most famous paintings they have in the museum." When Elena later approved the communiqué, it looked like a museum catalogue. "The works of some great artists, such as Botticelli, Giotto, Velazquez, Goya, Cranach, Van Eyck, David, Utrillo, Matisse were also presented," was just one sentence in the 200-word press release.[2]

We got back just in time for the reception given for Ceausescu by the U.S.-Romanian Economic Council and the Foreign Policy Association at the Waldorf. After being generously praised—everybody had learned his weakness—Ceausescu gave a long, demagogical speech. He included everything he could think of, from his discussion with Jimmy Carter to the (false) 12.5 percent growth rate of Romanian industry, from economic cooperation with 140 countries around the world to national independence and sovereignty, not forgetting Romania's over 2,000 years of history.

While we walked from the Waldorf's lobby to the Presidential Suite, Ceausescu caught my elbow and asked: "How did you like my speech?"

"One hundred percent 'Horizon'!"

"I delivered the sermon. It's up to you to take up the collection for their money. And their technologies."

After the luncheon, Elena went back to her jewels. I accompanied Ceausescu to his meeting with William Norris, the president of Control Data Corporation. Ceausescu considered this an important occasion, and he instructed me to assemble all the official members of his delegation for it. The company "Romcontrol Data," set up together with Control Data Corporation, was not only the first Romanian-U.S. joint venture; created for the production of American electronic equipment and computers in Romania, it was considered by Ceausescu to be one of the most important doors for getting in to steal American microelectronics technology.

INTELLIGENCE OFFICERS FOR JOINT VENTURES

Cooperative and joint ventures with the West became fashionable in the Soviet bloc after they proved their usefulness at providing new technology by both legal and illegal means. The general rule is that all bloc citizens involved in such joint ven-

[2]Ibid., p. 186.

tures should be intelligence officers. Ceausescu ordered the DIE to make intensive use of every new cooperative venture for infiltrating small armies of intelligence officers into the West, and he personally supervised these operations. A joint venture with a West German firm provided Romania access to technological intelligence on various turbotransmissions for armored cars and tanks, including Ceausescu's favorite Leopard. A French-Romanian cooperative venture for producing the Renault 12—known as the "Dacia" in Romania—was used to obtain significant military technologies found at Renault plants. It also provided a way to steal more than 13,000 additional options for the basic car that had not been included in the contract, thus saving Romania several million dollars. After a joint venture had been signed with Citroën a few months earlier, a team of more than 150 Romanian engineers and technicians was sent to France to learn how to build Citroën cars. Most of them were intelligence officers or agents, armed with newly built minicameras and photographic contact paper. When the photosensitive materials sent back to Romania were read, they revealed many secrets that Citroën had tried to keep out of the new joint venture. Some of the intelligence officers recruited Citroën employees for more in-depth technological intelligence.

Romcontrol Data was the product of a DIE operation and was now being intensively used for industrial espionage. Two officers, one under cover as a Romanian engineer, the other an illegal with a Western identity, had developed valuable sources there and were now extracting significant classified data on such things as high density computer discs for military use. Ceausescu's desire to make this meeting as public and as festive as possible was nothing but additional cover for the under-the-table operations he was running inside the American corporation.

After the meeting I found a few minutes for pressing Elena to make her final choices, although when it came to jewelry she never made "final" decisions.

"Let's take these along with us. In Bucharest I'll have more time to look at them carefully and pick out the nicest ones," said Elena, pointing toward more than two dozen boxes holding sets of jewelry and a few solitaires. That was what she always said, but she never sent anything back. In a quick look, I saw no box with a pricetag under $20,000.

When we returned to the Presidential Suite with the boxes she had selected, Ceausescu had just wound up his last business meeting and was looking for me.

"If your emigrés are ready, bring them here," he ordered.

The three emigrés chosen by the station to meet Ceausescu were waiting in a nearby room; one had brought his wife along. According to Florea, who was with them, all three were docile DIE agents. When I brought them to Ceausescu's salon, he was standing there with Elena and just one photographer, who had gotten only one shot before being rushed out by Ceausescu. One after the other, the emigrés droned out the speeches given to them by Florea. Every text praised the Romanian president, vehemently condemned the "slanderous and irredentist" demonstrations against Romania, and assured that the leaders of Romanian emigré organizations would send telegrams to President Carter in the name of all Romanian emigrés, asking him "to put an end to the activity of the fascist circles" in the United States.

This done, Ceausescu had Celac called in to take notes. That was the tipoff that he intended to make a propaganda speech for the press. He did just that, accusing the demonstrators of being Nazi war criminals who had "sent over 200,000 Jews to concentration camps."

"Your dominie was right up to the mark again, Pacepa," Ceausescu said after the emigrés had left. He was referring to "Avram," the one described by Florea as an agent-priest sent from Romania to take over an Orthodox church in Detroit.

"Who was the tall one?" Ceausescu asked.

"The editor of *Dreptatea.*" That was an emigré newspaper.

"The one we fund?"

"That's what Florea said."

Ceausescu ordered that nothing appear in the Romanian press about the demonstration but that his own speech be published in its entirety, together with a summary of the speeches given by the tame emigrés. "They had better not keep the texts. We may need to doctor them up for the press," said Ceausescu, sending me off to catch the texts of their speeches.

The text of Ceausescu's speech was published in the April 19, 1978, issue of the official Romanian newspaper, Scinteia, *together with a photograph of the meeting showing Ceausescu receiving "a group of American citizens of Romanian descent." I was in the middle, with Elena and Ceausescu on the left side, and the emigrés on the right. The same picture was used in a 260-page book about Ceausescu's visit, printed in English, which in July 1978—just before the United States granted me political asylum—was all ready to be shipped to the United States for propaganda purposes. Because I was depicted next to Ceausescu and Elena in most of the photographs, all its 30,000 copies were destroyed, and the book was reprinted, after I had been deleted from all of the photographs. In the picture showing Ceausescu's meeting with the Romanian emigrés, an expert eye can spot the place where I was removed and the background painted in. That was the opposite technique from the one used in Trifa's case, when his head was added to a picture.*

BACK TO BUCHAREST

I could not catch up with the three emigrés until the lobby, where I got their speeches back. When I tried to return upstairs, the elevators were blocked because Ceausescu was ready to leave. I climbed the stairs all the way to the 29th floor, only to see the door of the elevator close in front of my nose with the last of Ceausescu's group in it. I raced back down the stairs, but when I got to the front door the motorcade was pulling away from the hotel. Once more, Ceausescu had made an unforeseen move. The manager of the Waldorf Astoria, who understood my predicament, approached two police officers and asked them to drive me to the airport. It was one of the most exciting rides I have ever had. For a good half hour we raced through New York at rush hour, occasionally jumping onto the sidewalk or dashing the wrong way down a one-way street. When we entered Kennedy Airport through a back gate, the police car whizzed along side roads at 80 miles an hour and crossed several runways before coming to a halt at the back door of the Romanian presidential plane.

"Here we are," said my driver, dripping wet but proud of his performance.

"Faster than the Secret Service," the other police officer remarked, pointing to the flashing lights of the official motorcade, which was just entering the airport area.

"I hope the fate that put me in your hands today will give us a chance to meet again," I said, giving both of the friendly officers a hug, and inwardly hoping that I was truly being prophetic.

When Ceausescu got out of his limousine, I was standing with the State Department officials. Followed by Elena, he went down the row shaking hands. Upon seeing me he suddenly remembered: "You were still in the hotel when we left, weren't you?" Giving Elena a wink, he bragged: "Now will you admit that my security is better than your army?"

At six-forty that Monday evening the presidential Boeing 707 took off, made a wide turn over the city, and headed for Bucharest, leaving the Statue of Liberty behind. In Bucharest it was already Tuesday.

The airplane had just reached its cruising altitude when Ceausescu sent for Oprea, Andrei, Pungan, Avram, and me.

"What's new?" he began as usual.

"Glad to be on Romanian soil again," Oprea squeaked, stamping the floor of the presidential Boeing 707 several times with his right foot.

"You think you're so clever, Oprea. Don't you know it's an American plane?" Elena noted acidly, taking him down a peg. She kept one eye admiring the picture of herself at the NASA Space Center that was reproduced on the front page of a *Scinteia.*

"Until Pacepa and Avram start producing our own airplanes, we'll have to fly capitalist ones. But you're right, Oprea, we are on Romanian soil," Ceausescu decided.

"Take Oprea's side just once more, Nick, and you can sleep with *him* tonight," Elena snarled.

"Rosenthal's speech outdid all expectations," Andrei ventured, referring to Milton Rosenthal, the American chairman of the U.S.-Romanian Economic Council, who had given a speech at the business luncheon that day.

"He was so delicate," Oprea jumped in, eager to perform his

share of the adulation, "when he explained how the Comrade had started serving the people of his country even as a young man."

"My eyes got all misty. Especially when he told how the Romanian people, known for their intelligence and skill, had learned to turn out high-tech products," was Avram's uninspired contribution.

"Isn't he clever," Elena's sharp tongue broke in. "The Romanian people, huh? Without the Comrade, his 'talented' Romanian people would still be barefooted shepherds. Isn't that so, Andrei? You ought to know that better than I."

"I'm going to put this up in big letters in the lobby of my ministry," Andrei changed the subject, reading from a small notebook. "'As the leader of his great nation, President Ceausescu has not only brought tremendous progress to Romania but has also taken on a role of leadership in the entire international community.' That's what Carter said with his own lips. I'll post it there for everybody to see what the American president said."

"I have a beautiful collection of what Carter said," Pungan contributed, reading from his notebook. "'Ceausescu has a unique ability to relate easily to leaders of nations, regardless of their political commitment or orientation.' Here's another: 'Ceausescu has provided a bridge for the easing of tensions and the better understanding on a worldwide basis.' Or: 'His influence in the international arena is exceptional.' Or. . . ."

"Just don't make a hero out of the Peanut Head," Elena interrupted. "Don't you remember his idiot wife and the luncheon she gave me in a museum, and her bright pink suit?"

"It was an excellent visit," Ceausescu decreed, whereupon he immediately started issuing orders, running roughshod over the accompanying chorus of "yesses" and "of courses." "We should call an extraordinary meeting of the Council of Ministers, Oprea. Devoted just to the visit. It should express its full and unanimous approval of the results."

"Marvelous," Oprea exclaimed.

"The prime minister should give an address, and all those Hungarians and Germans and Jews we've still got should also give speeches there."

"I'll work on their speeches as soon as we get back to Bucharest. I won't even go home first," Oprea assured him. As first deputy prime minister the job fell to him.

"I should receive a telegram from the Council of Ministers about the visit."

"I'll write it right now, on the plane."

"You aren't going to forget me, are you, Oprea?" Elena wheedled sweetly.

"Give him a hand, comrades. Put your pens to work. I should also receive telegrams from all around Romania. Use your imagination, comrades. We should have the whole people expressing their full approval of this visit." Ceausescu wound up his enthusiastic tirade, twinkling his eyes at me: "From Westerners, too, of course.

"From Nicu, too, and his Communist Youth Union," Elena added. "And from the women's committees, Nick."

"You're tired, comrades, but make one last effort. Go write up these telegrams now, so that they can be broadcast immediately upon my arrival in Bucharest."

When General Stan reported that, "the comrades have gone to bed," Andrei pulled a bottle of Scotch out of his larger-than-ever briefcase, stuffed with everything he had been able to lay his hands on at Blair House and the hotels, from bottles of booze to soap, toothbrushes, and shower caps.

Pungan got off an enciphered telegram to Dumitru Popescu, the Party secretary for propaganda, telling him that, "at the airport the Comrade should have the largest and most enthusiastic crowds ever to welcome him," and that, "all radio and television stations should transmit patriotic programs about the visit and should be prepared to broadcast the special material we are bringing with us."

Oprea, Pungan, Andrei, and I spent the rest of the flight to Bucharest composing hundreds of laudatory telegrams to Ceausescu from various regional Party committees, from some ministries and other governmental agencies, from a few universities and institutes of culture and art, and from several embassies abroad. It was a firm rule that, after his every visit abroad, *Scinteia* had to run two pages of adulatory telegrams for some time. After his earlier visits to the United States, the telegrams of praise had gone on for more than three weeks.

On our arrival in Bucharest, almost 100,000 people were waiting at the airport. There were schoolchildren wearing brand new pioneer uniforms, peasants in their folk costumes, workers in fresh overalls, priests in their black soutanes, and bureaucrats in their gray suits. As usual, they had been bussed from their schools and workplaces out to the airport. They were now carefully lined up, with those responsible for each group wearing red armbands and directing the "enthusiastic and spontaneous" welcome to Ceausescu and Elena. Hundreds of pictures of the royal couple were held on high, and the crowd was dotted with countless posters proclaiming things like "Ceausescu and the People!" or "The Most Loved and Esteemed Son and Daughter of the Romanian People!" Television cameras transmitted the festive occasion live.

When Ceausescu and Elena got off the plane, the rank and file were lined up together on one side, with the diplomatic corps on the other. Pioneers were chanting "Long live the president!" and folk groups were dancing in the middle of the runway. Over the loudspeakers a solemn voice was explaining that "the cheers and ovations of those present express the feelings of satisfaction of our whole people for the remarkable results of the visit of the head of the Romanian state to the United States of America, for this new and valuable contribution. . . ." Far at the back I saw Popescu the Lord, together with Ion Dinca, the mayor of Bucharest, organizing yet other "spontaneous" activities. Their job is no longer so complicated as it used to be, however. Now every one of the eight administrative sectors into which Bucharest is divided has its own standing plans for bringing people to the airport for Ceausescu's departures and arrivals. Popescu and Dinca have to say only the number of people each sector should supply, the text of the placards they should carry, and the wording of the slogans they should yell out.

XXIII

As soon as my chief executive officer reported to me that Silvo Gorenc had already landed in Bucharest on a special Yugoslav airplane, I left to meet him. His precipitate arrival had to have a good reason.

"To 'Km. 12,'" I ordered my driver. Gorenc had been taken there because it was a safehouse he already knew, and also because it was located very near the airport where he had landed.

A VISIT WITH TITO

I had first met Silvo Gorenc a few years earlier on the island of Brioni, where I had accompanied Ceausescu to one of his many meetings with Josip (Broz) Tito. After the break between Belgrade and Moscow, Yugoslavia was always a DIE target. It was only after the 1968 Soviet invasion of Czechoslovakia that Ceausescu directed the DIE to make a secret overture to Yugoslavia, and in the early 1970s a first cooperation agreement was signed between the two foreign intelligence services. That was one of the reasons Ceausescu took me with him to Brioni. The other was that he had recently given me the additional title of state secretary in the Ministry of Interior and the task of preparing all his future visits to foreign countries.

During the lunch given on Monday, by Tito at his Brioni residence, I was seated between two Yugoslavs. On my right was Luca Banovic, the federal secretary for internal affairs, who always described himself as Tito's oldest and closest friend. On my left was Silvo Gorenc. "After lunch," Banovic said, "Comrade Tito will invite Comrade Ceausescu onto his personal yacht for coffee and cognac. He," pointing at Gorenc, "and I will be there. Comrade Tito asks that you also be present. Just us. Nobody else. Comrade Tito wants to develop our incipient intelligence cooperation. So be prepared."

After we had boarded the yacht, Tito directed Ceausescu to a large, comfortably cool guest suite filled with exotic flowers and bowls of fruit. "Make yourself at home here. We'll get together up on the bridge, whenever you're ready," Tito said in parting.

Taking my arm, Banovic shoved Gorenc and me toward a teak table on the deck and asked for cognac. Milling around us were dozens of men, all dressed in formal white-tie. They were busy setting up a large round table in the middle of the bridge, cleaning imaginary spots off the floor, wiping the railings, or just doing nothing. "Don't worry. They're all security officers," said Banovic through his interpreter. "And me, too," the interpreter added on his own behalf. In no time Ceausescu came up from below and started rapidly pacing around the deck. As he passed our table I heard him muttering something in my direction about "their stupid air conditioning."

When Tito came out he was dressed all in white, except for a light blue scarf at the neck, and he was holding a glass of something on the rocks, as if posing for a flattering picture in a magazine. Ceausescu, in his dark gray, striped suit and heavy black shoes with thick leather soles, looked like a poor relation invited to visit on a luxury yacht. In those days Ceausescu, who was only in his eighth year in power, looked up to Tito as an idol, his ideal of a bright and shining Communist leader who had made an international name for himself during 25 years of unshared power. At that time their relations were excellent. It was only later, when the two men started to know each other better, and when Elena was put down by Jovanka's festive elegance, that their personal relations started to deteriorate.

"May I take your jacket, Comrade Ceausescu?" Tito broke the ice. "And your tie. I want you to feel at home here. What about a drink?"

Ceausescu loves his favorite yellow wine, his aromatic cognac, or Elena's Cordon Rouge champagne, but he almost never drinks in public, where he is at pains to portray himself as ascetic and teetotaling. This, together with the fact that he knew far too much about Tito's drinking habits, made up his mind.

"A glass of mineral water. Not cold," Ceausescu replied.

"That's not encouraging," Tito tried to jest. He took Ceausescu by the arm and seated him at the large round table in the middle of the main deck, then motioned with his hand for Banovic, Gorenc, the interpreter, and me to come over. A fat diamond ring gleamed on one of his fingers; it had not been there during lunch. After one of the white-tie bodyguards had placed coffee, cognac, mineral water, cigarettes, and cigars on the table, Tito started to speak.

He praised Ceausescu for his initiative in establishing the cooperation between their two intelligence services. "We should, my dear Comrade Ceausescu, push our services to do more than just exchange information. We should direct them to run joint operations as well. . . . The cooperation between our foreign intelligence services is not the same as cooperation between internal security services—it cannot be accused of interfering in our internal affairs."

Tito not only opened the discussion, he also kept the initiative during that whole meeting. He spoke coherently and in short sentences. "Both of us are building up an arms industry in our country. We say it is for the protection of our independence, and that is good enough for a public statement. But both of us know, and we can say it just between ourselves, that building Communism is expensive and presupposes hard currency. We," said Tito, including his two officials with a gesture, "concluded that nothing but a modern arms industry could provide that hard currency." He broke off for a moment, taking a noisy slurp of coffee. "We decided to become exporters of military airplanes to the Third World. Now I'm proposing that you join us in secret cooperation." Tito explained that his new aeronautics industry was entirely based on technological intelligence and on the illegal or semi-legal import of Western equipment forbidden to Communist countries. "Both of us enjoy privileged positions because of our public attitude toward Moscow. It is at least ten times easier for both of us to get our hands on Western military secrets than it is for the Soviets." Tito then proposed that the Romanian foreign intelligence service join him in his own efforts to develop a military fighter airplane, as a starter.

One hour later, Ceausescu accepted a glass of cognac. "To our eternal friendship. To our new ROM-YU fighter," he toasted.

"To our friendship. Doesn't YU-ROM sound better, though?" said Tito, chalking up one more point for himself that day. After that, the YUROM company became a vital part of the relationship between the two intelligence services. One year later the agreement was extended to include both Ministries of Defense, which set up a joint military organization for research and the construction of six prototypes. When the first YUROM fighter crashed on its test flight in March 1978, the intelligence cooperation intensified, rather than slackened.

The discussion continued after a break during which Tito showed Ceausescu around the yacht. Both presidents came back visibly overheated by the prospects of their new cooperation. "Now that we're partners," Tito began in a low voice, "I would like to raise another matter. I have reliable information that my assassination is on the drawing board of some Yugoslav emigrés. Today it's me, tomorrow you, Comrade Ceausescu." Although my eyes were on Tito, I could feel Ceausescu shifting around uneasily in his chair. Tito went on, "I think that you, Comrade Gorenc, should tell the story."

According to Gorenc, some Yugoslav emigrés were setting up a national separatist group targeted against Tito. He stated that the head of the new operation against Tito was the Yugoslav emigré Wladimir (Vlado) Dapcevic, who had been one of Tito's collaborators during and immediately after World War II. In 1948, he was condemned in Yugoslavia, but he was set free in 1956, whereupon he emigrated and settled in Brussels, becoming a Belgian citizen.

"Luca, would you like to have the chief of my protective security service come here?" Tito said to Banovic, seeming to stress the man's official position.

A few minutes later a gray haired officer came to the table. He was wearing a well-cut general's uniform with rows of ribbons displayed on the front of his jacket. "At your service, Comrade President," he addressed Tito.

"Hi! Tell Comrade Jovanka to be ready for dinner at nine."

After the general had left, Tito said: "Do you know his name?" Seeing Ceausescu's puzzled expression, he continued, "Dapcevic is his name. He's the brother of Vlado Dapcevic. I've got to neutralize his brother. I need the brother here, to make him spill out every single name he's been given by the other side." Tito went on to explain that Vlado Dapcevic would never try to set foot on Yugoslav soil again, and that to kidnap him from Belgium might be difficult, because he always had bodyguards around him. It could also generate political heat directed at Tito personally. "I'm asking you, Comrade Ceausescu, to lure him to Romania, secretly arrest him and then turn him over to us. That would put me in your debt for life. Banovic and Gorenc are ready and able to have any persons you indicate kidnapped from the West or even assassinated there. You wouldn't have to lift a finger."

I saw Ceausescu squirming in his chair. He always wants to have foreign hands do the job against his political opponents in the West. "Helping you, Comrade Tito, is helping myself," Ceausescu began. "Your intelligence service should lure Dapcevic to Romania and then take him secretly to Belgrade. I won't see anything. But I don't want to touch Dapcevic myself."

Toasts to a New Friendship

"I would like to thank you from the bottom of my heart, Comrade Ceausescu. I was sure you would understand me," Tito said, getting up and embracing Ceausescu. "We won't worry about the details now. Our men will have to iron them out," Tito finished, gesturing toward Banovic, Gorenc, and me. Then he ordered cognac for all and asked Ceausescu to drink with him "to our new friendship."

Ceausescu tossed the cognac down his throat and signaled to a waiter to refill everybody's glass. "To our secret cooperation and work together," Ceausescu toasted in turn, emptying his glass at one swallow and asking for a new one. "Let's drink this glass to our intelligence services."

Tito enjoyed this game. "And one more glass for each of our boys," he toasted, pointing toward Banovic, Gorenc and me.

When the ritual was completed, Ceausescu's eyes were glistening. He began in a very low voice, after loudly filling his lungs with air. "D-Dorogoy T-Tovarishch Josip Broz!" Russian is Ceausescu's only foreign language, and he uses it only among intimates or as a sign of the greatest respect. After he had made this point, he snapped his fingers in the direction of the interpreter and continued in Romanian. "I see that the foreign intelligence service is as important for you as it is for me." Then Ceausescu started to explain, in a lower voice, that in 1972 he took the DIE under his personal control and made changes not only in its personnel but also in its mission. He described how the DIE that he took over in 1972 had fewer than 1,000 case officers and was organized along KGB lines. He did not change that, he explained, but he simply added 2,000 officers to carry out what he considered to be the main mission of a modern Communist intelligence service in today's world: "to build Communism with capitalism's political help, money, and technology, through influence operations."

"Influence is what we do best," Tito interrupted, looking pointedly at his two officials.

"I have to admit that you are better at it. I admire how your service has attracted Western political goodwill, money, and technology. How it portrays you in the West."

It was obvious that Ceausescu had hit one of Tito's soft spots. With slow gestures, Tito took a Cuban cigar from the box that was lying on the table and deliberately lighted it with a gold Dunhill lighter. Then he ceremoniously emptied his cognac and, while holding the glass with his pinkie sticking straight out and his ringfinger ostentatiously showing off its solitaire diamond, turned toward Ceausescu. "You are right, dear Comrade. That's what we do best."

"You certainly do," said Ceausescu, egging him on.

"We wouldn't be able to get anything from the West by riding on Moscow's coattails," Tito went on, "and without Western money and technology there wouldn't be any Communist society in our countries. That's why we should have our own way of dealing with capitalism."

"Letting the West believe that we're different, that we don't want its scalp," Ceausescu added.

"They call it 'Tito's Triangle.' I set up three basic guidelines: friendly smile toward the West, maximum take from it, and no contamination from capitalism. And these men"—Tito pointed to his two fellow Yugoslavs—"constructed a whole strategy and tactics based on that." Tito paused only to drain another glass. "But that's not something we want to talk about out loud—not here on this yacht, and not even in our deepest sleep. Let our men work together. They know what we need, and they can keep their mouths shut." Then Tito ordered "cognac for all" and made a toast "to our new cooperation."

We got back to shore just in time for the official dinner, and Ceausescu walked along with a swinging stride. Tito's Rolls-Royces were waiting. One for him, one for Ceausescu.

"Every president has a yacht," Ceausescu said after the dinner. "Nixon has one. Tito has one. I want one, too. And a Rolls-Royce."

After that, a personal yacht and a Rolls-Royce limousine became matters of prestige for Ceausescu. The DIE got him the Rolls—two, in fact, one limousine and one convertible—but a kind of restraint unusual for Ceausescu made him drive both of them mostly inside the grounds of his residence. I recall only one time outside. A yacht, however, was more than even the DIE could bring off. In 1976, he ordered that a presidential yacht be built in Romania, based on blueprints obtained by the DIE; it had reached an advanced stage by the time I broke with Bucharest.

In early 1985, the Greek media announced that the Romanians were in secret negotiations with the Greek government to buy the Christina *as a personal yacht for President Ceausescu. The 325-foot vessel had been Aristotle Onassis's private yacht. After his death it was donated to the Greek government by his daughter Christina and used for state entertainment. Probably the most publicized yacht in the world when Onassis was courting Jackie Kennedy on board, and with a rich history of guests from Winston Churchill to Maria Callas, the* Christina *evidently appealed to Ceausescu's vainglory and his sense of history. Her unique touches, such as a lapis lazuli fireplace, a canary-yellow amphibious airplane on the upper deck, and barstools covered in whale foreskin, undoubtedly appealed to Elena's taste.*

A KIDNAPING AT TITO'S REQUEST

On July 30, 1975, Drasko Jurisic, another Yugoslav deputy federal secretary for internal affairs, together with Gorenc and a small staff, arrived unannounced in Bucharest in four Mercedes sedans. They brought an oral message from Tito to Ceausescu stating that the Yugoslavs had lured Dapcevic to Romania, where he and his bodyguard Stojanovic, also a Belgian citizen, would arrive on August 1 to visit Svetislav and Djordje Markusev. The latter were Yugoslav emigrés, now Romanian citizens. They lived in Bucharest and were allegedly active in the anti-Tito movement. Tito's request that Dapcevic be secretly arrested by the Romanian Securitate and handed over to the Yugoslavs at the border made Ceausescu furious, however. For him, Yugoslavia was "too liberal" to be able to keep a secret. "I *don't know* and I *don't* want *to know* any Dapcevic," he insisted. "The Yugoslavs are welcome to take him, but they will have to do it with their own hands. The only thing I'll do is close my eyes."

Informed of this decision by Drasko Jurisic via a special telephone hookup, Tito, who did not want to let Ceausescu have the goods on him, refused to authorize a Yugoslav operation on Romanian soil and personally appealed to Ceausescu. Finally Ceausescu gave his approval, based on Tito's solemn promise that the Yugoslavs would keep silent concerning Romanian assistance. For greater secrecy, however, Ceausescu ordered that the kidnaping be organzied by the DIE's anti-terrorist unit, not by the internal Securitate. Altogether, only six Romanians, including Ceausescu, were fully informed about this operation and knew Dapcevic's identity. According to Ceausescu's order, the operational team was to act "blind" against "two Serbian terrorists" and was not to speak a single word out loud in Romanian, so as to allow for subsequent disinformation attributing the action to the Yugoslavs.

The kidnaping was scheduled for August 7, the night before Dapcevic and Stojanovic planned to leave Bucharest. It was to take place during their walk between the Markusev house, where they had been invited for dinner, and their hotel. At about ten in the evening, Dapcevic and Stojanovic, accompanied by Markusev, left the house, but because of a heavy rain they took a taxicab. This changed the plans, and the kidnaping took place at the Hotel Dorobanti, in Dapcevic's room, where some of the DIE's team were stationed. While trying to resist, Markusev received a fatal blow on the head, and Stojanovic was severely injured. Dapcevic and Stojanovic, together with Markusev's body, were taken to "Km. 12," the DIE safehouse in Baneasa, where the Yugoslav team was waiting.

Ceausescu, who personally coordinated the operation throughout the night, ordered that the Yugoslavs could have Dapcevic and Stojanovic only together with the body of Markusev, who had "suffered a heart attack," and only if they would take them from Bucharest in their own cars. When Jurisic objected, Ceausescu called Tito. Shortly after that, the captives were taken to Belgrade in Jurisic's and Gorenc's cars, accompanied by only two Romanians: Colonel Marcel Popescu, the chief DIE doctor, and Ion Sablici, an interpreter. On his return from Belgrade, Popescu reported that he had given Stojanovic blood transfusions during the trip, but that Stojanovic had then been put in a Yugoslav prison, where he had soon died from hemorrhaging and lack of medical attention. Late that same night, Ceausescu ordered that two DIE illegal officers leave Bucharest on a scheduled flight to Brussels the next morning using the Dapcevic and Stojanovic passports and tickets, and then return on two false West German passports under different names.

When the first inquiries about Dapcevic were received from his family and the International Red Cross, Ceausescu ordered a "full investigation." A few days later the Ministry of Interior replied that, according to its border records, Dapcevic and Stojanovic had entered Romania on August 1 and left Bucharest on August 8 on a commercial passenger airplane, giving the flight number. Seizing upon the testimony of a Hotel Dorobanti doorman who reported that, coincidentally, a Yugoslav canoeist group had left the hotel in a motorcade bound for Yugoslavia during the night of Dapcevic's kidnaping, Ceausescu ordered the DIE to put out some "protective disinformation," in case the Yugoslavs did not keep the secret. It spread the rumor that Dapcevic and Stojanovic might have been secretly kidnaped by the Yugoslav canoeists, while two other Yugoslavs had left Romania legally using the passports and flight tickets of Dapcevic and Stojanovic.

The Western press devoted a good deal of attention to the mysterious disappearance of the Belgian citizens Dapcevic and Stojanovic, and various hypotheses were postulated, including a Yugoslav kidnaping, but no news media learned anything substantive. In Bucharest, Markusev's wife reported her husband's disappearance to the Romanian minister of interior. The only response she got was a statement that Markusev's disappearance had been looked into, with no result.

The luggage belonging to Dapcevic and Stojanovic found in the Hotel Dorobanti rooms was minutely searched by the DIE. Hidden inside a double wall of one suitcase was a notebook containing several hundred names. A few days later it was handed over to Gorenc. Ceausescu was subsequently informed by Tito that, based on that material and further interrogations, the Yugoslavs had arrested or secretly liquidated many "enemies of Yugoslavia." In accordance with a joint agreement, on December 26, 1975, the Yugoslav press agency Tanjug officially acknowledged that Vlado Dapcevic had been arrested on Yugoslav territory while carrying out hostile activities. He was described as a Yugoslav citizen who would be tried in Belgrade once the investigation of his case was completed. No word was said about the two men killed in the operation. In July 1976, Dapcevic was convicted of high treason and Cominformist activities and sentenced to 20 years in prison. In an oral message, Tito assured Ceausescu that Dapcevic would never leave jail alive. The joint Dapcevic operation, like the bilateral Influcommunism actions, has remained one of the best-kept secrets in Romania and Yugoslavia.

In early 1978, Ceausescu asked to be paid back for the Dapcevic operation by having Faust Bradescu lured to Belgrade. Bradescu is a French citizen and political opponent of Bucharest who lives in Paris and who had begun smuggling "hostile propaganda" into Romania and distributing it. Ceausescu, who did not want to be caught red-handed by the French, planned to have the Yugoslavs kidnap Bradescu. A press communiqué prepared on Ceausescu's orders, stating that Bradescu had been "arrested on Romanian territory while carrying out hostile activities," was ready to be publicized several months after his kidnaping. Also prepared were counterfeited declarations with Bradescu's forged signature, supposedly made during his interrogation in Bucharest, in which he accused the CIA and the French foreign intelligence service, the SDECE, of secretly plotting against the Bucharest government and planning Ceausescu's assassination. These documents were ready and waiting for Bradescu's arrival. They could then be dated and put to use for publicity or political blackmail, as needed. So far, however, Bradescu has resisted all attempts to lure him to Yugoslavia.

AT SAFEHOUSE "KM. 12"

When my car stopped at the front door of the safehouse, I could hear Gorenc's hearty voice and laughter. At the sound of my car, he came to the door. "It's so nice to see old friends and familiar places," he said, embracing me and pounding my back with his hands, a Yugoslav custom. Of course he knew the house. It had been his headquarters during the kidnaping of Dapcevic.

Tito's message for Ceausescu that Gorenc brought was an answer to Ceausescu's earlier request that the Yugoslavs help to free Aldo Moro. It said flatly that they were not able to influence the Red Brigades' leaders to release Moro, and that a decision for his "exemplary execution" had just been made. "You know," Gorenc elaborated, we have excellent relations with the Red Brigades' leadership. I personally spoke with one of them on behalf of Comrades Tito and Ceausescu, and I just got their final response last night. That's why I am here now, ready to answer any questions Comrade Ceausescu may have."

Secret military and financial support for the Red Brigades was a significant part of the Yugoslav intelligence operations for undermining the political stability of Italy, Yugoslavia's NATO neighbor. According to Banovic and Gorenc, Yugoslav involvement in the Red Brigades started in the mid-1960s, when his service infiltrated a Marxist group at the University of Trento and secretly guided its political indoctrination. In 1970, the group took the name *Brigate Rosse* and organized the firebombing of several plants and warehouses in Northern Italy. Gorenc repeatedly and proudly emphasized the "Yugoslav connection" of the new terrorist wave in Italy. This could be seen in the Red Brigades' symbol—a five-pointed red star identical to the one in the Yugoslav flag, complemented by a machine gun—and in its self-proclaimed goal of undermining the Italian state and paving the way for the proletarian revolution.

From the safehouse I telephoned Ceausescu, who decided to receive Gorenz immediately. "Too bad," said Ceausescu, when Gorenc finished relaying his message. "Helping to get Moro released would have been a masterstroke of Influcommunism." He was, however, neither shocked nor impressed by what he heard. For Ceausescu, as for Tito, Moro was merely a filthy capitalist leader who might have helped them and the Italian Communist Party make spectacular points in the West.

"Comrade Tito suggests you send a telegram of condolences to the Italian Communist Party when Moro's death becomes public. For public consumption," added Gorenc.

"Not bad," Ceausescu mused. Then he immediately called Andrei on the telephone. "Have condolence telegrams prepared, in case Moro dies. Include one for Berlinguer also."

"Inspired," I could hear Andrei's admiring remark on the other end of the line.

A few minutes later, Ceausescu got up from his chair. "Stop mourning, start working." He smiled. "I'm going bowling in Snagov," he said to Manea, as he left the office.

I went back to the safehouse with Gorenc, where Pop had prepared a formal luncheon for us, including black-tie waiters. They were actually DIE officers specially trained as waiters and scheduled to be sent abroad in the near future.

When he drinks, Gorenc is far from taciturn. He chattered away almost the whole time, and, as always when two intelligence officers get together, the main subject was the intelligence business. "Do you remember the Dubrovnik restaurant my service opened in Vienna? The one where our officers are working as waiters, and where we have microphones on every table? Where we picked up the first tipoff to the plot to mine our beaches, and where we've been able to identify a whole slew of emigrés recruited by Western services?" Without waiting for my reply, he went on. "That turned out to be a fantastic experiment! Now we've gotten control of several restaurant chains in Austria and West Germany. We're also working on France and Italy, and we have plans for the United States." Gorenc paused just long enough to finish his soup and let out a noisy belch. "The West is going to start sprouting lots of Dubrovniks and Balkan Grills all over the place. You ought to try it with some Romanian restaurants. It's just fabulous."

Gorenc rambled on and on about his work. By dessert he was telling about the training centers his service had set up in Yugoslavia for the PLO. According to Gorenc, these centers were also paying off. They provided not only insurance against Arab terrorism on Yugoslav territory but also professional foreign hands to carry out the Yugoslavs' "dirty jobs," as well as unexpectedly useful connections with the Red Army, the Baader Meinhof group, and other similar organizations in the West.

Although it had been almost three years since his kidnaping from Romania, Dapcevic was still one of Gorenc's favorite topics. "I remember it like yesterday," he said. "There was Dapcevic blindfolded, handcuffed, and covered with blood, lying in this very room. He never did figure out what had happened to him, how he had been captured in his hotel room. It's still a mystery to him." Pointing to the room next to the one we were in, an office, he went on. "Stojanovic was lying in there, unconscious, with a big hole in his head. When we got to Belgrade, he was thrown into a cell and 'forgotten.' Keeping him alive would've brought us nothing but headaches. He was cremated that same day. Nobody knew and nobody will know anything about him." Gorenc went to the window. "Do you remember how Comrade Ceausescu reacted that night, when he learned that Markusev had been killed? He said, 'I don't know any Markusev, or any Dapcevic.' When we insisted that Markusev, as a Romanian citizen, was not under our authority, he exploded. 'The only thing I know,' he said, 'is that if you don't clean the place up this minute and take both the living and the dead with you to Belgrade, I'll get Comrade Tito on the line right now.' He meant it, and he did! Pointing toward the window, Gorenc added, "There was a terrible rain that night. After Comrade Tito called, I gave the order to put Markusev's body outside, to wash the blood off of his clothes, so I could put it in the trunk of my Mercedes. It was brand new."

After Gorenc left, I went for a walk in the woods behind the house. Dapcevic was the beginning of a new policy era for Ceausescu. His Influcommunism was now more often "bloody" than not. After Dapcevic, political crime became an almost daily habit for Ceausescu. It was as if he had just been waiting for a precedent to be set.

Footsteps behind me suddenly cut short my musings. It was Iosza, the manager of the safehouse, who was running to catch up with me. "For a long time I've been trying to see you alone, Comrade General," he blurted out, catching his breath. "I have a delicate personal problem I'd like to ask you about." And he began to ramble on in his uneducated way, telling me how he had been with the DIE as a gardener and safehouse keeper since

1948, and how his wife was old and sick. "She got terribly sick the winter of '56/'57. Around the end of November that year we got Imre Nagy here—God rest his soul!—with a lot of Soviet officers. They interrogated him night and day for more than a year. You were young then," he said, trying to find an excuse for me. "They ordered that the house be kept cold, and here in the middle of the woods it's like an icebox in winter. Whenever they liked Nagy's answer, they would give him a jacket or blanket. When they didn't, they would take it away again. And they did the same thing with the food," Iozsa went on. "That winter was a killer. The Soviets had thick fur coats, but we didn't. It was that winter that killed my wife and me. We both got terrible rheumatism from it, and now we can hardly move." His bottom line was that he and his wife had gotten sick "in the line of duty," and now they were asking for early retirement "with full pension and a little house with a garden, where we can finish out our days."

HELPING THE SOVIETS HANDLE IMRE NAGY

I had always been interested in the Imre Nagy story, because of its connection with an entirely different Ceausescu than the one he pretends to be today. That Ceausescu was the one who studied in Moscow, who expressed Moscow's ideas better than the Kremlin itself, who made his political name in a period of indisputable and total Romanian subordination to Moscow, going all the way from apprentice during the war to secretary of the Central Committee of the Romanian Communist Party by 1955. In 1956, as a young captain in the foreign intelligence service, I was chief of the German desk—covering West Germany and Austria—when Nikita Khrushchev and Georgy Malenkov secretly came to Bucharest for "consultations" about Hungarian insubordination and possible military intervention against Imre Nagy's government. The Romanian participants in these ultrasecret conversations were the late leader Gheorghe Gheorgiu-Dej, the "Old Bolshevik" Emil Bodnaras, and the youngest member of the Politburo, Nicolae Ceausescu, who was in charge of the armed and security forces.

Between Ceausescu and Bodnaras there existed long-standing and very close ties. As one who had been given political asylum during World War II in the Soviet Union, where he became a member of the Soviet Communist Party, Bodnaras was made general and minister of defense after the Communists took over Romania. One of his priority measures as new minister of defense was to dispatch a small team of fanatic Romanian Communists to a special military school in Moscow to be hastily trained and to become his closest aides. Among them was the young Nicolae Ceausescu. When the team graduated, Moscow indicated that Ceausescu was the most dedicated and asked that he be made general and appointed to the most important job at that time, "political commissar of the military forces."[1]

Thus Ceausescu became Bodnaras's closest collaborator and the most zealous general involved in transforming the traditional Romanian military forces into a Soviet-style Red Army. In April 1954, during the tense days following Stalin's death and the fight to wash away all public trace of his hideous personality cult, the Kremlin proposed that Bucharest abolish the position of general secretary of the Party and replace it with a four-man secretariat. At Bodnaras's suggestion, the Kremlin insisted that the Moscow-educated General Ceausescu be one of the four, and that he supervise the military and security forces.

The Romanian trio that participated in the secret 1956 discussions with Nikita Khrushchev and Georgy Malenkov were unanimously pushing for a swift and firm military intervention against Imre Nagy's government. From Gheorghiu-Dej I later learned that Ceausescu vehemently supported a military intervention, emphasizing that Romania had already secretly started to provide arms and information to the Hungarian security forces in some of the border regions in self-defense against the "counter-revolutionary virus." Khrushchev and Malenkov insisted that there was no need to internationalize the Hungarian crisis by involving any troops other than the Soviet forces already stationed in Hungary in accordance with the Potsdam agreement.

Khrushchev did, however, ask the Romanian government to use the Hungarian minority in Romania, then amounting to over two million people, the largest minority in Europe, for se-

[1]In those days, the Romanian name for this position was chief of the General Political Directorate. The name of this body was later changed to Higher Political Council, as it is called today. As of 1985, its chief was Ceausescu's brother, Lieutenant General Ilie Ceausescu.

cret but intensive intelligence operations among intellectuals and students in Budapest, on Hungary's border with Austria, and of course on its border with Romania. Ceausescu became the political supervisor of this operation, helped by a KGB advisor who came to Bucharest to organize and coordinate the DIE operations in Hungary. Several hundred Securitate agents of Hungarian origin were sent as visitors to Hungary to identify as many Hungarian "counterrevolutionaries" as possible. Around a hundred DIE legal and illegal officers were sent to the West and from there to Hungary on false Western passports, most of them Austrian, West German, French, and Italian, and used as Trojan Horses against the revolution. They collected valuable information about the heart of the Hungarian resistance, its leaders, illegal groups, contacts inside the Communist Party, in the government, and in the military. Ceausescu ordered that Wilhelm Einhorn, a deputy director of the DIE, be hastily dispatched to Budapest under cover as a counselor of the Romanian embassy, becoming chief of the newly created DIE station in Budapest and liaison officer with Yuri Andropov, the Soviet ambassador, and with the KGB chief there. Einhorn was a native Hungarian who had been a volunteer in the Spanish Red Army during the Spanish Civil War, a Soviet citizen, undercover Soviet state security officer, and a member of the French maquis during World War II. In 1948, he became an officer of the Romanian security forces, retaining his undercover rank in the Soviet service.

The DIE's most important task at this time was to organize 24-hour radio contact with its forces in Hungary. Volumes of information came in daily and were immediately given to the special Soviet advisor, who also had around-the-clock radio contact with Moscow. The material especially contained names: names of the main organizers of the September revolt; of the most rebellious students, including the ones who proposed the rejection of the Youth League as their organization and prepared the street demonstrations on October 23; of the anti-Communist officers in the military forces; of the people around Jozsef Cardinal Mindszenty, who had just been freed.

On November 4, Soviet troops openly attacked Budapest, and on November 13, Imre Nagy sought refuge in the Yugoslav embassy. Gheorghiu-Dej accepted Khrushchev's confidential de-

mand for cooperation in luring Nagy out of the embassy and
secretly keeping him under arrest in Romania until a new Hungarian government could be consolidated. He put Ceausescu in
charge of the operation. After the Romanian embassy in Budapest officially pledged that no criminal charges would ever be
brought against Nagy, he agreed to be taken to Romania. Nagy
was put in the DIE safehouse where Iosza was the keeper,
located some seven miles (12 kilometers, whence its name) north
of Bucharest on the highway to Ploesti, where he was soon informed that he was under arrest. Only Gheorghiu-Dej and Ceausescu were kept informed about Moscow's intentions in Nagy's
case.

In March 1957, Kadar paid his visit to Moscow and, when he
came back, denounced Nagy as an enemy. On May 27, an agreement signed in Budapest legalized the presence of the Soviet
troops in Hungary. The DIE station and most of its illegal groups
were still active there. Posing as Western citizens or Hungarians
living in the West, they continued to provide long lists of people
who were acting, speaking, or thinking against the Soviet invasion. According to the special Soviet advisor, quite a few of the
people on these lists were secretly deported to the USSR. Later
I learned that Nagy was sent on a Hungarian airplane to Budapest, where he was tried and executed in June 1958. At that time,
I was the chief of the DIE station in West Germany. After I came
back, no Romanian leader, Ceausescu included, was willing to
talk about the Romanian role in the Soviet invasion of Hungary
or the Imre Nagy case. In recent years, Ceausescu began representing himself within his circle of intimates as the only one
among the Romanian leaders of that time who opposed the Soviet invasion of Hungary, claiming that his position was definitive
in keeping Romania "out of the Soviet mess."

"We know that Comrade Einhorn and the others who participated in Nagy's case are no longer members of our service,"
Iozsa went on. "We also know that today nobody even wants to
remember that Nagy was once in this house. But we are little
fellows. All we did in those days was to ruin our health," lamented Iozsa.

I stared at this man who was probably the only person alive in

Romania to have witnessed Imre Nagy's ordeal. I promised to see what I could do, and a few weeks later I signed the papers authorizing his retirement.

I was driving toward Bucharest when the radio telephone came on. "Sixty-two is asked to call fifty-eight. Orders from zero one. Urgent matter." That was Pop, telling me that Oprea wanted to see me, on orders from Ceausescu.

"Let's stop there," I ordered Paraschiv, as we were approaching the headquarters of the Party's Central Committee, where Oprea had his office.

Oprea had Pungan, Andrei, and Luchian in his office. "The Comrade ordered me to call all of you together. We are to draft a message to Brezhnev about the Comrade's visit to the United States. Luchian is the only outsider involved, because the Comrade wants it to be a political document, and he considers Luchian's style the best suited for that."

"Everything?" I asked.

"Oh, yes. Including verbatim reports of his private discussions with Carter and Andrei's with Vance."

It was late in the evening by the time we left, but I stopped a moment to chat with Luchian outside. He was eager, as usual, to tell me what had happened in Bucharest during my absence. Luchian has a good sense of humor and can tell a good story. Everything and everybody in Bucharest had been relaxed while Ceausescu was abroad. The minister of defense and his deputies had played tennis every day. The mayor of Bucharest had gone fishing in the afternoons. He himself had been off on a three-day hunt in the mountains with Maurer. "When we got back, I had another chance to glance at his manuscript. The Comrade may not like it much, and *Madame* certainly won't. But it's true, Mike. I know Maurer. He wouldn't put a single comma in there if it distorted the truth." Then Luchian began talking about the new favorite, Postelnicu. "Do you know what Marcu told me yesterday? You won't believe it. While you were in America, Marcu took your place, as he usually does. So he went to visit Postelnicu and have a chat with him about espionage, to make friends with him. When Marcu finished, Postelnicu was sublime. He said he wasn't sure he had really understood what a deaddrop was. So he took Marcu over to his bathroom, the one on the corridor. Inside he pointed to the water tank of the toilet and asked if it could be used as a deaddrop. 'Why not?' Marcu said, proud that he had gotten through to the idiot, when guess what Postelnicu said? He said, 'Why don't you load it with a bottle of Scotch every other day? I don't want my executive officer to see you coming with packages to my office. Here's a key to the door.' Marcu says he just stood there with his mouth open. It was so incredible!"

Luchian stopped for a minute, looked cautiously around, and then continued in very low voice, telling me that his house had been surreptitiously entered a few days earlier. "Could I have microphones, Mike?"

"So what? Are you a spy?"

"You know I'm not. But, I don't know why, this time I'm afraid. Afraid of Postelnicu."

Luchian left on foot for his car, which was parked on the other side of the Central Committee building, a few hundred yards away. Two shadows appeared out of the dark and started following him at a prudent distance. It was my turn to be afraid, for Luchian.

XXIV

IT was well before seven in the morning when I arrived at the headquarters of the Securitate Troops, where the military exhibit was set up. This exhibit was conceived by Ceausescu as a major step toward development of Romania's military technological intelligence. The whole Soviet bloc arms industry was more and more based on espionage, as a result of the growing technological gap between East and West. The heart of each Soviet bloc modern arms system was now being developed in the KGB's technological cities, where intelligence stolen from the West by all seven bloc countries was being transformed into Communist might. Romania's role in this process had increased greatly, her trumpeted independence from Moscow having opened far more doors to Western secrets for her than for all the rest of the Warsaw Pact together. Ceausescu, however, wanted to raise Romania even higher, to an indisputable number two place in the Warsaw Pact. He also wanted to create a new arms industry producing new types of equipment independently of Moscow and the Warsaw Pact, which could therefore be freely exported.

THE TWO PARTS OF ROMANIA'S ARMS INDUSTRY

In Ceausescu's view, Romania's military industry should have two main parts. First was the existing arms industry, which had to continue producing equipment for the Warsaw Pact and Romania's own military forces, according to her obligations within the Soviet bloc. The second part was to be an entirely new industry, producing Western military equipment for export to the Third World, seen by Ceausescu as the most important arms market of the future. A multifunctional military airplane—for bombing, transport, parachuting, reconnaissance—based on the Fokker-614, a tank based on the Leopard II, and a Western-style, jointly developed Romanian-Yugoslav fighter were its most important components.

Seven years later, The Washington Post *reported: "Figures prepared by the U.S. Arms Control and Disarmament Agency on the World's leading arms exporters were published last October in* Business Week. *They listed Romania as the fifth largest exporter in 1982."*[1]

The military exhibit had been set up inside both the Securitate Troops' sports hall and a number of military tents, and was divided into two parts. The first and largest contained weapons and equipment being designed, manufactured in prototype, or mass-produced in Romania on the basis of technological intelligence. The second part displayed recent technological intelligence and Western samples that had not yet been copied. In ordering the exhibit, Ceausescu not only wanted to stimulate cooperation from the DIE and the DIA with the industrial ministries producing military equipment, but he also intended to issue orders and deadlines for the future.

The ministers and other top officials concerned were already there to give out last minute orders, because before eight o'clock they had to attend the opening of the National Conference of Women. General Dumitru Dumitru, the chief of the DIA, spotted me and rushed over. Standing six feet tall, he had the masculine charm of a Clark Gable and the affected elegance of an operetta general, dressed up for the occasion in a brand new uniform and clutching a brown leather glove in his gloved left hand. Dumitru could be taken for anything but the chief of a military intelligence service, except that when he speaks he becomes mysterious, barely whispering his words. Elena had selected him for this position two years before, based on the fact that his home town was close to hers and on his appearance.

[1] *The Washington Post,* May 15, 1985, p. A1.

Dumitru stopped a few yards in front of me, saluted ceremoniously, looked around suspiciously, and then came up and started speaking in a very low voice. During the night the DIE had received a complete engine for the Leopard II tank, which had just been set up in a separate tent. It was not a new one but a still functioning, used engine from a West German tank that had just gotten a replacement. Dumitru came even closer and started whispering in my ear. The DIA agent who had gotten the engine was one of Kirschfeld's representatives in Bucharest, and Kirschfeld was a West German trade organization with headquarters in Düsseldorf. A native Romanian, the representative had been recruited a couple of years earlier thanks to his involvement with a Romanian girl who was cooperating with the DIA. The price he had asked for the engine was an exit visa for his girlfriend, and Dumitru now wanted my help to get it. Shifting over to my other ear, perhaps considering it more secure, Dumitru murmured two names into it, those of the agent and his girlfriend. He gave me an envelope, stating that it contained the two names and nothing else, and then he went back over his story, to be sure I had understood.

Because it was not easy to turn Dumitru off once he got going, I always preferred meeting him in his office, not in mine, so at least I would be able to walk out, after I had made my points or grasped his. On this day Oprea came to my rescue. Wearing his dark gray raincoat, unbuttoned as usual, over a black pin-striped suit and ostentatiously waving a copy of *Scinteia*, he bore down on us at his rapid pace.

"'Your recent visit to the United States, Comrade Supreme Commander,'" Oprea started reading the newspaper out loud as he approached, "'provides further evidence of the clearsightedness and firmness with which you, Comrade Nicolae Ceausescu, the beloved leader of our socialist nation, eminent personality of contemporary political life. . . .'[2] Isn't that sensitive?" Oprea said, jamming the newspaper into his raincoat pocket. *Scinteia* was still running two full pages daily on Ceausescu's visit to the United States. "I hope we can give the Comrade a very good day. He's so fond of military equipment!" said Oprea, proposing we take a quick turn around the exhibit together.

[2]*Scinteia*, April 21, 1978, p. 3.

AT THE NATIONAL CONFERENCE OF WOMEN

A few minutes before eight we all arrived at the Radio-Television Concert Hall, where the conference was taking place. The charming concert hall, paneled in light wood, had been filled since long before seven with the 790 women delegates from around the country, who had been put up at student hostels and bussed over to the hall. Only the front rows were empty, waiting for the high ranking Party and government representatives. The stage had been fixed up like a presidium, with chairs for Ceausescu, Elena, and the most important members of the Political Executive Committee. The backdrop behind it showed a huge portrait of Ceausescu, flanked on each side by the Romanian flag and the Communist red banner with its hammer and sickle. Ceausescu had gradually changed the Soviet bloc custom of posting all three portraits of Karl Marx, Friedrich Engels, and Vladimir Ilyich Lenin at major public demonstrations. A few years after he came to power he dropped Engels, and then later Lenin went, leaving just Marx and Ceausescu. In the last two years he had kept only his own portrait.

When Ceausescu and Elena appeared at the door, everyone was lined up by position. The women delegates, dressed in folk costumes, gray proletarian overalls, or print dresses, were standing and chanting "Ceausescu and the people," while clapping frenetically. Photographers ringed the Ceausescus, their cameras flashing, while television crews did a live broadcast.

Lina Ciobanu opened the conference: "With deep esteem and high value, with love and happiness, we welcome the presence in our midst of the Party and government leadership, headed by the most beloved son of our people, Comrade Nicolae Ceausescu, . . . fiery revolutionary and patriot, experienced nationalist, who has done and is doing everything for his people for the cause of peace and socialism. . . . To you, brilliant personality of the modern world, indefatigable militant, we owe the full manifestation of our motherland's independence and sovereignty."[3] Ciobanu ended in an explosion of "Ceausescu and the people," answered by the rhythmic clapping of all the participants, now standing up.

[3]*Ibid*, April 22, 1978, pp. 1 and 5.

It lasted more than ten minutes, until Ceausescu raised both arms, asking for silence.

After sucking the air in between his teeth several times, Ceausescu started off his speech in a low voice, as usual, reeling off a batch of statistics and stressing the contribution to the Romanian economy made by women: 40 percent in the overall industrial labor force, with much more in some branches, such as 80 percent in light industry; 58 percent in the agricultural labor force; 64 percent in commerce and public services. No names, no personalities. Then he ventured into a number of "we should's" for the further "flowering of our motherland," winding up with some ways to make women's lives easier. "Our industry should develop a more diversified production of ready-cooked and semi-prepared foods to save women time and allow them to devote themselves to multifaceted activities."

Then Ceausescu turned to issue orders for the artistic and literary fields. "Of course it is nice to hear a good love poem, but that is not enough. . . . The working people demand that our literary and art works promote the new, revolutionary concepts, the opposite of the concepts of the old society of capitalists and landowners," Ceausescu ordered. The participants, egged on by Prime Minister Manescu, chanted "Ceausescu and the poeple!" for many minutes, until Ceausescu again raised his arms. He moved on to international matters, eulogizing Romania's relationship with the other Communist countries, demanding that Israel withdraw from all the territories it occupied during the 1967 war, and claiming Romania's devotion to a Palestinian state.[4]

When finished, Ceausescu modestly took his chair, while the participants stood and broke into wild applause, chanting "Ceausescu and the people!" intermittently interspersed with "Ceausescu—RCP!"—RCP being short for the Romanian Communist Party.

After more than ten minutes, during which Ceausescu pretended to be studying a file he had on the table in front of him, he waved both arms in a call for silence. Lina Ciobanu took the floor, embarking on another course of flattery. She was interrupted only by a loud blare of trumpets followed by an invasion

[4]*Ibid.*, pp. 1 and 3.

of children dressed in their Pioneer uniforms with red ties at the neck. After showering Ceausescu and Elena with flowers, they delivered an ode in chorus:

> Comrade Nicolae Ceausescu, all children
> Are bringing you burning love from their souls,
> Because you, leading the Party and the people,
> Are teaching us to move forward.
> When we say Ceausescu, we all know
> That we say liberty, truth and steadfastness.
> That's why we love you with ardor,
> With all that is heart in us and in Romania.[5]

Ceausescu and Elena took their departure amid a rousing, "spontaneous" demonstration and blare of trumpets, through a corridor formed by the children tossing more flowers. Oprea and I went back to the military exhibit in the same car with the Ceausescus. "How was it?" Ceausescu asked as usual, thirsting for the praise he always needs after giving a public speech.

PLANNING ARMS SALES TO THE THIRD WORLD

The car slowed down only slightly when entering the Securitate Troops headquarters, continuing past a string of soldiers presenting arms. Each of them gripped a submachine gun with a red flag sticking out of the end of its barrel.

After General Luigi Martis, commander of the Securitate Troops, had given his report to the commander in chief, Ceausescu, accompanied by Elena, reviewed the honor guard. She had fussed around a great deal, until she had finally won this right also. Once they had finished, the soldiers cheered "hurrah!" three times and then burst out into a loud and long "Ceausescu and the people, Ceausescu RCP!" chanted simultaneously not only by those present but also by several thousand more voices coming from the remote surrounding barracks. That was Martis's surprise part of the show. The cabinet ministers, lined up in military formation, were clapping to the same beat.

Ceausescu and Elena, accompanied by Oprea and the Minister

[5]*Ibid.*, p. 5.

of National Defense, Ion Coman, started their visit with Avram's first tent. The centerpiece was a full-scale prototype of a Leopard II. Although it did not yet have its engine, turbo transmission, or any kind of arms, Avram presented it as a huge Romanian success. Ceausescu walked around it, admired it, touched it. Clearly impressed, he started issuing orders. The tank assembly line should be not in Bucharest, but hidden in a mountainous area, even if it cost twice as much. Secrecy was what mattered in the arms business. Production should start immediately. The tanks for Libya should be called "Cega," the ones for the Third World "Independence." Its entire production should be for export, half to Libya, the rest to the Third World. They should play an important role in reducing Romania's foreign debt and balancing its budget in hard currency.

"We have a surprise for you," Ion Coman said when Ceausescu had finished. "Last night we snagged a complete engine for the Leopard II. Brand new," he added, capping his story with a lie.

"Where is it?" Ceausescu turned toward him, quick as a flash.

"I hope it will be in our tent by the time you get there," replied Ion Coman, adding more spice to his story.

Behind the tank was a Yurom fighter plane co-produced with the Yugoslavs. Its sister plane had just crashed a couple of weeks earlier in an experimental flight. Ceausescu became excited again, christened the plane "Liberty," and doubled the production of the Craiova airplane factory on the spot, although it had not even been finished yet. "There are fewer than ten countries on earth with their own aeronautics industry. Within a five-year plan Romania should join their number. Nuclear power, microelectronics, and an aerospace industry should crown Romania's 2050 years of existence!" he declared dramatically.

With his infectious enthusiasm, Florescu gave a presentation on the chemical contribution to the military industry. He presented new, NATO-type gas masks being mass produced in a just completed factory in Buzau, and ended up by displaying an experimental solid propellant to be used in future rockets. Outside the tent he showed off a spectacular incendiary rain and emphasized the role of Elena's institute in producing "Ropalm," a powerful new Romanian super-napalm. Ursu's tent climaxed with a high-powered carbon dioxide laser, which, he said, would eventually become a powerful weapon. At the Ministry of Defense booth, General Nicolescu culminated his show by simulating a laser-guided anti-aircraft attack on balloon targets anchored outside the exhibit area at a height of several hundred feet.

Finally it was my turn to be the guide. I described the second part of the show, containing recently received and as yet unused intelligence and samples, most of which were displayed inside the Securitate Troops' sports hall under heavy security. Rows of tables held samples of military equipment. On display were dozens of handguns, rifles, submachine and machine guns, and self-guided anti-tank systems, each with ammunition, that were being stolen from all over the Western hemisphere. They were followed by samples of military radio communications equipment and a few portable enciphering machines. Farther along, other tables contained military computers and an automated, computerized command center for the artillery. Indefatigable, Ceausescu went from table to table, listening, then issuing orders and setting deadlines.

A booth containing American and West German military infrared and light-amplifying equipment for nighttime use caught his attention even more than the previous marvels. "Do you remember what I once asked you?" he said, suddenly turning on me.

"Yes, comrade!" I answered. I knew exactly what his vague question was about, so I handed him a precision rifle fitted out with night vision equipment.

"Is that it?" he exclaimed, as he eagerly caught at the rifle. Bear hunting is his favorite pastime, and bearskin trophies are his greatest pride. Small armies of forest rangers all around the country do nothing but prepare Ceausescu's bear hunts. They tie down half a dead horse in places where bears are known to look for water at daybreak or after sundown, and then they watch the bait. When a large bear makes a habit of feeding there, Ceausescu is notified. He arrives by helicopter before three o'clock in the morning and leaves with the bearskin well before five. Because of the dark at that hour, he had missed a few bears, and that was why he had ordered a special rifle to shoot with during the night. "How can I try it out?" Ceausescu asked.

"Everything is ready," I promptly came back. The Securitate Troops' headquarters had a firing range designed for practice in nighttime shooting.

"Let's go!" he cried, leaving the building at his fast clip, closely followed by the waddling Elena. The visit did not get back on track again until after he had gotten used to firing the new rifle and had ordered that a bear be "prepared" for him Sunday morning.

I moved from the samples to the technical documents. Blueprints on various Fokker aircraft including the VTOL reawakened Ceausescu's appetite for issuing orders, instructions, and deadlines. When he had finished, he whispered into my ear: "You've got to take a whole bunch of them with you and go back to the 'Bedouin.' No later than next week," he ordered, preparing me for another trip to Tripoli.

After I had presented the last blueprints and technical documents, I conducted the Ceausescus over to a British Centurion tank that had just arrived in Bucharest. It had been sent by Yitzhak Yesahanu at Marcu's request, and in return Marcu had promised him that such a gesture would be followed by an increase in Jewish emigration from Romania. The Centurion tank had its engine running, and Ceausescu went for a ride. He came back ecstatic.

"Isn't this better than the Leopard, Coman?"

"The same class of tank, Comrade Ceausescu. The Centurion is more massive and built to last forever—typically British. The Leopard is faster and more maneuverable—typically German."

"Maybe we ought to produce both."

"I don't think we can manage to produce two heavy tanks just now."

"Have you forgotten Gadhafi's money?" Ceausescu scolded Coman, searching around with his badger eyes until he found Marcu. "Let's ask your friend for the blueprints and technical documentation. If we don't get them, kkkkkch!" he said, drawing his forefinger across his throat. Only Marcu and I understood that this meant the cutoff of Jewish emigration from Romania.

After finishing with the Centurion, Ceausescu personally drove the light tank that had been captured by the PLO in Lebanon and sent to Romania by "Annette." He considered it ideal for use against riots, rebellions, and other uprisings and ordered that it be immediately copied and mass produced both for export and for domestic use by the Securitate Troops. Avram and the two Comans industriously took notes.

The Ceausescus moved on to the DIA tent. There they found

the Leopard tank engine indeed functioning, causing Avram and me to be showered with new orders and deadlines for hastening the joint venture with the West German firm that was to produce the basic tank engine in Romania. A holographic fire control system prompted a sermon on the advantages of producing microelectronics and optics instead of toilet paper, washing machines, and dryers. And finally, a live demonstration of a radar-absorbing camouflage coating gave new horizons to Florescu's research institutes.

A GIFT FROM CHINESE INTELLIGENCE

A few more booths, and the visit came to an end in a tent where the ground was covered with Persian rugs, the walls decorated with dozens of red flags bearing the hammer and sickle, and a table had been set for a military-style feast. Two free-standing, life-size color photographs, one of Ceausescu and the other of Elena, taken during their visit to the exhibit, were in the center of the tent.

"The first color film and color paper ever produced in Romania, used for the first son and the first daughter of the Romanian people," said Florescu, presenting the photographs and chalking up another point for himself. "Original Kodak," he added.

"I thought we hadn't yet bought the Kodak license, Florescu," Ceausescu joked with a wink.

"We haven't, and we won't. Kodak is outrageous—twice as expensive as Fuji's offer, which was bad enough: more than $12 million. Now we have everything for nothing. We've spent only lei."

"Are you going to divulge the secret?"

"A gift from Comrade Hua Go-feng. Chinese intelligence got it from Kodak, and now it's becoming a Romanian industry," Florescu rattled off.

"Color pictures may give the idiots a taste for color TV," Elena snarled.

"It's only for export, dear, and for tourists. Just for dollars." Ceausescu was trying to tone her down. He had already approved everything.

"We're not being consistent, Nick. Instead of spending for heavy industry, they're wasting money on luxury gadgets."

"We're being very consistent," Ion Coman intervened, opening a folder he had just gotten from General Nicolescu and holding up an intricate color photograph with both hands.

"What the hell is that?" asked Elena.

"An aerial photograph of the exhibit, taken during your visit here."

"It looks like the satellite picture Carter just gave me," Ceausescu exclaimed.

Coman explained that the process for producing the film used in air reconnaissance had also come from Chinese intelligence and had been reproduced in the same plant built to make ordinary color film. The plant was only partially civilian. More sections for military applications would be created on top of the original base.

"Two birds with one stone," a smiling Ceausescu pointed out to Elena.

"And also consistent, Comrade Elena," Ion Coman added.

"Don't be a smart-ass!"

A row of soldier-waiters dressed in perfectly tailored black-tie, one for each guest in the tent, paraded in, bearing silver trays loaded with bacon rind, grilled over charcoal, and glasses of tsuica, Ceausescu's favorite dishes during his years in the military, as had been carefully researched by General Martis. This gesture, intended to impress Ceausescu, passed unnoticed. In his paranoia, shortly after becoming Romanian leader Ceausescu made it a rule never to eat anything that had not been prepared by his own chef, tasted by his own protective service, and served by his own waiter. Over the years he had become adept at simulating eating at official dinners during visits abroad, and a master at dropping his food under the table, then kicking it with his foot as far as he could. From time to time, such as at the dinner President Carter had just given for him at the White House, Ceausescu would even praise the host for his delicious menu. Here, however, he was without diplomacy. Bajenaru simply replaced the plates and glasses with Ceausescu's favorite salad of tomato, onion, and feta cheese and his own yellow wine. Bajenaru was always prepared.

In an excellent mood, Ceausescu went on to his main topic of conversation, the country's bright future. In that overdecorated tent, Romania was not a place that perpetually had long lines outside the stores, where food was still rationed, and where people had to tighten their belts. That was a side of Romania that Ceausescu never wanted to hear about. What Ceausescu was describing now was a country with dozens of nuclear power plants pulsating with electricity and servicing all of Europe, a country unable to meet the worldwide demand for its commercial airplanes, a country whose microelectronics were being exported to both hemispheres and whose medicines were being used in the farthest corners of the earth, a country whose "Independent" tanks and "Liberty" airplanes were arming the tiniest Third World nation.

DESTROYING THE HEART OF BUCHAREST

Next, Ceausescu animatedly described the new administrative center he desperately wanted to build in Bucharest as a monument to his personal reign. He had decided to locate it in the very center of downtown, without caring a fig that it would be at the cost of razing part of the city's historic heart. To the contrary, he declared himself overjoyed at the prospect of getting rid of musty old churches and synagogues.

"Who needs bourgeois vestiges of the past?" agreed Minister of Interior Coman.

"Churches and synagogues are poison," declared Florescu, a confirmed atheist. "All of them should be torn down."

"All in good time, comrades," said Ceausescu prophetically, lifting both arms. With the fervor of a visionary, he began describing the future headquarters of the Communist Party, with the hammer and sickle carved into its granite and red marble facade, making what Ceausescu termed "Communist lace." Building after building took shape before our very eyes, up to the last one, a red marble pantheon where his body would lie in state for all eternity, as Lenin's did in the Kremlin mausoleum. Ceausescu called his future administrative center "this Acropolis of ours" and a revolutionary urban achievement.

Florescu, who had spent his youth in France, compared it with

Baron Haussmann's redesign of the city of Paris in the last century.

"The symbol of our Age of Pericles!" Avram's tenor voice burst out enthusiastically.

"This most Romanian of men raising our motherland up to join the great family of the most civilized and most highly esteemed countries of the world!" said Ion Coman, topping everybody. He had followed Ceausescu as military political commissar.

When Ceausescu left, he took Oprea and me along with him in his car.

The demolition of the center of Bucharest started on a large scale in 1984. The Brancovenesc Hospital, the Vacaresti complex, the Cotroceni monastery, and the Old and New Spirea churches, invaluable architectural treasures, were only a few of the unique historical monuments to fall victim to Ceausescu's ambitions. By June 1986, some 15,000 old dwellings and public monuments had been smashed to make room for the new complex, dominated by a new presidential palace. Prominent architects and art historians have signed protest letters decrying the destruction. Few aspects of Romanian life have received so much recent commentary in the Western media as the razing of old Bucharest. The New York Times, The Wall Street Journal, The Washington Post, The Washington Times, The Los Angeles Times, and British, French, West German, and Swiss magazines and newspapers have termed the demolition not only an expression of the Romanian Communists' disrespect for the country's cultural heritage, but an action unparalleled in 20th century Europe. The West's vehement reaction at first took Bucharest by surprise, but soon it launched a counterattack, accusing the Western press of outright lies. Didier Fauqueux, for example, the Agence France Presse correspondent in Vienna who covered Bucharest, was banned from Romania for five years. [6]

When Ceausescu arrived at his office, Manea reported that the Soviet ambassador, V.I. Drozdenko, was waiting to be received. "Give me ten minutes, and then show him in," Ceausescu or-

---

[6]"Romania Responds to Western Criticism of Urban Demolition," *Romanian Situation Report/3*, Radio Free Europe Research, February 24, 1986, pp. 9–11.

dered. Then he ordered Oprea and me immediately to form an innocuous-looking Western firm for dealing in military equipment. It should be "owned" by an illegal officer who was already a Western citizen and staffed with other illegal officers documented as Westerners. The new company was to specialize in selling Western weapons built in Romania to the Third World. After Oprea had left and the waiter had brought in a cup of medicinal tea, Ceausescu ordered that General Marcu ask for an immediate meeting with his Israeli connection, Yitzhak Yesahanu. "The Centurion tank is the incontrovertible proof that Yesahanu is willing to add NATO secrets to his dollars to get more Jews. Marcu should make it clear to Yesahanu that he won't be able to put out the welcome mat for any more Jews until we have the blueprints for the Centurion. And then Marcu should use the same tactic with 'Eduard' in Bonn."

When I left Ceausescu's office to go to Elena's, Drozdenko was chatting with Manea, waiting to be received. He was there as usual after one of Ceausescu's visits abroad, to receive a detailed report for Brezhnev about its results. Only in very rare cases does Ceausescu go around the Soviet ambassador and send a special messenger directly to Moscow.[7]

A SESSION WITH ELENA

As I entered Elena's office, she was standing at the window.

"Look who's here!" she said in her nicest voice, eager for some exciting news. "Tell me, what did my dearest friends do while we were away in America? I suppose the prime minister spent all those days in Snagov?"

"Yes, comrade."

"Did Coman play tennis with his generals?" That was Ion Coman.

"Yes, comrade."

"And Pana went fishing."

"Exactly."

[7] The following article, translated in its entirety, was carried at the bottom of page one in *Scinteia* of April 22, 1978: "Comrade Nicolae Ceausescu, general secretary of the Romanian Communist Party, president of the Romanian Socialist Republic, received V.I. Drozdenko, the ambassador of the Soviet Union, at noon on Friday at his request. A cordial, comradely conversation took place on this occasion."

"The shits!" Elena spat out with venom. "Let's take a look at these *messieurs*. Give me Manescu. He's started putting on airs."

She read every transcript from the microphones Prime Minister Manescu had in his office.

"Pish tosh! Give me the ones from his Snagov villa. I want to know what his Barrel's been saying." The "Barrel" had been Manescu's secretary up until ten years earlier, when he married her. Since Manescu had become prime minister three years ago, she had packed on a lot of extra pounds.

Today Elena displayed unusual patience. She asked countless questions, read with glassy eyes the tale of Violeta's latest amorous adventure, cursed Pana's wife for her chastity, derided Ursu's for her peasant behavior, and made all her usual remarks about "the idiots."

"When's our visit to London?" Elena finally asked, going over to her safe and locking up the whole bunch of cassettes she took from me. She would certainly while away her time in the coming days listening to sexual adventures, pornographic discussions, and political jokes in the room behind her office.

"It starts on the thirteenth of June."

"Are you such an idiot?"

"The British picked the date," I said defensively.

"What are you planning for me there, darling?" she asked coyly, in her most honeyed tones.

"Buckingham Palace. You'll be staying there."

"Forget about Queen Popinjay!"

"The Tate art gallery."

"Who cares?"

"Professor *honoris causa* of the Central London Polytechnical Institute."[8]

"What a fiddler you are! I won't leave London without becoming a member of the British Academy."

"I tried, Comrade Elena. There's not a chance of changing their rules."

"Go ahead and tell me about how old and stodgy everything is there. I want to be made a member of their academy," Elena insisted, her eyes shooting daggers at me.

"I'm trying to get an 'Honorary Member of the Royal Institute

[8]*Scinteia*, June 15, 1978, p. 4.

for Chemistry,'" I said, playing my last card.[9] The *Royal* in the name apparently did the trick.

"Is it prestigious enough?" she asked, already placated.

Then Elena started thinking out loud about the presents she was hoping British companies would give her during the visit and ticking off the various kinds of jewelry she wanted to "take a look at in the privacy of Buckingham Palace."

I left Elena's office on foot. It was probably the stillness of the April night and the perfume from the trees in blossom that dredged Shelley's verses up from the depths of my schoolboy memory:

> "My name is Ozymandias, King of Kings:
> Look on my works, ye Mighty, and despair!"
> Nothing beside remains. Round the decay
> Of that colossal wreck, boundless and bare
> The lone and level sands stretch far away.

The Ramasseum funerary temple in Egypt, with its toppled, 50-some-foot tall seated colossus of the pharaoh Shelley called Ozymandias, seemed to represent the perfect prediction for the future of this first Communist dynasty in world history: Pharaoh Ceausescu, with Elena the number two, and her son Nicu the third in line.

[9] *Ibid.* Elena did receive this honorary title as well.

CHAPTER

XXV

AT three in the afternoon I left my office and went to the National Center for Enciphered Communication, called CNTC from its Romanian name *Centrul National de Transmisiuni Cifrate,* for a last look around before the inaugural visit there by Ceausescu and Elena, scheduled for four o'clock.

The CNTC was the most terrifying secret of my life: a national cipher system I personally put together over many years consciously knowing that sooner or later it would be deciphered by the United States, with West German help. The thought, though, that the least indiscretion on the part of either Washington or Bonn might lead to my execution in Romania, caused me many sleepless nights.

It had all started in November 1962, soon after the withdrawal of the Soviet advisors from the DIE. As a new deputy chief of the DIE, I submitted to the then Romanian leader, Gheorghe Gheorghiu-Dej, a personal report suggesting that the Romanian cipher system was being routinely deciphered by Moscow. This view was based on reporting from a number of valuable DIE agents in the West to the effect that they had recently been contacted by undercover KGB officers attempting to lure them into cooperating with Moscow instead of Bucharest and offering them substantially greater rewards than the DIE did. Gheorghiu-Dej ordered me to conduct a full investigation. The results, which I submitted some months later, concluded that Moscow was indeed monitoring Romanian enciphered traffic.

My final report to Gheorghiu-Dej stated that the Soviet KGB had had its fingers in Romania's cipher systems since 1949, when

Soviet communications experts had been sent to every Soviet bloc country to create Soviet-style cipher services. In Romania, the new organization, called "Service H," was set up as a super-secret component responsible only to a Soviet advisor, who cloaked it in deepest secrecy and Draconian rules. The mystery around Service H was so profound that only a chosen few were allowed to know that the heart of the system—the one-time pads containing random numbers for enciphering and deciphering— arrived periodically from Moscow. Even fewer knew that, in addition to the pairs of cipher booklets sent to Bucharest, a third copy remained in Moscow for "emergency" purposes. The rest of my report was full of Romanian military and civilian intelligence cases amply demonstrating that the KGB was currently using the third copy of the cipher key to monitor Romanian traffic.

CREATING A CIPHER THE AMERICANS COULD BREAK

When Gheorghiu-Dej finished reading my report, he was in a quiet rage over being deceived by his Soviet friends. On the spot he put me in charge of creating a new central cipher service unconnected with Moscow to produce random-number pads in Romania in place of the ones being received from the KGB. The scientists we consulted, however, claimed that Romania did not yet have the know-how to produce its own modern random generators. Nevertheless they noted that, in the prehistoric age of cipher systems, rows of random numbers had been produced by the throw of dice. In the absence of anything better, Gheorghiu-Dej ordered that a hastily assembled group of Securitate officers start rolling ten-sided dice in around-the-clock shifts to produce Romanian one-time pads. Later he introduced lottery-type machines instead of dice, but the basic system remained essentially the same for years, until after the mid-1960s.

In November 1964 I reported to Gheorghiu-Dej that I had personally made contact with "Reinert," the owner of a West German company called EMI, which reportedly produced cipher machines for NATO military forces, and that "Reinert" had agreed to supply the DIE. Gheorghiu-Dej approved my proposal to buy an EMI random generator to produce the one-time pads for all Romanian institutions handling enciphered communications. He also signed off on my report proposing the purchase of a number of EMI electronic enciphering machines for the DIE to study and then modify and secretly reproduce in Romania under the patriotic name "Romcif." In my proposal, the Romcif machines would become the heart of a future electronic cipher system, replacing the manual one used by the DIE and the Ministries of Foreign Affairs, Trade, and National Defense in their enciphered communications abroad. Gheorghiu-Dej evidently paid little attention to the fact that the future Romanian cipher might be vulnerable to the West, as in those days no Soviet bloc leader had ever been deposed from that quarter. Moscow's assassinations of Communist leaders were what was primarily causing him concern. At that time Gheorghiu-Dej was in a public conflict with Moscow and was afraid that the Kremlin would use some of the deciphered Romanian telegrams as "criminal evidence" against him, brand him an anti-Soviet, and serve a secret death sentence on him. That very day Gheorghiu-Dej officially put me in charge of creating a new Central Cipher Service responsible for electronically producing random materials for all the cipher services of the various Romanian ministries and other institutions.

On Monday, March 19, 1965, Gheorghiu-Dej died of a galloping cancer. The new leader, Nicolae Ceausescu, reconfirmed my task of building a new Central Cipher Service and, in February 1972, expanded my assignment. Ceausescu wanted to gather into one single component—the CNTC—all the cipher services with contacts abroad, meaning primarily those of the Ministries of Foreign Affairs and Foreign Trade, the Ministry of National Defense's Directorate for Military Intelligence, and the Central Committee of the Romanian Communist Party, and to subordinate them to his DIE. Ceausescu had recently increased by more than tenfold the DGTO's capacity to monitor international mail, telephone, and telex communications; now the DIE was his choice for monitoring the Romanian cipher traffic.

In 1973, Ceausescu formally approved my project for the new national Romanian cipher center, based exclusively on the Romcif machines developed and produced in Romania, as well as its secret subordination to the DIE. In 1977, my newly created National Center for Enciphered Communications officially went into operation. By Romanian standards it was a modern behemoth, employing over 1,000 engineers and technicians.

There were only two hitches in my system. The first was Ceausescu's secret: On the sly, the CNTC was connected with an ultra-secret monitoring center where batteries of telexes and electronic typewriters automatically banged out copies of every telegram sent to or received from abroad by any Romanian organization, including the Central Committee. There, monitors analyzed the traffic and prepared weekly reports for Ceausescu, suspicious telegrams being sent to him immediately. He has never trusted his ministers and the rest of his *nomenclatura.*

The second hitch was my secret: Although the Romcif machines looked entirely different, on the inside they were almost exact copies of the EMI, which the DIE had been unable to modify to any significant extent. To remove the last evidence of Romcif's Western origin, I arranged for Algeria to be provided with all the original EMI equipment as a fraternal gesture.

In order to protect myself, I assembled an impressive collection of covering documents. The Romcif machines were certified as absolutely secure by the Romanian Central Institute of Mathematics and by the Central Institute of Physics, and their use was approved by the National Council for Science and Technology, under Elena's signature, and by a presidential decree signed by Ceausescu himself. I also obtained Ceausescu's approval for the DIE periodically to give samples of the one-time random tapes produced by the Romanian generators and samples of enciphered texts to one of its trusted agents in West Germany to have them secretly analyzed by a NATO computer center specializing in cryptology with which the agent was professionally connected. The agent was instructed to represent the Romanian samples as West German military cipher materials. He always returned them to the DIE with accompanying written certifications from the NATO center stating that the tapes were indeed random and that the enciphered texts could not be deciphered. I showed Ceausescu most of these NATO documents, but I never reported to him that the DIE agent involved was the same "Reinert" who had given the DIE the EMI machines ten years earlier.

* * *

Now on this day in 1978, I took a last look around the CNTC before Ceausescu's visit. The building, anonymous on the outside, was gleaming on the inside. Although everything was brand new, the rooms scheduled to be visited by Ceausescu had been repainted overnight. The officers were resplendent in their new black suits and red neckties worn under their new dark gray labcoats, for the center was under cover as a civilian installation. Lifesize portraits of Ceausescu and Elena had been installed in the marble lobby between two red flags with the hammer and sickle. Above them stretched a long red banner with the slogan "Architects of Our Grandiose Times" written in large gold capital letters.

After I finished checking everything, I went to pick up Ceausescu and Elena, returning with them a few minutes after four in the afternoon. A group of communications officers, crowded into the lobby and onto the staircase, were chanting in unison: "Ceausescu and the people!" Standing in front of them, aligned in military order, were Stefan Andrei, Cornel Burtica, Colonel General Ion Coman, the minister of national defense, and Minister of Interior Teodor Coman, representing the ministries that were using the CNTC. They were rhythmically clapping their hands, performing the ritual that is the unwritten rule for welcoming the Ceausescus on visits anywhere from a kindergarten to the Party Congress.

After General Vasile Goga, the DIE officer supervising the CNTC, had given his formal report to the "Supreme Commander" and the "Most Esteemed and Beloved Daughter of the Romanian People," I took the Ceausescus on a tour of the center. Only the building was new for Ceausescu, as he was more than familiar with everything else concerning the Romanian cipher system. Before approving my proposals for the new installation, Ceausescu had asked for a scale model of the center. There is a general rule in the Soviet bloc that every major economic investment, from a remodeled residential district to a new nuclear power plant, can be approved only on the basis of a scale model. Scale models and facades are the most important Communist criteria for economic projects, as the question of profits has always been considered a degrading capitalistic consideration.

Along with the scale model for the new CNTC headquarters, I had given Ceausescu live demonstrations of the new cipher system. In two rooms next-door to his office, I had set up one Romcif random generator, together with a headquarters cubicle and an embassy cipher room, both fitted out with real equipment and in communication with each other. Ceausescu had spent many mornings and evenings there learning the new system.

"Let's take a look at a cubicle," Ceausescu commanded. "That'll make everything clear to everybody."

"Because you've just come from America, I invite you to visit the U.S. cubicle," said Goga, accompanying the Ceausescus upstairs.

The "U.S. cubicle" was on the fourth floor and was run by Colonel Jeleru. After a formal greeting, he started explaining the job of maintaining enciphered communications with both the embassy in Washington and the mission to the United Nations in New York.

"My cubicle is a little different from the others, because the U.S. government does not allow us to have a radio link with New York. That's why I have both radio with Washington and telex with New York," said the colonel in conclusion.

"Is this something else you don't understand, *monsieur?* Or isn't it the foreign minister's job to make Romania respected by foreign governments?" Elena croaked in Andrei's direction.

"I know about the problem, Comrade Elena. It is not the American government. It's the New York mayor who won't allow us to transmit by radio from New York, so as not to disturb their television reception around our mission."

"The Jew? The spy?" screeched Elena.

"We don't pay any attention to that rule," Goga broke in, to change the subject, "because international telex is very expensive. To save money, we transmit everything to New York by radio. There is no easy way for them to catch us at it, and especially to prove it. From New York, we do use the telex, but only to Washington, which then forwards everything on by radio."

"Inspired," said Andrei, grateful for the relief.

"You'd better do your job, *sir,*" Elena barked out acidly, not yet through with him, "and make the filthy Jew respect us." To address someone by anything other than "comrade" was always considered an insult by Elena. *Sir* and *monsieur* were her highest forms of insult.

TRIAL MESSAGE TO WASHINGTON

"I want to send a telegram to Washington," said Ceausescu, ignoring Elena's rantings, "and to see the whole process down to when it's deciphered. Let's suppose that Andrei is in America and I send him a telegram."

"I'm ready to take it down," said Goga.

"Comrade Stefan Andrei, ask the State Department to receive you and our ambassador immediately. There you should express, on behalf of my wife, Elena, and on my own behalf, the warmest wishes for good health and personal happiness to President Carter and to the highly esteemed Mrs. Carter, together with our satisfaction over the successful outcome of our stay in Washington. Also express our thanks to the State Department, the Secret Service, and the FBI for their contribution to our historic visit to the United States. Inform them also that in June I will be making an official visit to Great Britain."

"Signed by you, Comrade Ceausescu?"

"Yes. I want to see the text as it appears on arrival in Washington."

"It will take only a few minutes. In the meantime the colonel would like to show you the system and the flow of traffic," said Goga, leaving to encipher the telegram elsewhere and to transmit it back to our cubicle for deciphering.

Jeleru did not have time to finish his short, prepared presentation, when a buzzer went off and a red lightbulb started flashing. "I have the telegram," he said a few minutes later.

"Give it to Andrei to read," Ceausescu ordered.

"'COMRADE PROFESSOR, ASK THE DEPARTMENT STORE TO RECEIVE YOU AND OUR DEAN IMMEDIATELY. THERE YOU SHOULD EXPRESS, ON BEHALF OF MY WIFE, ATHENA, AND ON MY OWN BEHALF, THE WARMEST WISHES FOR GOOD HEALTH AND PERSONAL HAPPINESS TO THE CROCODILE AND TO THE HIGHLY ESTEEMED MRS. RABBIT, TOGETHER WITH OUR SATISFACTION OVER THE SUCCESSFUL OUTCOME OF OUR STAY IN WALNUT. ALSO EXPRESS OUR THANKS TO THE DEPARTMENT STORE, THE BROTHER-IN-LAW, AND THE MOTHER-IN-LAW FOR THEIR CONTRIBUTION TO OUR

HISTORIC VISIT TO THE BIG DIPPER. INFORM THEM ALSO THAT IN JAGUAR I WILL BE MAKING AN OFFICIAL VISIT TO THE LITTLE DIPPER.' Signed, 'SUPREME GUIDE.' Inspired!" Andrei finished.

"What's all this nonsense?" Elena exploded, disconcerted.

"It's not nonsense, Elena."

"It's a farce."

"It's only a supplementary security measure, my dear comrades. You may tell them the trick, Goga. Tell them, and then change it. Secrecy should be our watchword in matters of cipher," finished Ceausescu, pumping the air with his right hand.

Goga explained that the new national cipher system was based on one-time materials produced by the Romcif generator; the key was used only once and then immediately destroyed, making it theoretically invulnerable. If, contrary to all expectations, the enemy should be able to decipher one telegram, that would not help him to decipher a second one. Even in such an unthinkable situation, the enemy would still not be able to understand the full contents of the telegram he had deciphered, as the most important words would have been super-protected according to a periodically changing memory code system. "In our test case we used *professor* for foreign minister, *dean* for ambassador, *department store* for the State Department, *Crocodile* for President Carter, *Rabbit* for Mrs. Carter, *brother-in-law* for the Secret Service, *mother-in-law* for the FBI, *Big Dipper* for the United States, *Little Dipper* for Great Britain, and *jaguar* for June," Goga finished his explanation.

"The code name for the Comrade is inspired," Andrei remarked. "It should never be changed."

"Why am I *Athens*, darling?" Elena turned on me.

"It wasn't *Athens*. It was *Athena*, the goddess of wisdom. Isn't that right, Pacepa?" said Burtica, coming to my help. "I wonder what my code name might be?"

"*Gizzard* at best," snapped Elena. The name Burtica means "little belly" in Romanian. She was evidently unhappy that her code name was not *Supreme Goddess* or something else much closer to her husband's.

Ceausescu raised his hand, immediately making for silence. He began speaking in a low and slow voice, as he usually starts most of his speeches, and expressed his admiration for the new cipher system. "Here we are, comrades, six members of the Political Executive Committee and at least one who may soon be elected to it. I consider that we are enough to make a decision. I consider that the Executive Committee should unanimously approve the new cipher system, comrades. Is there anyone against it?"

Everybody applauded.

"In that case, let's leave this temple of secrecy and lock its door again. This is the first and last time that anybody not employed by it is allowed to set foot in here. That should be the law, comrades, and you should consider it to have also been approved by the Executive Committee. As a matter of fact, tomorrow I'll sign a decree establishing this and other rules."

On leaving the cubicle, Ceausescu whispered into my ear: "Change *Athena* to *Academician.*"

The foyer was full of communications officers. At Goga's discreet signal they began chanting with all their lungpower: "Ceausescu and the people!" while beating time with their handclaps.

Ceausescu stopped short in the middle of the foyer, as if surprised, for a few minutes bestowing a grateful look on the crowd, whose fervor and enthusiasm kept growing louder and louder. Certainly none of them had ever seen Ceausescu up close before. When he raised his hand, the crowd stopped in mid-breath.

"Dear comrades," he started, keeping his right hand up in the air, an unmistakable sign that he was demanding attention. "Today we have visited one of the most important bastions of our independence and sovereignty."

The officers again began frenetically shouting "Ceausescu and the people" and clapping in time to their chant.

After a few minutes, Ceausescu again raised his hand. "You, comrades, are a symbol of our new policy toward capitalism. You have been sent here by the Communist Party to be its soldiers. A special kind of soldiers, without guns in your hands. Your main weapons should be a diplomatic passport, a perforated tape, and a broad smile on your face, as you look toward the enemy. Let him believe that we like him. Smile with your mouth, and hit him with your brains, with your cleverness. That is your historical duty for the time being."

The crowd of officers exploded again, as Ceausescu was shaking hands. The four ministers, Goga and I, also all clapping rhythmically, accompanied Ceausescu and Elena to their car, while from the foyer resounded a final thunderclap of "Ceausescu and the people!" I left with the Ceausescus.

ANOTHER USELESS SHOWPIECE

"Let's give Goga the Star of the Republic, Pacepa."

"Why not a medal for me too, Nick," Elena piped up. "I signed off on Romcif's certification."

"Come on, Elena. We can't make that public knowledge."

"May I make a suggestion," I interposed.

"Go ahead, Pacepa."

"What about a marble plaque in the lobby of the CNTC stating that it had been conceived, designed, and inaugurated by Comrades Elena and Nicolae Ceausescu?"

"Who says Pacepa is nothing but a fiddler, Nick?"

For the rest of the drive, both Ceausescus could not stop admiring their own handiwork. Back at his office, Ceausescu ordered Manea to prepare a presidential decree authorizing the DIE to install the plaque and also to face the outside of the CNTC building's first storey with marble. "It's the eighth wonder of the world, isn't it?" he exclaimed, signing off on the decree.

With Ceausescu's blessing, the CNTC was to become another marble-fronted Communist enterprise that was anything but useful: like the mammoth, ultra-elegant Romanian tractor factory in Brasov, which is shown off to every important foreign delegation but cannot find free-market buyers for its products; or like the monstrous *Scinteia* publishing house, which stretches out over acres and acres and yet publishes nothing but newspapers and books written about or by Ceausescu that nobody wants to read.

When I finally got home it was past ten, and the S telephone was ringing.

"General Pacepa speaking."

"Hi, Boss. This is your humble slave, Constantin Manea. Sorry for calling so late. I was busy with the Comrade at his residence." His voice dropped to a low, conspiratorial tone, as if he were afraid the telephone might be monitored. "Do you know what he asked me tonight? When your birthday was and how old you would be. And when he heard that you'd be fifty, do you know what he said? You'll never believe it, Boss." His voice dropped even lower. "The Comrade said he wanted to make you a Hero of the Republic and give you your third star as a general."

When Manea hung up I went over to Fedot Lily. His eyes reflected a fear I had never seen in them before.

"Yes, Fedot. I know the danger," I said, without moving my lips.

CHAPTER

XXVI

"GENERAL Pacepa speaking." It was shortly after one in the afternoon when I answered the S telephone. I was almost certain it would be Elena. Unlike Ceausescu, she never takes a midday nap.

"Why didn't you tell me that we were going to take up your TS in the Political Executive Committee today?" Elena's sour voice spat out at me from the receiver. *TS* was a term inherited from the Soviets, standing for *technological* and *scientific* intelligence. "I won't be able to say anything in there," she complained.

"I can send General Sirbu over right now. He can explain everything you need to know."

"Who the hell is this Sirbu?"

"The chief of TS. You met him at IPRS."

"Are you nuts? You get yourself over here right this minute." The awful noise coming out of the receiver reflected the violence with which she hung up on me.

JEWELS ON THE TA-78 ACCOUNT

I got over to Elena's office in nothing flat and went straight in to her, without having her executive officer announce me. I knew that the longer she was alone, the more furious her rage would become, soon bringing on hysterics. When I opened her door, Elena was at her desk skimming through *Scinteia*.

390

"Why don't I have the report, you fiddler?" she erupted again, with me standing at attention before her desk.

"Here it is, Comrade Elena. Handwritten in only one copy, as it was approved by the Comrade."

"How many pages?"

"Only twelve. The Comrade cut it."

"How am I supposed to read twelve pages in one day?" Elena threw me a baleful look, before starting to read the report. After a few minutes, I cast a discreet glance at her and saw that her eyes were focused on something behind me, as her pinky finger bored around in her nose. I waited.

"I've taken another look at the sets we brought with us from New York, and I just can't make up my mind, darling," Elena suddenly burst out in her sweetest voice.

"The jewelry?"

"Uh huh. I just can't bear to part with any of it."

That was the real reason Elena had called me in. I could not recall any occasion when she had sent jewelry back, once she had gotten her hands on it. I already had the accounting for all of the jewelry in my briefcase, ready for Ceausescu. As usual, he would shred the accounting and the original receipts himself, asking me not to retain any copies, and would order the payments to be made out of the TA-78 account.

"I may need a few more days to look at the things," Elena continued. "In the meantime you should try to bring the price down."

I knew this tactic, too. After two or three more weeks, Elena would again murmur something about how she could not yet make up her mind, and then she would never, ever mention the jewelry again. I always suspected that in the depths of her mind she would become convinced that, by the time she had "forgotten" about the jewelry, the jewelers would also forget that they had yet to be paid.

Elena kept me there until a few minutes after 2:30, when she left to wake Ceausescu up. By that time I had a good sized list of clothes and other things she wanted me to get her, not only from New York, but also from London and Paris.

"Take your report from my desk, Pacepa," Elena said as she went out. "I think we're going in the right direction. We should concentrate more on your Texas Instruments, though. Aren't they the filthiest pigs you've ever heard of?" Elena had soured on Texas Instruments during the visit there, when she understood that they would not be giving her the fur coats she had asked for.

BRIGADE SD FOR TECHNOLOGICAL ESPIONAGE

In Romania and the other East European countries, technological espionage was created at the request of the Soviet Union in the early 1950s. In 1959, I became the chief of the Romanian technological intelligence component and remained in that position until 1962, after which I was the deputy director of the DIE responsible for coordinating that field, among others. In those years Soviet bloc technological espionage became a piece of sophisticated machinery kept permanently charged up by the incapacity of Communist regimes to produce their own technology by other means. Without private ownership, competition, and personal incentive, the Soviet bloc has been unable to make any genuine technological progress. It has, however, amply proved its ability to steal and reproduce Western technology.

Romanian technological espionage was organized and functioned identically to that of the KGB, having its main emphasis on military technology. In 1972, when Ceausescu took over the DIE, he reorganized it as an independent directorate called "Brigade SD," the designation SD having no significance, and he more than doubled the number of its officers, almost 300 of whom would be assigned abroad—as many as the KGB had in the West for technological intelligence. Ceausescu left unchanged the mission established by Moscow, military production, but added new ones intended to transform Communist Romania into a strong nuclear and industrial power and an important, independent exporter of arms. Brigade SD was organized geographically by target country, and inside each country by industrial area. The main SD services were those for the United States, Japan, West Germany, Great Britain, Canada, France, Italy, and the Benelux countries, but there were also individual or group services for all other NATO countries as well as for some of the most representative non-aligned target areas. Several specialized services for the main types of military equipment were created on top of the geographical ones, coordinating the whole DIE intelligence potential that could be useful for the arms industry. Their activity was based on both Romanian and Soviet special requests. The Soviet ones, made by the Military Industrial Commission, known as the *VPK*, from the Russian *Voyenno-Promyshlennaya Kommissiya*, were sent to Bucharest by the KGB. As in the Soviet Union, the Romanian requests for military technology were made not only by the Ministry of National Defense but also by every civilian ministry involved in producing arms, among which the most important were the Ministries for the Machine Building Industry, for the Metallurgical Industry, and for the Chemical Industry.

The results of Romania's theft of Western technology were dramatic, by 1978 becoming the single most important component of the country's economy. On the Warsaw Pact scale, Romanian technological espionage rose from an obscure place in the 1960s to one of the top three in the 1970s. In 1978, the largest technological espionage effort was the East German, based on its record numbers of illegal officers and agents documented as West Germans working everywhere in the Western hemisphere. According to Brezhnev and Andropov, the second place was now being disputed in Moscow between the Poles and the Romanians, considered the most efficient at obtaining high-tech military technology. These results were what Ceausescu wanted to present to the Political Executive Committee, together with his desire to transform Romanian technological espionage into a mass operation, and then to share Romania's experience with the rest of the Soviet bloc countries.

Ceausescu's new pragmatic approach was to stress that technological espionage had been one of Romania's most important dollar producers and money savers in recent years, and that it should be developed to the point that foreign trade would become subordinated to it. That was in full accordance with the principle widely proclaimed throughout the Soviet bloc that it was not only morally admissable for a proletarian government to steal from its mortal enemy, but it was also a lot cheaper than to buy from capitalism. He considered the results of the DIE's TS operations nothing less than the crowning glory of this principle.

* * *

Just before three, Gheorghe Oprea and I were called in by Ceausescu, who was with Elena.

"After Pacepa presents his report," Ceausescu decreed, "we should have some questions, and you have to set the tone, Oprea. For instance, ask Burtica about the total number of commercial representatives he has in the West and about how many of them have collected technological intelligence or helped the DIE to recruit Westerners. He'll make the point for us. Or ask the minister for the food industry how much he paid for the license to produce the French Camembert cheese the foreign tourists are so crazy about now. When he says it was TS intelligence, then you can turn around and ask the minister of domestic trade why he is still importing French perfume for tourists. But make it very clear what you're driving at—he's an idiot *boanghen*. Understood, Oprea?

"Yes, comrade."

"I've prepared the prime minister for the discussion. Whom have you talked with?" said Ceausescu.

"I have Avram and Agachi as main speakers," Oprea answered.

"I've talked with Florescu and Lina Ciobanu," Elena added.

"That should be enough," Ceausescu decided. "The rest will have to catch up by themselves."

A Meeting of the political Executive Committee

The Political Executive Committee room, adorned only with the Communist Party seal and a photograph of Ceausescu, was located just a few steps away from his office. Although the meeting had been set for three o'clock, everyone was in place long before two, trying to pick up hints about the drift of the meeting. The full and candidate members were seated around a long rectangular table. The deputy prime ministers and the ministers who were not members of the Political Executive Committee lined the walls. As always, everyone was anxious and uneasy before the meeting started. Many a time a miscalculated word uttered at such a meeting had aroused Ceausescu's fury or Elena's hysterics and brought about the author's dismissal from his position.

Ceausescu came to the meeting with Elena, at one minute past three, and everyone jumped to his feet. In opening it, he said that "we are here to analyze the excellent and impressive results of our technological intelligence and to establish new ways of expanding its secret but very important role in our society." No sooner had he finished saying this, than a palpable feeling of relief spread over the crowded meeting room. "Excellent," "impressive results," and "very important role" were clear signs that those present should not criticize but rather praise and imitate.

The substantive part of the meeting started with my report on the past five years of technological intelligence, which I presented precisely as it had been modified and approved by Ceausescu. It began by stating that, since the Comrade had taken over the DIE, technological intelligence had entered a new era, expanding broadly to include almost anything that could replace imports and save hard currency. The most favored area had been the chemical industry, "because of Comrade Elena's personal, boundless assistance," and there whole factories had been built on technological intelligence, without buying foreign licenses or paying Western royalties. Among the examples I gave were a large, automated installation for producing polystyrene inside the huge petrochemical complex in Borzesti, a factory for polyurethene and synthetic leather in Iasi, one for melamine in Brasov, one for films and photographic paper in Targul Mures, one for plastic explosives in Victoria, one for radial tires in Bucharest, and new sections for coloring agents in Codlea. The medical-pharmaceutical industry, also blessed with Elena's personal interest, had been completely modernized, using stolen American, West German, French, and Italian technologies. New antibiotics enterprises had been built in Iasi and Bucharest, including production plants for cephalosporin and a wide variety of aureomycines. The metallurgical industry came next, with quite an impressive number of Western technologies for high-alloy steel, metal carbides, and non-metal alloys, as well as for modernized steel mills and rolling mills, together with a new aluminum industry. American integrated circuits and specialized chips were now being produced by the electronics industry based only on technological intelligence and embargoed equipment secretly smuggled into Romania. New digital machine tools, diesel engines, and a large variety of Bosch injection pumps were also exclusively based on intelligence.

My list was much longer. Based on the production figures of the Romanian industrial ministries for this five-year period—with the exception of agriculture and the military industry—it was estimated that a net annual savings of $600 to $800 million had been realized by replacing legal but expensive imports with illegal but inexpensive intelligence. The figures had been exaggerated both by the ministries and in Ceausecu's final retouching.

"Have you ever estimated, Pacepa," Ceausescu interrupted my report, "how much hard currency each TS officer sent to the West brings in and saves us on an average?"

"Yes, comrade. Three million dollars per year for each TS officer abroad has been the average over the past two years. That is explained in detail over there," I replied, pointing toward a chart. Ceausescu himself had made the estimate a few days earlier, grossly exaggerating the true figures, and had ordered me to present it in a special graphics display.

"If we take the official exchange rate of 15 to one, we get the amazing net sum of 45 million lei produced annually by every TS officer. If you consider that their average salary is 45,000 lei a year per head, you have a ratio of salary to benefit of 1:1,000, which is by far the highest in the world." For a few minutes, Ceausescu looked at us one by one, as if to be sure that we understood. "Now run through the same calculation taking the real exchange rate we use in our internal books, which is—let's keep this just among ourselves—40 lei to the dollar. Aren't the results astonishing? Can you imagine, comrades, what it'll be like on the day when our motherland has 3,000 TS officers abroad, instead of only 300?" The room suddenly buzzed with murmured approval, some of those present even going over to read the charts and statistics displayed on several free-standing panels. "And that's only the beginning of this new era, comrades," Ceausescu added.

The second part of my report stated that these results were minimal, however. Only 35 percent of the inventory and development of the Romanian civilian industry, no more than 50 percent of the military industry, and just about 60 percent of the agricultural production was due—totally or in part—to intelligence operations, leaving a huge margin for further improvement. The third part of the report treated measures for substantially broadening the use of technological intelligence. Special attention was given to the secret new government decision, HCM-272, initiated by Ceausescu, that required all economic ministries to obtain detailed reports from each of their employees traveling in the West, describing all companies, institutions and factories they visited and every Western specialist or technician they met, and to send these reports to the DIE. I wound up promising solemnly that "the intelligence officers all around the world will work harder and better to fulfill the important tasks given to them by the most esteemed son of the Romanian people, its brilliant, shining leader, Comrade Nicolae Ceausescu."

"Questions, comrades?" Ceausescu asked.

Only Oprea raised his hand. There was an old, unwritten rule within the Political Executive Committee that nobody would ask the first question, unless specifically instructed by Ceausescu to do so. Every member knew that before opening his mouth he should first see which way the wind was blowing. "With your permission, Comrade Ceausescu, I'd like to ask a few questions."

"Go ahead, Oprea, ask. That's why we're all here. We won't leave this room until everything is clear to everyone."

"I'd like to ask our minister of foreign trade if he knows how many of his representatives in the West are now something more than simple buyers from capitalism. I don't know if I make myself clear enough for you, Comrade Burtica. You're brand new at your job."

The minister of foreign trade, Cornel Burtica, answered as Ceausescu had expected. He castigated himself and his ministry for having many representatives in the West that were not paying enough attention to technological espionage and begged the other ministers not to repeat his mistakes.

After Oprea had launched "his" pointed questions about Camembert cheese and French perfume, the minister of domestic trade, Janos Fazekas, beat his breast over his political short-sightedness and committed himself to collaborating with the DIE for the production not only of French perfume in Romania but also of everything else aimed at Western tourists, from Scotch whiskey to American cigarettes. Another three ministers voluntarily followed, flagellating themselves and promising to do away with all imports from the West.

Before opening the discussion, Ceausescu emphasized that the meeting was not intended to analyze military-technical intelligence, and he asked the participants strictly to avoid any reference to such secrets. The first to speak was the prime minister, Manea Manescu. His speech was a lesson about class struggle. Based on the principle of Marx and Lenin that "everything is ethical if it is for the benefit of the proletarian dictatorship," technological intelligence as an institution should not have to have any scruples; we should reap everything we can from capitalism; the practical methods of accomplishing this transfer should be limited only by the imagination. Manescu went on to transport his listeners to a very secret, invisible world, the world of technical intelligence, producing science and technology at an incredibly faster rate than even the most efficient research organizations anywhere. With great pathos he presented the struggles of anonymous DIE heroes to smuggle not only prohibited technology out of the best defended American fortresses, but also American-built, strictly embargoed equipment and machinery. Manescu's speech ended with an ardent appeal for a drastic change in mentality. "We should stop paying capitalism for technology and equipment developed by Western proletarians. That belongs to us, to the proletarian world revolution." Then he asked the participants to express once again their gratitude to the "most brilliant son of the Romanian people, who today is opening new horizons for his beloved motherland."

In his loud tenor, Ion Avram delivered a lesson on how the joint ventures with Western companies should be used for harvesting the bounties of capitalism. He started by describing a joint venture with a West German firm for producing turbotransmissions in Romania, under which a relatively large number of West German specialists came to the city of Craiova. With them they brought quantities of various technical documents "for unforeseen circumstances." Avram evoked with compassion the long nights spent there by the DIE and local security officers to photograph them. "Do you know what we found there? An incalculable treasure trove! Buried among the hundreds of thousands of documents we photographed, we found ones on turbotrans-missions for Western tanks, for example. For Western tanks, comrades! Can you imagine our surprise? That alone made up for all that we had invested in this joint venture." A murmur of appreciation swept through the room.

Ceausescu waved both arms to call for silence. "Need I say, comrades, that what we are discussing here involves state secrets, which should not only be kept but should also be defended with your lives?"

Avram continued, now describing the cooperative venture with the French Renault company for producing their Renault-12 in Romania as a Romanian car called Dacia. In the past, Romania had not been able to export the Dacia to the West, even at prices as low as $1,000 a car, because, to save hard currency, the French license had been purchased only for the stripped down car, with almost no optional equipment. Avram then related that everything Romania had not bought from Renault had later been obtained through intelligence channels. Avram said that the Ministry of the Machine Building Industry wanted to express its gratitude to the DIE for the clandestine procurement of all those French documents, which made it possible to avoid importing from France more than 13,000 options and improvements on the basic car that were not included in the cooperative contract, representing a savings of more than three million dollars. He also emphasized that some of the Renault documents containing improvements that could be applied to any similar make of car should be sent to the Soviet Union and to other Socialist countries producing their own cars. "This operation will enable us able to export our Dacia to Western Europe, comrades. Someday we may even be able to export it to America!"

On the CBS Evening News of May 7, 1986, Dan Rather had a special report called, "Dacia, as in Gotcha." It was an evaluation of the Romanian Dacia car, which had just gone on the market in the United States. Although the Dacia seemed to be a bargain, its performance was found to be so poor that Rather chose to do a humorous skit on it, showing how everything went wrong when someone tried to drive it. The final straw was when the demon-

strator could not turn the Dacia's motor off, even after taking the key out, until he had turned the headlights on.

"Furthermore," Avram continued, "we now have a brand new joint venture with Citroën to produce one of their newest compact cars in Romania. I have just sent over one hundred engineers and technicians to France to learn about this Citroën car. Only a few of them are my men, though; the rest are from the DIE, armed with new mini-cameras and photographic contact paper. It's not that I've made a sacrifice. To the contrary, comrades, it was a calculated move. When they get back, we'll have ten times more information than if I'd sent only my men to Citroën."

TRANSFORMING AMERICAN BLUEPRINTS INTO ROMANIAN PRODUCTS

"Let's hear from someone else," Ceausescu addressed the meeting.

The minister of the metallurgical industry, Neculai Agachi, is a good storyteller and uses a picturesque Romanian spiced with a strong Moldavian accent. He began by noting that in the early 1970s, on Ceausescu's orders, Romania had started to exploit its large bauxite deposits to become an aluminum producer. Because of political restrictions, and especially because of the prohibitive prices set at that time by the aluminum monopoly, his ministry had not been able to import rolling mills from the West for processing the aluminum. Romania had therefore been exporting the aluminum ingots to both Eastern and Western countries. One day, however, a confidential report drew his attention to a West German firm that was negotiating for the purchase of three aluminum rolling mill projects from the United States— ones for sheet, textured, and foil aluminum. That same day he reported it to Ceausescu and sent the report over to the DIE. "I don't want to go into any details. I only want to say that today I have a very special, unique, and unmentionably secret design institute, set up in several DIE safe houses, that is working to transform American blueprints and projects into Romanian products. By 1983 or 1984, Romania should have the three ultra-modern aluminum rolling mills in operation. 'Don't spend the people's money to fatten up capitalism,' is what our country's foremost son keeps telling us day after day. We should write this in gold letters and hang it up in each of our offices, comrades," Agachi wound up.

The atmosphere was much more relaxed when the minister of the chemical industry, Mihai Florescu, took the floor, focusing more on Elena than on Ceausescu. A volunteer in the Red Brigades during the Spanish Civil War and a member of the Romanian government for more than 25 years, Florescu had long ago forgotten his training as a chemical engineer. To make up for it he had the gift of gab. Now his subject concerned the art of luring Western companies to Bucharest with as much technological documentation as possible. He told how Ceausescu had ordered him to eliminate Romania's first polystyrene plant from the five-year plan for imports from the West and instead to build it with his own resources, based on Romanian research and design. "It was like reinventing the radio again, after Popov had already done it, if I may say so," Florescu lamented, looking guiltily over toward Ceausescu. In the Soviet bloc, the policy is to replace Western inventors with Soviet ones. All the history books there have wiped out Marconi's name and now proclaim that the radio was invented by a Russian named A. Popov.

"Merely designing a large polystyrene plant to be built in Romania would mean at least four or five years of intensive and expensive efforts," said Florescu. "But the Comrade in his wisdom found an incredible solution for us. He instructed me to write phony letters to the most important chemical firms in West Germany, Great Britain, France, and Italy, expressing Romania's firm interest in purchasing the production license and a very large automated polystyrene plant." Florescu explained that six Western companies came to Bucharest to make bids, and that the negotiations dragged on over more than one year, during which time each of them went back and forth bringing more and more blueprints and technological documentation asked for by the Romanian negotiators. Everything was secretly and punctiliously photographed by the DIE, but the results were still considered insufficient to allow the plant to be completely designed in Romania. That was until a French company, ultimately wanting to demonstrate its superiority, brought a whole polystyrene project to Bucharest that it had just sold to another Western country. Understandably cautious, the French asked that their key documents be locked up every night in the safes of the Athenee Palace Hotel, where they were staying. These documents were more than enough for a "Romanian solution" to the problem. "Without purchasing any foreign project, license, or know-how," Florescu trumpeted, "our country was able to build a huge polystyrene plant within the Borzesti Petrochemical Combinat." And he, too, added a final flourish. "I cannot finish here without expressing my boundless gratitude to the most brilliant son of our people, to Comrade Ceausescu, and to our greatest scholar and academician, Comrade Elena. They are opening up new and, as always, original ways for leading their Romania on to glory and Communism."

"In the 1960s," Ceausescu addressed the meeting, "Bucharest was full of Western businessmen signing contracts to export industrial equipment to Romania. Nowadays, Western companies still travel here with bids, supported by impressive technical documentation, but fewer and fewer contracts are actually being signed. Florescu's example should be taken by everyone as a real-life model for the future."

"You're getting old," Elena said sweetly, looking over affectionately at Florescu, who was her principal favorite. "Didn't I tell you to tell that story here you told me about that big Nazi company that had forgotten all about the fact that we had nationalized their factory here in Romania?"

"The I.G. Farben Industry, Comrade Elena. You're right, I am getting old," admitted a servile Florescu. He then told about how the Colorom-Codlea factory producing coloring agents had formerly been a subsidiary of I.G. Farben, which became Hoechst after World War II. "During a visit I made to Hoechst some years ago I met a German who had been born in Romania and who addressed me as 'Herr Genosse' or 'Mister Comrade.' He was very interested in Colorom, where he had worked before emigrating. . . ."

"Watch your tongue, Florescu," Ceausescu broke in.

"I won't say anything more about that man. Only that for a good number of years now we have been getting data every month on what Hoechst is doing in its production of coloring agents. The other day I tried to make a joke about it for Comrade Elena. I said it looked as though Hoechst hadn't yet heard that Colorom had been nationalized: They still send Colorom every new formula they develop, just as if it were still one of their affiliates."

The minister of light industry, Lina Ciobanu, was up next. Elena had personally selected Ciobanu from a group of Party activists to be the only other woman member of the Political Executive Committee. In choosing her, Elena's main concern was not only that "the other woman" not try to compete with her but especially that she should make Elena look good by comparison. Ciobanu looked like an old-time Soviet political activist, with her hair tightly drawn back into a bun, her enormous, jutting chest fairly bursting the buttons off of her military-style, high-buttoned jacket closed right up to her chin, her calf-length straight skirt, and her sturdy boots. Furthermore, she even read her speeches like a commissar.

"In the early 1970s," Ciobanu began, "an American citizen who was the chairman of an American company in California and a DIE agent reported that the chief engineer of a Ford glass factory was prepared to sell a complete technical project for a new Pittsburgh Plate Glass process under the table for the sum of $200,000. . . ."

"Let's skip over such details, Ciobanu," Ceausescu admonished the speaker. "Names and positions do more harm than good when given here," he calmly counseled. He is courteous when talking to a woman.

Ciobanu, however, kept rattling on like a machine gun, reading the speech one of her advisors had prepared for the meeting. "Romania, traditionally a glass producer and exporter, was very interested. A meeting was set up at a hotel in America to exchange $200,000 for the project, but before it could be concluded the participants were all arrested and. . . ."

"Comrade Ciobanu, we are not interested in American propaganda stories. We are here to decide what we should do for the future. Is that clear?"

"Yes, Comrade Ceausescu. The engineer was fired from his job. Two years later an American came to Bucharest, asked to see me, and proposed designing a Pittsburgh glass factory in Romania for $300,000. It was the same engineer, only his price was higher! I immediately reported the case to the DIE, and the engineer was contacted by his former case officer, the one who had been declared *persona non grata* by the Americans. . . ."

"Shush! Put your idiotic papers down on the floor, right now! On the floor! On the floor!" Elena screamed hysterically, until Ciobanu did finally put her speech down on the floor. "Now tell us the story, darling, in your own words. You can do that, can't you?"

Ciobanu shifted nervously from one foot to the other, then started up her machine gun again. "It was John Akfirat, Comrade Elena, the Turk who was an American citizen and was the chief engineer of the Ford glass factory, and you know him, because I told you about him so many times. . . ."

"You'd better read us your paper, Comrade Ciobanu. Just do that!" Ceausescu cut in, to the satisfaction of Ciobanu, who immediately grabbed up her speech and tried to find where she had left off when she had been interrupted by Elena.

"A large team of engineers, translators, and draftsmen moved into several DIE safe houses and, under the American engineer's direction, designed a huge Pittsburgh glass factory. A few days ago it was put into experimental production within an existing plant, Scaeni Glass Factory. The American engineer received his 300,000 tax-free dollars. That is all the hard currency we had to spend for this factory. If it had been imported legally, it would have cost $14 million, plus 15 years of royalties. The American has begun another 'consultation' project for us concerning a new type of American glass called 'float,' which we'll start to produce at three large factories in no more than two years. Soon you'll find Romanian glass items in every department store in Western Europe and the United States, putting some of the old European and American corporations out of business. That's Comrade Ceausescu's Communist way of creating our glass industry without capitalist licenses or royalties. That's why I want to add my voice to those of ten million other Romanian women: We thank you, Comrade Nicolae Ceausescu! We thank you, who are for us more than father, brother, husband, and son put together!"

TOTAL ECONOMIC ESPIONAGE

It was around six o'clock when Ceausescu started to present his "new economic order" and his firm directives for the future of Romania's technological and economic relations with the West. As he usually does when beginning an important speech, he started out in a very low voice, almost a whisper. "What we have discussed here today may be new to some of you comrades, but not to all of us. As in many other domains where Romania leads the way, our Communist Party developed its own original concept of technological intelligence a few years earlier. It proved to be substantially superior to the one that we inherited from Moscow."

Ceausescu then put forth his principle of total technical and scientific espionage against the West; imports from the capitalist world should become the exception now, not the rule. "During my 1975 visit to Tokyo I was told a very interesting story. It was about how a Japanese company started to build a photo industry. I won't tell you if it was Canon or Nikon or Minolta or something else, because I promised to keep it a secret; let's just call it 'Tokon.' When it started, it didn't even have the couple of lathes in an abandoned garage that Sony began with. 'Tokon' went out and hired 160 optical and mechanical engineers and gave each of them a sealed envelope. Inside was the name of the Western company where the engineer was to manage to get hired for three years and the name of the photographic equipment part he was to learn how to produce. Some, for example, went to Leica or Rolliflex to learn how to produce the body, or the mechanical, electronic, or photoelectrical component of a camera. Others went to Zeiss-Ikon to learn about lenses. During this period they were paid by 'Tokon' in addition to receiving their salaries from Leica or Rolliflex or Zeiss. When they came back to Japan, they designed several camera models based on what they had stolen from Western Europe, built a modern factory, and bang! All of a sudden 'Tokon' started to flood the world market with very good cameras that were far less expensive than the European ones. No time had been wasted on research, no license or know-how had been bought, no royalties paid. That's the way we should go in the future. With only one difference: We are not going to have our engineers paid twice. We are Communists, not capitalists. We are called to enrich our motherland, not our own pockets, comrades," he brought his story to a close.

Afterwards, Ceausescu started giving out orders with the agility of a lifelong intelligence professional. Foreign trade should be reorganized so that imports would be completely subordinated to the principle of total economic espionage. Every trade representative in the West should have a dual role. Every contact with Western firms should be analyzed for intelligence purposes. Every Western specialist met in trade negotiations should be reported to the DIE. Every cooperative and joint venture with Western companies should be subordinated to the purpose of obtaining new technology by intelligence means. Romanian industrial ministries should lure a greater number of Westerners to Bucharest and get them to bring sensitive documents. The internal Securitate and the DIE should see that virtually every Western technical, commercial, and financial visitor had his luggage examined and any valuable documents secretly photographed.

"Florescu told us an interesting story about a Romanian emigré who became a very useful agent," Ceausescu said. "I want to tell you another story. Not long ago I sent Patan to Peking to propose to Comrade Hua Go-feng that our foreign intelligence services work together." Ion Patan was a deputy prime minister who, until March 1978, had also been minister of foreign trade. "Do you know what Comrade Hua said? 'We do not have spies in the West!' Can you believe that? When Patan insisted, Comrade Hua replied: 'Tell my friend Ceausescu that we don't have spies in the West, but we do have a lot of patriots there.' That's what we should be doing, too, comrades. We have over 600,000 Romanians living in the West, most of them in America. Detroit and Cleveland are the next largest Romanian cities after Bucharest. And we have lots more Germans living in West Germany who are either Romanian-born or of Romanian descent. I'm not counting the Romanian Jews living all over the world. We should make every one of them into a patriot working for the motherland abroad, a soldier in the service of our Communist Party!" Ceausescu climaxed in a very loud voice, pounding the table. For another half hour or so he continued in the same vein, describing his vision of the future Communist Romania, which should become one of the first ten industrial powers on earth, based on technological espionage.

Ceausescu then summed up his message. "In his unmatched genius, Lenin phrased the future of his proletarian revolution in a simple mathematical formula: 'Communism equals political power plus electrification.' Today, sixty years later, I would add a new building block to Marxism-Leninism: Modern Communism equals national Communism plus technological intelligence and money from capitalism. That, comrades, is the Romanian contribution to Marxism!" Ceausescu ended. His face had turned bright red, and his forehead was dripping with perspiration. The participants had stood and were clapping with a rhythmic beat. Ceausescu waved his arms, and the participants froze. "I have heard voices raised in some other Warsaw Pact countries calling for certain liberalizations, for a greater degree of industrial autonomy."

"That's anarchosocialism," Manescu shouted, trying to anticipate Ceausescu.

"That's correct, comrades. We should today call once more for greater Party discipline on all levels. Here we have reported, questioned, criticized, discussed. Now we have to make a decision, comrades. A unanimous decision, as always, which should become the letter of the law for every single Romanian living inside and outside of our borders. Who is for approving the new concept of technological intelligence, comrades?"

Everyone broke into applause, which soon turned into the ritual clapping. For quite some time Ceausescu busied himself with the papers he had in front of him on the table, searching for some, rearranging their order, organizing his folder. Then he waved his arms again and continued, without looking at us, speaking rapidly, like an American tobacco auctioneer. "Is there anyone against? Any abstentions? In full unanimity the Political Executive Committee of the Romanian Communist Party approves the new concept of technological intelligence as it was described in the report presented here and in the conclusions to our meeting."

A few minutes after leaving the meeting, Ceausescu called me into his office. He was standing in the middle of the room with Elena.

"How many of the directors of foreign trade enterprises are officers?"

"Eleven DIE and one DIA out of forty-one. Twenty-six are cooptees."

"By the end of the year all of them should be deep cover officers. Bring them back here one by one. I'll give them their military rank. Understood?"

"Yes, comrade."

"The same with the Ministry of Foreign Affairs," Ceausescu added. "We should keep it a secret from Andrei and Burtica. The ministers are rotated every couple of years or so anyway, aren't they?" he said with a wink.

XXVII

"GENERAL Pacepa speaking."

"Hi, Boss. You'd have been better off eating shit than answering the phone. The Comrade wants you here immediately. You've no idea what terrible weather we've got, Boss."

"I'll be there in nothing flat, Professor."

ANOTHER SOVIET SPY?

It was a few minutes after ten in the morning when I left my office for Ceausescu's. Waiting at the top of the stairs as usual, Manea gave me his report in that flat, emotionless monotone of his that has never betrayed either anxiety or satisfaction. "Postelnicu was already here waiting for him when the Comrade arrived this morning. Comrade Elena was with him—she never comes so early—and went right in with them, as if she knew what was coming. Postelnicu said it was urgent. The Comrade was a shriveled heap. Almost the way he was that day when he tore up the decree making Militaru chief of the General Staff."

When I entered Ceausescu's office, he was still yelling violently and pounding the desk with his fist. His face was purple with rage. Elena and Postelnicu were seated at a table in front of his desk. A cassette recorder sat in the middle of the table.

"Wh-Why h-haven't you r-reported that L-Luchian was a K-KGB officer?" Ceausescu screamed at me.

After that evening at the Athenee Palace, when Luchian had picked Nicu up by the nape of the neck and deposited him outside the door, I had been waiting for something to happen. This, however, was more than I had bargained for.

"T-Tell h-him, P-Postelnicu. Sh-Show h-him wh-what you've l-learned," Ceausescu thundered.

"I caught General Luchian speaking fluent Russian!" Postelnicu said, dropping his bombshell into my lap.

"W-With h-his w-wife! B-both are KGB illegals plotting against me!" Ceausescu smashed his fist down on the table.

"Turn on the recorder!" Elena barked out.

Postelnicu, who never waited to be asked twice by Elena, obediently reached over to the cassette player. A man and a woman could be heard discussing some guests that had just left. Although the cassette had a lot of background noise, I could recognize Luchian and his wife, Silvia. Then they faded out completely. It made no sense to me that the quality should be so poor, because Luchian had concealed microphones in all of his rooms.

"There it is!" Elena screamed.

I could make out a few words in Russian, but, since my knowledge of that language was next to nothing, as was Elena's, I could not understand anything. Nor could I identify the two very low voices as being those of the Luchians.

"T-Two K-KGB i-illegal o-officers! And one of them right here in th-this v-very b-building, just above my office!"

Ceausescu's fury raged for a long time, Elena all the while adding fuel to the fire and turning the recorder off and on several times.

"Luchian and his wife are a Soviet illegal couple, infiltrated into Romania during the turmoil of the 1944–45 period," Ceausescu declared an hour or so later, the disappearance of his stutter being a sure sign that he had gotten hold of himself. He said both were Soviets of Romanian descent, and that was where their faultless Romanian language came from. The KGB had documented them as Romanian citizens born in Tighina, had armed them with false birth certificates that could not be verified, because Tighina was now in the Soviet Union, and had even created false graves for their parents here in Bucharest. No doubt about it. The conversation in Russian was proof positive. The Luchians should not be arrested; they should be neutralized in a different way. Until a final decision was reached, they should be kept under rigorous coverage.

As I left with Postelnicu, Elena was still sitting there in the same chair, both hands gripping the tape recorder. At his desk, Manea was busy shuffling his papers, indifferent to everything around him. He merely remarked in his flat monotone: "Is the Comrade going to tear up another decree?"

To Neutralize Radio Free Europe

I was on the way back to my office when my car's radio telephone spoke up. "Sixty-two should immediately report to zero one. Repeat, sixty-two should report to zero one."

"Sixty-two is on his way to zero one," I answered.

When I arrived at Ceausescu's office, Manea was outside waiting for me. "There's a new cyclone raging in there, with Coman, Postelnicu, and Plesita in the eye of the storm, and Comrade Elena pumping the bellows. It's over something about Radio Free Europe from your bulletin. I hope it won't go on too long. I've got opera tickets for tonight. Massenet's *Manon*, Boss. I don't want to ruin my evening the way Manon Lescaut ruined his life." *Manon* was Manea's favorite opera. He thought of himself as a kind of Manon, throwing away his life on a courtesan named Ceausescu.

I had been expecting an outburst over that day's bulletin giving Radio Free Europe's report on new and exceptionally violent attacks on Ceausescu's personality cult. When I went in, a scowling Ceausescu was seated at his desk, with Elena standing behind him. He was in the midst of dictating orders, a sign that he was already in the process of cooling down. Coman, Postelnicu, and Plesita were assiduously scratching away in their notebooks.

Ceausescu went on talking, without even deigning to look at me. He said he never wanted the name of Radio Free Europe pronounced in his office again. It should be replaced with a code name, something like "Yakkity-yak." Or even better, "Chatterbox." A special Securitate unit should be created and put in charge of nothing but "Chatterbox." The unit's main task was to identify every one of "Chatterbox's" listeners. The Militia and Securitate confidential informants from all around the country were to be involved in this operation. Total censorship of the mails to the West, with seizure of everything addressed to or connected with "Chatterbox." The DGTO should immediately report everyone identified by its microphones, telephone intercepts, and mail censorship as listening to "Chatterbox" broadcasts. Today "Chatterbox" burned like poison ivy. But the day when its broadcasts no longer simply attacked the Party and government activists but actually appealed to them, trying to twist them around its little finger and lure them over to the other side, that was when it would become a deadly poison. And we had to be prepared for that day.

"We must rebuild our jamming center," said Ceausescu, finally addressing me. The Romanian jamming center had been dismantled years earlier, and its buildings turned over to the DIE school. The dismantled jamming equipment, mostly provided by the Soviet Union in the 1950s, had been preserved, ready to be used again any time. It was being kept with newer and more powerful Soviet jamming transmitters received from Moscow over the years. Ceausescu ordered that the jamming center be operational within six months. Bucharest and the areas with ethnic German and Hungarian populations should be jammed with maximum intensity. If more equipment was needed, it should be imported right away. A few minutes and a couple of orders later, Ceausescu raised his hands, signaling that he had finished. "You stay here, Pacepa," he added.

Ceausescu got up from his chair, came from behind his desk and started pacing around his office, eyes lowered and following his feet, long arms swinging rigidly and close to his body, hands cupped and facing backwards. Elena fell in behind him, waddling to keep up. Ceausescu beckoned for me to follow. We traipsed around in quiet procession, making me think of the march to the gallows in Berlioz's *Symphonie Fantastique.*

Ceausescu finally broke the silence, his voice exceedingly soft. "I would rather neutralize 'Chatterbox' from inside than jam it on this end. Jamming would only stir up more interest in it. I want to get rid of Bernard," he went on, his voice dropping even lower. Noel Bernard was the director of Radio Free Europe's Romanian Department.

Ceausescu was afraid that Bernard would change the Radio Free Europe policy of discrediting only Romania's top leadership and replace it with one aimed more at turning the heads of some important functionaries and getting them to defect to the West. Ceausescu dreads the thought of any kind of defectors, but the idea of high-level ones is a nightmare for him.

"And Georgescu, Nick," Elena added loudly. Bernard was Ceausescu's *bête noir;* Georgescu was Elena's.

I reminded Ceausescu that he had personally charged Luchian with handling the Georgescu matter, and that Luchian had seemed optimistic about soon having some results.

"L-Luchian is d-dead. Th-The D-DIE sh-should take over G-Georgescu and f-finish with him," said Ceausescu even more softly.

When I left, Ceausescu's mood was still black, but he had calmed down to the point of knowing just what he wanted.

Preparing the Trip to London

Back at my office, I tried to catch up with the normal routine of managing a foreign intelligence service that had been constantly growing, becoming involved in almost everything from espionage, influence, disinformation, and trafficking in arms, drugs, and people, down to the daily monitoring of the microphones concealed in the offices and homes of every Romanian leader. The traditional civilian institutions of government had proved incapable of rescuing the country from economic disaster, and in his own mind Ceausescu believed the whole country ought really to be run like a "Horizon" operation, fueled by deception.

It was already dark when the *S* telephone rang. In Bucharest the days of April are still short.

"General Pacepa speaking."

"This is your slave, Boss. How's the weather there?"

"The calm after the storm, Professor."

"Here, too. Comrade Elena just left, and when she opened the door you could feel how stifling it was in there. She had a cassette player under her arm, but she didn't look as if she were going to a dance. Now the Comrade is about to leave. Do you know what's next?"

"Constantin Manea is going to see *Manon.* He has opera tickets for tonight."

"And you, Boss, are going to see the Comrade. At his residence."

"Oh, no!"

"Oh, yes! Manea's forecast is for hazy and sultry weather, but no more thunderstorms."

Ceausescu was walking at a fast clip in his enormous garden, lighted only by the "dwarfs."

"What's new?" he asked conventionally, when I had fallen into step with him. He went on, however, without waiting for me to reply. "Have we gotten any answer from Rolls-Royce?"

"Yes, comrade. There's an affirmative one in directly from Keith," I reported. Sir Kenneth Keith was the president of Rolls-Royce. He had just agreed to Ceausescu's visiting the Rolls-Royce aircraft engine plant on his official trip to England in June, which I was preparing.

"That's excellent. Excellent. Our Yurom crashed because of its engine. And from BAC?" he went on, here referring to British Aerospace, a corporation created in 1976 after the nationalization and merger of British Aircraft Corporation, Hawker Siddeley, and Scottish Aviation.

"Yes, comrade."

"Very good. During the visit I want to sign the contract for the production of both the airplane and its engines." Ceausescu had decided to import the license and the equipment for producing the commercial passenger airplane BAC 111 from British Aerospace, and for manufacturing its turboengines from Rolls-Royce, in order to open intelligence doors into them.

"It won't be easy."

"I want to have both joint ventures signed while I'm in England. And I want our officers to be inside there right after we get back," Ceausescu ordered, marching along at his steady, rapid pace. "From Rolls-Royce I want to get complete intelligence on their military jet-engines. From BAC I want blueprints on their fighters." He now turned to walk along the unilluminated paths. "And I want the Harrier. I'm sure that Brezhnev would pay a very good price for it." The British Royal Air Force Harrier was the first operational military aircraft ever with vertical takeoff and landing. "Try to arrange a live demonstration with it during my visit there." Ceausescu proceeded to snow me under with an avalanche of other orders in preparation for the trip to London. The last one was to arrange, apart from the visit's official schedule, a meeting with Gordon McLennan, the secretary general of the British Communist Party, at the Romanian embassy, out of earshot of British microphones. "After one week of my being at Buckingham Palace, he may believe I've caved in to capitalist influences."

Ceausescu abruptly switched subjects. "Any news from Dobreanu?" Mihail Dobreanu was the son-in-law of Ion Marcu, a deep cover DIE colonel working as the chief of the Romanian commercial agency in Tehran. Marcu had played the most important role in the recruitment of the Shah of Iran's brother and had become his case officer in Tehran, responsible for everything connected with him, including the 10 percent payments made to him in cash. A year earlier Marcu had defected with his wife, daughter, and son-in-law, the latter couple having been given permission to spend a short vacation in Tehran, and this defection had provoked the most terrible burst of rage from Ceausescu that I ever witnessed. A few months later the DIE located the whole family in Canada, where Marcu had been given political asylum. According to "Popovici," the DIE agent who had tracked him down, Marcu's son-in-law had become homesick for his parents in Romania. Immediately, Ceausescu ordered that he be lured away from Canada and brought to Bucharest, which the DIE had just recently accomplished.

"Yes, comrade. Dobreanu is now in Bucharest."

"Has he said anything?"

"He's being interrogated about Marcu."

"The dirty crook! Ask the shah's brother to have Savak get him out of the way. Say it's a personal request from me. Understood?" Savak was the shah's infamous intelligence service.

"Yes, comrade."

"When is my visit to Peking?"

"The beginning of May."

"If so, *I* can ask him. Arrange a stopover in Tehran on my way to Peking. Have the shah and his brother meet me at the airport. I'll get Marcu's scalp. Understood?"

"Yes, comrade."

"You twist Dobreanu's arm to lure his wife and child here. All of them should croak in jail." When we passed the bench in front of the two story house he had built for his mother, Ceaucescu automatically said, "Good evening." He still could not believe that the octagenarian woman wearing a black shawl tightly wrapped around her shoulders and a black kerchief tied under her chin would never again be there on that bench waiting for him.

After a few more steps, Ceausescu paused, reached for one of my buttons and started twisting it. Very, very softly he said, "I want to put 'Radu' in Bernard's office."

"We have never had a portable 'Radu,' comrade."

"Let's make one."

When we passed the entrance, Elena was on the marble steps looking out for Ceausescu. Shuffling along in her slippers, she tried to catch up with us.

"We've got to get rid of Georgescu, Nick," she puffed. "I beg you. Enough is enough!"

"Uh huh."

"Goma and Tanase, too! They hate our guts, Nick."

"Let's have dinner now, and afterwards a *Kojak*. Ten o'clock," he tossed back at me, as he and Elena went off hand in hand.

THE CYCLE BEGINS ANEW

Ceausescu, wearing his favorite white turtleneck sweater, arrived at the movie theater on the dot of ten and started pacing around the room, waiting for Elena. When she came, she was draped in a long gray velvet dressing gown, buttoned only halfway up. The waiter rushed in with the Moldavian yellow wine kept at room temperature and then opened a cold bottle of Cordon Rouge champagne for Elena.

At the end of the movie, the cruel lights came on to spotlight Elena sleeping soundly, her head nestled softly on the gray velvet back of her chair and her mouth drooping open to let out a slight, regular wheeze.

Ceausescu drained his glass of wine, threw a glance at the sleeping Elena, and then set off at a rapid pace, making a sign for me to follow him. Once in his private study, he went over and put on the stereo, turning it up loud.

"You'll have to go to Germany and twist Beitz's arm to get the

Fokker for us. Our bears aren't to be had for free." Berthold Beitz, the general manager of the famous Krupp concern and on Fokker's board of directors, was an avid hunter and a close acquaintance of former Prime Minister Maurer and of Luchian. After his numerous hunting trips to Romania Beitz took marvelous bearskin trophies home to West Germany with him, but he also left behind several very fine, custom made Krupp hunting rifles for both Ceausescu and Maurer.

"You'll have to twist Wischnewski's arm, too." Hans-Juergen Wischnewski had the title of minister of the chancellery and was the number two man in Helmut Schmidt's cabinet. In the past few years I had met him several times to hand him personal messages from Ceausescu to Schmidt, asking for prohibited technology to help Romania preserve her independent stance toward Moscow. Of an open mind and unflinching character, Wischnewski had stubbornly fought giving Ceausescu access to West German military aeronautical technology. So it was also with Beitz, who, despite the vague promises made to Luchian and me over friendly lunches and dinners in Krupp's executive villas, was not about to put his own prestige on the line for Ceausescu. "And don't forget the Windbag himself." That meant Willy Brandt. "Push him to come here before my visit to London. *I'll* twist his arm."

As Ceausescu was speaking, the heavy door to his study flew open and slammed against the wall. Elena stumbled in, with eyes puffy, hair tousled, dressing gown askew, obviously having just come from the movie theater.

"Try to leave for Bonn tomorrow, Pacepa. That's what we have to do first," Ceausescu called back to me, as he was being dragged off by Elena.

ONE MORE PARTY

When I finally got away, it was just past midnight. "To the Party's guest house," I ordered the driver. I had promised Burtica that I would not miss his dinner. The occasion was to celebrate his appointment as minister of foreign trade. When I got there, everyone was already feeling no pain.

"Can anybody tell me how many different dishes we've had

this evening?" I heard Cornel Burtica's voice asking, as I took the seat that had been saved for me.

"At least ten," blubbered Stefan Andrei through a full mouth.

"It's a big mess!" Burtica went on.

"Why? I saw at least ten more waiting in the kitchen."

"I'm talking about something else. Can you believe it, comrades? We still have first class restaurants for tourists that have only four or five main dishes on the menu. That's what's such a mess."

"What a disaster for our foreign relations," Andrei contributed.

"I had some of my men collect menus from the tourist restaurants we have in Bucharest. And when the Comrade got back from the United States, I reported the whole mess to him. Do-cu-men-ted. And do you know what he did?"

"Had the restaurant managers arrested?" guessed the minister of national defense, Ion Coman.

"Why have them arrested? They're all either political appointees or our own officers," said the minister of interior, Teodor Coman, defending them.

"The Comrade again proved he's without equal! Right there on the spot he ordered that a presidential decree be drawn up obligating every tourist restaurant to have a minimum number of main entrees on its menu. I proposed thirty-five for a luxury class restaurant, twenty-five for the rest."

"Marvelous. How can they manage that?" asked Ion Coman.

"It's the Comrade's idea: cans, canned food. Every restaurant should have several thousand cans in stock, with the dishes listed on its menu. If somebody wants goulash, you just open up a can of goulash and serve it to him. If somebody wants sausages and beans, you open up another can. Pork and sauerkraut? There it is. And the quality's always the same. The Comrade could easily make a million in the West, with the ideas he has."

"Isn't it expensive for a restaurant to serve canned food?" Teodor Coman dared to ask.

"It's a matter of national prestige, not money," Andrei put in.

"All our restaurants run on a deficit, comrades. All we have to do is double the subsidy, and we can have thirty-five entrees on the menu. Money isn't the problem; the tourists are. There's nothing that makes better propaganda for our Communist Romania than a happy tourist."

The discussion continued desultorily. People at this level are not used to listening to others. They only want to make their own contributions to the adulation of Ceausescu. There is always somebody around who will tell the Comrade tomorrow what you said today. And that's without even counting the microphones.

"The poor comrade. As if Washington and the White House weren't enough. Now he has to go to London and sleep in a royal palace and have the queen looking down her nose at him as if he were a country cousin," commiserated Ion Coman, uninspired.

Burtica stiffened. "What do you think we are, Coman, troglodytes? The Romanian people have been able to give the Comrade more in twenty years than the British Empire has given its royal dynasty in a whole millennium. How many offices does the queen have? One, Coman. Our comrade has three, and one is the former royal palace. How many official residences does the queen have? Three, Coman, that's all she has. The Comrade has five. Five, Coman. Five. And that's without counting the thirty-nine special guest houses we built for him in each of our districts and keep just for when he goes there on a visit, or with a hunting party."

"And twenty-one presidential apartments in our embassies," Andrei chimed in, chomping noisily. "Nobody else ever sets foot in them. They're only for the Comrade."

"How many personal airplanes do you think the queen has?" Burtica went on. "Two, Coman, that's all she has. The Comrade has nine, *and* three helicopters. And don't forget, one is a Boeing 707 and two are those giants, the Ilyushin-62. All fitted out with presidential apartments, salons, and offices. How many personal trains does the queen have? One, Coman, only one, and a very old one at that. The Comrade has three. Not three coaches, three whole trains, and all ultra-modern. How many ambulances does the queen have? Two, Coman, just two—I know that. The Comrade has four, all custom ordered in America and West Germany. How many of her own hospitals does the queen have, Coman? None, that's how many. The Comrade has one for himself alone. And doctors who treat only him and his family."

"And that's without counting the new Administrative Center," the minister of interior added proudly, as he filled a tumbler with Scotch and emptied it in one gulp.

"You're right, Coman," Burtica agreed. "Do you suppose the

queen can demolish the center of London to build palaces for herself and her government? But we can, comrades. And we will. And we'll call it the 'Ni-co-la-e Cea-u-ses-cu Administrative Center.'"

"I'm going to London with the Comrade," said Andrei. "He just told me. He said we'd all be staying at Buckingham Palace. Is that true, Pacepa?"

"True."

"I'm dying to see myself there, where Queen Victoria reigned for almost sixty-five years. As foreign minister I ought to have one of the best apartments in the palace. I can't wait to pee on its imperial walls and on King George IV's furniture. It should be a lot more fun than Blair House!" Andrei dazzled us with his eclectic knowledge of history.

The animation of the conversation grew in direct proportion to the number of bottles emptied, skipping around to touch on the most unexpected subjects. The party finally came to its usual end, with the two Comans well sloshed, Andrei unsteady on his feet, and Burtica tipsy but in full control.

As usual, my apartment was dark. Only Fedot Lily, with his wrinkled peasant face softly illuminated, was up waiting for me. His large, warm, friendly, and always inquisitive eyes stared me full in the face.

Lying on the large cocktail table next to Fedot I found a printed invitation to the closing day of Dana's show. "My beloved Dad" had again been entered on the line for the name, penned in Dana's firm yet feminine hand.

Epilogue

ON Sunday, July 23, Dana came to the airport with me. Ceausescu had ordered me back to West Germany to try once more to obtain Bonn's approval for the joint venture with Fokker, so that he could start building the Fokker planes and would have an entree for stealing VTOL technology. I had his personal messages for Chancellor Helmut Schmidt and for Prince Bernhard of the Netherlands, the most prominent member of the Fokker board of directors, firmly assuring them that any Western technological secrets deriving from the venture would not be shared with Moscow. Ceausescu ordered me to be back in a couple of days to start working on the plans he and his wife had for assassinating three dissident emigrés in Western Europe.

As I held Dana and kissed her goodbye, I knew that I would not be back. Not in a few days, not ever. Suddenly, I had had enough. Enough duplicity, enough plotting, enough of life at the top of a society that I detested more every day, enough postponing my hopes of escape to freedom. "Forgive me, Dana," I said after kissing her. "Forgive me for all the wrong I may have done you, and for all the things I may have left undone."

"Come on, Dad," Dana replied, her eyes searching mine and seemingly trying to penetrate my mind. "With my father on board, there's no airplane in the whole world that could go down." When the plane was far out on the runway, she was still standing in front of the terminal waving to me. Dana could not know, and to protect her I could not tell her then, that the night before I had said goodbye to my life in Romania.

It had been shortly after midnight when I had returned home that last evening. Everything was the same as usual. The militiaman at the Polish embassy came out of his booth for a formal salute, and Mrs. Groza was peeking out from behind her window

421

curtain. The only light burning in my apartment was Fedot Lily's, and I pulled up a chair to talk with him. To this day I have no idea whether I sat there one minute or one hour, but I know that his black eyes asked me harder questions than they ever had before. Having made up my mind, I quietly went to my study, pulled up a certain piece of the parquet floor and removed a small envelope. It contained the membership card I had been given in 1945 when I joined the Association of Young Friends of the United States, an organization sponsored by the United States embassy in Bucharest that the Communists had later declared treasonous. I slowly burned the envelope with my lighter, then left the house and took the wheel of the service car that was always parked at the door for emergency purposes.

A full moon was shining brightly when I reached the cemetery and knelt down beside my father's grave. It was he who had sown the first seeds of love for America in me. Most of his life was spent working at the General Motors affiliate in Bucharest, where he developed a great enthusiasm for America. Firmly determined to emigrate with his family to Detroit, as one of his uncles had done, he had had the bad fortune to become trapped in Romania, first by World War II and afterwards by the Soviet occupation. The best he could do was to pass his love for America on to me and to keep reinforcing it in me as long as he had a spark of life left in him.

When I returned home, I got out my violin and stood in front of my mother's portrait. The strains of Dvorak's "Humoresque," her favorite piece, seemed to beat down with the force of a spring rain. When I finished playing, I kissed her forehead and hair. It took her a moment to understand, and then her wide black eyes became frightened. "You are going to leave me," I seemed to read her lips whispering. I quickly spun around. There was no one there but the microphones concealed in the walls.

I spent the rest of the night silently bidding farewell to Dana's paintings, touching some, caressing others with my eyes. When I got to my books, it was almost dawn. Deeply buried in their pages were other years of dashed hopes and unfulfilled dreams.

On the airplane the next day, it was only after we had broken through the cumulus clouds that a tear rolled down my cheek. I love Dana far more than my own life. For many years I had done everything I could to have her with me in the West. Only there, far from Communist microphones and the ever present Romanian Securitate, would I have been able calmly to explain to her what I wanted to do, where I wanted to go. I know Dana as well as I know myself, and I did not have the slightest doubt that she would also have chosen freedom. Not only is she my daughter, but she is also an artist who has always wanted to express what she herself feels, not what she is told to feel. I was certain that, once together in the West for even a single day, we would never have returned to Romania. Ceausescu consistently refused.

To protect Dana's future days and nights, her life and freedom, even now I had told her nothing of my plans. That was why I also could not tell her that my whole new life over there in "our America," as my father used to call it, would be devoted to getting her and her fiancé released from their bondage and helping them to become Americans, too. The airplane was high in the skies, crossing over the Romanian border, when I closed my eyes. As the image of Christ crucified came slowly into focus, I asked for forgiveness for my past, freedom for my daughter, and strength for the lives ahead of us.

When I arrived at the Frankfurt/Main airport, I was met by Ambassador Ion Morega and the DIE chief of station, General Stefan Constantin. They reported that a meeting had been set for the following afternoon with West German Chancellery Minister Hans-Juergen Wischnewski, so I could give him Ceausescu's message to Chancellor Schmidt. My welcoming committee took me to an old castle on the outskirts of Frankfurt for lunch, and we passed the remainder of the day at the ambassador's residence in Bad Godesberg, near Bonn. When Constantin finally drove me to the Intercontinental Hotel in Cologne, I told him that I wanted to spend the next morning loafing around its health club. I was notorious for being a fanatic lover of tennis, swimming, and the sauna.

Early the next morning I left my hotel alone, caught a train to Bonn, and then took a taxi to the United States embassy, where I requested political asylum. A couple of days later it was magnanimously granted to me. Despite the 27 years I had served Communism from increasingly high positions, the United States of America generously accorded me the privilege of becoming a part of this wonderful nation. For my part I was determined to do whatever I could to repay this generosity.

On the night of Thursday, July 27, I secretly left West Germany on board a United States Air Force Hercules aircraft sent from Washington to get me. For this special trip, a wooden cabin containing a dining and a sleeping area was hastily set up inside the empty belly of the huge airplane. We had just reached the Atlantic Ocean when its commander came back to my wooden cabin. "Welcome to freedom, sir." It was the first time in many years that I had been called *sir,* instead of *comrade.* As I gave him a hug, I had a sudden urge to burst into tears, but I had not yet learned how to cry for joy.

When the commander left me, my thoughts automatically turned back to Bucharest. It would take Ceausescu a few weeks to pull together the "hard evidence" showing that I had been recruited by the CIA when I was a gullible teenager, unable to comprehend the advantages of Communism over capitalism. Then Ceausescu would sentence me to death as a CIA agent and do whatever he could to erase all evidence that General Ion Mihai Pacepa had ever existed. The Soviet bloc has its own rules for writing and rewriting history. And indeed, the general has ceased to exist, except in the memories of a few people. He remains forever on that huge airplane, isolated inside the wooden cabin built for him in its belly. He was exactly three months short of attaining the round age of 50.

The man who got off the Hercules airplane at Andrews Air Force Base near Washington, D.C., on July 28, 1978, had a brand new identity, attested to by his new American documents. The firm set of his jaw betrayed his fierce determination to begin a new, free life, as so many other immigrants had done before him.

A few days after General Pacepa's disappearance, the United States embassy and other Western diplomats in Romania described Bucharest as a city under siege. The headquarters of the Romanian Communist Party's Central Committee and the residence of its leader were under heavy guard, while security troops patrolled Bucharest day and night. Nicolae Ceausescu, reportedly ill and confined to his residence, canceled all activities and disappeared from public view.

In September 1978, Western press and diplomatic sources in

Bucharest reported that General Pacepa's disappearance was followed by the greatest political purge in post-war Romania. A third of the ruling Council of Ministers was demoted. Twenty-two ambassadors were replaced, and more than a dozen high-ranking security officers were arrested, while several dozen more simply vanished from sight in the turmoil. General Eugen Luchian was among the latter.

In October 1978, with DIE officers and agents throughout the West under investigation by counterintelligence services, Bucharest was fully engaged in a furious operation aimed at withdrawing most of the DIE legal and illegal officers, evidently to avoid further international embarrassment. Some of them chose freedom then and there, others later, and all reported that only hours after General Pacepa's disappearance the DIE entered a state of desperate confusion and soon began to disintegrate. Numerous investigating commissions, all directed by Elena, started dissecting the DIE and its personnel. By the end of the year, Elena had reportedly disbanded the DIE and started to build her own new organization on its ashes. The Western intelligence community was later in agreement that the DIE had become the first espionage service in history to have been entirely destroyed by the defection of a single man.

Pacepa's daughter, Dana, married her fiancé, sculptor Radu Damaceanu, on July 14, 1979. Completely isolated by the Romanian Securitate, they have not been able to receive any direct news from the United States. It was not until early 1985 that Dana and Radu first learned from an open letter to them her father published in France that he had not been found dead in a New York subway station, as Bucharest's rumor had it, but that he was still very much alive and fighting for their freedom. In defiance of orders given them by the security forces, on July 5, 1985, Dana and Radu courageously filed an official request to leave Romania, registered as no. 2668. Many members of the United States Congress have written to President Ceausescu asking for their release, but the letters have all remained unanswered.

Periodically, Romanian attempts to locate Pacepa surface in the most unexpected ways. Over the years a steady parade of odd characters have come to notice—Westerners, Palestinians, and Romanian emigrés—who have let it be known that they could make a fortune for Pacepa by going into commerical deals with him, or by employing him as an economic advisor, or by writing a book together with him. There have also been attempts by people representing various international groups to recruit retired CIA officers with tempting offers of financial reward for the least scrap of information about Pacepa's new identity or his whereabouts. A closer look at all these efforts has always betrayed either the gloved fist of Ceausescu himself or of his best friends, the PLO's Yasser Arafat or Libya's Moammar Gadhafi.

Since General Ion Mihai Pacepa's defection in 1978, Nicolae Ceausescu has not received any more invitations to set foot in the United States. Romania's most favored nation trading status, however, continued to be renewed by the United States government, giving Bucharest significant political and financial benefits. Thanks to "Horizon" and other similar influence operations, Ceausescu is steadily transforming Romania into an outstanding monument to Marxism and to himself, as symbolized by the triumphal arch he erected in 1986 at the entrance to Bucharest's International Fairgrounds, inscribed: "The Golden Epoch—The Epoch of Nicolae Ceausescu."

APPENDIX:

Where Are They Now?

Given below are the publicly reported positions of the principal Romanian figures in this book as of 1986. The current positions of DIE officers are, of course, not available.

Aghachi (Ah-GAH-kee), Neculai—Member of Central Committee of the Romanian Communist Party

Andrei (Ahn-DRAY), Stefan—Central Committee Secretary for Economic Affairs

Apostol (Ah-POS-tole), Gheorghe—Ambassador to Brazil

Aslan (Ahs-LAHN), Ana—Vice Chairman of Romanian-French Friendship Association

Avram(Ah-VRAM), Ion—Minister of Electric Power

Burtica (Boor-TEE-kuh), Cornel—Unknown

Ceausescu (Chow-SHES-koo), Elena—Member of Permanent Bureau of Political Executive Committee; Chief of Party and State Cadre Commission; First Deputy Prime Minister; Chairman of National Council for Science and Technology; Chairman of Classification, Standardization, Norm-setting and Quality Control Council

Ceausescu (Chow-SHES-koo), Ilie—Deputy Minister of National Defense

Ceausescu (Chow-SHES-koo) Ion—Minister State Secretary of State Planning Committee

Ceausescu (Chow-SHES-koo), Nicolae—Secretary General of Romanian Communist Party; President of Romania

Ceausescu (Chow-SHES-koo), Nicu—Candidate Member of Political Executive Committee; First Secretary of Union for Communist Youth; Minister for Youth Problems

Ceausescu (Chow-SHES-koo), Zoia—Chief of Mathematics Department of Scientific and Technical Creation National Institute

Ciobanu (Cho-BAH-noo), Lina—Chairman of General Union of Trade Unions

Coman (KO-mahn), Ion—Central Committee Secretary for Armed Forces and Security

Coman (KO-mahn), Teodor—Ambassador to Jordan

427

Datcu (DAHT-koo), Ion—Ambassador, permanent representative to the U.N.— European Office (Geneva)

Dinca (DEEN-cuh), Ion—First Deputy Prime Minister

Domokos (DOH-moh-kosh), Geza—Director of Kriterion Publishing House

Florescu (Flo-RESS-koo), Mihai—Minister State Secretary of National Council for Science and Technology

Kiraly (Kee-RAH-lee), Carol—dissident living in Romania

Lipatti (Lee-PAHT-tee), Valentin—Ambassador at Large

Luchian (Loo-KYAN), Eugen—Unknown

Manea (MAH-nay-uh), Constantin—Ceausescu's Chief of Staff

Manescu (Mah-NESS-koo), Manea—Vice President of Romania's State Council

Maurer (MOW-rer), Ion Gheorghe—Honorary Chairman of International Law and International Relations Association

Mihulecea (Mee-hoo-LAY-chay-uh), Cornel—Chairman of State Committee for Nuclear Energy

Milea (MEE-lya), Vasile—Minister of National Defense

Militaru (Mee-lee-TAH-roo), Nicolae—Unknown

Olteanu (Ole-tay-AH-noo), Constantin—Colonel General and Member of State Council

Oprea (OH-pray-uh), Gheorghe—First Deputy Prime Minister

Pacepa (Pah-CHE-puh), Dana—Married to Radu; both are trying to emigrate from Romania, so far without success

Pacepa (Pah-CHE-puh), Ion Mihai—Living happily in the United States and trying to have Dana and Radu join him

Pacoste (PAH-kos-tay), Cornel—Deputy Prime Minister

Pana (PAH-nuh), Gheorghe—Chairman of Committee for Problems of People's Councils

Plesita (PLEH-shee-tsuh), Nicolae—Member of Party's Central Auditing Commission

Popescu (Po-PESS-koo), Dumitru—Member of the Political Executive Committee; Rector of Party Academy for Social and Political Training

Postelnicu (Poh-STELL-nee-koo), Tudor—Minister State Secretary of Interior and Chief of State Security Department

Pungan (Poon-GAHN), Vasile—Ambassador to Bulgaria

Stanescu (Stuh-NESS-koo), Ion—Minister of Tourism and Sport

Ursu (OOR-soo), Ioan—First Vice Chairman of National Council for Science and Technology

Verdet (Ver-DETS), Ilie—Chairman of Romanian Communist Party's Central Auditing Commission

Index